JINGJI XUE

Jingji Xue

The History of the Introduction of Western Economic Ideas into China, 1850–1950

Paul B. Trescott

The Chinese University Press

Jingji Xue: The History of the Introduction of Western Economic Ideas into China, 1850–1950
By Paul B. Trescott

ISBN 978–962–996–242–5

THE CHINESE UNIVERSITY PRESS
The Chinese University of Hong Kong
SHA TIN, N.T., HONG KONG
Fax: +852 2603 6692
+852 2603 7355
E-mail: cup@cuhk.edu.hk
Web-site: www.chineseupress.com

Printed in Hong Kong

Contents

Preface

This book originated in 1983–84 when I served as Fulbright professor in the World Economy section at Peking University. "Jingji xue" is the Chinese term for Economics. Toward the end of my stay, we learned that Wang Jianye and Yan Zhijie would be coming to the United States under Fulbright sponsorship. To facilitate a rendezvous, we agreed to prepare a paper for the meetings of the History of Economics Society. My expectation was that my two colleagues would do all the heavy lifting while I would come along at the end, adjust the grammar and adjectives, and become a co-author. They did in fact prepare a large and scholarly draft, parts of which are embodied in the present document. In working through it, however, I was soon utterly captivated by the topic and unable to resist trying to find out more about it. My goal was simple—identify the Chinese who studied Economics in the West and find out what happened to them on their return to China. Both of the original collaborators have continued to provide assistance and encouragement. So also my Beida supervisors Hong Junyan and Chen Daisun, colleagues Fang Wei and Lai Rongyuen, and students Wang Yijiang, Ma Guonan, and Tian Xiaohua.

Our Fulbright year was a life-changing experience, in large measure because my wife Kitty also became very engaged with China. She studied the language, and succeeded in developing friendships with a virtual army of Chinese students and colleagues who have provided the indispensable language skills which I do not possess. She also accompanied me on innumerable visits to libraries and archives, always ready to search and photocopy resources. This project has taken us all over the world and has been (mostly) a wonderful adventure.

This project has generated an enormous data base identifying individual Chinese economists, students, and faculty. Each student and faculty member is represented by at least one sheet of paper; the essential data are summarized in computer files. These resources are available for researchers. Copies of much of the paper file have been deposited with the Shanghai University of Finance and Economics.

After Beida, the project benefited greatly from my opportunity to teach in the Ford Foundation special training program at People's University in 1992. This brought the extraordinary assistance of Xiao Zhijie in ransacking archives and libraries. His meticulous translations of course lists and faculty rosters have been at my fingertips daily. Renda colleagues Wang Chuanlun and Gao Hongye patiently answered questions and helped arrange interviews.

Before we left in 1983, Jean Fan introduced me to Wang Jizu, who in turn hosted us at Nankai University on several occasions and arranged interviews with many of their senior faculty.

While the project has been mainly self-financed, important assistance has come from the Luce Foundation (thanks to Arthur Waldron), the Rockefeller Archive, and Taiwan's Ministry of Education (thanks to Lee Wenfu). Our Fulbright visit to Poland in 1996 gave us a base from which to pursue research in England, France, Germany, and Austria. Through the hospitality of Franklin Chaomin Li, we were able to visit the Shanghai University of Finance and Economics for helpful seminars and archival visits.

Our Beida colleague, the late Charles Wyvill, led us to Harold Shadick, who in turn aided my Yanjing connection, particularly with Hilda Tayler Brown and her sister Gladys Tayler Yang. Beida colleague Lu Chungtai provided valuable material on the elusive Furen University. Our HES discussant Jim Chang shared his experiences at wartime Nanda and in JCRR. Harry Price shared recollections of Yanjing and the Kemmerer Commission.

I was aided in researching Nanjing's CAF by interviews with Stanley Warren, Ardron Lewis (who kindly gave me his copy of the silver report), Wang Yinyuen, and Wang Xixian. My SIU colleague Bill Herr, a Cornell PhD in Agricultural Economics, gave a helpful review of Chapter 9.

At Taiwan's Tsinghua University, Professor Lai Cheng-chung has been a full collaborator in work involving Liang Qichao and Yan Fu, and also aided in choreographing our visits to Taiwan. Sun Chung-hsing sent me away with not only a copy of his helpful dissertation but a ream of precious photocopies. Chapter 14 reflects his input. Chiang Yung-chien shared his dissertation and source materials.

In Carbondale I ruthlessly exploited Chinese students, guests, and friends: Wu Naichun, Zhou Shudong, Chen Zaiping, Liu Yixin, Lin Suren, Ma Lingjie, Wang Xingyu, Yin Hong, Hu Hualing, Chen Zhihong, Wang Zhimin, Peng Zhifang, Zhang Zhongyang, and Zhong Litao. Yu Xiaoyang linked us with Lu Xiaoyan at the National Library in Beijing. I was grateful for correspondence with Ruth Hayhoe, Ramon Myers, Arif Dirlik, Dwight Perkins, Wei Wou, Alfred K. Ho, Chuhei Suguyama, Anthony Koo, and Mabel Li Chang.

Southern Illinois University provided support in many ways: sabbatical leave, library resources, congenial teaching assignments, and the cheerful assistance of Nancy Mallett and Sandy McRoy in the preparation of endless successive drafts.

The many libraries and archives are acknowledged in the text or reference list, but special thanks go to Martha Smalley and the staff of the library of Yale Divinity School.

Editors of scholarly publications have been gracious enough to publish some fragments of this research, and have granted permission to reproduce these. These include *The American Journal of Economics and Sociology*, *Annals of Cooperative and Public Economics*, *History of Political Economy*, *Journal of Economic Issues*, *Taiwan Journal of Political Economy*, *Journal of the History of Economic Thought*, *International Journal of Social Economics*, and University Press of America.

The leadership of US-China Peoples Friendship Association have been a constant source of encouragement and a willing audience, notably Barbara Harrison, Barbara Cobb, Bob Sanborn, and Jon Saari.

Special thanks also to Esther Tsang and Lisa Tang, my editors at The Chinese University Press. They have been consistently upbeat and indulged many of my grandiose fantasies for this project.

List of Plates

1. John and Pearl Buck on their wedding day
Source: *Pearl S. Buck: A Cultural Biography*, Peter Conn. Cambridge University Press, 1996, p. 60.

2. Chen Da
Source: *Who's Who in China*, volume 3, 1931, p. 62.

3. Wu Jingchao
Source: *Who's Who in China*, volume 3, Supplement to the Fifth Edition, p. 50.

4. Li Quanshi
Source: *Who's Who in China*, volume 3, 1931, p. 231.

5. D. K. Lieu
Source: *Who's Who in China*, volume 3, 1931, p. 284.

6. Four former Harvard students, 1984. From left to right: Zhang Peigang, Chen Daisun, Chen Biaoru, and Tan Chongtai.
Source: *Chen Daisun Jinian Wenti*. Fujian People's Publishing House, 1998.

7. Chen Daisun and the author, Beida, 1984
Source: Author's personal photograph.

8. H. D. Fong (Fang Xianting), circa 1950
Source: *Social Engineering and the Social Sciences in China, 1919–1949*, Yung-chen Chiang. Cambridge University Press, 2001.

9. Franklin Ho (He Lian), circa 1947
Source: *Social Engineering and the Social Sciences in China, 1919–1949*, Yung-chen Chiang. Cambridge University Press, 2001.

10. Li Zhuomin
Source: The Chinese University of Hong Kong.

11. Liang Qichao
Source: *Dragon Lady*, Sterling Seagrave. Alfred Knopf, 1992, p. 332.

12. Sun Yat-sen
Source: *The Search for Modern China*, Jonathan Spence. W. W. Norton, 1990.

13. British Economics faculty and students, 1941. Rear, second from the left: S. C. Tsiang (Jiang Shuojie). Center, seated: Professor Friedrich A. Hayek. On his left: Professor Nicholas Kaldor. Front, first on the right: Puey Unphakorn, later head of Bank of Thailand, and the author's mentor in 1965–68.
Source: *The Reminiscences of Dr. S. C. Tsiang*. Institute of Modern History, Academia Sinica, 1992.

14. Wu Baosan, on his 90th birthday
Source: Photograph courtesy of Wu Baosan's family.

15. Yan Fu

16. Yanjing economists, 1928–29. From left to right: Li Binghua, John B. Taylor, Augusta Wagner.
Source: *The Yenchinian* (yearbook), 1928–29, UBCHEA archives. Special Collections, Yale Divinity School Library. Reproduced with the permission of Yale Divinity School Library.

17. Zhao Naituan
Source: *Biographies of Contemporary Chinese Social Scientists*. Shanxi People's Press, 1982.

18. Ma Yinchu
Source: *Biographies of Contemporary Chinese Social Scientists*. Shanxi People's Press, 1982.

List of Tables

Abbreviations

ABD	All But Dissertation
AEA	American Economic Association
ALLFAC	All Economics Faculty in China
AS	Academia Sinica
BOTHFAC	Economics Faculty holding appointments in Both Christian and Chinese Universities
BTH	Berlin Technische Hochschule
CAF	College of Agriculture and Forestry, Nanking University
CAS	Chinese Academy of Science
CASS	Chinese Academy of Social Sciences
CHINFAC	Economics Faculty in Chinese (non-missionary) Universities
CHRSFAC	Economics Faculty in Christian Colleges
CIER	Chung-hua Institution for Economic Research
CIFRC	China International Famine Relief Commission
CNC	Chinese National Currency
CNRRA	China National Recovery and Relief Administration
CPI	Central Political Institute
CSPSR	*Chinese Social and Political Science Review*
CYB	*China Year Book*
ECAFE	Economic Commission for Asia and the Far East
FCU	Fujian Christian University
HY	Harvard-Yenching Library
IMF	International Monetary Fund
IOE	Institute of Economics

IPR	Institute of Pacific Relations
IUD	Intra-Uterine Device
JCRR	Joint Commission on Rural Reconstruction
KMT	Kuomintang
LSE	London School of Economics and Political Science
LU	*Land Utilization in China*
NARB	National Agricultural Research Bureau
NCC	National Christian Council
NCU	National Central University
NEC	National Economic Council
NSEQ	*Nankai Social and Economic Quarterly*
NTU	National Taiwan University
NYU	New York University
PPE	Philosophy, Politics, Economics
QJE	*Quarterly Journal of Economics*
RA	Rockefeller Archive
SWAU	Southwestern Associated Universities
TVA	Tennessee Valley Authority
UBCHEA	United Board for Christian Higher Education in Asia
UNRRA	United Nations Relief and Rehabilitation Administration
UTS	Union Theological Seminary
WCUU	West China Union University
WN	*The Wealth of Nations*
YDS	Yale Divinity School

1

Introduction

During the critical period of the Renaissance and Reformation in the West, China was relatively isolated from the rest of the world, economically, politically, and intellectually. Then the West forcibly disrupted China's isolation, particularly through the Opium Wars of 1839–41. From that point on China entered a turbulent and painful process of modernization.

The introduction of western economic ideas into China began in the nineteenth century and accelerated in the last decade of that century. Our initial chapters deal with Chinese intellectuals who played a major role around 1900 in transmitting and interpreting these western ideas—Yan Fu, Liang Chi-chao (Qichao), Kang Yu-wei (Youwei), and Sun Yat-sen.[1] Yan and Liang were much impressed with the ideas of Adam Smith and tried to promote his emphasis on the potential benefits of free markets and profit-seeking business for China's economic development. In contrast, Sun was skeptical of private enterprise and urged a centralized, collectivist approach to economic policy. His ideas were more congruent with traditional Chinese attitudes, seasoned with influences from Japan and Germany, and were very influential both before and after 1949.

In the twentieth century, a remarkable feature of the Chinese experience was the large number of Chinese who studied Economics in the West and returned to China to teach, to do research, or to work in other positions. We have assembled information on approximately 1,600 named individuals who studied Economics in the United States (about 1,200 at graduate level) and Europe (about 400).[2] This data set is the heart of this book, providing a uniquely detailed picture of the flow of western economic ideas through the literal movement of persons. Chapters 4 and 5 examine their student experiences, with particular focus on the western universities they attended. Chapter 6 reviews data on their careers, and particularly their absorption into the faculties of Chinese universities. We have assembled a data set of more than 900 Chinese who taught Economics in Chinese universities up to 1950. Of these, 544 achieved some foreign study. Of the Chinese faculty listed, about 27 percent had studied graduate level Economics in the United States and an additional 16 percent studied in Europe. In addition, we have identified about 100 westerners who taught Economics in Chinese universities in this period. Of these, missionary economists John Lossing Buck and John Bernard Tayler received much attention. Their activist roles went far beyond classroom instruction.

The later portions of the book present detailed information on the development of Economics programs in major Chinese universities, identifying the elements of western Economics. We deal separately with the missionary colleges and with the indigenous Chinese universities. The missionary colleges were an important channel for bringing in western-trained economists to teach in China and for sending Chinese students to the United States for graduate study in Economics.

About three-fourths of the Chinese who studied Economics in western universities came to the United States. Most of the westerners who taught Economics in Chinese universities before 1950 were also from the United States. Chinese universities became in large measure outposts of American Economics, using American textbooks and American course structuring.[3] However, a significant contribution also came in combination from Japan and Germany. Both Liang Qichao and Sun Yat-sen displayed the effects of their long residence in Japan. Combined, Germany and Japan provided more than ten percent of our sample of Economics faculty.

No other less-developed country of that period displayed an experience comparable to that of the Chinese. To be sure, many students from India attended British universities, and British economic ideas became the staple fare of Indian universities. But the number of Indians studying Economics in Britain was far smaller than the Chinese representation in the United States.[4]

The large flow of Chinese to graduate study in the West occurred across the academic spectrum. Table 1-1 summarizes the total number of U.S. doctoral degrees in humanities, social sciences, and education awarded to Chinese students during the period 1900–49. This makes clear the prominent role of Economics.

The appeal of Economics was wide because it offered opportunities in business and in government departments, as well as in academic institutions. Most western-educated Chinese economists took positions in business and/

Table 1-1. U.S. Doctoral Degrees Awarded to Chinese in Humanities, Social Sciences, and Education, 1900–1949

Discipline	Doctoral Degrees	Percentage** (%)
Economics	134	24
Education	95	17
International Law & Relations	63	11
Political Science	59	11
Sociology	37	7
Psychology	36	6
Law	33	6
Philosophy	29	5
History	23	4
Religion	17	3
Literature	11	2
Miscellaneous*	17	3
Total	554	100

* Geography (6), Library Science (4), Linguistics (4), Music (3).
** Rounded to nearest whole number.
Source: Tabulated from Yuan Tung-li 1961.

or government departments. About one fifth of our listed U.S-trained, and one third of the European-trained, economists entered university teaching in China. Most department chairs and many deans were western-trained.

The influx of western economics coincided with an explosion in research and publication about China's economy, a topic explored in Chapter 14. Table 1-2 displays data on publications on China's economy by Chinese authors during the period 1900–49. Data on the flow of publications are compared with the potential stock of returned economics students.[5]

Prior to 1924, there were very few publications. Beginning in the mid-1920s, however, there was a veritable explosion of publications. Between 1924 and 1936, published output grew at an average annual rate of about 25 percent, while the population of western-trained Chinese economists grew by 9 percent annually.

While western-trained economists dominated university faculties, they contributed a relatively small share to this published output. Only about one-seventh of the authors were in our student lists, and only about one-seventh of our students published items on China's economy. Very similar proportions were observed for the Chinese authors of a sample of 230

Table 1-2. Publications on China's Economy by Chinese Authors, 1900–1949

Year	Publications	Returned Economics Students
1910–14	24	15
1915–19	50	57
1920–24	55	157
1925–29	314	318
1930–34	958	540
1935–39	1,310	755
1940–44	360	1,003
1945–49	362	1,169

Sources: Returned students—numbers taken from our student files (Chapters 4 and 5); publications tabulated from Skinner and Hsieh 1973. See Chapter 14 for details.

translations of economics materials into Chinese: only 32 (13 percent) were in our student lists. This was also true for economics textbooks. We identified 35 Chinese authors of widely used economics textbooks, or similar items. Of these, 20 were not educated in the West. Thus the prominence of "returned students" from the West did not prevent the development of a vigorous and diverse literature on China's economy by Chinese who did not study overseas. Much of this literature emanated from research organizations, such as those affiliated with the China Foundation and Academia Sinica, and those embedded in government departments and in banks. These are described in Chapter 14. Such studies embodied research techniques imported from the West, notably survey research and index numbers. Leadership in such organizations typically came from western-educated economists, while the vast majority of the research workers had not studied abroad. Many had studied with western-trained economists in Chinese universities. To adapt an idiom familiar in other branches of Economics, the return of western-educated economists produced a "multiplier effect" seen in the emergence of a highly productive community of China-educated economists. The explosion of publications can be viewed as a lagged effect of the rapid expansion in the number of "returned economists" after 1915.

The flow of translations of western economic works closely correlated with the publication output noted in Table 1-2. The flow increased rapidly in the 1920s. Table 1-3 identifies some prominent items translated.[6]

Table 1-3. Some Western Economics Works Translated into Chinese, 1920–1949

Date	Author	Work
1920	J. M. Keynes	*Economic Consequences of the Peace*
1924	Karl Marx	*Value, Price and Profit*
1927	Lewis Haney	*History of Economic Thought*
1929	J. N. Keynes	*Scope and Method of Political Economy*
1929	Friedrich List	*National System of Political Economy*
1930	Henry George	*Progress and Poverty*
1930	Karl Diehl	*Socialism, Communism, and Anarchism*
1931	Irving Fisher	*Purchasing Power of Money*
1931	Adam Smith	*The Wealth of Nations*
1932	Alfred Marshall	*Principles of Economics*
1933	Gustav Cassel	*Theory of Social Economy*
1933	Ralph Hawtrey	*Gold Standard in Theory and Practice*
1933	Thomas N. Carver	*Distribution of Wealth*
1933	T. R. Malthus	*Essay on Principle of Population*
1933	J. B. Say	*Treatise on Political Economy*
1934	J. B. Clark	*Distribution of Wealth*
1934	David Ricardo	*Principles of Political Economy*
1934	Eugen Böhm-Bawerk	*Karl Marx & the Close of His System*
1936	W. S. Jevons	*Theory of Political Economy*
1936	J. S. Mill	*Principles of Political Economy*
1936	Gustav Schmoller	*Mercantilism*
1936	A. R. J. Turgot	*Reflections on the Formation and Distribution of Wealth*
1936	Thorstein Veblen	*Theory of the Leisure Class*
1937	Eugen Böhm-Bawerk	*Positive Theory of Capital*
1937	Werner Sombart	*Modern Capitalism*
1938	Karl Marx	*Capital*
1938	Lionel Robbins	*Essays on the Nature and Significance of Economic Science*
1947	Arthur C. Pigou	*Socialism and Capitalism*
1947	Johann von Thünen	*The Isolated State*
1948	Karl Marx	*Theories of Surplus Value*

Sources: See note 6.

Because of longstanding terminological problems, it is not clear how much Chinese readers could derive from the translations. But their number is significant as a measure of the effort to introduce western economic ideas, and the fact that much of that effort came from people who had not studied in the West.

This configuration was reflected in the Chinese Economic Association, which was formed in 1923. Attendance records for their meetings during the period 1928–36 listed 514 different participants. Only 62 of these—one eighth—appeared in our lists of western-educated economists.[7] However, the latter were among the most frequent and influential participants.

Similarly, the individual authors who published prolifically about China's economy were overwhelmingly western-trained. By 1949 China was producing world-class economists such as Li Choh-ming (Li Zhuomin), Tsiang Sho-chieh (Jiang Shuojie), Liu Ta-chung (Liu Dazhong), Pu Shan, and Chang Pei-kang (Zhang Peigang). Numerous Chinese economists emigrated during the war-torn decade of the 1940s, enriching academic life in the United States and Taiwan and providing productive staff for international agencies. Some are described in Chapter 15.

In an influential study of China's returned students in all academic fields, Wang Yi-chu (1966) was highly critical of their achievements. They became, he felt, "an elite unconnected with the life surrounding them and . . . not really aware of actual conditions in the country at large." (p. 374) He claimed that "Few Anglo-American-trained specialists wrote". If they did, "their topics were often specialized, and the substance unintelligible to the public . . . [T]hey made no attempt to communicate their findings in simplified versions to the public." (p. 420) Our findings regarding economists differ strongly from Wang's claims. Western-educated economists made extensive efforts to study and teach about China's economy. Their teaching attracted large numbers of students, many of whom were motivated to become teachers and researchers themselves. Besides publications in learned journals, Chinese economists wrote extensively for newspapers and magazines of general circulation.

Shortcomings

However, both in university teaching and in their writings, most Chinese economists were clearly selective in what they used from western economics. They retained negative attitudes toward private business enterprise and free markets, sharing populist stereotypes regarding merchants, landowners, and moneylenders. They maintained a naive faith in collectivist economic policies, perhaps reflecting influences from Germany and Japan. They greatly exaggerated the damage from foreign products and foreign investment. And Chinese economists failed to develop a proper appreciation for the quantity theory of money. The hyperinflation of the 1940s, which was so destructive of the public's morale, might have been less severe had Chinese economists had a better grasp of monetary theory.

By the end of the 1930s western economists (notably J. L. Buck and J. B. Tayler) and western-trained economists (particularly those at Nankai University) were working valiantly to adapt western economic ideas to Chinese conditions. But these efforts were largely derailed by war and revolution. Civil war was an endemic condition. Warlord conflicts dominated the period from 1911 to 1927, and conflict between Kuomintang and Communists became dominant in the 1930s. The Japanese invasion followed in 1937. Economists in China did not have much opportunity to advise in a context of internal peace, law and order, or to have access to well-formulated statistical data.

Western Economics

The introduction of western economics into China occurred in a confluence of three interacting trends of the late nineteenth century. The first was the emergence of Economics as a relatively scientific academic discipline suitable for graduate study. The second was the dramatic upsurge in Protestant missionary activity in the United States and Britain, much of it directed toward China. The third was the rise of western-style universities in China, stimulated by China's military humiliations in the Sino-Japanese War (1894–95) and the Boxer Rebellion (1900).

Economics as a specialized intellectual discipline took shape over the nineteenth century, responding to Adam Smith's *The Wealth of Nations* (1776). Smith's most significant contribution was the notion of an economic system, in which the pursuit of self-interest by individuals, disciplined by competition and by a suitable system of law and administration, would yield beneficial outcomes. Smith's treatise strongly emphasized a vision of economic growth in which private saving and investment would lead to technological improvement and greater productivity, raising wages and improving living conditions for the common people. In contrast, he felt that government intervention typically degenerated into special-interest programs ("rent-seeking behavior", in the modern idiom) in which political power would be used to divert income rather than create it.

Important as Adam Smith's work was in western economics, the first Chinese translation of *The Wealth of Nations* did not appear until 1902.[8]

How Smith's ideas were presented to the Chinese audience is an interesting case study in intellectual diffusion, which is explored in Chapter 2. The most important contribution may have been the moral legitimation of business activity rather than the analysis. The 1949 Communist triumph was a measure of how limited that legitimation was, even by 1949.

Nineteenth-century British classical economists explored the interactions of population growth, productivity, and people's real income. Malthus, Ricardo, and John Stuart Mill feared that population growth would make it difficult to improve people's living conditions. Twentieth-century students of Economics, in China as well as in the West, were usually exposed to a course in the history of western economic thought and thus had some acquaintance with the important ideas of Smith and Malthus in particular. By the 1940s, many Chinese academics favored birth control programs, but these were generally opposed by officials, reflecting Sun Yat-sen's opposition to Malthusian ideas (MacNair, 1944, pp. xxiv, xxxii). A recent study has argued that the drastic Chinese population-control measures since 1980 were a direct response to the Malthusian view.[9]

China's most urgent economic need was to increase productivity and experience rapid economic growth. But these considerations were not a central part of western economic analysis between 1900 and 1950.[10] And western economic growth analysis presupposed an institutional framework of law and order, property rights and contractual obligations, restraints against the predatory impulses of government officials, and monetary stability. China did not have these conditions prior to 1949, and securing them was not the sort of problem that western economists addressed.

Pre-1950 western economics possessed two "Great Truths". The first was that economic resources were scarce and it was important to use them efficiently. Mainstream microeconomics stressed the element of optimization, arguing that private ownership and profit maximization would achieve social efficiency. The second "Great Truth" was that the incomes of the "owners" of factors of production—land, labor, and capital—reflected the marginal productivity of those resources, which depended, inter alia, on their relative supplies. A country like China, with an enormous poorly-educated labor force relative to its land and capital, would inevitably have very low wage rates and high returns per unit to land and capital. A better understanding of these matters might have mitigated the emphasis on "class warfare" which produced much of the cruelty of the Maoist regime. Better understanding might also have directed more attention to efforts to reduce China's birth rate.

Unfortunately, these "Great Truths" were not a prominent part of the western economics imported into China. Chinese who studied in the West learned a vast amount of descriptive information about economic policies of western countries. Their western instructors were typically critical of the defects of market economy—poverty, injustice, depression, and unemployment. After 1929, the Great Depression weakened everyone's faith in the benevolent tendencies of free markets. Many Chinese studied Economics at Columbia and Wisconsin, schools where "institutional economics" stressed the defects rather than the virtues of free markets (Persky 2000; Rutherford 2004; Yonay 1998).

The most widely publicized theoretical innovations in mainstream economics in 1900–1950 were Keynesian economics and the theory of imperfect competition. Both focused attention on "market failure", and neither had much relevance to China. Both were particularly stressed at Harvard, which attracted many Chinese students. They were even more influential for the 33 Chinese students who studied Economics at Cambridge University in Britain.

Much of *The Wealth of Nations* commented on issues of public policy. Smith advocated relative freedom of international trade and payments as a way of promoting international specialization, economic efficiency, and high productivity. After the 1840s, Britain not only adopted free trade for its own residents, but also imposed it on China. A series of "unequal treaties" brought foreign domination of China's import tariff, the principal source of Chinese government revenue. Until the 1920s, Chinese tariff rates could not ordinarily exceed five percent. The Chinese bitterly resented this foreign domination and free trade as well.

American economists played a major role in the development of agricultural economics. Leading figures such as Thomas Nixon Carver and George Warren had grown up on farms. Warren helped develop the subject at Cornell. Several of his students, notably John Lossing Buck, developed the subject at Nanjing University, a leading missionary college. These matters, which were very relevant to China's economic development, are described in Chapters 4 and 9.

By 1900 an important dimension of economic study was the accumulation and manipulation of statistical data (Biddle 1999). The trained economist was soon expected to be familiar with the techniques of descriptive statistics. The spread of survey research to China was a major development in the 1920s and thereafter. Another challenge to economic statisticians was aggregation. By 1900 experiments were under way in making index numbers, especially for prices. Irving Fisher's pioneering efforts at Yale were aided by Ho Lien (He Lian—Franklin Ho), who subsequently played a major role in developing index-number work in China. Efforts to estimate China's national income got under way in the 1940s, by Ou Pao-san (Wu Baosan) and Liu Dazhong, and involved American national-income pioneer Simon Kuznets as an adviser. The role of western analysis and western-trained economists in Chinese economic research is explored in Chapter 14.

Western economics prior to 1949 was a diffuse and diverse body of ideas. The core of analytical concepts usually known as neo-classical economics, centering on marginal analysis, optimization, and perhaps mathematics, was challenged by many skeptics in the profession. There were a significant number of socialists of various persuasions, and many more who favored substantial government intervention to alter the processes of market economy.

The Chinese Environment

During the period covered by this study, China was one of the poorest countries of the world, judged by per capita income and productivity. By the nineteenth century its population had probably reached 400 millions, of which as many as 90 percent lived on farms. Although there were some large absentee landlords, most farms were small and the majority were owner-operated. "Chinese farmers did not live in a subsistence economy, but were engaged in a web of commercial activity carried on in rural market areas to which virtually all villages had access." (Maddison 1998, p. 33.) They were relatively quick to develop cash crops such as cotton, sugar, tobacco, tea, and soy beans. But rural transportation was primitive, and productivity and incomes were very low. While Communist jargon refers to nineteenth century China as "semi-feudal", the term seems inappropriate. There was no hereditary (Han) aristocracy, with large estates and special privileges, and no serfdom.

Comparing Chinese and western economic growth, Angus Maddison reached some striking conclusions:

> Already in the tenth century [China] was the world's leading economy in terms of per capita income and this leadership lasted until the fifteenth century. [China] outperformed Europe in levels of technology, the intensity with which it used its natural resources, and capacity for administering a huge territorial empire. In the following three centuries, Europe gradually overtook China in

> real income, technological and scientific capacity. In the nineteenth and the first half of the twentieth century, China's performance actually declined in a world where economic progress greatly accelerated.[11]

Prior to the 1840s, China had been for more than a century quite isolated from the West. Consumers in Europe and America had developed a taste for Chinese tea, silk, and porcelain. But the attitude of the Chinese elite toward the West was one of disdain and repugnance. The inflow of western goods, people, and ideas after 1840 came as a relatively unwelcome intrusion, based on western military superiority.[12]

There was no significant system of public education in nineteenth-century China. Small private academies prepared students for the competitive examinations by which government officials were chosen. These examinations emphasized familiarity with traditional Chinese literature and philosophy, as well as facility and felicity in self-expression. According to Teng and Fairbank (1963), officials were "drawn from the small literate element of the Chinese population, the literati who could transact public business using the intricate Chinese writing system . . . [T]he ideal men of distinction were landlord-scholar-officials, rather than generals or merchants." (p. 4)

The status of an official was much sought after in China, as it still is. Until the imperial examinations were abolished in 1905, intellectual life in China remained fixated on the studies central to the examinations. Neither private intellectual inquiry nor public policy devoted much attention to economic productivity and growth. According to Maddison (1998), the bureaucratic Chinese government was a major obstacle to economic development before 1950, because of rent-seeking behavior and insecurity of property rights (p. 14). Dwight Perkins, in contrast, argued that "the policies of the Chinese government in the nineteenth century were not so much wrong as inadequate" (1967, p. 486). Prior to 1950 the Chinese government was fiscally unable to spend significant amounts on such vital infrastructure components as transportation and education. The government was also incapable of maintaining civil order. The country was torn by such violent episodes as the Taiping Rebellion, the Boxer Rebellion, the civil disorders of the 1920s and 1930s, and of course the Japanese invasions beginning in 1931 (Hou Chi-ming 1963, pp. 604–605).

The Treaty of Nanjing (1842) was the first of a series of "unequal treaties" which embodied western imperialism to Chinese historians. It gave the British possession of Hong Kong, and opened Canton (Guangzhou) and four other seaport cities for foreign residence and trade. The number of these "treaty ports" was repeatedly extended, until by 1911 there were 48 of them. Foreign residents were given the privilege of "extra-territoriality"—meaning they remained under the jurisdiction of their home laws and courts, rather than those of China. Foreign residents were given permission to build houses, hospitals, schools, and places of worship in the treaty ports. The treaties protected the opportunity for missionary activities and for foreign ownership and management of business.

Two responses occurred as a result of the Treaty of Nanjing. The first was the literal invasion of China by western individuals—merchants, missionaries, administrators—who learned the Chinese language and transmitted western ideas. The other was the "self-strengthening movement" among Chinese officials and intellectuals, who advocated cultivating western knowledge so that China could become strong and protect itself. Reformist intellectual Feng Kuei-fen put it thus: "Would not the best of all possible stratagems be to retain the social relationships and the illustrious moral principles of China as the foundation, and to reinforce them with the techniques that the various countries [of the West] have used to attain wealth and power?" (Quoted Grieder 1981, p. 73.)

The early introduction of western economic ideas into China can clearly be decomposed into a "push" component and a "pull" component. The "push" involved the efforts to westerners to spread mainstream economic doctrines. The first known economics book published in the Chinese language was prepared by a German missionary, Karl Friedrich Gutzlaff, around 1840. Formal instruction in western economics was initiated by an American missionary, William A. P. Martin, director of the Tongwenguan, a government school established in 1861 to train diplomatic interpreters (Biggerstaff 1961). English and American missionaries in China also wrote extensively on economic matters.

More interesting to the student of intellectual diffusion were the efforts of Chinese intellectuals to understand, transmit, and adapt western economic ideas. Ma Chien-chung (Ma Jianzhong) was the first Chinese known to have studied Economics abroad, as part of his study of law and commerce in Paris in 1876–77. Four major figures in Chinese intellectual history were leading participants in the "pull" of western economic ideas into China. Yan Fu, who studied science and technology in England in 1877, undertook a series of interpretive translations of major western writings on social and economic topics. His translation of *The Wealth of Nations* appeared in 1902. His friend Liang Qichao became a prolific commentator on all aspects of western social and political thought. In 1902 he published a brief history of western economic ideas, drawing mainly from the Japanese translations of western works. Liang's mentor, Kang Youwei, struggled with economic concepts of competition and inequality in writings directed partly at practical policy advice and partly at utopian speculation. Sun Yat-sen often wrote on economic topics in his political career, giving attention to economic growth and advocating a large role for the government.

These four figures will be examined at length below. Each of them attempted to select and interpret western economic ideas to suit his visions of what China needed—and these processes often changed the focus of prominent western works such as *The Wealth of Nations*. And each of the four was particularly concerned with the weakness and ineptitude of China's government. Japan's example demonstrated that vigorous economic growth required some constructive input from government (Hsiao 1975, pp. 356–365).

Rise of Universities

China's defeat by Japan in 1894–95 prompted the imperial government to renew efforts at national self-strengthening. These efforts included the creation of the first modern universities in China. Beiyang College in Tianjin was founded in 1895, and a comparable institution in Shanghai, the Nanyang College, opened the following year.[13] Both emphasized science and technology. A landmark measure was the creation of the Imperial University in 1898, absorbing the Tongwenguan. After 1911 it was known principally as National Peking University, and more recently, simply Peking University, commonly abbreviated as "Beida".[14] Since the 1920s it has been China's premier institution of higher education. A number of "normal schools" (teacher-training colleges) were initiated soon after 1900, often with Japanese input. There was also a brief and transitory fad for two-year colleges of law and political science, in which Economics was taught (Sun 1987, pp. 86–87).

Tsinghua (Qinghua) College opened in 1911 with the specific charge of preparing Chinese for study in American colleges and universities. Its early operations provided powerful stimulus toward such study. By the late 1920s, it had evolved into another leading national university, a status which it still maintains. By the mid-1920s, China had a fairly extensive network of government universities and other institutions of higher education. Their Economics programs are reviewed in Chapters 10 to 13.

Much of our research has been devoted to identifying Economics faculty in Chinese universities and their study in the West. Table 1-4 shows data for six leading universities: the number of Chinese whom we have identified as teaching Economics and how many of these had studied Economics in the West, and students graduating from each university who went to the West to study Economics.

Table 1-4. Western Economics Study: Major Chinese University Faculty and Students

University	Listed Chinese Economics Faculty				
	Total	Studied in U.S.	Studied in EU	Western Faculty	Students to the West
Nanjing (Ch)	94	35	16	20	64
Fudan	91	26	21	0	36
National Central	81	31	26	0	54
Nankai	81	38	14	1	54*
Yanjing (Ch)	78	33	9	7	60
Beida	74	24	16	3	78*

Some faculty are listed for more than one university.
Ch: Christian college.
* Includes 9 students prorated from Southwest Associated Universities.

Roughly half of the faculty in these universities had studied in the West. These six schools provided about one fifth of the Chinese students who studied Economics in the West.

The first Economics doctorate awarded to a Chinese person was conferred in 1906 by Yale University on Chen Chin-tao (Jintao). We have identified over 1,600 Chinese who studied Economics in the United States (graduate level) and in Europe. We examine this group in detail below. Some 335 Chinese received doctoral degrees in Economics (or closely related areas) in Europe and America between 1900 and 1950. The majority of these did their doctoral research on topics relating to China. Most of them returned to China. Some became mainstays of university Economics departments. The most impressive roster of American-educated "returned students" teaching Economics was assembled by Nankai University, a private institution in Tianjin. Wuhan University employed numerous British-trained economists. In Chapters 7 to 13 we offer case studies of a number of the Economics programs in leading Chinese universities.

The Missionary Enterprise

By 1900 a number of Christian colleges had been established in China, and these soon became a significant element in higher education. Economics was typically a major component of their curricula, and was often taught by westerners. We have identified 89 westerners who taught Economics in China's Christian colleges. Of these, 58 were from the United States. John Lossing Buck and John Bernard Tayler were two missionary economists whose work figures prominently in our study. Their contributions went beyond teaching and research into an activist role, aiding in the development of cooperatives and in promoting "rural reconstruction". Their research, writings, teaching, and institution-building in regard to rural China are explored in Chapters 7, 8, 9, and 14. Missionary colleges also contributed a disproportionate share of Chinese who went to the United States for graduate study in Economics, often returning to teach in their college of origin. The number of colleges ranged between ten and twenty, and in the period 1900–25 they probably accounted for 20–30 percent of university enrollments in China.

Emergence of the Kuomintang

Sun Yat-sen was a principal organizer of the Kuomintang (KMT), a political organization which aspired to national leadership. Sun's strongly collectivist and nationalist economic ideas, which are discussed at length in Chapter 3, became an important component of KMT doctrine. After his death in 1925, leadership in the KMT passed to Chiang Kai-shek, a military figure with training in Japan. In 1927 Chiang led the overthrow of the weak and corrupt national government headquartered in Peking. He moved the national capital to Nanjing.[15] Chiang turned against his former communist allies, and the Chinese Communist movement retreated into remote areas of the countryside. Efforts to exterminate them remained an obsession for Chiang. In its initial phases, the KMT attracted the allegiance of many bright, energetic, and educated Chinese. The new government offered the prospect of an effective campaign for social and economic modernization.

These prospects were undermined by the encroachments of the Japanese. In 1931 they seized Manchuria. In 1932 they gained effective military presence in Shanghai. And in 1937 full-scale war broke out, followed by extensive Japanese invasion. The most prosperous and highly developed regions of China fell under Japanese rule. China's higher education system was seriously disrupted.

The war exposed the weakness and corruption of the KMT. Monetary inflation grew into a post-war hyperinflation. When the war ended in 1945, despite a major effort at economic reconstruction by the United Nations Relief and Rehabilitation Administration (UNRRA), Communist influence grew rapidly. Civil war in China ended in 1949 when Chiang and his KMT remnant evacuated to the island of Taiwan. In October 1949, Mao Tse-tung (Zedong) proclaimed the formation of the People's Republic of China.

China's Economics Profession before 1949

The professionalization of economics proceeded in China along familiar western lines, particularly from the 1920s onward. In 1920 the Peking government organized a Bureau of Economic Information (Sun 1987, pp. 118–120). Its research director for the period 1920–28 was D. K. Lieu (Liu Dajun), a Michigan Economics graduate who produced many important studies of China's economy. Liu helped organize the Chinese Economic Association in 1923. Professional journals began to appear both in English and Chinese.[16] Some of the U.S.-remitted Boxer Indemnity money financed the China Foundation. One of its numerous research divisions was the Social Sciences Research Institute, which produced its first economics publications in 1928. Other research organizations emerged, some associated with the government or with universities. Government agencies began to employ Chinese economists as administrators and as researchers. Output of publications on China's economy expanded rapidly until the war broke out.

A major focus of our study is on Economics instruction in Chinese colleges and universities. Economics probably attracted about ten percent of the students. It became a common practice for outstanding students to be invited to stay on as junior faculty members. By the 1940s, the typical Chinese university Economics faculty would include a few senior professors with foreign graduate degrees and a number of junior instructors who had received their degrees from the employing institution.

Because academic jobs did not pay well, it was not uncommon for faculty members to hold appointments at more than one institution in the same area. And universities often engaged government and business officials as adjunct faculty.

What Is Western Economics?

Present-day historians of western economic thought tend to concentrate their attention on the theoretical core of the subject. But this core was not much stressed even in western graduate programs in Economics before 1949. Much of the content of such programs was institutional-descriptive material. Students might learn about the organization and finance of corporations, the structure and functioning of labor unions, and how commercial banking operations might affect the money supply. Public policies, laws, and administration were surveyed in the context of the United States, Britain, France, or Germany.

In many cases, Chinese studying Economics in western universities approached these materials for possible guidelines as to how Chinese institutions and policies should develop. There was an implicit assumption that China could beneficially imitate western practices. Although economic theory often called attention to the benefits of free-market activities and institutions, a large part of western economics both in the United States and in Europe either argued or assumed that governments could and should intervene to improve the performance of the economy. In the early twentieth century these interventions might involve measures to improve the condition of the poor or (primarily in the United States) to limit the power of monopolies. During the 1930s, interventionist focus shifted to measures to remedy or avert disastrous depressions. With the coming of war, this concern was broadened to include the control of inflation and the mobilization of national resources for war.

The majority of economists both in the West and in China were, in the 1920s, 1930s, and 1940s, not strongly devoted to the superiority of free markets.[17] Nor were they very skeptical about a major economic role for the government. In China, this attitude was reinforced by elements in the Chinese classics. Chinese economists were probably not much different from the rest of the Chinese people in accepting the political triumph of Mao's communism with equanimity and perhaps even enthusiasm.

One subject area which Chinese economists did not learn much about in their western studies was economic development—an area which logically could have occupied a position of great importance. Among leading Chinese economists one can see a clear struggle to try to create such a field. Sun Yat-sen's work had the merit of addressing this topic directly, but with a heavily collectivist focus. Development—more specifically, industrialization—became a major area of research by Nankai University economists, especially H. D. Fong (Fang Xianting).[18] Chang Pei-kang's (Zhang Peigang) doctoral research at Harvard in the 1940s provides an interesting case study of this search for guiding principles (see Chapter 14).

Issues of economic development were not just a matter for verbal attention. Leading economists at Nankai, Yanjing, and Nanjing universities were directly involved in efforts to promote both increased productivity and social justice through programs involving "rural reconstruction" and cooperatives. The program to promote industrial cooperatives during the war with Japan arose directly from these efforts.

Interacting Intellectual Traditions

This study does not undertake to be a comprehensive history of Chinese economic thought. However, Chinese intellectual and moral traditions influenced the way in which western economic ideas were received. Confucian traditions stressed obedience to hierarchical authority and the responsibility of rulers to promote the welfare of their subjects. These and other traditional views certainly affected the way in which Kang Youwei, Liang Qichao, Sun Yat-sen, and Liang Shuming (one of the founders of the rural reconstruction movement) responded to western ideas.

On the other hand, this study attempts to add to the knowledge of the history of economic thought in the West. Chapters 4 and 5 review the leading professors and ideas which confronted Chinese students in western graduate schools. Several chapters examine exactly what intellectual capital the Chinese students took back to China with them. This is a particular focus for Chapter 14, which details Chinese research on China's economy.

This study also attempts to contribute to the history of higher education in China. Our study demonstrates the large role which the missionary colleges played in many aspects of the introduction of western economic ideas into China. For both missionary and indigenous universities, we have tried to illuminate the elements of academic instruction in Economics—courses, textbooks, ideas, and activities of faculty.

Socialism and Communism

This study does not deal systematically with the evolution of Chinese Marxism or the ideas of Mao Zedong and other Chinese Communist leaders. There is no dearth of literature on these matters. Marxist influence was especially strong in pre-1949 study of the condition of

China's impoverished farmers, who constituted the vast majority of the Chinese population. Land issues, which were dramatized by Sun Yat-sen, became the subject of an extensive literature in the 1920s and thereafter. A significant contributor was Chen Han-sheng. Chen was a western-trained Marxist historian who subsequently studied in Moscow, held academic appointments in Economics and directed a research institute which nurtured two of Communist China's leading economists, Sun Ye-fang and Hsueh Mu-chiao (Xue Muqiao).

At Beida, Marxist ideas were represented in the 1920s by Li Ta-chao (Dazhao) and Chen Chi-hsiu (Qixiu). At Amoy University, two prominent Marxist professors, Wang Ya-nan and Kuo Ta-li (Guo Dali), translated many of Marx's writings and also those of the English classical economists on whose work Marx's ideas were built. By the 1930s, numerous universities offered courses in which Marx's ideas (among others) were described.

Both the Peking government before 1927 and the subsequent Nanjing government tried to suppress communism among university faculty and in publications, but with uneven success. One prominent item which escaped purge was Shen Chi-yuan's (Zhiyuan) textbook *Outline of New Economics*. It was initially published in 1934 and was in its tenth printing by 1949. Shen had studied in Moscow and taught at Jinan, Peiping, and Northwestern universities before joining Yanjing after the Communist take-over.[19]

Even so, Marxist ideas did not figure prominently in the pre-1949 economic literature of China, nor were there many professed Marxists in university positions. Government pressure was one reason for this; Li Dazhao was executed by order of warlord Zhang Zuolin in 1927.

Much of the popularity of the Communists in China by 1949 arose from their patriotic heroism in the war against Japan. They had also gained a reputation for honesty and competence in administering the areas which came under their control. But there was also an important economic element in the appeal of Chinese Communism—the prospect of a better life for the poor, especially the farmers. Furthermore, the Marxist emphasis on the evil influence of the "bourgeoisie" dovetailed closely with the traditional Chinese dislike for merchants, landlords, moneylenders, and other "exploiters"—a dislike which was shared by many non-Marxist Chinese economists. Beyond this, the pre-1949 pronouncements of Mao and other Communist leaders did not provide a clear blue-print for economic policy.

How well did the study of western economics before 1950 provide Chinese people and their leaders with a realistic assessment of Communist economic organization? Even though the Communists did not gain power through any sort of formal election process, they undoubtedly enjoyed the support or acceptance of most Chinese people in 1949. The people were eager for a strong government able to get rid of foreign domination, a relatively honest and competent government for dealing with domestic affairs, economic development to bring a higher level of real income, and social justice to reduce poverty and inequality, particularly for the rural population.

Long before 1949, these issues had been addressed in the writings of Sun Yat-sen, which are explored in Chapter 3. Sun was strongly influenced by Henry George and by Lenin's experiments in the newly-formed Soviet Union. He observed first hand the Japanese government's success in promoting economic development. And Sun absorbed German ideas associated with Adolf Wagner and German-educated Richard T. Ely. Although Sun died in 1925, his ideas maintained near-religious status over the next quarter-century. His viewpoint was a relatively collectivist one, and was the basis for national government ownership and control of many sectors of the economy, particularly after the outbreak of war in 1937. While Sun was hardly a representative of mainstream western economics, his confidence that a strong government could successfully pursue economic growth and social justice was shared by many American institutionalists and their European counterparts.

In 1956, soon after the Communist take-over, Wu Yuan-li observed that "Because the [Chinese] government had played an increasingly important role in the actual allocation and use of resources both before and after the war, and because inadequate attention had been given to the development of the economy through individual initiative within a well-ordered economy and established rule of law, there was not a broad and vigorous capitalistic economy in China at the time the Communists took over. The transition to the system of greater regimentation . . . was made all the easier both physically and ideologically." (Wu 1956, pp. 42–43)

Post-1949

Our final chapter reviews developments after the Communist take-over in 1949 and attempts an overview and evaluation. The Communist seizure of power in 1949 was largely a response to the war against Japan, which overwhelmed the Kuomintang government of Chiang Kai-shek. It is doubtful whether a better understanding of western economics would have impeded the Communist take-over. But such an understanding might well have improved the disastrous policies followed by Mao Zedong.[20] A regime based on force and fraud largely suppressed the wisdom of western economics. One response was a notable exodus of Chinese economists to the West and to Taiwan, where they made valuable contributions to the discipline.

The creation of Mao's new government in 1949 brought radical changes in the areas with which this study is concerned. The missionary colleges were abolished as separate entities; their facilities and remaining faculties were absorbed into government institutions. Marxist materials came to dominate instruction in Economics. Russian instructors came to China to teach. Soviet textbooks were adapted for Chinese students, who were also pressed to learn the Russian language.

By 1951, most western missionaries and teachers in China left or were driven out. Western-trained economists, and all other academics, were subjected to a crash course in Marxism. By 1952 it had become very difficult for Chinese people to leave the country. Whereas a large number of Chinese had been enrolled in American Economics graduate programs in the 1940s, virtually none came after the early 1950s. Western-trained economists shared the persecution which the regime systematically directed at all Chinese exposed to foreign ideas. This was conspicuous in the "Anti-rightist Campaign" of 1958, when several prominent western-trained economists were major targets. Systematic persecution of intellectuals was an important part of the Cultural Revolution, which reached peak intensity during the period 1966–69, but continued in various ways until 1976.

Mao's death in 1976 led to a thaw. Gradually the radical totalitarianism was relaxed. Interactions with foreign governments and individuals were resumed. Universities, many of them closed for as much as a decade, reopened and began to develop curricula more in line with those in the West. China's economy, under the direction of Deng Xiaoping, adopted many of the trappings of capitalism. A surprising number of older western-trained Chinese economists survived these vicissitudes and were still professionally active into the 1980s. Perhaps the quarter-century under Maoist rule made Chinese economists and political leaders more receptive to western ideas of free competitive markets.

The ideas of both Malthus and Keynes received a lot of attention during acrimonious debates of the 1950s. Proponents of their views (largely western-trained economists) lost the battle. But their ideas ultimately prevailed. China's extreme measures to limit population growth owed much to the Malthusian tradition. And demand management in a strongly

Keynesian vein became a major element of Chinese economic policy after 1980.[21]

The remarkable developments in China since 1949 help provide a motivation for studying the materials presented in this book. Regardless of the degree of diversity in the western economics studied by Chinese before 1949, the material dealt consistently with situations of market economy. Thus the pre-1949 economists were dealing with the same issues which now concern economists in China and in the West as well.

2

Preliminaries: Missionaries and Westernizing Chinese

The first recorded economics text published in Chinese language came at the time of, and by a person associated with, the Opium War. Karl Friedrich Gutzlaff (1803–51) was a German missionary who came to Asia in 1826 and learned the Chinese language. Around 1840 he published *Outlines of Political Economy* and *Treatise on Commerce*, both apparently only in Chinese.[1] Gutzlaff was a colorful and outrageous figure who was willing to accompany opium-smuggling ships in order to distribute Christian literature. He believed that free markets would lead to economic and social progress if organized "under a system of law and justice similar to the British" (Lutz 1985, pp. 82–83). Gutzlaff also published a magazine in which he and fellow missionary E. C. Bridgman advocated similar views. Articles in 1837 "cited the pre-Confucian work Kuan-tze for ancient Chinese arguments in favor of international commerce", and presented "the principles of laissez-faire . . . and a short history of world commerce . . . [which] illustrated the benefits that accrued to trading partners" (Drake 1985, p. 97).

The Treaty of Nanjing (1842) which followed the Opium War opened China to the influx of western missionaries. In addition to the Christian gospel, they introduced western attitudes toward education, sanitation and health, women's rights, and concern for poverty and inequality. Although most Chinese intellectuals viewed Christianity with disdain or outright disgust, some missionaries became sufficiently "Chinese" to win acceptance and support from Chinese leaders.

In 1861, the Chinese government opened a school in Peking to train diplomatic interpreters—the Tongwenguan. An American missionary, William A. P. Martin (1826–1916) was its first director (Duus 1956; Spence 1969). In 1867 Martin initiated a course in "Richer Nations'

Policy"—meaning, political economy.[2] For the class, Martin and Wan Feng-chao (Fengzhao) subsequently (1880) translated Henry Fawcett's *Manual of Political Economy*, originally published in England in 1863.

The Chinese government opened another language school in Shanghai in 1863, and a translation bureau was added in 1868. It was headed by English missionary John Fryer (1839–1928) (Bennett 1967; Spence 1969). In his 28 years with the bureau, Fryer and his Chinese collaborators were responsible for a large output of translations, including a number of social science items. These included *Money*, by James Platt (originally 1880); Thomas H. Farrer's *The State in Its Relation to Trade* (originally 1883); and a compilation of writings on mints and coinage.

"Homely Words"

The most intriguing of Fryer's translations was a small book designated in Chinese as "Homely Words to Aid Governance", which appeared in 1885.[3] It was a translation of *Political Economy for Use in Schools and for Private Instruction*, by John Hill Burton, originally published in 1852 in Edinburgh. Of the book's 154 pages, nearly 50 at the beginning were devoted to a very broad survey of the evolution of social institutions. Here Burton dealt with the family, individual rights and duties, equality and inequality, the origins and interactions among nations, development of types of government, laws, and government activities. These sections were apparently of greatest interest to Chinese intellectuals.

In the more conventional economics sections, Burton defended the notions of private property and free competition, but neglected such standard topics as the law of diminishing returns, the Malthusian theory of population, and the wage-fund concept.

The translators had difficulty with many economic terms,[4] and the translation toned down Burton's confidence in the beneficial evolution of political and legal institutions. Burton had waxed lyrical in support of British free trade (1852, p. 20) but in the translation, Britain's dismantling of import taxes was completely ignored. Chinese intellectuals resented the imposition on China of a low-tariff policy by western nations. Burton's passages stressing the spontaneous tendency of market forces to harmonize private self-interest with public benefit were repeatedly toned down.[5] His clear statement that the reward to labor reflected workers' productivity (p. 68) was not clearly translated.

The Burton translation had an obvious influence on major Chinese intellectuals of the period, notably Kang Youwei, Liang Qichao, and Tan Ssu-tung (Tan Sidong).[6]

Other Missionary Writings

An important outlet for western missionaries writing on economic topics was a monthly missionary periodical entitled *Wan Kwok Kung Pao*, variously translated as *International News Bulletin* or *Review of the Times*. The articles did not attempt technical economic analysis, but aimed to alert the readers to the dimensions of economic life and policy. Hsiao summarizes a few representative items as follows: an article by Joseph Edkins (1889) "suggesting that the existing railway system be expanded"; an article by customs director Robert Hart (1889) "arguing that foreign trade should benefit China and that railroads, electric power, mining, steamship navigation, and banks should be developed"; two articles by Ernst Faber (1890) "recommending machine manufacturing, development of a transportation system, abolition of likin, and issuance of government bonds" (Hsiao 1975, p. 332).

Joseph Edkins (1823–1905) came to China from his native England around 1848. He resigned from missionary service in 1880 and became a translator for the (British-dominated) Imperial Maritime Customs Service (Barr 1972, pp. 20, 57, 81). There he collaborated in translating William Stanley Jevons's *Primer on Political Economy* (originally 1878), which was published in 1886.[7] About 1900 Edkins was commissioned by the Customs Service to write a series of monographs on financial topics. He produced a volume on Chinese currency (1901), one on government revenue and taxation (1903), and one on banking and prices in China (1905).

Chinese Traditions

The ideas and activities of "westernizing" or "modernizing" Chinese of the nineteenth century developed against a background of traditions. These were institutionalized in the imperial examinations, success in which was a stepping-stone to becoming an official. The rewards were very great—power, prestige, comfort, and wealth. Success in the imperial examinations required a mastery of the "classics", and the ability to write in accepted literary modes.

The Chinese classics, some of which dated back about two thousand years, contained many disparate and sometimes conflicting elements.[8] The

Confucian writings were concerned with virtue and propriety. The Confucian image was one of a hierarchical world involving the duties and responsibilities of such relationships as rulers and subjects, parents and children, and husbands and wives. "Filial piety" amounting at times to ancestor worship was an important element. The powerful family bonds among Chinese remain an important economic factor. For a long time, China experts condemned Confucian values as a source of backwardness and stagnation. Then as Asian countries demonstrated extraordinary economic achievements (particularly China after 1976), emphasis shifted to extolling Confucian values as a source of both prosperity and social solidarity.[9]

Virtue and propriety were, in the Confucian teachings, the essential qualifications of suitable rulers and officials. Paul Cohen noted that "expertise, as such, never became an acknowledged pathway to social prestige and status" (1974, p. 159). The Confucian texts did not ignore economic concerns. In some passages, Confucius supported a laissez-faire approach to economic activities. At the same time, the ruler had a responsibility to aid the public in achieving economic sufficiency (Hu Jichuang 1988, pp. 42–47, 56). Confucianism could be used to defend a hierarchical non-achieving status quo, or to argue in favor of much more ambitious government economic intervention.

Other Chinese classics offered divergent viewpoints. The eminent historian Ssu-ma Chien (Sima Qian), writing around 200 B.C., offered an astonishingly clear view of the economically integrating role of market economy. The legalist scholar Han Fei provided very specific content to the economic responsibilities of the government (Cohen, p. 187). However, for the most part, Chinese scholars did not envision the economy as a system worthy of attention in itself.

"Westernizing" Chinese Intellectuals

The forcible opening of China to western influences in the 1840s soon provoked responses from Chinese who were eager to protect their culture. Initially they emphasized the need to upgrade Chinese military force and to adopt western weapons. That in turn brought attention to western technology in general, and then to western science. Individual Chinese began to travel abroad and to report back not only their descriptions of conditions in the West, but also their recommendations for China's economic system.

Wei Yuan (1794–1857) pioneered in describing the West to Chinese readers. He argued that a major basis for western success was the development of commerce, a pursuit not highly esteemed in China. He enumerated many sectors of production in which China might imitate the West, and advocated private enterprise as the chief form (Hu Jichuang 1988, pp. 516–526). Wang Tao (1828–97) had a long association with western missionary scholars and lived in Britain and continental Europe for four years. His writings often dealt with economic topics. He described many western industries and enumerated specific types which he felt China could and should develop. He was an early advocate of railway development, at a time when most Chinese retained a deep emotional antipathy to it—sufficient that in 1876 the Chinese government bought up an early private railway line in order to destroy it (Cohen 1974, p. 192)! Whereas Chinese tradition praised agriculture and disparaged merchants and commerce, Wang stressed the importance of commerce as a source of western power, and argued that commercial development would aid, not damage, agriculture (Cohen 1974, pp. 185–208). Wang Tao met Sun Yat-sen in 1894, early in the latter's career. There are substantial similarities between Wang's view on China's economic development and those which Sun eventually systematized (Cohen 1974, p. 3). Hsueh Fu-cheng (Xue Fuzheng) and Chen Chiu (Qiu) strongly defended private enterprise as a means toward economic development (Hsiao 1975, pp. 319–324, 327 ff). Several writers extolled Japan's economic progress as a possible model for China (Feuerwerker 1958, pp. 31–34).

Ma Jianzhong was probably the first Chinese to study Economics overseas, as part of his law studies in Paris in 1876–77. Writing in 1890, he urged the importance of increasing China's exports and decreasing imports. Since China could not increase import tariffs, this goal should be sought through modernizing production (Hsiao 1975, pp. 324–325).

Kang Youwei

One of China's most active intellectuals at the turn of the century was Kang Youwei (1858–1927).[10] Kang became convinced that China must become familiar with western learning for self-improvement and self-preservation. He never learned a western language, but read extensively in Chinese and Japanese translations and commentaries on western materials.

By 1890 Kang had become a prolific writer on social and political matters, advocating reform of China's political, economic, and educational institutions. In a series of practical memorials and essays, Kang urged that the government try to promote economic development in order to strengthen the state and to improve the people's economic well-being. However, the role of government was to be one of cultivating and encouraging private enterprise. Experience with government enterprises in the West showed it was often inefficient and unproductive (Hsiao 1975, pp. 302–303; Lo 1967, pp. 150–151).

The year 1885 was also the starting point for extensive philosophical writings in which Kang appears to have contradicted many of the themes just noted. Most interesting was a book entitled *Ta-Tung-Shu* (*Dadongshu*), variously translated as *The Book of Great Unity*, *Great Harmony*, or *Great Community*. Completed in 1902, parts appeared in print in 1913, but the entire text did not appear until 1935, eight years after Kang's death.[11]

Ta-Tung-Shu outlined a utopian socialist society, comparable to western works by Robert Owen, Edward Bellamy, and Charles Fourier (whom Kang cited as "Mr. Fu").[12] Kang argued that much of the harmful division of the world came from competitive striving after gain animated by the family system. However, he recommended retaining competitive elements, such as differential rewards of honors and money to persons distinguished for their contributions to the public welfare (Thompson 1958, pp. 204, 242–244, 258). Kang also envisioned a system of "Public Institutions for the Poor", which seemed to be modeled after the British workhouses provided by the notorious Poor Law of 1834: "the institutions must stress the punishing of laziness, and exhortations to work" (Thompson 1958, p. 200).

We know that Mao Zedong was familiar with Kang's ideas, and some scholars have suggested that Mao's concept of the people's communes (briefly and disastrously introduced in 1958) was based in part on Kang's *Ta-Tung-Shu* (Hsiao 1975, pp. 478, 494–495).

Kang's practical memorials urging modernization gained him the attention of the Guangxu Emperor. But in 1898, officials took drastic action against leaders of the reform movement. Kang and Liang Qichao both escaped from the country. Kang's travels in the United States caused him to lose his enthusiasm for western ways. He opposed the overthrow of the monarchy in 1911–12, then worked to promote its restoration and to have Confucianism adopted as a state religion.

Yan Fu and Adam Smith

A milestone in China's intellectual history was reached in the work of Yan Fu (1853–1921), whose translation of Adam Smith's *The Wealth of Nations* (WN) was published in 1902. Yan Fu learned English at the Foochow Shipyard School, then went to England for further study. Upon reading Herbert Spencer's *Study of Sociology* in 1881, Yan became convinced that Social Darwinism held a key to the relative wealth and power of Britain and offered guidance for strengthening China. His writings stressed the idea that economic power and progress contribute to the strength of the state. This theme took on greater urgency after China's defeat by Japan in 1894–95. Yan Fu published translations of relevant major western works, including John Stuart Mill's *On Liberty* and *A System of Logic*, and Jevons's *Primer of Logic*, accompanied by his own extensive commentaries.

Yan Fu's translation of Adam Smith was not easy reading. Although Yan sensibly abridged his translation of the 900-page original, his style was deliberately esoteric, aimed at the scholars.[13] For all its shortcomings, Yan's translation did influence Liang Qichao and Mao Zedong.[14]

Professor Lai Cheng-chung of Qinghua University in Taiwan is the leading Chinese authority on Yan Fu's Adam Smith.[15] He has generously collaborated with the present author. We chose sections of Smith's work which would have been of particular value to Chinese readers and examined how well Yan Fu did in translating them. Professor Lai re-translated relevant passages back into English for comparison with the original.

The Morality of the Market Economy

Yan was well aware that among his audience, "the prejudice against a revaluation of the merchant and his presumed ethos was still bone-deep" (Schwartz 1964, p. 123). Adam Smith was a moral philosopher. To show how individual self-seeking behavior would promote the welfare of the entire community, Smith had first to explicate his title.[16] The wealth (= economic welfare) of a nation was identified with its real output per capita, which is provided by "the annual labour of every nation" (Smith, p. 10). Smith wrote:

> According therefore, as this produce . . . bears a greater or smaller proportion to the number of those who are to consume it, the nation will be better or worse supplied with . . . necessaries and conveniences . . . (Smith, p. 10)

Compare it with Yan Fu's rendering:

> All that is needed by a group of people for living is produced by the labor of its people. The expenses of a nation are supposed to be the same as its national production. When the production exceeds consumption, there is surplus, and with this surplus the people will be comfortable. On the other hand, if there is a deficit, the people will suffer. (Lai 1997, pp. 40–41)

Several of the ideas are presented with admirable clarity and brevity—the first sentence, for example. But Smith's references to proportions were blurred, and the focus on per capita consumption was largely lost.

Smith next celebrated the high productivity which results from "division of labor" (specialization). But specialization is not beneficial unless products are exchanged. One of Smith's most famous passages linked this process with the market mechanism. In modern society, said Smith, each individual:

> stands at all times in need of the co-operation and assistance of great multitudes, while his whole life is scarce sufficient to gain the friendship of a few persons . . . [M]an has almost constant occasion for the help of his brethren, and it is in vain for him to expect it from their benevolence only . . . It is not from the benevolence of the butcher, the brewer, or the baker, that we expect our dinner, but from their regard to their own interest. We address ourselves, not to their humanity but to their self-love, and never talk to them of our own necessities but of their advantages. (Smith, pp. 26–27)

Yan Fu condensed these ideas but stated the central theme clearly, as follows:

> Since we are living in a community, on most occasions we need supplies from many others to satisfy our needs. If you expect all these supplies only from those people who like you, it will be very rare in all your life that someone can please you and satisfy your needs at the same time . . . If we need help from the society but we cannot rely on others' supplies all the time, then how can we make our living? The answer is: it is sufficient to pursue one's self-interest . . . The butchers, the wine sellers, the grain suppliers in the market all satisfy our needs in food. They do so not because of their morality but because of their self-interest. (Yan Fu, p. 12)

Smith's most famous passage in support of the morality of market economy came almost halfway through WN, as follows:

> [E]very individual who employs his capital in the support of domestic industry, necessarily endeavours so to direct that industry, that its produce may be of the greatest possible value . . . In proportion as the value of this produce is great or small, so will likewise be the profits of the employer . . . As every

> individual, therefore, endeavours . . . both to employ his capital in the support of domestic industry, and so to direct that industry that its produce may be of the greatest value; every individual necessarily labours to render the annual revenue of the society as great as he can . . . [H]e intends only his own gain, and he is in this, as in many other cases, led by an invisible hand to promote an end which was no part of his intention. (Smith, pp. 455–456)

In this passage, Smith presented a rudimentary marginal analysis in which capital investment is drawn to those activities which add the most to the value of both private output and the national product. Yan Fu struggled with this passage, perhaps because of Smith's ambiguous use of the word "industry" which conveys a mix of entrepreneurial effort and capital investment. Yan Fu wrote:

> People who invest their capital to seek profits will devote all their efforts to this task. If so, the benefits [to the society] will be maximized. When a specific skill is used to produce goods, this skill will be applied to many other materials which will increase the price [value] of the transacted goods. So the level of profit earned by manufacturers [producers] depends on the price-added that they have created. Those who invest capital to seek profit will never say that the profit is too high; the same is true for those who work on the materials to increase the price [value] of the product. However, above all, the profitable thing is to let the workers seek their own outlets and let the people be thus organized.
>
> The value of output in a nation (which depends on the fertility of the land and the labor devoted) depends on the product that they can exchange. If the merchants of the country try to maximize their profits in local business . . . , if the manufacturers seek to maximize their value added, then what these people are doing is to increase the annual revenue of a nation. They do that not for the interest of the public nor for the benefits to the nation. All that they are doing is simply for self-interest . . . (Yan Fu, pp. 449–450)

Yan Fu had no difficulty stating the punch line—which the self-interested activities of entrepreneurs lead to public benefit. But his exposition was murky—nowhere in Yan's text do we clearly see an increase in the national output. He relates "the value of output in a nation" to products exchanged, when one would have preferred a reference to products produced. The social benefits are expressed in terms of the "annual revenue" of the nation, which lacks the implied dimension of real national income. Yan Fu is most disappointing in rendering the "invisible hand" sentence. He tried to convey the message, but the result was not comprehensible.

Economic Growth and Development

In Smith's vision, economic growth was a benign process, raising demand for labor and benefiting workers through higher real wages. Smith wrote:

> The same cause . . . which raises the wages of labour, the increase of stock [physical capital], tends to increase its productive powers, and to make a smaller quantity of labour produce a greater quantity of work. The owner of the stock which employs a great number of labourers, necessarily endeavours . . . to make such a proper division and distribution of employment, that they may be enabled to produce the greatest quantity of work possible. For the same reason, he endeavours to supply them with the best machinery which either he or they can think of . . . More heads are occupied in inventing the most proper machinery for executing the work of each, and it is, therefore, more likely to be invented. There are many commodities, therefore, which in consequence of those improvements, come to be produced by so much less labour than before, that the increase of its [labour's] price is more than compensated by the diminution of its quantity. (Smith, p. 104)

In Yan Fu's words:

> The reason why wages increase is because the capital for employment is increased . . . When more skilled, people will use the skills more deeply: the needed labor is less but the production is larger. When more capital is invested and more workers are employed, the entrepreneur will allocate all these . . . such that the resources will be efficiently used and production will be abundant. They also will develop skillful techniques to save labor and improve production . . . It is possible only when labor is abundant and new inventions are created. An activity which needed ten workers previously now needs only a single person to perform; what previously took a year now takes only a day. Although the wage rate is higher, the required labor for the same production is less; the difference increases profit. That is why the wage is higher but the commodity price is lower, such that the general living is improved and people need not worry about unemployment. (Yan Fu, p. 96)

Yan Fu certainly had no difficulty dramatizing the increase in productivity. And he translated clearly Smith's descriptions of basic categories of capital goods. Yan coined the term "mother capital", probably as a way of dramatizing the importance of capital goods for productivity and economic growth. The term recurred often in Yan's text.

Adam Smith was convinced that economic growth, driven by capital formation and technological improvement, would raise wages and bring benefits to the working class. Yan Fu clarified Smith's discussion by adding explicit references to the supply of and demand for labor.

Smith recognized that improvement in the real wage could improve the health and nutrition of the working class and reduce infant mortality, leading to population growth (WN, pp. 97–99). Unlike the subsequent concern of Malthus and Ricardo for diminishing returns, Smith anticipated that food supply could keep ahead of population, as has been the case in the developed countries (WN, pp. 206, 235, 259).

Yan Fu rendered Smith's discussion as follows:

> As the rewards to labor improve, the living condition of the people improves and the breeding of children will be easier. The mortality of children is also decreased . . . As the population increases, the supply of labor also increases such that the demand and supply are made equal. The improvement of workers' living is the result of national wealth increase. A better living induces more population. (Yan Fu, pp. 86–89)

The priority of capital investment in promoting economic growth, to which Smith and Yan devoted so much attention, became a standard feature of Chinese discourse for much of the twentieth century, involving authorities ranging from Sun Yat-sen to Fang Xianting to Mao Zedong. But it took a long time before people appreciated the importance of an optimizing framework to use capital productively.

Value and Resource Allocation

Smith's work was a powerful polemic in favor of international free trade, and his position was strongly endorsed by Yan Fu. Smith supported his case for free trade and free markets by lengthy and sophisticated analysis of the interplay of product and factor markets. Smith argued that there existed "natural" [equilibrium] prices for labor, land, and capital. Workers and other input suppliers would shop around for the best deal until the rewards in various employments would be equalized (Smith, pp. 72–74).

Modern economists have recognized that such factor-price equalization across different products is a condition of economic efficiency. Yan Fu's rendering missed it entirely. But he reproduced very competently the general notion of the adjustment of quantities toward equalizing supply and demand in product and factor markets (Yan Fu, p. 115).

Smith's analysis of factor prices—wages, interest, and rent—was of very uneven quality. However, in his section on colonies he developed a very sophisticated analysis relating factor prices to the relative supplies of productive factors (Smith, pp. 564–566). Yan Fu transmitted these ideas quite faithfully, as follows:

> European countries established colonies in regions which had only a few inhabitants . . . These colonies were developed and enriched, far more than the old countries could expect. Why? . . . The land that a man can occupy is often much more extensive than his ability to farm. There is no landlord, hence no rent is necessary . . . They enjoy their entire harvest . . . If a country is old enough, rent and profit are usually high while wages are low. Those who possess rent and profit will be rich and noble. But the inferior class consists of minor citizens who live by the efforts of their hands and legs. These minor citizens are often under the control of the rich and noble. However, everything in the new territory is different: there is no slave labor to be used [!], so they have to be generous to workers, and it is only by so doing that they can generate more profits. The lands are fertile, but the price of land is normally cheap. Those who are diligent are often able to earn profit. What they need more is labor, but since the population is not abundant, wage rates are usually high. (Yan Fu, pp. 556–557)

Yan might have noted that this analysis was very relevant to China, indicating that low labor incomes were a result of the factor imbalance in the economy, rather than such politically popular explanations as the abusive behavior of landlords, moneylenders, middlemen, foreigners, etc. Unfortunately, these passages occurred deep into Smith's book, by which time most readers had already been muddled by his earlier factor-price discussions.

Smith used his formidable analysis of competitive markets to show the disadvantages of restrictions on international trade. Again, Yan transmitted the central ideas clearly, as follows:

> The idea that accumulating gold and silver through trade will benefit the nation has been proved wrong . . . There are two major benefits [of international trade]. One is to export the surplus commodities; the other is to import what is insufficient. (Yan Fu, pp. 440–442)

> If a foreign country can supply a product cheaper than one can obtain it at home, then it is evident that this product is not the advantageous specialization for our land and our people. In this case, it will be more beneficial to exchange these products with those of our specialization. (Yan Fu, pp. 450–451)

Yan Fu's was one of the few voices in China raised in favor of unrestricted imports. Forced into a low-tariff policy by the "unequal treaties", most patriotic Chinese were eager to restrict imports to promote domestic manufacturing.

The Role of the Government

Yan Fu clearly identified Smith's basic agenda for the government, which should provide for defense, domestic law and order, and public goods (Smith, pp. 687–688; Yan Fu, p. 684). In Great Britain, the government was already addressing the problems of national defense and the maintenance of domestic law and order. In China, however, neither of these was adequately provided. China's military weakness had been conspicuous throughout most of the nineteenth century and was to remain a problem for another half-century. Similarly, domestic law and order were poorly protected.

Smith emphasized the urgency of adequate legal protection for property and contracts (p. 910), and Yan Fu reproduced this urgency:

> Unless the law is fair and the people are well protected, the industries and commerce of a nation cannot last long . . . If justice cannot be maintained, people having property will not feel reliable. If contracts cannot be enforced, functionaries do not protect the right side. (Yan Fu, p. 935)

Smith's agenda emphasized public works to improve transportation, and Yan Fu transmitted these ideas faithfully. However, such advocacy was already commonplace in Chinese commentaries.

Smith's Book Four devoted much space to describing and criticizing British mercantilist policies regulating trade and navigation. Smith's sharp-edged critique of "rent-seeking behavior" led Yan Fu lamely to remark in his translator's notes, that the reader can "see how the old mercantile system was harmful to national economy; it is also evident that when people were in search of self-interest, the results were in conflict with the real interest [of the whole society]" (Lai 1997, p. 7 of ch. 4). Yan failed to stress that self-interested behavior was harmful when organized pressure groups achieved monopoly gains through state action.

Adam Smith and China

Adam Smith referred to China at several points, particularly in his analysis of economic growth. China illustrated the problems facing a country where capital did not grow very fast. Smith painted a grim picture of economic conditions in China—too grim, according to some recent scholarship (Pomeranz 2000). Yan Fu's relatively accurate rendering of Smith was as follows:

> China was a bountiful country where people's living was affluent, though requiring hard work. The land is abundant but not unexplored. She has, however, not progressed for several hundred or a thousand years . . . The miserable conditions of the ordinary people in China are worse than the poorest European countries. In the Canton area hundreds and thousands of people are living in floating boats on the river. These boat people have very meager subsistence such that when a Western ship comes by, they will surround the ship waiting for their discarded food to be dropped into the river . . . Their children are numerous but infanticide is the rule; they are killed as animals. This is the most cruel thing in the world, but it has been a common practice in China . . .
>
> Although China did not progress, she also did not degenerate. The tilled fields are still under cultivation, and the farmers are still doing the same thing as usual. Even the lowest people and the poorest workers can find ways to get married and breed their children. Otherwise the population would have decreased and could not be so active as one observes. (Yan Fu, pp. 75–77)
>
> In China commerce and business are considered as mean professions. Sailing on the sea is prohibited. Trading with foreign countries is a shameful business such that Western ships are allowed in only one or two ports. In this kind of country commerce is seldom developed, and many commodities are not fully circulated. Moreover, politics is another problem. The leading houses [families], having political and economic powers, tend to take over others' properties; the middle-level businessmen are exploited by the general administrators. Contracts are not reliable, and when disputed, people will lose much more. (Yan Fu, p. 107)

In these passages, Smith and Yan closely paralleled the recent judgments of Maddison (1998) on China's economic evolution noted in Chapter 1.

Despite its antiquity, many sections of *The Wealth of Nations* were worthy of the attention of Chinese readers. However, the passages we have selected must often have seemed to Chinese readers to be afloat in a vast sea of relatively shapeless statements.

Yan's translation was most often on target with descriptive statements, but he struggled with analytical passages. Yan had trouble rendering the concepts of increase or decrease, referring instead to magnitudes being "high" or "low". Yan relied much on *ipse dixit*, substituting authority in place of analysis. Free trade and free markets were good because Smith said so.

Yan is better viewed as a crusader defending the values of business enterprise in free competitive markets, rather than as a purveyor of technical economic analysis. His crusade had disappointing results. A primitive populist antipathy toward business persisted in China, manifested both in Sun Yat-sen's writings and in the appeal of the Communists. One can imagine Yan's Chinese reader noting that China already had a relatively unrestrained market economy and very low tariffs on imports. If things were so good, why were they so bad?

A new translation of *The Wealth of Nations* was published in 1931 by Wang Yanan and Guo Dali. The translators were Marxists and undertook the translation to aid readers in understanding Marx.[17]

Liang Qichao

An important dimension of Yan Fu's influence was exerted through his friend and collaborator Liang Qichao.[18] Although he never learned to read any western language, Liang took on the role of an intellectual intermediary, reading voraciously in Chinese or Japanese renderings of western ideas and then writing about them to a wide audience in China (Nathan 1985, p. 48).

Liang developed intellectually as a protégé of Kang Youwei.[19] In 1896 Liang became friends with Yan Fu, with whom he shared an enthusiasm for Social Darwinism. Liang drew on Yan Fu for his own comments on Adam Smith (Schwartz 1964, pp. 47–48, 70, 83–85; Lai 1997). During the reform movement of 1898, the emperor appointed Liang to head a newly formed government translation bureau. When support turned to persecution, Liang and many others fled to Japan.

Liang immediately set about learning the Japanese language and gained access to the large volume of western intellectual materials which had been translated into Japanese. During his time in Japan, Liang published a number of Chinese-language newspapers which circulated on the mainland and overseas. Mao Zedong was one of many Chinese intellectuals who testified to the eagerness with which they read his writings. According to Hao Chang, Liang can be considered "the most popular writer in China" during the decade following 1898 (Chang 1971, p. 142).

The overthrow of the monarchy in 1911–12 gave Liang the opportunity to return to China, where he entered national politics. He served briefly as Minister of Justice (1913) and Minister of Finance (1917), and attended the

Paris Peace Conference (1919). From 1920 he held various university teaching positions in China, writing and lecturing chiefly on philosophical and literary topics.

Liang's "Concise History"

In 1902 Liang published a series of newspaper articles which were subsequently collected under the title "Concise History of Economic Thought". This was probably the first such survey presented in a manner accessible to a significant number of Chinese readers. A full translation of this study has been prepared by Dr. Wang Zhaoping. The bulk of Liang's survey was devoted to Adam Smith and his predecessors. The essay did not carry the reader into the realm of nineteenth-century economics.

Most of Liang's 1902 material was drawn from Japanese translations of works by Luigi Cossa and John Kells Ingram.[20] Liang bypassed Cossa's comments (p. 88) on the "statesmen and learned men of [ancient] China". He did endeavor to provide his readers with some of the institutional background of classical civilization, medieval times, and the ages of Renaissance and Reformation.

Liang enumerated many shortcomings of mercantilism, particularly primitive bullionism. But he forthrightly urged that China follow a mercantilistic policy:

> Although mercantilism hindered economic development in Europe in the sixteenth century, it seems to be the only remedy for today's China. With rich natural resources, China can be self-sufficient in her daily needs. Therefore, a tariff barrier against goods to be imported and a high price level of the imported goods will not affect the general living-standard of the Chinese people. Having the cheapest labor force and a sufficient supply of raw materials, China is able to produce low-cost commodities. It is therefore a good policy to encourage exports . . . Compared with European businessmen in the fourteenth and fifteenth centuries, whose ability of doing business took a lot of government effort to foster, Chinese businessmen are more talented and enterprising. China is therefore expected to be more effective in implementing a mercantilist policy. Unfortunately, no mercantilist statesman like Cromwell has ever appeared . . . in China.

Liang's discussion of Adam Smith drew extensively on Yan Fu's understanding, going far beyond the inadequate treatments given by both Cossa and Ingram. Liang's exposition of Smith proceeded smoothly and sequentially, stressing first the division of labor. The mutuality of economic exchange is well expressed: "While a person has his needs fulfilled, he helps fulfill the needs of society as a whole." Efficient specialization in turn requires exchange, which is the motivation for the institution of money. And he summarized the self-regulating market succinctly.

Liang stressed Smith's conviction that economic development would raise the demand for labor and thus cause wages to rise. This led Liang to the following discussion:

> Take China as an example. Wages have now been rising substantially. In Guangdong Province, Peking and Tianjin, wages have doubled over the years. This is evidence of the economic development of this country. If, however, we look deeper into this fact, we will find that the capital supporting the economic development is not the capital of our country but from foreign countries. It is the foreign countries—the capital providers—that are the first to benefit from our economic development . . . They are more of a beneficiary of than a contributor to China's economic development. With the ever-increasing investment of foreign capital, there are more and more job openings in the labor market. But, because of transportation problems, the labor force in inland provinces of China is not readily available to meet the demand. As a result, wages are going up dramatically. On the other hand, although business is good and the employment situation is improving, people still live in destitution. What is even worse, prices are rising together with wages and salaries. The higher wages can do little more than cover the rising prices. Meanwhile, domestic small capital owners, unable to employ workers, would offer themselves as wage-workers . . . India and other colonized countries had the same experience following the economic invasion from the Western powers. The overturned cart ahead is a warning to the carts behind. I shudder at the mere thought of the future of my country.

Liang's emotional distress over China's weakness and the supposed damage from imperialism swamped his analysis; real and money wages became hopelessly muddled, and people apparently became better off and worse off at the same time. Free-trade convictions he had displayed in earlier writings were now replaced by a strident support for protectionism. The conviction that Chinese business enterprises were being destroyed by foreign competition came to be shared by observers as diverse as Sun Yat-sen and distinguished Nankai economist Fang Xianting.

Liang regained his equanimity to reiterate Smith's vision of a self-adjusting system, paraphrasing as follows:

> It is wise to let people make decisions for themselves. Those who exert themselves to make a living will get compensation for their hard work. If a

> particular line of business is on the rise, more and more people will go in for it. If it is on the decline, people will abandon it. People themselves are a self-regulating mechanism and they will take care of their livelihood. There is no need for the government to have a hand in their economic affairs.

Liang felt that Smith's attack on mercantilistic regulations was appropriate for its time and place, "for economies were dislocated and people became less enthusiastic about their economic pursuit. However, things are different in China. The Chinese government had shown very little concern for the undertakings and well-being of its people. In this sense the Chinese people are extremely 'free', but unfortunately they are far behind the western countries in economic development. What Adam Smith prescribed was a good remedy for yesterday's Europe, but not the remedy for today's China. The way to save China is to follow what Cromwell did in England."

Liang's discussion of Book Two brought him to two topics to which he gave particular emphasis; the growth of capital, and the distinction between productive and unproductive labor: "the nation can produce more and more output on the strength of ever-growing capital stock" generated by diligence and frugality. Furthermore, "increase of capital raises demand for labor, increasing wages but lowering profits". Interest is a reward for productive saving and investment, and thus should not come under disapproval.

Liang's discussion of Smith was quite a competent survey—better by far than the treatment given by Cossa and Ingram. Having identified Smith as an intellectual creator of western progress and strength, Liang probably did not feel the need to extend his narrative of the history of economic thought. It is ironic that Liang gave Chinese readers a clear statement of the virtues of free markets and free trade, but then proceeded to argue for import restrictions for China.

Other Essays

Liang dealt with matters involving the history of western economic ideas in several other essays. In a lengthy analysis of Jeremy Bentham, Liang expressed his concern about the degree to which private interests would spontaneously come into harmony with a public interest.[21] According to Liang, "Public interest and private interest not only cannot coincide with each other, they also clash with each other in nine out of ten cases." (Hao Chang 1971, p. 207) Liang was unfair to Bentham, who was aware that harmony often did not occur spontaneously, and whose work was rich in schemes of social engineering designed to direct private interest toward public benefit.

Another article of the same period briefly summarized Malthus's analysis of population. As Levenson (1959, p. 69) noted, Liang garbled Malthus's contrast between arithmetic and geometric progressions, but cautioned his readers that this was a contrived theory. Liang stated the central theme in this manner: "If there is no way of preventing it, the calamity of excess population is unavoidable and war, plague and suicide will become widespread."[22] But his article gave no indication that he saw China as manifesting the problems depicted by Malthus. Rather, he applied the analysis to Europe, where he felt that rapid population growth had become a powerful force behind imperialism and colonization.

Liang also took a strong interest in monetary affairs. In 1904, an American economist, Jeremiah Whipple Jenks, visited China and prepared a report urging China to adopt a gold-exchange system. Liang wrote a book explaining and supporting the proposal (Hou and Wu 1984). During his brief tenure with the Monetary Bureau in 1914 and as Minister of Finance in 1917, he tried without success to implement some of these ideas.

After 1904 Liang engaged in a political competition with Sun Yat-sen in an effort to organize overseas Chinese into programs for Chinese political change. This led to controversy concerning socialist proposals from Sun and his followers. The debate is summarized in the next chapter and is reviewed in detail in Lai and Trescott 2005. Liang and Sun both started their discussions with strongly negative assessments of capitalism and industrial development in the West. Both relied in part on Richard T. Ely's *Outlines of Economics* (1893), which had been translated into Japanese (Scalapino and Schiffrin 1959, p. 335, n. 22).

Liang began the debate supporting a considerable degree of socialism along German lines, citing Adolf Wagner, Gustav Schmoller, and Lujo Brentano in support (Bernal 1976, pp. 158–159). But in the heat of argument Liang receded considerably from this position. While Sun was advocating that China adopt socialist policies to bypass capitalism, Liang argued that the problem facing China was primarily inadequate production. Liang urged that China rely on private property and free markets, except that domestic capitalists needed protection against imperialistic foreign capital. Despite earlier remarks supporting nationalization of utilities and natural monopolies, Liang in 1907 unleashed quite a formidable arsenal of arguments against government ownership and management, even of tramways.

In the 1920s, after the emergence of a genuine revolutionary Communist movement in China, Liang reiterated some of his fears of 1907: "If we desire to transplant to China the centralized socialism conceived of by Marx and put into practice by Lenin, then it, too . . . because it runs counter to the national character, must fail in the end." (Quoted Levinson 1959, p. 212.)

The Japanese Link

Discussing Liang and Sun Yat-sen affirms the importance of Japan in transmitting western economic ideas into China. Following the Sino-Japanese War in 1894–95, large numbers of Chinese went to Japan to study. Japan was perceived as a model to be imitated. Between 1898 and 1911, at least 25,000 Chinese studied in Japan—an unprecedented educational migration, though only a small percentage received the equivalent of a modern university education (Reynolds 1993, p. 226). However, the contributions of Meiji, Keio and Waseda universities to Chinese economic education were not trivial. A prominent product of the early experience was Li Dazhao. Later Japanese-educated figures in our narrative include Gideon Chen, Wang Yanan, Lu Guangmian, Yang Tuan-lu (Duanliu), and Jiang Shuojie. Chao (Zhao) Lanping graduated from Keio University in 1922 and held teaching positions in several Chinese universities, notably the Central Political Institute. He published several widely used textbooks transmitting mainstream western economics, particularly an elementary text which went through 20 editions between 1932 and 1947. Tang Yu-jen (Youren), another Keio graduate, became director of economic research for the Bank of China (*China Year Book 1935*). Wu Ting-chang (Dingzhang) became a prominent banker and government official, and was president of *Ta Kung Pao* (1926–35), an influential newspaper which published a lot of economic material (*China Handbook 1937–45*, p. 701).

Economic scholarship in Japan was a generation ahead of China, and many western economic works had been translated into Japanese by 1900. An early example was the translation into Chinese of the Japanese version of *The Wealth of Nations* in 1896. It was translated by Kojo Teikichi, a Japanese engaged by the newly-formed Nanyang University in Shanghai (Reynolds, p. 111). There occurred a wholesale transference of technical terms from Japanese into Chinese—including central ideas in economics.[23] Tsien (1954) estimated that between 1850 and 1899, 567 works were translated into Chinese, of which 46 were in social sciences other than history and geography. Of these 46, 28 were in English and only 6 were in Japanese. In contrast, of 533 translations studied during the period 1902–04, 136 were in social sciences, of which only 16 were in English and 83 were in Japanese. For 1912–40, 5,299 translations were tabulated. Of these, 1,351 were social sciences, of which 491 were in English and only 53 in Japanese. It is likely that the earliest recorded Chinese textbooks in Economics were taken from Japanese sources. These included *A Textbook of General Economics* (c. 1903) edited by Wang Tsai-shan (Caishan); *A Textbook of Economics*, compiled and translated by Chou Kuei (Zhou Gui, c. 1903); *Outlines of Economics*, by Tsai Cheng-huan (Cai Zhenghuan 1906) (Huang Fu-ch'ing 1982; Hu Jichuang 1988, p. 530). These textbooks were probably used by the colleges of law and political science which sprang up in large numbers, imitating Japanese institutions. A Japanese publishing firm in Shanghai listed 608 Chinese-language items in its catalogue for 1904–05. Of these, 27 were in political economy (Peake 1932, p. 52).

Conclusions

The translations and transmissions of John Fryer, Yan Fu, and Liang Qichao helped alert Chinese intellectuals to western economic scholarship. However, there were major linguistic obstacles. Furthermore, even as late as 1902, none of these went much beyond Adam Smith in exposing Chinese to economic science.

Both Yan Fu and Liang Qichao enthusiastically supported Smith's conception of a beneficent self-adjusting free market system. They endorsed the importance of saving and investment to promote economic growth and improved well-being. Yan followed Smith's support for unrestricted international trade, but he was relatively alone among Chinese intellectuals in this posture. Most, like Liang, resented the free trade that was imposed on China by the western powers.

Liang's nationalistic concerns led him to support a kind of "welfare mercantilism" for China that showed the influence of Bismarck and the German Historical School as well as circumstances in Japan, where Liang lived in his most prolific period. This viewpoint became probably the consensus position among Chinese economists in the years up to 1949, not so much because they were influenced by Liang, but because they shared many of his values and views of the evidence. In many respects, Liang, rather than Sun Yat-sen, may deserve to be regarded as the intellectual precursor of Taiwan's post-World-War-II economic miracle.

Liang's work dramatically illustrated the forces which led to the introduction of western economic ideas into China. The process was not a mere academic exercise. Rather it was animated initially by a powerful motive to find the intellectual sources of western wealth and power and to harness those for China's improvement.

3

Sun Yat-sen

Sun Yat-sen (1866–1925) played a major role in modern Chinese political history. He helped overthrow the monarchy in 1911–12, was the first president of the new Chinese republic (if only provisionally) and was a major founder of the Kuomintang (KMT) as a powerful political organization.[1]

Sun wrote extensively on economic questions. His best-known writings occurred in 1919–25, stressing economic development and social justice for China. However, these had important antecedents published before 1911. Sun's work reflected much influence from Henry George, from Richard T. Ely, and indirectly from German economists, filtered through Japan. Sun is another interesting example of how Chinese intellectuals attempted to adapt western economic ideas to Chinese values and problems. The western influences on Sun's later writings were diverse. But his writings were widely read and had substantial influence in China during the period of Kuomintang dominance after 1927. As Wu Yuanli put it in 1946, "Chinese economic policy, finding expression through all the programmes and plans that have been evolved under the present government, has invariably owed its inspiration to Dr. Sun Yat-sen's doctrines." (Wu 1946, p. 29)

Early Life and Ideas

Born in Southeast China, Sun studied in Hawaii and Hong Kong, trained in western medicine and the English language, and professed belief in Christianity. Thus his background was very different from those of Yan Fu, Kang Youwei, and Liang Qichao, all of whom experienced the traditional "scholar's education". Those three intellectuals had only disdain for Sun.

Sun spent much of his life prior to 1912 outside China, some in study in the United States and Britain, and nearly ten years in Japan, much of that devoted to efforts to overthrow the Qing (Manchu) monarchy.

In 1894, before he became identified as a rebel, Sun composed a brief plan for China's economic development, which he submitted to government leaders, perhaps in hopes of gaining an appointment.[2] Sun stressed efforts to improve education and to introduce technological improvements. He urged government programs to improve transportation and management of water resources, themes which he was to elaborate in later work. Private trade should be stimulated, in his view, by abolishing the burdensome tax barriers to internal trade and by improved protection for persons and property. Sun was one of the first Chinese to point to the pressure of growing population on limited land resources (Chen Chang-heng 1931). To increase rural productivity, he recommended establishing agricultural schools, with international exchanges to send Chinese abroad for study and to bring in foreign experts.[3] This early document was a list of areas needing attention rather than a detailed agenda. As such, it had many things in common with similar memoranda prepared by other Chinese intellectuals, including Kang Youwei.

Influence of Henry George

Soon after this presentation, Sun decided that the Manchu regime was hopeless, and began his long organizational campaign to try to overthrow it. He began to put together economic ideas related to "min-sheng": the people's livelihood. Among these was a belief in a vaguely defined socialism, combining ideas taken from western utopias and also from the traditional Chinese idea of "Great Harmony".[4] Sun also absorbed general notions of socialism from the Japanese environment.

Sun repeatedly acknowledged that his thinking was influenced by the work of Henry George (1839–97), an American journalist and social reformer. George's best-known work, *Progress and Poverty*, was originally published in 1879. George argued that private property in land caused a disproportionate share of the fruits of economic progress to go to landowners, to the detriment of wage earners. He advocated taxing away the "unearned increment" in land values.

Sun probably read *Progress and Poverty* around 1897, and was also interacting with people in Britain and Japan who were interested in George's ideas. He persuaded his colleague Liao Chung-kai to translate *Progress and Poverty* into Chinese and arranged for publication of part of it in 1905 (Chang and Gordon 1991, p. 118). Subsequently, Sun was also influenced by Chinese who were involved in the experiments with land value taxation in the German-held port city of Tsingtao (Qingdao).[5] Sun began to advocate "equalization of land rights" as a policy goal, using a phrase taken directly from *Progress and Poverty* (George 1960, pp. 403–407).

Progress and Poverty abounds in references to China and Chinese people.[6] Sun must have felt he was reading a diagnosis directed toward his own people. George spoke with great respect about traditional Chinese culture, but stressed that this great civilization had seen its progress halt and reverse (George 1960, pp. 482–484).

Henry George devoted a large segment of *Progress and Poverty* to a denunciation of the Malthusian theory. While acknowledging that population could be too large relative to resources, he argued that in the real world overpopulation was not generally the basic cause of economic misery (George 1960, p. 104). In China as in India, economic problems arose from unequal land ownership and foreign oppression.

Sun Yat-sen drastically altered his own views on China's overpopulation. In an essay "China's Present and Future" which appeared in 1897, just about the time he read *Progress and Poverty*, he attributed agrarian problems to inadequate transportation, internal trade barriers, and unfair import competition—but not to overpopulation (Gregor, Chang, and Zimmerman 1983, pp. 12–13).

Henry George placed much of the blame for China's economic distress on bad domestic government and on imperialism. In his 1924 lectures, Sun claimed that "the European powers are crushing China with their imperialism and economic strength" (1943, p. 36). Both George and Sun argued that the existence of a government with democratic form would not assure good policies. For Sun, it was the weakness, rather than the wickedness, of the state which seemed most deplorable (1943, p. 198).

Sun Yat-sen spent several years in the United States and Great Britain. He observed first hand that many people there lived in conditions of hardship, notably the Chinese immigrants.[7] He wrote:

> The industrial revolution in the European and American countries produced a sudden change in [people's] living condition . . . Its effect on society is exactly similar to that which Henry George described in his book: *Progress and Poverty* . . . The results of the industrial revolution bring happiness only to a few members of society, but inflict pain and suffering on the great part of the people. (Sun 1921, pp. 36–37)

Sun Yat-sen's vision of an ideal society was strongly influenced by traditional Chinese images of "Great Harmony" (Chang 1983, pp. 10–11; Wang 1966, pp. 331, 340–341). Henry George's vision contained many of the same elements. George waxed lyrical about the potentialities for a society which took maximum advantage of the high productivity which could be achieved by modern technology. In 1914, Sun was defending a similar vision:

> I shall work . . . for the introduction of a system whereby the creators of wealth, the laborers, will be able to receive their fair share of the production, and this must be based upon a common ground of justice and fraternity. They would be able to cultivate the mind, have adequate recreation, and procure the blessings which should be in all men's lives, but which, on the showing of other nations, are largely denied the workers and the poorer masses. (Sun 1914, pp. 659–660)

Moreover, both Henry George and Sun Yat-sen sometimes cast their vision in Christian terms (George, pp. 549–555; Handy 1966; Barker 1955). Sun had been raised as a Christian, and a close associate asserted that "Sun became a Christian purely because of the Christian concern for the welfare of mankind" (Wong 1986, p. 209, quoting Feng Ziyou).

The foregoing help to demonstrate why Sun Yat-sen would have regarded Henry George as a very credible guide, and why in 1912 Sun could tell an interviewer, "The teachings of your single-taxer, Henry George, will be the basis of our program of reform." (Quoted Leng and Palmer 1960, p. 25.)

Debate with Liang

After 1904, Sun and Liang Qichao became Japan-based rivals, competing for the allegiance of the numerous Chinese students in Japan and for financial support from wealthy overseas Chinese.[8] In July 1905, Sun organized the Tungmenghui ("Alliance") as a vehicle for his anti-Qing campaign. On a visit to Belgium in May 1905, Sun asked to affiliate his Chinese groups with the Bureau of the Socialist International—the "Second International" (Bernal 1976, pp. 65–66). He and his associates were enthusiastic about the social experiments which had been undertaken under Bismarck in Germany, which included pension programs and public housing as well as government ownership and management of railroads.

Sun and his colleagues collaborated in developing policy proposals which appeared in the newspapers they sponsored. In 1905 Sun's colleague

Feng Ziyu articulated a number of positions which became staple fare in Sun's subsequent writings. One was that class conflict was rising in the West, but that economic class divisions were not yet severe in China and could be averted by appropriate policies. Feng recommended that the government take over all land rent or acquire it through taxation (George's "single tax"—Scalapino and Schiffrin 1959, pp. 326–329). The Alliance urged that government should "assess the value of all the land in the country. The present value of land will still belong to the owner. But all increases in value resulting from reform and social improvements shall belong to the state . . ." (Quoted Bernal 1976, p. 69.)

In 1906 Liang vigorously attacked the Alliance positions, drawing heavily on the Japanese translation of *Outlines of Economics* by Richard T. Ely.[9] Liang felt that China should give priority to economic growth and increased production, rather than to problems of inequality. He felt that "the primary point for the future of China's economy is to encourage capitalists, and the second endeavor is to protect laborers". These goals should be sought through restricting imports. He feared the power of foreign capital in China.

Eventually, Sun was to adopt much of Liang's viewpoint—emphasis on economic growth and import restrictions. For the moment, however, Sun's associates Hu Hanmin and Wang Jingwei (writing under the pseudonym Minyi) disagreed with Liang's attack on foreign capital: "Those foreigners who can do profitable business in China are also beneficial to us; they are not the only winners." Minyi also disputed Liang's protectionism. If protected against import competition, domestic firms would be less strongly motivated to innovate and sharpen their competitive vigor (Minyi 1907, pp. 69–70).

Sun's Views on Land Policy

As early as 1905, Sun wrote "The present value of land will still belong to the owner. But all increases in value resulting from reform and social improvements shall belong to the state to be shared by all people in order to create a socialist state . . ."[10] Each landowner would be required to report the value of his land. To destroy the incentive for underassessment, the government would have the option to buy the land at the self-assessed value. Sun also sensibly proposed in 1912 that China change the existing land tax from one based on area to one based on value.[11] This would reduce the incentive to overstate the value.

Liang observed that Sun and his associates appeared to oscillate between two very different proposals. One was the actual Henry George single-tax proposal, where land would remain privately owned but subject to a capital-gains tax. The other was that government would acquire land and rent it out for private use—a position Henry George had strongly opposed. Liang asked how the government could afford to purchase a large amount of land (1906a, p. 25). The government would need to determine rents for many different qualities and different locations. How would they distribute lands among competing demands? These issues became very real after 1950, when China's government seized ownership and control of land.

Sun's associates replied that "when land nationalization is implemented, the production of the nation will progress significantly. There will be no more unproductive rentiers [landlords], or uncultivated or wasted land; all factors will be invested in production." (Minyi 1907, p. 86) With the projected rich inflow of tax revenue, "we may do something to develop railroads, mines, post offices, electric power, water supply, etc. without worrying about the capitals involved." (pp. 75–76) "With rent revenue alone the state will be a big capitalist. This will enable the state to run the business of national monopolies. Other business will remain in private hands . . . Land nationalization will improve income equality in several ways. First, since land cannot be privately owned, there will be no landlord to receive the output of the land without making any contribution or to dominate industries with their wealth. Second, capitalists therefore cannot use their two weapons [land and capital] to control laborers . . . Third, where there is no private land, all capital will be used in production rather than in profit-diluting activities [land speculation] . . ." (p. 101)

These passages display a commendable attention to economic growth (reflecting Henry George's influence), but invoked the traditional Chinese antipathy toward landlords and displayed a lack of concern for economic efficiency and resource allocation.

Liang, in response, pleaded that "if people's property rights in land are taken away, this would take away their most important property right. Half of the personal motivations toward creativity and industry would be lost." (1906b, p. 24) He urged instead that private land remain private and that existing government holdings be privatized (Scalapino and Schiffrin 1959, p. 339).

While Sun Yat-sen's proposals with regard to increments of land value clearly followed Henry George's, his most famous land proposal did not. This involved the slogan, "All land to the tillers", which Sun was using in

1924 (Sun 1943, p. 456; Leng and Palmer 1960, p. 154). As early as 1899 he was urging that "all who till should receive land". These statements appeared to contradict the idea of land nationalization.[12] In 1923–24, he refused to endorse a proposal for land confiscation and redistribution.[13] "Land to the tillers" certainly did ultimately become public policy in both the mainland and in Taiwan.

Sun's Views on China's Economic Development

Sun Yat-sen was out of China and was not directly involved in the revolution which overthrew the monarchy in 1911–12, but his prestige was sufficient that he was chosen as provisional President of the new republic. He held this position only briefly before yielding power to Yuan Shikai, who had the support of the fallen empire's military forces. Yuan appointed Sun Director of National Railways, a position he held for about a year. It was during this time that Sun began to formulate plans for national economic development—or "reconstruction", one of his favorite terms. From this time until his death in 1925, Sun was primarily engaged in political struggles to gain and, occasionally, to exercise power. His writings on economic topics must be seen primarily as an evolving political platform, rather than a scholar's attempt to discover economic wisdom.

Sun's writings on economic development are available in English chiefly in four volumes. *The International Development of China*, initially published in 1920, was largely an extension of the transportation program which Sun had been developing since 1912. At the end of World War I, Sun believed that China could and should attract a large inflow of foreign capital. However, Sun's grandiose proposals went unnoticed by the western powers. His second major publication, his famous *San Min Chu I* (the Three People's Principles), was published in 1925 as a transcription of lectures delivered in 1924 on the themes of nationalism, sovereignty, and livelihood. The lectures were probably influenced by the willingness of the Soviet Union to assist Sun's political organization, the Kuomintang. The text is a rambling patchwork of political rhetoric, but most commentators agree that it presented ideas which Sun had maintained consistently for twenty years or more.[14] At the same time it reflects his favorable view of Lenin's New Economic Policy. Additional writings appeared in English in a volume inappropriately titled *Memoirs of a Chinese Revolutionary*, originally published in 1918, and in *Prescriptions for Saving China* (Wei 1994).

The International Development of China grew out of Sun's efforts to interest the western powers in providing capital and expertise to aid China's development at the end of World War I. Sun envisioned a vast network of state-owned and state-dominated enterprises:

> I suggest that the vast resources of China be developed internationally under a socialistic scheme . . . It is my hope that as a result of this, the present spheres of influence can be abolished; the international commercial war can be done away with; the internecine capitalist competition can be got rid of, and . . . the class struggle between capital and labour can be avoided. (Sun 1928, p. 6)

The bulk of *The International Development of China* was concerned with railway and waterway development. The waterway plans, often presented in loving detail, embodied the mixture of good sense and fantasy so often characteristic of Sun's economic ideas. He proposed the development of three major seaports. Two of these were proposed for relatively undeveloped locations, probably to enable the development authority to capture much of the rise in land values to be engendered (Sun 1928, pp. 28, 31). For inland waterways, Sun stressed a multi-purpose approach concerned with flood control and reclamation as well as navigation.

Sun also devoted extensive space in *International Development* to railway proposals. He was particularly captivated by the vision of a transcontinental trunk line beginning at his proposed Great Northern Port near Tianjin. "This will be the shortest line from the Pacific Coast to Europe", and "will command the most dominating position of world importance . . . The Trunk Line from Dolon Nor [in Mongolia] to Kashgar and beyond, about a distance of three thousand miles . . . is on the most fertile plain and encounters no natural obstacles . . . If there is a railway connecting these vast territories the waste labour of the congested provinces can go and develop these rich soils." (Sun 1928, p. 21) For the entire country, Sun proposed an ambitious rail network of about 125,000 kilometers. This can be compared with the official estimates that about 22,000 kilometers were in place by 1949 and about 52,000 in 1985.[15]

Sun's discussion of highways was perfunctory, but hardly modest: he called for no less than a million miles of road to be built ("as if by a magic wand") through some vaguely identified form of corvée labor (Sun 1928, p. 151; also 1943, pp. 469–472). Sun utterly failed to anticipate the importance the bicycle would attain in modern China; it was not mentioned in his writings.

Sun Yat-sen devoted only a small proportion of his books to projects outside transportation, but the proposals were no less breath-taking. Four regional plans involved government development of heavy industry, to include iron and steel, coal, cement, and transportation equipment (Sun 1928, pp. 26, 54, 61, 97, 138). Sun also advanced perceptive proposals for extractive industries. He felt that China could aspire to produce 200 million tons of coal a year, a level ultimately reached in the 1950s (Sun 1928, p. 154; *Encyclopedia* 1987, p. 311). He predicted accurately that China had the potential to become a major petroleum producer and recommended oil field and pipeline developments accordingly (Sun 1928, p. 155).

Sun's industrial program was largely a wish list. It gave little concern to priorities or to the vast requirements of capital and managerial skill. No attention at all was given to the labor needs that would be entailed. With the exception of a brief acknowledgement of private enterprise in mining, Sun's blueprint called for state ownership and management of the industrial facilities.

Sun's socialist vision was a bold plea for international capital and expertise, anticipating by a generation the kind of international development program we now associate with the World Bank. But to pay interest and principal of the resulting debts, domestic resources within China had to be mobilized. Here Sun envisioned a major role for land-value increments. Sun's construction proposals involved substantial reclamation of lands initially under water. By selling these, government could obtain some of the revenue needed to finance the projects (Sun 1928, pp. 31, 36, 41, 57–58, 70, 75, 81).

International Development devoted barely two pages to agriculture, recommending only scientific land surveys and agricultural mechanization (Sun 1928, pp. 140–142). In *San Min Chu I* Sun reiterated his support for mechanization and added sensible suggestions for use of fertilizer, crop rotation, pest eradication, improved transportation and processing, and better protection against natural disasters (Sun 1943, pp. 463–476). But by the early 1920s these were hardly novel ideas even in China.

Although Sun's earliest writings had suggested China was overpopulated in relation to food supply, in *San Min Chu I*, Sun argued that, if anything, China's population was too small. He feared China would be dominated by other "races" which were growing more rapidly.[16]

In 1981, Gregor, Chang, and Zimmerman asserted, "Rather than embarking immediately on an effort to fabricate a heavy industrial base . . . to the neglect of agriculture, Sun proposed a systematic upgrading of agriculture, infrastructural development, mass education, an expansion of labor-intensive industries under a regime of tariff protection, and final effort to create a heavy industrial foundation for a new society." (1981, p. 41) This is very inaccurate. Sun gave priority to rapid development of heavy industry and to capital-intensive projects, and dealt only superficially with education and with agriculture.[17] Sun certainly supported protective tariffs (largely out of anger against imperialism), but nothing in his discussion endorsed labor-intensive methods of production; indeed, he explicitly condemned the results of labor-intensive production of linen (1943, p. 495).

Commentators have also misrepresented the role of the private sector in Sun's vision. Gregor, Chang, and Zimmerman attribute this view to Sun:

> "An interventionist government would create an environment favorable to private economic activity . . . The program for development . . . would involve a large private sector and an attendant market economy." (1981, pp. 41–42; see also Fei 1988, pp. 38–39.)

These comments do not remotely convey the sense of Sun's proposals, which gave overwhelming emphasis to state ownership, state control, state investment, and state management. In his three-phase development schema noted above (transportation, mining, and manufacturing), Sun hastened to add "If we do not use state power to build up these enterprises, but leave them in the hands of private Chinese or of foreign business, the result will be simply the expansion of private capital and the emergence of a great wealthy class with the consequent inequalities in society." (1943, pp. 48–49)

Indeed, Sun's references to a private sector were so few and brief that it was easy to enumerate them (Sun 1928, pp. 14, 139, 156–157). His general view was well expressed in the concluding sections of *International Development*: "It was once thought by the economists of the Adam Smith school that competition was a beneficent factor and a sound economic system, but modern economists discovered that it is a very wasteful and ruinous system . . . Therefore China should make all the national industries of China into a great Trust owned by the Chinese people . . ." (Sun 1928, p. 160) Sun proposed state ownership and operation of railways and waterways, electric power, iron and steel, fertilizers and the machinery to make them, agricultural machinery, locomotives and railway cars and the equipment to make them, cement and other building materials and the equipment used for them, boats and ships, consumer durables and the equipment to make them, clothing, automobiles and gasoline, printing and publishing and inputs used therein. Government is projected to dominate the marketing of food products and their storage and processing, as well as producing the relevant equipment. There will be large-scale public housing, serviced by government utilities which in turn are serviced by equipment produced by the government.

Sun's general attitude toward free markets and capitalist development was so negative that any private sector must have had a very precarious existence.[18] Sun was obviously impressed with the Russian Revolution and looked upon the Soviet system as a possible model (Sun 1943, pp. 18–19, 87–88, 278, 349–351; Bedeski 1977, pp. 343–347). He accepted uncritically a "stage" theory of economic evolution along Marxian lines. Socialism was simply a more advanced stage than capitalism, and China should move directly to socialism. "Our min-sheng principle aims at the destruction of the capitalist system." (1943, p. 478)

The Influence of Sun Yat-sen: China, 1925–1949

The cult of Sun Yat-sen was quick to form following his death in 1925. Sun's personal protégé Chiang Kai-shek was able to generate the military power which enabled him to dominate the Kuomintang, carry through a bloody purge of its Communist element in 1927, and overthrow the moribund Peking government in 1928. Chiang did all in his power to emphasize his role as Sun Yat-sen's heir (Sheean 1969, p. 197). Sun's writings became sacred texts, and a compulsory weekly memorial service to Sun was instituted throughout China (Holcombe 1930, pp. 252–257, 303). The draft constitution of 1936 declared that "The Republic of China is a San Min Chu I Republic." (*China Handbook 1937–1943*, p. 120) In Moscow, the Sun Yat-sen University was founded in September, 1925, designed to serve (revolution-minded) Chinese students. A notable early student was Chiang Ching-kuo, son of Chiang Kai-shek (Seagrave 1985, pp. 232–233). Deng Xiaoping attended in 1926 (Deng Maomao 1995, pp. 104–109).

As Communist insurgent groups instituted radical land redistribution programs in their interior "base areas", the issues of land ownership in particular and social-economic development and reform in general became widely publicized throughout China. The Chinese Association of Land Economics was formed in 1932, largely to follow up Sun's ideas. The Sun Yat-sen Institute for the Advancement of Culture and Education was established in 1933 in Nanjing, with his son Sun Fo as life trustee. The government created a Commission on Land Research and Planning in 1934, which undertook extensive rural surveys (Chen Li-fu 1934). In 1935, economist Fang Xianting identified 89 books and pamphlets and 251 periodical articles on land policy, most published after 1930 (Fong 1935, p. 326).

The new government put forward transportation proposals related to Sun Yat-sen's programs, and his son Sun Fo became Minister of Railways in 1927. But severe financial constraints kept them from going very far. Huenemann (1984) pointed out that the national government directly created only about 1,600 route miles of railway in 1928–37 (pp. 94–97).

Even lower priority went to waterways, to which Sun had devoted even more space. His proposal led the government to create in 1928 a Construction Commission. But their operations seemed to have an adverse effect on the relatively localized programs already in existence.[19] As for highways, Fang Xianting noted in 1937 that "The total length of roads in China is officially given as 84,809 kilometers, but only a small part of it is surfaced, and . . . a good part of the other is not much better than the tracks and furrowed lanes which for ages have served the traffic between towns and provinces." (Fong 1937, p. 939)

H. H. Kung, as Minister of Industries, outlined in 1928 a proposal for state development of major industries which was obviously inspired by Sun Yat-sen.[20] The Japanese invasion of Manchuria spurred the government toward a more systematic pursuit of a "planned, national defense economy" reflecting Sun's emphasis on heavy industry and on foreign capital (Kirby 1983, p. 44–46).

Outbreak of war with Japan in 1937 moved the government further toward Sun's image of state socialism. According to Eastman, "war made the government the leading economic entrepreneur . . . By 1942 . . . the Ministry of Economics reported that state-controlled enterprises accounted for 17.1 percent of all factories, 70 percent of the capital, 32 percent of the workers and 42 percent of the horse-power in the Nationalist area." (Eastman 1986b, pp. 599–600; see also Ho 1978, p. 117.) But many observers felt the Nationalist economic program was designed mainly to enrich government officials (Reynolds 1975) and that its contribution to industrial progress was disappointing (Sun Fo 1944, pp. 138–142, 199). He Lian (Franklin Ho), the Yale PhD Nankai professor who headed the government's Central Planning Board, had initially expressed enthusiasm for Sun's development ideas. But after he entered government service in 1936, this evaporated. He concluded that "although formulators of policy claimed *San Min Chu I* as the basis of their action, there is no basic principle of development outlined there." (Ho 1967, p. 148; also pp. 294–300.)

Sun Yat-sen's Influence in Taiwan after 1949

There have been numerous attempts to credit the economic success of Taiwan to the application of Sun Yat-sen's principles.[21] However, most of the economic policies crucial to Taiwan's success seem to have involved departures from Sun's recommendations. The closest link between Taiwan's development and Sun's ideas was political: Sun Yat-sen was the chief founder of the Kuomintang and the principal architect of its central political doctrines.

Consider Taiwan's famous land reform program, which received high praise for contributions to economic growth, political stability, and social justice. Beyond slogans about "all land to the tillers" Sun had no land-reform proposal. He did suggest that government could carry out compulsory purchase of land, but the purchase would take place at a price set by the landowner, and the threat of compulsory purchase may have been mainly a method of preventing under-assessment for tax purposes. A major element of the Taiwan program was the 1952 law which provided for compulsory government purchase of land from all private holdings exceeding approximately 7 acres in magnitude, to be resold to actual tillers. The purchase price was only 2.5 times the annual yield and was paid not in cash but in depreciated commodity bonds and shares of stock in government corporations (Gregor, Chang, and Zimmerman 1981, pp. 30–34). The program was thus confiscatory, with one estimate placing the loss to landlords on the order of 13 percent of Taiwan's gross national product (Ho 1978, p. 166). Thus the policy did not carry out any blueprint of Sun Yat-sen.[22]

However, Taiwan adhered more closely to Sun's program in regard to land taxation. The constitution of 1947 provided for land-increment taxation based on his ideas, and the tax was imposed in 1954. It differed in detail, providing for a progressive rate structure based on the size of the proportional capital gain. The tax was imposed only on realized gains, whereas Sun had envisioned it to be based on accruals as well (King 1977, pp. 59–66).

Taiwan's policy also deviated significantly from Sun Yat-sen when it undertook to bring down the initially high rate of population growth. Discussions of family planning programs began in the 1950s and a large-scale campaign to promote use of the IUD began in 1963.[23]

Taiwanese policy was consistent with Sun in the extensive investment made in infrastructure in the 1950s. Large-scale shipbuilding, one of Sun's goals, developed after 1957. However, Taiwan did not follow Sun's prescription for rapid build-up of heavy industry immediately after 1949. Government sponsorship of an integrated steel plant did not come until the six-year plan for 1976–81 (Gregor, Chang, and Zimmerman 1981, p. 69). Ho (1978) suggested that the Nationalist government would have preferred that economic development after 1949 be dominated by the public sector, a view consistent with Sun Yat-sen's outlook.[24] Because of financial constraints and the influence of the United States foreign-aid administration, however, the relative role of the private sector expanded steadily (Ho, pp. 117, 128–129).

For a decade after 1949, Taiwan maintained an international trade policy consistent with Sun's proposals for import restrictions and generous welcome for foreign capital and expertise. A complex mixture of direct government controls included a multiple exchange rate system and direct regulation of foreign exchange transactions and imports. But this autarchic policy led to inefficiency and sluggish growth. Consequently a major transformation took place. The direct controls were relaxed and markets were liberalized. Export promotion became a major instrument for renewed vigorous growth (Ho 1978, pp. 4, 117–119, 248). This radical adjustment owed nothing to Sun Yat-sen's statist convictions. Important influence came from two brilliant western-educated Chinese economists, T. C. Liu (Liu Dazhong) and Jiang Shuojie. Beginning in 1954, they proposed a series of measures to restore monetary stability, stimulate private savings, and open the way for relatively free international trade and payments.[25]

Viewing all the crucial policy inputs to Taiwan's economic miracle, it is difficult to trace any of them in detail to Sun Yat-sen, with the exception of his emphasis on transport infrastructure, and of course the land tax. Steven Cheung concluded that "there is no truth to the claim . . . that Taiwan's economic success is attributable to the adoption of [Sun's] economic 'principles'." (Cheung 1982, p. 22)

Sun Yat-sen's Vision and Mainland China since 1949

Writing in 1954, Rewi Alley had no doubt that "the People's Republic . . . more than fulfills Sun Yatsen's vision of a new China."[26] Sun's vision of an industrialized China did anticipate many features of the post-1949 People's Republic (Hofheinz and Calder 1982, pp. 221–222). Industrial development was in fact pursued after 1949 with relative disregard for optimal factor proportions or appropriate technology. Heavy industry was given priority. Foreign experts and foreign capital from the Soviet Union played a significant role. There was a preoccupation with large centralized systems of control and management. Sun's dislike for private enterprise was reflected in the periodic PRC campaigns to wipe out "capitalist tails" and limit trade and transportation to bureaucratic state monopolies. Public housing did play a major role in urbanization, with high-rise apartment buildings of standard construction achieving some economies of scale in providing units of at least hundred-family, if not thousand-family, dimensions. Sun's eye for detail was sufficiently sharp to anticipate the Yanhee-Gezhouba multiple-purpose dam project on the Yangzi (1928, p. 60) and to spot the potential attractiveness of the area near Guangzhou for retired overseas Chinese—a consideration embodied in the design of the Shenzhen Special Economic Zone (Sun 1928, p. 70; Putman 1983, pp. 71, 73). However, transportation development, so dear to Sun's heart, was relatively neglected, as the World Bank study of 1985 made clear (see also *The Economist* November 29, 1992, p. 32; Edmonds 1987, p. 432).

To be sure, the inspiration for most Maoist policies lay more in the Stalinist tradition of the USSR than in Sun Yat-sen's writings.[27] One may doubt that Sun would have approved of the atmosphere of violence and coercion, of class conflict and "struggles" which characterized so much of the Maoist era. In particular, the PRC land reform measures of 1949–51 involved much more violence and confiscation than occurred in Taiwan, and the principle of "land to the tillers" was soon totally rejected in favor of agricultural collectivization (Leng and Palmer 1960, pp. 154–162).

After Mao died in 1976, economic policy in the People's Republic moved closer to a market system. The assignment of land-cultivation rights under the rural responsibility system did embody the spirit of Sun's motto, "all land to the tillers". The "open policy" associated with Deng Xiaoping sought the inflow of foreign capital and foreign expertise, also very much in line with Sun's vision. While the PRC conceded a steadily expanding role for a private sector, government domination continued in heavy industry and infrastructure. And the oppressive political atmosphere of Maoism was replaced by a milder form of one party dictatorship.

If we associate Sun Yat-sen with the "spirit" of responsible government, social justice, and economic productivity spearheaded by private enterprise, modern Taiwan deserves his mantle. But if we read the literal words of his vision of a modern industrial China, it seems much more nearly approximated in the People's Republic.

4

Graduate Study of Economics by Chinese in the United States

The materials we have presented so far deal primarily with Chinese intellectual developments around the turn of the century. Major intellectual and political figures struggled to grasp and adapt western ideas about economics in an effort to strengthen the Chinese state against the imperialists and to promote economic growth and social justice inside China.

A remarkable element in the introduction of western economic ideas into China was the vast number of Chinese who studied Economics in western countries and then returned to China. From the 1920s onward, "returned students" came to constitute a large element in the Economics faculties of Chinese universities. In this chapter we present information on roughly 1,200 Chinese who studied Economics at the graduate level in the United States in the years prior to 1950.[1] The next chapter looks at roughly 400 Chinese who studied Economics in Britain and western Europe. A third chapter analyzes the research subjects of both groups, their prior studies in Chinese universities, and their employment on returning to China. Subsequent chapters look in detail at their roles in economics programs in the missionary colleges and in the indigenous Chinese universities.

The Boxer Settlement

The flow of Chinese students to the United States was stimulated as an aftermath to the Boxer Rebellion of 1900. The resulting treaties obligated the Chinese government to pay indemnities to the victorious invading powers. In 1908, the United States government agreed to devote a portion of its indemnity to support Chinese educational development. Financial assistance was extended to Chinese students coming to the United States, and funds were provided for the creation in 1911 of Qinghua College, explicitly designed to prepare Chinese to study in the United States.[2] Additional financial support came from national and provincial governments in China (Wang 1966, p. 55).

A critical step in validating modern (i.e. western) education in China occurred in 1905, when the imperial government abolished the traditional classical examinations as the qualification for government positions. This opened the way for western-educated Chinese to find government positions, and many of them did.

The overthrow of the monarchy in 1911–12 disrupted educational conditions only momentarily. The new regime was more favorable to overseas study by Chinese. In 1917 one Chinese commented "from the government down through all walks of Chinese life, the returned man or woman is sought after to direct, or to assist in, the realizing of the potentialities of this nation . . . The returned student has, under the Republic, come into his own." (Quoted Wang 1966, p. 89.)

Table 4-1 compares the total flow of Chinese students to the United States with the number studying Economics in the United States and in Europe. The data are non-duplicating—each student is entered only once. After a slow start, the number of students in graduate-level Economics escalated to an astonishing level of one-seventh of the total in 1935–39. However, our dating does not match precisely with the China Institute totals, and their dated totals are on average one-third below the presumed true values. Elsewhere they estimated there were 1,122 Economics students in a population of 15,006 with identified fields—about 7.5 percent.[3] Table 4-1 can be compared with data in Wang Yi-chu 1966, pp. 510–511, which represent the "stock" of students for various years and thus contain many duplications. He found a total of 1,636 Economics students in a classified total of 31,432, which is 5.2 percent. There were 2,708 business students. About one third of all students and Economics students attended in the period 1945–50.

Our study concentrates on Chinese who studied Economics at the graduate level in the United States. However, even a student with a bachelor's degree could succeed as a professional economist in China. Some examples include the following:

Wang Chien-tsu (Jianzhu) studied at Beiyang University in Tianjin and Waseda University in Japan before completing a bachelor's degree at California (Berkeley) in 1905. He translated into Chinese portions of Charles Dunbar's *History and Theory of Banking* and Henry Carter Adams's *Science of Finance*. After brief stints in several government positions, he

Table 4-1. Chinese Students Coming to the U.S., Total and Graduate-Level Economics, 1900–1950

	All Chinese Students Coming to the U.S.	Students in Graduate Economics	Economics Students in Europe
1900–1904	51	0 (0%)	1
1905–1909	302	2 (0.7%)	2
1910–1914	604	28 (4.6%)	18
1915–1919	1,057	68 (6.4%)	7
1920–1924	1,994	130 (6.5%)	23
1925–1929	1,638	172 (10.6%)	49
1930–1934	977	132 (13.5%)	75
1935–1939	1,054	155 (14.7%)	109
1940–1944	1,064	103 (9.7%)	30
1945–1950	5,336	431 (8.1%)	41
Unknown	5,132*	7 (0.1%)	36
Total	19,209	1,228 (6.4%)	391

* Extends over 1951–53 as well.

Sources: Column 1 from data in *A Survey of Chinese Students in American Universities and Colleges in the Past One Hundred Years*, China Institute in America, 1954, pp. 26–27. Columns 2 and 3 from student data surveyed in Appendix and Chapter 5; some data are approximate. These are non-duplicating (flow) estimates.

became in 1915 Dean of the law school of National Peking University (*Who's Who in China* 1917).

D. K. Lieu (Lieu Da-kuin, Liu Dajun) attended Peking University before enrolling at the University of Michigan, completing a bachelor's degree in 1915. He taught English at Qinghua for a couple of years, but began almost immediately conducting research and writing about China's economy. His career as a leading researcher is reviewed in Chapter 14.

T. V. Soong (Soong Tze-ven) attended St. John's missionary college in Shanghai and graduated from Harvard in 1915 with a bachelor's degree in Economics. He worked in a bank in New York and took graduate courses at Columbia. He soon developed formidable family connections. One sister married H. H. Kung, soon to be a high official. Another married Sun Yat-sen, and a third married Chiang Kai-shek. T. V. Soong became Minister of Finance when the Kuomintang under Chiang came to power in 1927. Until his resignation in 1933 he exemplified the progressive, modernizing, reformist element in the KMT (Wang 1966, p. 441).

Chinese in Graduate Study in the United States

For this study, we have assembled data on approximately 1,200 Chinese who studied Economics (including Agricultural Economics) at the graduate level in the United States up to 1950. Table 4-2 summarizes the graduate schools they attended.

The students are listed in four categories. Students completing verified doctorates numbered 149. Another 88 were "ABD"—all but dissertation. Of these, 16 received Economics doctorates subsequent to 1950. The largest category consists of 572 students receiving master's degrees in

Table 4-2. U.S. Graduate Schools Attended, All Chinese Economics Students, 1906–1950

School						Percentage (%) of	
	GS	MA**	ABD	PhD	Total	Ch. GS	EcPhDs*
Columbia	59	142	43	29	273	21	10
Harvard***	64	30	8	28	130	10	13
Wisconsin	47	50	4	11	112	9	7
Michigan	39	56	2	2	99	8	3
Penn	21	55	7	14	97	7	4
Illinois	19	46	1	12	78	6	6
Chicago	24	14	8	3	49	4	6
New York	16	19	2	10	47	4	3
Cornell	7	21	1	14	43	3	6
California	10	29	0	2	41	3	4
Top 10	306	462	76	125	969	74	62
71 others	126	174	12	24	336	26	
Gross total	432	636	88	149	1,305	100	
(–) Duplicates	–13	–64			–77		
Total students	419	572	88	149	1,228		
Top 10 as % of gross	71%	73%	86%	84%	74%		

* Percentage of all Economics doctorates 1925–51, calculated from Bowen 1953, pp. 109–210.

** MA list includes 49 students who became ABD or PhD at a different school; these constitute the majority of the duplicates.

*** Harvard includes Radcliffe.

Sources: See Appendix. A similar tabulation for PhD students appears in Sun 1986, p. 353.

Economics as their highest status. In a few cases (32) students receiving MBA (master of business administration) degrees were included if they had a thesis topic which was clearly related to Economics. Of the 572, 20 completed Economics doctorates subsequent to 1950. The fourth category consists of 419 students who did not receive a verified graduate degree in Economics by 1950.

How complete is this sample? Our conjecture is that we have identified about nine-tenths of the Chinese who actually completed a graduate degree in Economics. However, of the non-degree students we have probably only one half.

Our survey counts only degrees received by 1950. Quite a few of the students who were in graduate schools in 1950 completed degrees later, including such notables as Alpha Chiang, John Fei, Cheng Pao-lun, and Anthony Tang. They are classified by their status in 1950.

These Chinese students were highly concentrated among a small number of schools. About three-fourths attended the top ten—a much higher concentration than for Economics doctorates in general. Columbia University was in a class by itself, with 273 Chinese students—one fifth of the gross total. Harvard, Wisconsin, Michigan, and Penn each accounted for about 100. The distribution of our Economics graduate students corresponded closely to the distribution of all Chinese students among American universities (Hsiao 1935, p. 102).

Compared to students from other foreign countries, it is likely that Chinese were the second most numerous after Canadians.[4] The 149 doctorates received by Chinese were 3.7 percent of all Economics doctorates in the United States in this period.

In 1906–24, the predominance of Columbia was even more pronounced, accounting for 39 percent of all the Chinese students tabulated, and 34 out of the 49 (69%) doctoral-level students (PhD plus ABD). Froman (1930) estimated that Columbia accounted for 32 percent of all U.S. Economics doctoral students in this period.

After rapid growth, the number of students in the United States declined in the 1930s in response to the economic depression and to a large movement of students to European universities. Columbia relinquished its top ranking in 1935–44 to Michigan, which granted a large number of master's degrees. Columbia granted only three Chinese doctorates in Economics in 1935–44. Nationally the total number of Chinese ABDs and PhDs fell from 68 in 1925–34 to 45 in 1935–44.

In the six years 1945–50, the number of students rose substantially, to

431. Many of these received degrees after 1950, so our GS and ABD categories are relatively large. Many schools appeared in the listings for the first time. Chinese students were enrolled in 50 different universities for Economics graduate study. Harvard reported an impressive 16 doctorates, nearly 40 percent of the total. Wisconsin received a large inflow of non-degree graduate students in Agricultural Economics sponsored by the U.S. Department of Agriculture.

Harvard and Yale

Harvard awarded its second Economics doctorate to Frank W. Taussig in 1883. He soon became its most distinguished economics professor until his retirement in 1935.[5] In 1900 Harvard's department came under the leadership of a former Ohio farm boy named Thomas Nixon Carver, fresh from graduate study at Johns Hopkins and Cornell (Carver 1949). Carver and Taussig became the backbone of the doctoral program (Church 1965, pp. 82–89). Carver's course in Agricultural Economics was one of the earliest in the United States, and attracted students from as far away as China (where Carver's textbooks were used in several colleges).[6]

One of Harvard's first Chinese graduate students was Luther Jee (Chi Shien-yien—Ji Shenen), who completed an MA in 1907. He returned to China to teach in Tangshan Railway and Engineering College (a predecessor of Jiaotong University) and the Imperial College of Finance in Peking, and later joined the Ministry of Finance (Chao 1917). Chen Changheng's graduate study at Harvard ended in 1917 without a degree, but his work there resulted in a book on China's population that went through numerous editions in the 1920s and helped focus attention on the problem of population control (Tien 1973, pp. 168–175).

However, it was not until 1920 that Harvard awarded its first PhD to a Chinese economist. This was Chu Chung-tao (Zhu Zhongdao), who presented a dissertation on salt taxation in five countries—but not including China, even though salt was an important revenue source there. In the mid-1920s Harvard typically enrolled ten to fifteen Chinese graduate students each year. Some of them went on to become the backbone of the Qinghua University Economics Department. The leader was Chen Daisun (Harvard PhD 1926), whose distinguished career did not end until his death in 1997.[7] The supporting cast included Chao Jen-tsun (Zhao Renjun—Harvard PhD 1928) and Hsiao Chu (Xiao Chu), who came to Harvard after completing a master's degree at Cornell in 1922. Economist J. B. Condliffe wrote, "Taussig told me at Harvard that he [Xiao] was the only Chinese post-graduate student who had been put on to do a piece of theoretical as distinct from descriptive work for his PhD."[8] However, Xiao did not complete his proposed dissertation on the theory of business profits. Another contemporary was Tang Ching-tseng (Qingzeng), who became a prolific scholar dealing with the history of Chinese economic thought. He taught in several Shanghai-area universities and was chair at Daxia (Great China) (Chan and Dirlik 1991, p. 135).

According to Byrd Jones (1988), the Harvard Economics faculty of the 1920s "were respected as gentlemen and scholars, not as iconoclasts or brilliant theorists . . ." (p. 130) Professor Charles Bullock, who directed the dissertations of Chen and Zhao, was influential in creating the Harvard Economic Service, directed in the 1920s by Warren Persons. Xiao Chu initially came to Harvard to work for them. They developed a well-regarded forecasting service which, unfortunately, failed dismally to predict the great downturn after 1929.

Nevertheless, from the mid-1920s Harvard ranked high in attracting Chinese students. A new star was John Black, a pioneer in the analysis of production functions, recruited from Minnesota to teach Agricultural Economics. His principal Chinese student was Alfred Kai-ming Chiu (Qiu Kaiming), whose 1933 dissertation on Chinese agricultural surveys we have used extensively in Chapter 14.[9]

By the late 1930s, Harvard's department had revived a great deal. One source of stimulus was Edward H. Chamberlin, who had developed his Harvard doctoral dissertation into the influential *Theory of Monopolistic Competition* (1933). Joseph Schumpeter joined the department in 1932, and Gottfried Haberler in 1936. In the 1940s Harvard became the leading center in the United States for Keynesian economics, led by Alvin Hansen and supported by junior faculty such as Seymour Harris and Lauchlin Currie. The new ideas attracted a number of Chinese graduate students and visiting faculty such as Fang Xianting.[10]

Three Chinese brothers received doctoral degrees in Economics from Harvard: Pu Shou-chang (1946—Shouchang), Pu Shou-hai (1946—Shouhai), and Pu Shou-shan (1950—Shoushan). All returned to China and took positions with the Communist government. The last-named (known subsequently simply as Pu Shan) was, according to schoolmate Anthony Koo, "considered the most brilliant economics graduate student in Cambridge . . . in the 1940s. He wrote his dissertation under Professor Joseph Schumpeter who offered him an assistant professorship at Harvard and at the same time offered him coauthorship . . . to write a book on Schumpeterian dynamics."[11] Pu Shan served as one of the Communist negotiators seeking to halt the Korean hostilities in 1953 and after. He was attacked as a rightist in 1957. After rehabilitation, he joined the Chinese Academy of Social Sciences and became director of its graduate school.[12]

Shih Chien-sheng (Shi Jiansheng), who attended Harvard in the 1940s, joined the National Taiwan University in 1949 and became a leader in the Economics profession on the island. His elementary textbook *Principles of Economics* was widely used, went through 12 editions, and earned him the nickname "Samuelson of Taiwan". Other distinguished Harvard doctoral graduates were Ou Pao-san (Wu Baosan), Chang (Zhang) Peikang, and Lo Chih-ju (Luo Zhiru). These three, all of whom remained in China after 1949, are discussed below.

The first Chinese student known to have received a PhD in Economics in the United States was Chen Chin-tao (Jintao), who completed his doctorate at Yale in 1906. Chen's dissertation on "Societary Circulation" was inspired by Irving Fisher, now widely regarded as the finest American economist of his generation for his path-breaking studies of money, interest rates, capital, and index numbers.[13] Chen returned to China for a career in government service, holding a number of positions related to finance. He also taught at Qinghua University (Boorman 1967, I, pp. 170–172).

In 1906 Yale established Yale-in-China, a teaching and social service program in Changsha (Holden 1964). This program produced one of Yale's most distinguished Chinese students, He Lian (Franklin Ho), whom we will discuss in detail in our chapter on Nankai University. The longtime treasurer of Yale-in-China, Dickson Leavens, assembled a vast collection of information on the monetary role of silver in China, a collection which formed the basis for a major book (Leavens 1939).

Yale did not attract many Chinese students in Economics. Aside from Fisher, its Economics faculty were generally undistinguished (Dimand 1998). However, three Yale doctorates—He Lian, Fang Xianting, and Rockwood Chin (Chin Quock-ping—Chen Guoping) became mainstays of the Nankai program. He Lian worked closely with Fisher in developing index numbers and helped expand their use in China.

Columbia

The second Chinese doctorate in Economics was awarded in 1911 at

Columbia University in New York City. Columbia at the turn of the century was bursting with vitality. Its enrollment skyrocketed from 2,000 in 1896 to 6,000 in 1909, including a thousand academic graduate students.[14]

John Bates Clark joined the Columbia Economics faculty in 1895, having studied at Heidelberg. Like Irving Fisher, he contributed to the development of the central doctrines of marginal analysis (Dorfman 1949, pp. 188–205; Persky 2000). Another Columbia leader was German-trained Edwin R. A. Seligman, on his way to becoming one of the country's leading authorities on government finance. Seligman became a mentor to many Chinese students, whose Columbia dissertations frequently pursued this specialty.

The Columbia Economics Department became distinguished for its heavy emphasis on statistics (Dorfman 1955, pp. 173–174, 188–189). Adding to the quantitative emphasis was the 1913 appointment of Wesley Mitchell, already a leading authority on business cycles. With the addition of John Maurice Clark (son of John Bates Clark) in 1926, Columbia became a major center for Institutional Economics.[15] After 1917, Columbia doctoral students were required to be examined in the history and theory of economics, statistics, and economic history, and in three of the following: public finance, money and banking, the labor problem, trade and transportation, corporations and trusts, business economics, insurance, and agriculture (Rutherford 2004, p. 37).

The first Columbia PhD awarded to a Chinese economist went to Chen Huan-chang (Huanzhang) in 1911 for his comprehensive study of Confucian economic ideas. Henry Seager was apparently his adviser, but both Clark and Seligman assisted (Chen 1911, pp. ix–xii). A total of nine Chinese received Economics doctorates from Columbia between 1911 and 1919, five of which involved government finance.[16]

One of these was Ma Yinchu, who introduced his 1914 study of New York City finances with the hope that its findings would prove useful for China. Ma returned to China to become a professor at Peking University and was, until his death, one of China's most prominent and outspoken economists. He held positions at several universities and served nearly 20 years in the national government's Legislative Yuan (assembly). He became an outspoken critic of the KMT government and was placed under house arrest for two years (Lutz 1971, p. 414). He used this time to compose a textbook in economic principles which became a bestseller (Sun 1987, pp. 152–153). Although he was not a Communist, Ma held several high positions under the Communist regime after 1949, becoming president of

Peking University in 1951. He was later dismissed for criticizing government programs he felt aggravated China's over population. Before his death his views were vindicated (Boorman 1967–71, II, pp. 475–478).

Another prominent public figure was Sun Fo, son of Sun Yat-sen. He received a master's degree in Economics from Columbia in 1917. He returned to China to join his father's political activities, serving as Mayor of Canton and Governor of Guangdong Province. When the KMT under Chiang established a new national government in 1928, he held several ministerial posts. As Minister of Railways, he attempted to implement elements of his father's ambitious construction program. He left China when the Communists took over, living in the United States and in Taiwan (Boorman 1967–71, II, pp. 162–165).

Sun's public career overlapped with that of Chen Kung-po (Chen Gongbo), who briefly joined the Communist party just after graduating from Peking University in 1920. Chen completed a master's degree in Economics at Columbia in 1924 with a thesis on the economics of the Communist movement in China. Returning to China, he taught briefly at National Guangdong University, then moved into the upper ranks of the KMT. In 1931 he was appointed Minister of Industry and joined the effort to put Sun Yat-sen's program into effect. He became a follower of Wang Jingwei and participated after 1937 in the puppet national government which collaborated with the Japanese. For this he was executed in 1946 (Boorman 1967–71, I).

Zhen's activities are in interesting contrast to those of Chi Chao-ting (Ji Chaoding), who completed a doctorate at Columbia in 1936.[17] He married an American woman and remained in the United States until 1941, chiefly as a member of the research staff of the Institute of Pacific Relations. Ji had joined the Communist Party in 1926, but this did not become known until much later. He returned to China in 1941 and held several high positions in the wartime Nationalist government, aided by family friendship with H. H. Kung. Ji served as Secretary-General of the Chinese delegation to the Bretton Woods financial conference in 1944. He became head of the large research department of the Central Bank of China in 1946. In 1949 he joined the newly formed Communist government as research director of the People's Bank and held a number of other prominent positions (Boorman 1967–71, I, pp. 293–297).

Among the many other Columbia students discussed in later chapters are Chen Ta (Da), Chao (Zhao) Nai-tuan, Li Chuan-shih (Li Quanshi), Lee Ba-en (Li Peien), and Cheng Lin-chuang (Zheng Linzhuang).

Columbia was the most popular site in the United States for Chinese students in general. A photograph of the Chinese Students Club for 1923–24 shows 158 students (six of them female—Hsiao 1935, p. 98). The Columbia students also seemed to have been more political and more controversial than those at Harvard and Yale.

Railway Studies

Concern for China's economic development led several of the early Chinese doctoral students to focus on railway problems. And the expansion of China's railways created a great need for staff with some knowledge of railway economics and management. Hsu Chih (Mongton Hsu—Xu Chi) received a doctorate in 1915 from Columbia with a historical survey (under Seligman) of Chinese railway developments and problems. While a student, Xu worked for both the Illinois Central and Pennsylvania railroads. He returned to work for the Peking-Mukden Railway and later the Chinese Eastern Railway before his untimely death in 1927.[18]

Railway economics was also a focus for early Chinese students at the University of Illinois. There Wang Ching-chun (Jingchun) completed his doctorate in 1911 with a study of the regulation of railway finance in Britain. Beginning in 1914 he headed the Department of Railway Accounts and Finance, working closely with Henry Carter Adams in modernizing China's system of railway accounting. He became interested in telegraph development and invented a phonetic system for telegraphing the Chinese language which was adopted by the government in 1928. From 1931 to 1949 he headed the Chinese Government Purchasing Commission in London (Boorman 1967–71, II, pp. 366–369).

Many Chinese studied railway and other transportation systems at the University of Pennsylvania. A prominent alumnus was Juwan Usang Ly (Li Chao-huan). Ly completed master's degrees in both Economics and Political Science. In 1921 he returned to China to a series of positions in banking, government, and railway administration. In 1930 he became president of the Jiaotong ("Communications") University, serving until 1949.[19] This institution, a highly regarded technical school with operations in Shanghai, Tangshan, and Peking, focused particularly on studies related to railways. Under Ly's administration, a strong connection was maintained between Jiaotong and Penn.[20]

High positions in railway management were also achieved by Liu

Ching-shan (Jingshan) and King Shih-hsuan (Jin Shixuan). Liu completed a master's degree at Penn in 1910 and held a long series of railway positions beginning in 1913. In 1921 he became Chief of the Railway Department in the Ministry of Communication, a post he held until 1927. He chaired the Hunan-Hubei Railway Rehabilitation Commission in the period 1931–33 and then worked for the National Economic Council.[21] King completed a doctorate at Penn in 1927. Reviewing a 1935 book of King's essays on Chinese railway problems, Leonard Ting (Ting Ge) remarked on King's "many years of active service and participation in the work of the improvement of railway service with a number of railway lines in China . . . The accounts of the improvement of administrative organization and transportation service and rate-setting are based on the author's extensive experience with the Peiping-Liaoning, the Hangchow-Kiangshan and the Peiping-Suiyuan Railways." (Ting 1935, pp. 404–405)

Wisconsin

Graduate Economics instruction at the University of Wisconsin began in 1892, when Richard T. Ely was hired from Johns Hopkins. Ely had studied in Germany and his ideas were very influential in China. He was a strong believer in the Social Gospel and was committed to government economic interventions in support of social reform (Bateman 1998; Lampman 1993). Wisconsin pioneered in developing a program in Agricultural Economics beginning in 1902. In 1904 labor economist John R. Commons, soon to become Wisconsin's most distinguished economist, joined the staff.

Ely and Commons exemplified a powerful reformist spirit which infused graduate study in Economics throughout much of the period 1900–1950. Robert Church (1974) documented the impulse by American social scientists to "contribute to social or individual betterment" (p. 573). "Problems and policies" were often the focal point for Economics courses dealing with such controversial topics as the tariff, money and banking, labor unions, taxation, monopoly, immigration, and government regulation of business (Biddle 1998). This emphasis carried over into the many thesis studies of Chinese economic policy by Chinese students.[22]

An early representative of Wisconsin in China was Clarence Dittmer, who taught Economics at Qinghua University in 1917 while doing doctoral research. One of his students was Chen Daisun, who was sufficiently impressed that he enrolled at Wisconsin to complete his undergraduate studies before proceeding to graduate study at Harvard.[23]

Ho Hao-jo (He Haoruo) completed a doctorate at Wisconsin in 1926 with a dissertation on "The Time Concept in Economics"—one of the few Chinese dissertations on economic theory. Returning to China, he became a high-ranking military officer, government official, and university professor.[24]

One of the most sophisticated dissertations by a Chinese was Li Teh-ying's study of "Development of Correlation Calculus and its Application to Economic Statistics" (1935). Li had taught mathematics in China for five years before coming to Wisconsin. He returned to a faculty position at National Central University in Nanjing (*Who's Who in China* 1936, p. 147).

Hsiang Ching-yuen (Xiang Jingyuen) completed a Wisconsin doctorate in 1941, writing about land tenure in China. After a number of research positions in China, he became a high official in CNRRA and its successor agency in the 1940s. After 1949 he remained in China with the National Resources Commission. He was attacked as a rightist in 1957 and spent a lengthy exile in Yunnan Province.[25]

Two Wisconsin students worked as underground Communist agents in 1947–49: Yung Wen-yuan (Yong Wenyuan) and Chow Ling (Frank Chou). Both returned to high positions under the Communist regime. Yung became Dean and Secretary-General of the Shanghai College of Finance and Economics, while Chow became a high official with the People's Bank (Loh 1962, p. 35).

Cornell

Cornell and Wisconsin played important roles in the graduate instruction of Chinese students of Agricultural Economics. At Cornell, the program was led by George Warren. Two of his students, John Reisner and John Lossing Buck, became important staff members of the College of Agriculture and Forestry (CAF) at missionary Nanjing University. Soon they began directing students to Cornell. Four Chinese (two from Nanjing) received doctorates from Cornell in Agriculture Economics in 1924. Feng Rui, whose dissertation offered "A Program of Chinese Agriculture", returned to teach at Lingnan and became Dean of Agriculture at National Southeastern University. In 1925 he joined the mass education movement headed by James Yen, pioneering in rural reconstruction, seeking "an across-the-board renaissance of village life".[26] After effective work in the Tinghsien area, Feng left to take a government post in Canton in 1934. "When that government fell, he was hanged, ostensibly for corruption in tungsten speculation, but more likely for being caught on the wrong political side." (Hayford 1990, p. 191)

Feng's classmate Tang Chi-yu (Qiyu), whose dissertation offered "An Economic Study of Chinese Agriculture", returned to faculty and administrative positions at several major universities and was also on the staff of the National Economic Council 1932–40 (*Who's Who in China* 1950, pp. 191–192). Tang's dissertation was reprinted in 1982 in the Garland Press series on China's economy.

A third member of the Cornell class of 1924 was Tung Shih-tsin (Dong Shijin), who wrote about "The Food Supply and Population of the World". On his return to China, he headed the rural improvement department of the China International Famine Relief Commission, and then held a series of academic appointments. He wrote a respected textbook on agricultural economics. After 1949 he escaped to Taiwan.[27]

The close link between Nanjing and Cornell is further explored in Chapter 9. In mainstream Economics, Cornell's most distinguished Chinese PhD was Liu Dazhong, whose 1940 dissertation dealt with "The Theory of Planning by the Individual Firm under Dynamic Conditions". Liu worked in the Chinese Embassy during World War II, helping to develop national-income estimates for China, then taught for two years at Qinghua. As the Communist take-over loomed, he left China for distinguished faculty positions at Johns Hopkins and Cornell, becoming one of the profession's most highly esteemed econometricians before his untimely death in 1975. He collaborated with Jiang Shuojie in helping to shape the effective economic policies followed in Taiwan.[28]

Business Administration

In the early twentieth century, university studies in business administration were expanding rapidly in numbers and improving in quality. There was substantial overlap with Economics. Many of the Chinese students who did graduate study in Economics returned to business careers in China, particularly in banking and in railway administration. Pan Shu-lun (Xulun), whose 1924 Columbia dissertation dealt with U.S.-China trade, returned to China and established his own accounting firm. In addition, he was president of Li Hsin Accounting College in Chungking. A *Who's Who* entry modestly suggests that Pan "introduced modern accounting in China".[29] Huang Han-liang completed a Columbia PhD in 1918 and returned to a successful career in banking in China. He retired to the United States in 1938. His son Philip (PhD, University of Washington) became a successful U.S.-based scholar of Chinese economy and history.[30]

A number of Chinese received graduate degrees in both Business and Economics, including Pan, Lee Ba-en, and Li Quanshi. Our MA file contains 32 MBAs, included on the basis of their thesis topics. Our GS file includes at least 13 persons with MBA degrees, but that was not the criterion for inclusion.

The next chapter takes a comparable look at Chinese who studied Economics in Britain and continental Europe. Chapter 6 then assembles information on both sets of students, particularly in regard to their role as faculty members in China.

Appendix

Sources

PhD listings were based on Yuan (1961). This gives an index entry for "Economics and Business Administration", and we separated the two on the basis of the topic's closeness to Economics. This source gives date of birth and name in hanzi. Our total of 149 compares well with Sun's total of 137 up to 1949.

ABD listings were derived from the American Economic Association's annual listings of dissertations in progress, removing those shown to have been completed. Topics outside Economics were deleted. The listings were dependent on reporting by individual universities which were far from uniform. Students who completed dissertations in 1951–53 were included as ABD as of 1950.

MA listings came from many sources. The China Institute published periodic surveys of master's theses by Chinese students. The first of these, published in 1928, covered all years to date (China Institute Bulletin, #4 and #7, 1928). Subsequent surveys appeared in the Bulletin in 1934 and 1937, while "Theses and Dissertations by Chinese Students in America 1931–1936" was published as a separate pamphlet by the institute. Of course many master's students did not submit a thesis.

Many students were identified from the 1917 and 1925 directories of returned students (Chao 1917; *Who's Who* 1925). These give names in hanzi as well as westernized forms, and identify employment after completion of study. Similar data for other Qinghua preparatory students were provided by the staff of the Qinghua Archives, arranged by Lai Rongyuen.

The *Handbook of Chinese Students in the U.S.A.* was published more or less annually beginning in 1912. Often students' major fields were not identified. We used volumes for 1914, 1918, 1933, and 1935. The *Directory of Chinese Students in America* was published in the period 1934–40; in a few cases graduate students are identified. Much more useful was the *Directory of Chinese University Graduates and Students in the U.S.* covering 1943–47. This gives names in hanzi, major fields, undergraduate schools and degrees, and current and previous employment. *Who's Who of the Chinese Students in America* (1921) is also valuable although it does not give names in hanzi. The *Directory of Chinese Students in Colleges and Universities in the United States* began in 1949, using data submitted by institutions. Though lacking hanzi, it identifies graduate students.

Kathleen Trescott and I visited the following universities to examine archival materials: California, Chicago, Columbia, Cornell, Harvard, Illinois, Indiana, Iowa, Iowa State, Michigan, Minnesota, Northwestern, NYU, Ohio State, Penn, Southern California, Stanford, Washington, Wisconsin, and Yale. We examined graduation lists and directories of students and alumni. Graduation records were relatively complete except for Michigan (ends late 1930s), Stanford (ends early 1940s), Harvard (ends mid-1940s), and Columbia, which did not identify student fields in either student directories or graduation records. Fortunately we were permitted access to a large card file of past Columbia graduate students maintained by the Economics Department. And the Columbia Archives has directories of master's theses by major departments. The best student directories (Harvard, Illinois, Wisconsin) identified undergraduate schools.

Additional listings came from who's-who types of sources. The various issues of *Who's Who in China* were studied; a four-volume consolidated reprint of the entire series was published in Taiwan in 1973. Additional listings were usually contained in *China Year Book* or *China Handbook*. The AEA handbooks gave data on academic training and employment for emigrant Chinese. We scanned issues for 1938, 1942, 1948, 1956, 1964, 1969, 1974, 1978, 1981, 1985, 1989, 1993, and 1997. These were supplemented by the *Directory of Chinese Faculty Members of American Colleges and Universities 1959–60* (Embassy of the Republic of China). Additional information came from faculty lists of Chinese universities which often identified their educational backgrounds. Details of these are in the chapters on Chinese universities. Biographical directories published in China give data on schools and degrees, names in hanzi, and subsequent employment (though often without dates). Useful sources include the following:

Biographical Dictionary of Professors in Chinese Universities and Colleges, 1990.
Social Science Biographical Directory, 1989 (Chinese language).

Longer biographical sketches of 53 economists appear in one or both of two Chinese-language multi-volume sets:

Contemporary Social Scientists in China, 1989.
Biographies of Contemporary Chinese Social Scientists, 1982.

Profiles of 132 economists (mostly post-1950) appear in *Biographies of Contemporary Chinese Economists*, 1987.

Neither the Chinese university faculty lists nor the more recent biographical reference works are entirely reliable regarding degrees actually awarded. I tried to verify these by writing to the respective universities. Where no verification was obtained, the individual was placed in the GS category.

5

Chinese Who Studied Economics in Britain and Continental Europe before 1950

The majority of Chinese who studied Economics in the West up until 1950 went to the United States. However, we have identified 391 who studied in Britain and continental Western Europe. The distinctions between graduate and undergraduate levels of study were not as clear as in the United States, and we have not attempted to distinguish them in the following analysis. Table 5-1 summarizes data on where they studied and when.

Table 5-1. Chinese Economics Students in Europe, 1904–1950

Date	Britain	France	Germany*	Miscellaneous	Net total
1904–09	3	0	1	0	3
1910–14	13	2	5	0	18
1915–19	3	3	2	0	7
1920–24	7	5	13	3	23
1925–29	18	18	13	5	49
1930–34	22	25	30	2	75
1935–39	48	30	31	4	109
1940–44	9	5	17	0	30
1945–50	27	8	3	3	41
Unknown	12	17	7	4	36
Total	162	113	122	21	391

Sources: See Appendix. Right-hand total is net of 28 duplicate entries.
* Includes Austria.

Britain

Despite the distinctive contributions of British writers to the development of economic thought, and despite the antiquity of Britain's distinguished universities, formal university programs in Economics were just beginning in 1900. The London School of Economics and Political Science (LSE), attached to the University of London, opened in 1895. LSE awarded its first Bachelor of Science (Economics) in 1904.[1] The Cambridge "Economic Tripos" produced its first graduates in 1906 (Harrod, pp. 129, 144). Oxford initiated its unique PPE (Philosophy, Politics, Economics) after World War I.[2] As late as 1945, "British economics was dominated by . . . Oxford, Cambridge, and the London School of Economics." (Backhouse 1997, p. 34; also p. 39)

To achieve an undergraduate degree in Britain required a higher level of scholarly achievement than in the United States. In particular, the BA (Honours) degree was often comparable to an American master's degree (Flexner 1930, pp. 253, 277–278). Instruction consisted primarily of relatively large lectures augmented by a weekly meeting of each student with his tutor, at which meeting the student often was required to present an essay (Johnson 1978, pp. 88–103). Prior to the 1940s, the doctoral degree was not an important part of British higher education. Separate graduate-level courses did not become common until the 1940s (Backhouse 1997, pp. 43–46). Degrees in business administration were also awarded.[3]

For this study we have assembled a file of 162 Chinese reported to have studied Economics in Britain up to 1950. Details are in the Appendix. Except for doctorates, the listings are incomplete, especially for non-degree students. Table 5-2 summarizes the British universities they attended.

Of the 162 students, a total of 92 studied at LSE—more than half. The preponderance was even greater for master's and doctoral degrees—28 out of 44. LSE catered well to overseas students. Academic life was less formal, and the London community offered more flexibility of housing and the ability to connect with an overseas Chinese community. Cambridge accounted for 33 students, including the largest number (16) of final bachelor's degrees. Oxford ranked a distant third. The undergraduate PPE degree did not represent as much of an Economics concentration as was the case at the other schools (Streeten 1997, pp. 196–197; Backhouse 1997, pp. 34–35).

The time pattern in Table 5-1 displays several interesting features. The 13 Chinese who matriculated in Economics in Britain in 1910–14 represents quite a high figure compared with the other countries we are examining. Three of the early LSE students came to form the nucleus of the Economics Department at National Wuhan University in the 1930s.[4]

Table 5-2. British Universities Attended by Chinese Economics Students, 1908–1950

University	PhD	MA	inc. th	BA (H)	BA	Others	Total
LSE	12	16	10	2	2	50	92
Cambridge	3	3	1	0	16	10	33
Oxford	0	0	0	2	5	5	12
Birmingham	0	3	1	0	1	3	8
Liverpool	2	3	0	0	0	0	5
6 others	1	3	0	0	1	11	16
Unknown	0	0	0	0	0	6	6
Total	18	28	12	4	25	85	172
(–) Duplicates	0	–2	0	0	0	–8	–10
Total	18	26	12	4	25	77	162

Only confirmed degrees are enumerated. BA (H): Bachelor's degree with honours (includes B.Litt.).
inc.th.: Thesis title was listed in *Economica* or *Register*, but degree was never completed.
Sources: See Appendix.

Both World Wars brought a drop in Chinese enrollments. The great bulge in numbers in 1935–39 may reflect the availability of Boxer Indemnity funds, and British Council funds help explain the revival in the 1940s.[5]

The London School of Economics

LSE was from its inception a powerful magnet for students from overseas, the largest element being those from India. Chinese were, during most of this period, the second largest group from outside the British Isles (Dahrendorf 1995, p. 174). By the time the LSE annual Calendar began publishing summary data on the number of Chinese students (1929), that number had reached 73. Annual data for the subsequent years are shown in Table 5-3.

There is quite a contrast between the large number of Chinese reported in Table 5-3 and the much smaller number in our sample in Table 5-2. Many of those reported in Table 5-3 did not complete degrees, and our enumeration of such students is quite incomplete. Further, students attending LSE had a wide range of social science and business major fields besides Economics. And of course the same individuals may appear in three or four

Table 5-3. Chinese Students Enrolled at the London School of Economics and Political Science, 1929–1950

Year	Chinese	All overseas students	All students	All Ec.Gr St.
1929	73	645	2,922	156
1930	56	582	2,937	163
1931	46	546	2,935	165
1932	62	652	2,939	195
1933	74	743	2,962	221
1934	93	719	3,029	228
1935	105	721	3,035	242
1936	104	717	3,000	256
1937	75	740	2,998	251
1938	73	697	2,891	240
1939	19	310	979	128
1940	9	171	683	66
1941	5	172	788	65
1942	4	130	825	52
1943	8	159	836	63
1944	12	181	1,066	66
1945	25	490	2,151	172
1946	18	511	3,225	252
1947	31	657	3,742	322
1948	29	588	3,811	333
1949	17	631	3,612	374
1950	7	669	3,510	379

Source: Compiled from annual issues of LSE Calendar, Prospectus.

successive years in Table 5-3. In the early years the most distinguished economists teaching at LSE included Edwin Cannan (economic theory, history of economic thought), Arthur Bowley (statistics), Richard Tawney and Lilian Knowles (economic history, which became one of LSE's strengths) (Dahrendorf 1995, pp. 113, 205–207). Tawney made two visits to China and wrote an influential study of Chinese agriculture.[6] Subsequent distinguished additions included Hugh Dalton (public finance, destined for political distinction in the Labour Party), Eileen Power (economic history), Theodore Gregory (money and banking), and Lionel Robbins (business cycles, history of economic thought).[7] Future Nobel Prize winner John Hicks joined the faculty in 1926 and produced his most innovative work while at LSE.[8] This was the reorientation of microeconomic theory based on ordinal preferences, indifference curves, and marginal rates of substitution, rather than marginal utility. Hicks left LSE in 1935. Other significant faculty from the 1930s were R. G. D. Allen, Nicholas Kaldor, Arthur Lewis (another subsequent Nobel laureate), George Shackle, Tibor Scitovsky, Brinley Thomas, Arnold Plant, and Frederic Benham.[9]

Another future Nobel laureate, Friedrich Hayek, came to LSE in 1931. He received much attention for his macroeconomic theories and disputes with Keynes. However, his Nobel award came for his insights concerning the informational basis of market economy and shortcomings of centrally-controlled economic systems—presented while he was at LSE.[10] One of the first Chinese students to respond to him was Chou Teh-wei (Zhou Dewei) who attended his seminar in 1933. Zhou published materials on the neutrality of money and on theories of credit policy. He returned to teach at Hunan, National Central, and Chongqing Universities.[11] Hayek left Britain for the United States in 1949. He had a major influence on Jiang Shuojie and Wu Yuanli (discussed below). While LSE had been founded through the efforts of noted Fabian Socialists, its Economics faculty also involved strong free-market advocates, ranging from Cannan through Robbins to Hayek.[12]

The most distinguished Chinese students at LSE came relatively late.[13] In 1937 Wu Chi-yuen (Qiyuan) received a PhD with a dissertation surveying theories of international prices, which was published in 1939 (Wu 1939). Wu had studied at Shanghai and did graduate work at Qinghua. He returned to China just in time to join the Qinghua faculty in Kunming, publishing a number of articles on China's wartime financial conditions. After the war, he left China to join the staff of the United Nations.

Jiang Shuojie came to LSE after studying at Keio University in Japan. His first Economics course was with Frederick Benham, whom he characterized as "well-known but not first-rate", and who displayed prejudice against Chinese students. Jiang had acquired a liking for philosophy since his studies in Japan and was drawn to Hayek, who helped him receive financial assistance. Hayek suggested his dissertation topic, for which he received a PhD in 1945.[14] His dissertation explored the behavior of real wages and profit margins over the business cycle, a topic which played an important part in Keynes's *General Theory*. Although Jiang was working under Hayek, who had been involved in much dispute with Keynes, the dissertation was not presented in a controversial vein. Jiang concluded that the statistical data weakly supported Keynes rather than Hayek (Tsiang 1947). His dissertation research was awarded the Hutchinson Silver Medal.

In other writings, Jiang had already challenged central elements of Keynes's thought. In 1943 he pointed out shortcomings of the Keynesian theory that the interest rate is determined by the interaction of money supply and stock demand for money.[15]

Jiang's later career demonstrates that he absorbed much of Hayek's skepticism about an extensive role for government. Jiang returned to China briefly to teach at Beida and other Peiping institutions. In 1947, as inflation was escalating, Jiang published two articles urging the government to create price-indexed savings certificates to assure savers a positive real rate of return on their funds. The proposal was not adopted at that time but was introduced by the new Communist government in 1949 (Tsiang 1980, p. 311).

Jiang, whose father was a high KMT official, left China as the Communist take-over loomed. He taught a year at National Taiwan University, then joined the International Monetary Fund. Later he taught at Rochester and Cornell. Beginning in 1954, Jiang played a major role in advising the government of Taiwan to follow a relatively liberal policy toward its international trade and payments, helping to stimulate the island's phenomenal economic growth (Tsiang 1980, pp. 310–333; Thorbecke and Wan 1999). Ultimately he moved to Taiwan and headed the Chung-hua Institution for Economic Research until his death in 1993.[16]

Wu Yuanli also wrote his dissertation under Hayek's direction, examining the relationship between capital formation, economic growth, and the organization of the economy. He emphasized that a policy to promote economic growth should improve people's economic welfare (a consideration often absent in Soviet-style forced industrialization). The program should promote saving and investment (giving attention to investment in knowledge and human capital) and developing the rule of law (Wu 1946a).

Wu returned to China to join the Central Bank, but like Jiang, left China at the time of the Communist take-over. He held professorships at several American universities, chiefly Marquette and San Francisco, worked for the U.S. State Department, and was a member of the research staff of the Hoover Institution, publishing extensively on China's economy (Sih 1970, p. 337).

Of the LSE students who returned permanently to Chinese academic life, Hu Chi-chuang (Jichuang) was noteworthy. He completed an MSc degree in 1939 and returned to a series of university positions, including Beida and Furen. After 1949 he taught at Zhejiang University (Hangzhou) and the Shanghai Institute of Finance. He became one of China's most distinguished historians of Chinese economic thought, producing a three-volume work published in 1962, 1963, and 1981. A condensed English-language version appeared in 1988 (Hu 1988).

English missionary John Bernard Tayler studied at LSE in 1919 before assuming his new duties as chair of the Economics department at the newly-formed Yanjing University in Peking. He returned for refresher study in the mid-1930s, "reading and discussing Institutional Economics with Professor [E. F. M.] Durbin".[17] His career is examined in Chapter 8.

Cambridge

Economics teaching at Cambridge University entered the twentieth century under the dominating presence of Alfred Marshall, who retired in 1908. His successor was his student Arthur Pigou. John Maynard Keynes joined the faculty at the same time, teaching monetary economics. Other faculty in the early days included John Clapham and C. R. Fay in economic history and Walter Layton on industrial economics (Harrod 1951, pp. 142–146).

By the 1920s, Cambridge had become associated with a series of revolutionary changes in orthodox economics, beginning with theories of imperfect competition in the work of Joan Robinson and Piero Sraffa. From 1930 the emphasis shifted to the transformation of monetary and macro-economics through the work of Keynes, supported by Mrs. Robinson and Richard Kahn. Though both of these topics were eagerly taken up in China, neither was very relevant to China, and both tended unduly to denigrate free-market institutions. This attitude was especially pronounced in Mrs. Robinson. After 1949, she took a great interest in China's experiments with communism and visited China several times.

Reported Chinese students at Cambridge were predominantly undergraduates.[18] This attendance began early, with Tseng Tsung-chien (Zeng Zongjian—1908), Lo Tsung-yi (Luo Zhongyi—1909), and Chang Wei (Zhang Wei—1910).[19]

The most important of Cambridge's three Chinese PhDs was Hsu (Xu) Yu-nan, whose 1940 dissertation examined the impact of the Depression on the British cotton industry. Xu returned to China to join the Qinghua faculty in Kunming. His teaching emphasized the innovations relating to imperfect competition and macroeconomics. He undertook to translate Keynes's *General Theory* into Chinese; it was published in 1957, just before he died of cancer. At the time he and other Chinese Keynesians were under attack as "rightists".

Keynes's ideas were promulgated in China even sooner through the work of Michael Lindsay. After spending some time as a research student at Cambridge (imbibing the Keynesian excitement), Lindsay joined the Yanjing faculty early in 1938 and developed a course on Keynesian economics. His career is examined at greater length in Chapter 8.

Fan Hong was a research student at Cambridge (1935–39) supported by the China Foundation for the Promotion of Education and Culture. In 1939 he published an article comparing Keynes and Marx on some major points of Keynes's analysis. Fan was already a Marxist and studied with Maurice Dobb who held similar views.[20]

Our data identified 68 Chinese who returned from Economics study in Britain to teach in Chinese universities prior to 1949. Of these, 44 had studied at LSE. Of the 68, seven had verified PhD degrees and another nine verified master's degrees.[21]

Information on the careers, research topics, and undergraduate backgrounds of the Chinese who studied Economics in Britain appears in the subsequent chapter.

Germany

In the last half of the nineteenth century, German universities had pioneered in the development of higher education.[22] University study in Germany focused on the doctoral degree. Often this was the only degree offered, and it did not entail the kind of lengthy and rigorous preparation associated with it in modern times. In the German universities, until well into the twentieth century:

> there was no BA, [and] no graduate school . . . In addition to writing a brief dissertation, candidates underwent examination in three broad subjects, such as history, geography, and mathematics. Neither the dissertation nor the examinations were very concentrated or demanding.[23]

Whether or not there really was a "German Historical School" among economists, there was certainly emphasis on evolutionary, institutional, and cultural factors, drawing heavily on historical and descriptive information. There was much common ground with American Institutionalism, particularly in support for government economic interventions; the influence of Adolf Wagner was noteworthy (Pearson 1999). In the early twentieth century, much Economics instruction in German universities was given in departments of law and political science, with a consequent bias toward interventionist policies.

Many Americans who became prominent economists studied in Germany or were heavily influenced by German economists. Most important was Richard T. Ely, who combined devotion to the Social Gospel with strong support for government interventions. Ely's work had a strong influence on Sun Yat-sen and Liang Qichao. His *Outlines of Economics* (original ed. 1893) was widely used in Chinese universities, both in its original and in the Chinese translation published in 1910. Other German-influenced Americans who had a China connection included Edwin R. A. Seligman and Henry Seager at Columbia, Charles Bullock at Harvard, who directed several Chinese dissertations, and Henry Carter Adams and Jeremiah Whipple Jenks, who went to China as advisers (Carlson 1999).

In 1897–98, the German government seized effective control of the Chinese city of Qingdao and surrounding portions of Shandong Province. The move brought to China facilities for teaching the German language and for brewing German beer. There were interesting experiments in land-value taxation which intrigued Sun Yat-sen.

German was taught in many Chinese universities. In 1907–10 a substantial number of Sino-German secondary schools were established in major Chinese cities. And 1907 also witnessed the creation of Tongji University in Shanghai, emphasizing medical science and using German as the medium of instruction. Tongji survived to the present and became a strong force in the teaching of science and technology. By 1949, Tongji had produced 2,251 graduates.[24]

German influence on China's educational system was promoted by German-educated Tsai (Cai) Yuanpei, who served as Minister of Education 1911–12 and President of Peking University 1916–26. The Beida Economics Department employed two German nationals (Friedrich Otte and E. Erde) in its early days and was headed for several years by Ku (Gu) Mengyu, who had studied in Germany.

During the 1930s, the Kuomintang government under Chiang Kai-shek cultivated relations with Germany in several dimensions. Sun Fo and other officials attempted (without much success) to combine German capital and technical expertise with the programs outlined in Sun Yat-sen's development program, and developed bilateral trading arrangements, particularly after Hitler came to power.[25]

These developments produced an increased interest in study in Germany by Chinese. By 1936 there were over 1,600 Chinese resident in Germany, most of them students (Kirby 1984, pp. 154, 202–205). There was no Boxer Indemnity money for study in Germany, but in the 1920s and 1930s, favorable exchange rates made Germany an inexpensive place for Chinese students (Liang 1978, pp. 24–26).

Chinese Economics Students in Germany

We have identified 122 Chinese who studied Economics in Germany between 1900 and 1950. Of these, 82 were recipients of doctoral degrees.[26] German universities most commonly taught Economics in the faculty of law, philosophy, or legal and political science (Rechtswissenschaft und Staatswissenschaft—R and S). The *Jahresverzeichnis* gives figures for total R and S doctorates for 1928–32, which moved upward from 1,721 to 2,215. However, Frankfurt had a Faculty of Wirtschaft- und Sozialwissenschaft. Jena, Cologne, and Tubingen all had faculties with Economics in the formal name (*Jahresverzeichnis* 1934). Sources for non-doctoral students are described in the Appendix; however, the tabulation is quite incomplete.[27] Table 5-4 identifies the German universities attended.

Table 5-4. Chinese Economics Students in German Universities, 1900–1950

	Primary university		Secondary university		
	Doctorate	Others	Doctorate	Others	Total
Berlin	26	24	8	1	59
Frankfurt	12	1	0	0	13
Leipzig	10	0	1	2	13
Jena	4	1	2	0	7
Vienna	3	2	2	0	7
Munich	4	0	2	1	7
20 others	22	5	10	1	38
Unidentified	0	8	0	0	8
Total	81	41	25	5	152
(–) Duplicates					–30
Total students					122

The largest number of Chinese students gravitated to Berlin, to what was formally the Friedrich-Wilhelm-Universitat. Frankfurt and Leipzig also attracted double-digit enrollments. The decade of the 1930s was by far the peak, influenced by the Sino-German rapprochement, and indicating the relative indifference of Chinese toward Hitler and the political turmoil in Germany.[28] A significant enrollment continued in 1940–44 despite the war, but evaporated when the war ended in 1945.

Reminiscences by prominent economists suggest that Berlin was not the most exciting school for Economics. Wolfgang Stolper entered Berlin University in 1930 and studied law for three semesters. "Except for Jastrow's seminar I did not visit any other economics lectures in Berlin. Part of this was certainly prejudice. My father [Gustav Stolper, an eminent economist] thought it was a waste of time . . . The only regrets I have is that I did not visit V. Bortkiewicz and perhaps Sering."[29]

Only three Chinese went to Freiburg, where the work of Karl Diehl (who directed the only Chinese dissertation) and Walter Eucken was much praised.[30] Kiel attracted three Chinese. But Andreas Predohl (who advised one of them) assembled the work of seven German-fluent Chinese for a 1937 symposium on China's industrialization (Predohl 1937).

From the examined dissertations, we obtained the names of the supervising professors, finding 23 at Berlin. Berlin's most noted professor, Werner Sombart, was involved with two.[31] Other Berlin professors who appeared more than once included Hans Weigman (5), Jens Jessen (8), and Horst Jecht (6); all relatively young scholars with numerous publications in the *National Union Catalog*.[32] Jessen directed one of the most unusual dissertations: "Mathematisch-statistische Untersuchung zur Chinesischen Industrie" (Berlin, 1937) by Wu Tao-kun. Following his graduation from National Central, Wu had worked as an assistant in statistics and experimental psychology at Hunan University. Moving to Germany in 1935, he studied statistics at the Berlin Technische Hochschule (BTH) in addition to his economic studies at Berlin University.[33] Wu used Chinese data to illustrate various statistical and econometric procedures. The most interesting exercise, following Erich Schneider's *Theorie der Produktion* (1934), generated parabolic cost functions and revenue functions for Chinese cotton mills. Presumably Wu learned most of these procedures at BTH; there is no evidence of them in the other dissertations.[34] The technische hochschulen were polytechnical universities. Several offered Economics courses and generated dissertations in our list, primarily on China's transportation system.

Hermann Schumacher, who had become "the professor" at Berlin in 1906, advised on three Chinese dissertations in the 1930s. He was a prolific writer whose publications ranged across monetary, international, and transportation. He had published a book on China's treaty ports (1898) and articles on foreign business in China (Pang 1937, p. 95). Another broad-ranging scholar was Friedrich von Gottl-Ottlilienfeld, who advised on two Chinese dissertations. His interests extended across history, economics, philosophy, and sociology, and he was sufficiently devoted to free markets to write *The Myth of Planned Economy* (Schumpeter 1954, p. 854).

At Frankfurt, Chinese students were advised by Paul Arndt (4), a labor economist who used two Chinese dissertations as the core of a book on wages in China (Arndt 1937). The book contained much useful descriptive information but lacked the crisp focus which would have been provided by a greater familiarity with marginal productivity theory. Karl Pribram advised two Chinese. He wrote extensively on cartels, labor and social insurance; ultimately he emigrated to the United States.[35] Students at Frankfurt were also exposed to Franz Oppenheimer: "a powerful teacher who shaped many growing minds and did much to keep the flag of economic theory flying by spirited controversy".[36] Oppenheimer's books occupy five pages in the *National Union Catalog*! He opposed Marxism but was critical of private property in land. The only Chinese dissertation he directed was entitled "Capitalism and Land Property in China" by Kuo Shien-yen (Guo Xianyan). Despite the title, it did not go very deeply into the problems of land policy.

Heinrich Schmitthenner, who advised on four dissertations at Leipzig, was something of a China expert. He was primarily a geographer who published two books on China as well as others on physical geography and on "living space and the conflict of civilizations".

Chang Ko-wei (Zhang Guowei) completed a doctorate at Berlin in 1930 on China's monetary system. He moved to Taiwan in 1949 for a distinguished career at the National Taiwan University.

We have included Vienna in our German section. Austria was German in culture and language. Moreover, Austria was forcibly incorporated into the German Reich in 1936, to be liberated in 1945. The University of Vienna had boasted many distinguished economists, but by the time Chinese students arrived in the 1930s, it had deteriorated badly. The chief remaining luminary was Othmar Spann, known for his Listian "universalism". He directed one known dissertation, by Tschang (Chang) Yen-yu (Zhang Yenyu—1935), dealing with attitudes and policy toward labor in Germany and in China. Zhang discussed views of several prominent German economists, but had no significant discussion of Marx.[37]

Gu Mengyu, Chen Hansheng, and the other German-trained people at Beida are discussed further in Chapter 13. Another early German-trained student of significance was Hsueh Hsien-chou (Xue Xianzhou). He completed his studies in Berlin in 1910 and returned to take a professorship at Fudan University, teaching German, Civics, and Economics. One of his students was Chen Guofu, later to become very influential in the KMT. Xue left Fudan in 1918, and founded the Shanghai Cooperative Bank, probably the first European-style cooperative in China (Lai 1988).

A notable product of study in Germany was Hsiao Cheng (Xiao Zheng), who completed his studies at Berlin in 1932. He returned to China to become a professor at the Central Political Institute and Dean of the Graduate School of Land Economics. Besides numerous government positions, he was director of the Research Institute of Land Economics beginning 1940. A strong advocate of Sun Yat-sen's policy for equalization of land rights, he moved to Taiwan and became Vice-minister of Economic Affairs, playing an important role in Taiwan's land reform.[38]

We have identified 46 of the Chinese who studied Economics in Germany as returning to teach in Chinese universities. Of these, 21 had verified doctorates (one in Switzerland) and 25 did not. This leaves 56 German PhDs whom we did not find in any Chinese university faculty list. Our lists are quite incomplete, to be sure, and some of the people undoubtedly taught in fields other than Economics. But it is likely that many entered government and/or business to take advantage of their language skills. Liang (1978) describes how Yang Shu-jen (Shuren) and Wang Chia-hong (Jiahong) studied Economics at Berlin while working in the Chinese embassy. Considering the light work-load usually involved in embassy work (then and now), it seems likely that a significant number of the Chinese who studied in London, Paris, and Berlin were embassy staff.[39]

Shen Djini (Shen Laiqiu—Lionel Shen) had a distinguished career in academic and government positions. After graduating from Tongji, he studied in Dresden and completed a doctorate in Frankfurt in 1924 with a dissertation on wages in China. He taught at Fujian Christian University and Amoy University in 1925–29, then worked for the Commercial Press (1929–33). Government positions followed, with the National Economic Council (1933–36) and National Directorate of Ordnance (1936–40). He then returned to academic positions at Tongji, National Yunnan University, and Huazhong (1945–49).[40]

Information on the research topics and undergraduate backgrounds of Chinese who studied Economics in Germany is presented in the subsequent chapter.

France

By 1900, there were secondary schools and colleges in China which provided instruction in many fields in the French or German language. French became the focus of much of the Roman Catholic missionary effort. In 1914, of the 1,500 Catholic priests in China, 850 were French. At the beginning of the twentieth century, there were over 3,000 French missionary schools in China, enrolling nearly 70,000 students (Hayhoe 1987, pp. 100–102).

In 1903 l'Université l'Aurore (Aurora University, Zhendan University) began operation in Shanghai. It was managed and largely staffed by French Jesuits, utilizing French and Chinese as media of instruction. French Jesuits also created the École des Hautes Etudes Commerciales et Industrielles (School of Advanced Studies in Commerce and Industry) in Tianjin, beginning in 1923 (Hayhoe 1987, pp. 104–107).

The French connection was intensified by the program which sent a large number of Chinese workers to France during and after World War I. Deng Xiaoping and Zhou Enlai were among the many subsequently influential Communists who shared this experience in France (Wang Yi-chu 1966, pp. 105–111; Deng Maomao 1995, pp. 52–103). In 1925 l'Université Franco-Chinoise was formed in Peking out of a number of separate specialized schools. The Franco-Chinese University was subsidized by French Boxer Indemnity funds, thus imitating the American support for Qinghua. The University was never very large—its total university enrollment was about 200 in 1933 and 500 in 1947.[41] French was also the first foreign language in the short-lived Labor University which operated in Shanghai 1927–32, discussed in Chapter 10.

The Franco-Chinese University in China was linked with another located within France—l'Institut Franco-Chinois in Lyon, established in 1921 and closed in 1947. The latter offered tutorial programs for Chinese coming to France for advanced study. The Institut aided a substantial number of Chinese students of Economics both in Lyon and in other French universities.[42]

Economics was taught in France primarily in colleges of law. Weisz notes that "political economy was deliberately introduced to the faculties of law rather than to those of letters so that its principles could be most widely and effectively disseminated" (Weisz 1983, p. 298; also pp. 113–115). As Clark has noted, by 1900:

> [T]his political economy emphasize[d] institutional and legal elements. Such "deforming" of political economy . . . was criticized by the few French economists at the time, most of whom held to a theoretical conception closer to their British counterparts . . . Thus, although chairs of political economy were increasing near the end of the nineteenth century, their incumbents seldom built on classical economic theory or utilized systematic quantitative analysis." (Clark 1973, p. 143; see also p. 122.)

The academics in this category resembled the American institutionalists—they tried to broaden their framework to include history, sociology, anthropology, and law; they were generally pro-labor and anti-business, favoring government interventions to aid the poor. Representatives of this group who were advisers on Chinese economic dissertations included François Simiand, Maurice Halbwachs, Célestin Bouglé, Marcel Granet, Jean Escarra, Henri Hauser, Paul Fauconnet, A. Demangeon, and Marc Bloch.

Chinese Students in France

We have identified 113 Chinese who studied Economics in France. Of these, 83 received doctoral degrees. Information on these comes from Yuan (1964) and from the annual dissertation lists published by the French Ministry of Education.[43] Details on the other students are in the Appendix; their listings are undoubtedly very incomplete.

Table 5-5 shows the universities attended by the Chinese studying Economics in France.

Table 5-5. Universities Attended by Chinese Students of Economics in France, 1900–1950

University	Doctorate	Others	Total
Paris	42	21	63
Nancy	15	0	15
Lyon	11	0	11
6 others	15	3	18
Unknown	0	6	6
Total	83	30	113

Sources: See Appendix.

Half of the doctoral students and more than half of the others studied at the University of Paris, primarily in the Faculty of Law. Probably Chinese in diplomatic service took the opportunity for such study. Nancy ranked second; they offered a specialty in Economics that was more focused than most of the other universities.[44] Lyon, with its connection to the Franco-Chinese Institute, ranked third.

The time pattern also shows a high degree of concentration: three-fourths of the students completed doctorates or reported study in the fifteen-year span 1925–39. War broke out in Europe in 1939, and Paris was overrun by the Germans in 1940, disrupting education.

The Paris dissertations which we examined reported 42 different professors as advisers. These included numerous figures familiar to the international economic community. Albert Aftalion (2 dissertations) made original contributions to business-cycle theory. Charles Rist (2) and Bertrand Nogaro (2) provided important commentaries on monetary questions. Gaetan Pirou (2) participated in the transformation of microeconomic theory, writing a book (1934) on the general equilibrium analysis of Walras and Pareto. William Oualid (6) published several studies on immigration and on foreign workers in France, as well as items on money, international trade, and wage theories.[45]

Many of the French advisers displayed an institutionalist quality. Henri Hauser (6) was a historian who emphasized social and economic factors. According to Weisz, "Hauser's brand of social history was [highly] political and closely linked to the interests of the moderate trade union movement because it focused on the history of the working class. Among other things, it described the exploitation of workers in the early capitalist system which often led to riots and revolution."[46]

Paul Fauconnet (5) combined sociology and law. A. Demangeon (3) combined sociology and geography. The combination of economics and sociology was demonstrated by Francois Simiand (2) and Maurice Halbwachs (4). Simiand produced monumental studies of the historical behavior of wages and prices.[47] Halbwachs published several studies on working-class consumption patterns, in which he "offered a sociological method to determine what is a social class, using wider criteria than those of the economist."[48]

The Chinese students in Paris also enjoyed access to two formidable French sinologists. Marcel Granet (1884–1940), a sociologist, spent two years in China in 1911–13 and wrote extensively about Chinese religion, culture, and history. His book *Chinese Civilization* (originally published in

1930) went through numerous translations and reprints.[49] Granet was an adviser on five of our dissertations. A good example of a dissertation under his direction was the study of the social work of the Chinese railways by Lou Yee-wen (Lu Yuwen—also advised by Halbwachs and Marc Bloch).[50] While primarily a social survey, this contains extensive economic data on wages, working conditions, and budgets.

Jean Escarra (1885–1955) was an authority on Chinese law, particularly as it related to commerce and to family relationships. Like Granet, he was conversant with the Chinese language and had spent considerable time in China. He served as an adviser to the Chinese government and published extensively on Chinese topics.[51] He was an adviser on seven Chinese dissertations in Economics. A representative dissertation in the "social economics" vein was Liu Nanming's *Contribution à l'Etude de la Population Chinoise* (1935), directed by Simiand and advised by Hauser, Demangeon, and Escarra. Liu believed China was in a severe crisis of overpopulation, and that the harmful effects had been aggravated by China's opening to the world. His proposed remedies were primarily aimed at increasing output. He did not emphasize birth control. Liu joined the faculty of National Central University.[52]

Lau (Lou) Tongsun studied under Charles Gide at Paris in the mid-1920s. He held a number of government and academic positions in China, including Secretary-General of the National Economic Council in 1936–37. Lou had been much influenced by Gide's advocacy of cooperatives. He translated several of Gide's books into Chinese and wrote biographies of Gide and of Robert Owen. He later became head of the China Cooperatives Association (*China Year Book* 1959–60, p. 746).

Outside of Paris, the largest concentration of Chinese doctoral students in Economics was at Nancy, with its focused "Mention Sciences Economiques". Four professors provided the bulk of the advising. Two of them, F. de Menthon (14) and Henri Lalouel (7) did little published research. Lucien Brocard (9) wrote on a wide range of topics, from the cooperative movement to the French metallurgical industry, as well as a principles textbook (Echinard and LeRoy 2000). Jean Marchal (9) completed his own doctorate at Nancy in 1929. His writings ranged over customs unions, financial markets, a history of French artisans, Marxism, budgets and fiscal policy, and extended to several principles texts in the post-war period.

From Chinese sources, we have identified 39 Chinese who studied Economics in France who returned to teach Economics in Chinese universities. Of these, only 18 had verified French doctorates. This means that 65 of our 83 doctorates do not appear in our faculty listings. No doubt some were teaching in fields outside of Economics. But it is likely that many used their language skills for work in business or government, particularly in the diplomatic service.

Information on the careers, research topics, and the undergraduate backgrounds of the Chinese who studied Economics in France is presented in the subsequent chapter.

Other European Countries

Besides the three major countries surveyed in this chapter, Chinese also studied Economics in a number of smaller European countries. We have identified 21 of these students, 13 being doctorates listed in Yuan 1964.[53] Of the 21, eight studied in Belgium (four at Louvain) and seven in Switzerland.[54] Eight of the 21 returned to teach Economics in China.

The best known was Paul Sih (Hsueh Kuan-tsien—Xue Guangqian) who completed a dissertation at the University of Rome in 1936 on China's banking system, studying under Professor Alberto de'Stefani, the former Minister of Finance. Sih worked for the Ministry of Railways and also participated in a diplomatic mission to Germany in 1937–38 as part of a futile effort to deter the German-Japanese rapprochement (Kirby 1984, p. 238). After 1943 he was part of the Ministry of Foreign Affairs, serving as ambassador to Italy. Moving to Taiwan, he continued in foreign service until 1959, when he joined St. John's University (Long Island, New York) and edited several books dealing with China's economy (Sih 1952; 1970, pp. 335–336).

Data on these 21 students are included in the summary tables in the following chapter.

Overview

Table 5-6 summarizes some important data from our survey of Chinese economics students in Europe. The similarity of the French and German lists is quite close. Doctorates were numerous—the 164 noted here for France and Germany exceeds the 149 recorded for the United States. Our non-doctoral lists are not as complete, since we did not use university archival materials except for Britain and the United States. The concentration of Chinese in the flagship universities (and diplomatic centers) was much

Table 5-6. Chinese Economics Students in Europe, 1900–1950

Country	Number of students	Doctorates	In largest university*
Britain	162	18	92
France	113	83	65
Germany	122	81	59
Others	21	13	4
Total	391**	195	220
U.S.	1,227	149	273

* University with the largest number of Chinese Economics students.
** Net of duplications.

more extreme in Britain, France, and Germany than in the other countries.

France and Germany were also paired in Nobel laureate George Stigler's remark (1990) that "France and Germany have made on the whole rather minor contributions to the evolution of modern economic analysis" (Breit and Spencer, p. 101). Leonard (2004) noted, referring to the 1920s, that "European social sciences were still highly speculative, . . . the universities were often torn by internecine strife" and plagued with bureaucracy (p. 298). Dissertations produced by top-ranking Chinese in Britain and the United States were superior to those produced on the Continent. In all fairness, however, Chinese who studied on the Continent were equally likely to return to teaching positions in China and to contribute to published research on China's economy as Chinese studying in Britain or the United States.

The nature of our source research suggests that our student lists are most incomplete for continental Europe, somewhat less so for Britain, and least so for the United States. The following chapter explores this issue; here we refer only briefly to some relevant data which appear in Table 5-7.

The proportion of our Chinese student lists who studied in the United States is higher than the share of U.S.-educated economists in our lists of Economics faculty in Chinese universities (ALLFAC). This is mainly a matter of timing, involving the disproportionately large flow to the United States in the 1940s.

Data on professors surviving in 1987 indicates proportions relatively close to those in our student lists, except for the relatively high number from Britain.

The ALLFAC data can be interpreted as indicating that our tabulations underestimate the proportion of students who studied in Western

Table 5-7. Relative Proportions (%) of Western-educated Chinese Economists

Country	From Table 5-6	ALLFAC	1987/90 Professors
U.S.	76	64	68
Britain	10	16	21
France	7	10	6
Germany	8	11	5
Other W. European Countries	1	2	0
Total	100*	100*	100

* Because of duplications, components exceed total.
Sources: Tables 6-1 and 6-6 in Chapter 6.

Europe. All of these matters are developed more fully in the following chapter.

Appendix

Sources for Students in British and European Universities

Britain: Data on PhD degrees were derived from Yuan 1963 and Bilboul 1975; the latter provided data on other thesis degrees. I examined as many theses as possible at the LSE Library to verify the inclusion of them as Economics. *Economica* published annually (1925–33) a "List of Theses in Economics and Allied Subjects in Progress at Universities and Colleges in Great Britain and Northern Ireland", which I scanned for Chinese students. Similar information appeared in the *Register of Research in the Social Sciences* for 1947 and thereafter. I scanned the LSE Prospectus, Calendar and Register. At the Bodleian Library I scanned the Oxford University Calendar. Mr. Anthony Twist kindly assembled data on Chinese who received Economics degrees from Cambridge.

In both France and Germany, the Ministry of Education published an annual list of all the doctoral dissertations completed in the preceding year. Kathleen Trescott and I scanned these for Chinese names beginning around 1910. Then I discovered Yuan (1964). At any rate, we achieved double coverage of the doctoral students. I also scanned the card catalogues for common Chinese names and included some Chinese authors of German-language and French-language publications about China.

Many of the entries were based on Chinese biographical references. These included the successive volumes of *Who's Who in China*, the *China Year Book* and the *China Handbook*. Faculty lists for individual universities sometimes identify their academic backgrounds; this is also true for the 1942 roster published by the Chinese Ministry of Education.

Biographical directories published in China gave data on schools and degrees, names in hanzi, and subsequent employment, although often without dates. These are listed in the Appendix to Chapter 4. The degrees recorded in my data set are those verified by Yuan, Bilboul, or university sources. Liang (1978) identifies some students connected with diplomatic positions.

6

Chinese Economics Graduate Students Overseas: Careers, Backgrounds, Research Areas

A large part of the introduction of western economic ideas into China came through the Western education of Chinese who returned to teaching positions in Chinese universities. The preceding chapters have documented about 1,600 Chinese who studied Economics in the West. In this chapter, we attempt an overview of those who returned to university faculty positions teaching Economics. Subsequent chapters fill in the detail for individual Chinese universities. This chapter also examines the undergraduate backgrounds of the students who studied overseas, emphasizing the major role of the Christian colleges and Qinghua College. We also summarize the research topics embodied in their theses and dissertations.

Role in University Faculties

We have identified over 900 Chinese who taught Economics in Chinese universities in our time period. Of these, over 500 achieved some foreign study. Data on Economics faculty are surveyed in Table 6-1.

Our faculty lists are divided into two categories. The data for the Christian colleges (denoted CHRSFAC) are almost complete, particularly for the 1940s. They constitute 43 percent of the gross total of 1,162 names, whereas their true proportion is more likely about one fourth.[1] Sources for these data are described in Chapters 7 to 9. Data for the Chinese universities are denoted CHINFAC. They are much less complete. Chapters 10 to 13 give details on sources for their faculty lists.

There were 122 Chinese whose names appear in both lists. They are an interesting group (denoted BOTHFAC). No fewer than 104 of them studied abroad, and 56 studied Economics at the graduate level in the United

Table 6-1. Overseas Study by Chinese Teaching Economics in Chinese Universities before 1950

	CHINFAC	CHRSFAC	BOTHFAC (deduct)	ALLFAC	1942
All Econ. Teachers	664	498	123	1,039	101
Foreign	9	89	1	97	0
Chinese	655	409	122	942	101
Studied abroad	415	233	104	544	82
U.S. grad. econ.:	200	133	56	277	26
GS	47	25	9	63	9
MA	68*	59	21	106*	7
ABD	15	9	5	19	1
PhD	56*	28*	20	64*	9
U.S. later**	14	12	1	25	0
Other U.S.	47	38	8	77	9
Total U.S.	247	171	64	354	35
GB & W. Eur.***	135	51	33	153	36
Britain	60	26	17	69	12
France	35	15	9	41	12
Germany	44	12	10	46	9
Others	9	2	1	10	3
Later or not econ.	8	1	0	9	0
Other foreign	57	16	10	63	18
Japan	50	13	8	55	16
USSR	6	2	2	6	1
Others	1	1	0	2	1
(–) Duplicates	24	5	3	26	7

* Three late PhDs were entered as MAs, since the MAs were received prior to their teaching in China.

** Students whose foreign study came after their recorded service as university teachers of Economics.

*** Total for GB and Western Europe is net of duplicates within Europe.

States. Removing the double counting represented by this group yields the net data denoted by ALLFAC, containing 942 Chinese names and 97 foreign.

The proportion of faculty reporting foreign study is high in both categories. Indeed, if we include foreign teachers, the proportions are nearly identical—about 64 percent for both Chinese and Christian institutions. Factoring out the foreign teachers yields 64 percent for CHINFAC and 57 percent for CHRSFAC.

Table 6-2 summarizes the percentages (of total Chinese faculty) for major categories of foreign study.

Table 6-2. Percentage Composition of Chinese Economics Faculty, 1900–1950

	CHINFAC	CHRSFAC	ALLFAC	1942 roster
Total Chinese faculty	655	409	942	101
Percentage (%) of listed Chinese faculty who studied in:				
U.S.: all grad. econ.	28	29	27	26
GS	7	6	7	9
MA	10	14	11	7
ABD	2	2	2	1
PhD	9	7	7	9
Western Europe*	19	12	15	36
Britain	9	6	7	2
France	5	4	4	12
Germany	7	3	5	9
Japan	8	3	6	16

* Net of persons listed for more than one country. Data in this table exclude persons whose foreign study came after their faculty service.

Table 6-2 indicates that over 40 percent of all the Economics faculty had studied Economics in the West. As noted above, another 20 percent had undertaken some study abroad, whether in Japan, as undergraduates, or in graduate fields (notably business) other than Economics.

The reliability of the big picture is strongly affirmed by the close similarity of the two subsets in Table 6-2. The two faculty lists were compiled almost entirely from separate and independent sources. Where they differ, it is in plausible directions: the Christian colleges had a higher proportion of American-educated economists, the Chinese universities a higher proportion of European and Japanese-educated people.

Another possible test of reliability is offered by the 101 economists listed in the 1942 roster of "certified" professors. This list is analyzed in detail in Chapter 10. The roster is only a small subset of the 1942 faculty and is a very biased sample. For all that, the 1942 roster contains 26 professors who studied Economics at the graduate level in the United

States—almost identical to the proportions shown in CHINFAC and CHRSFAC. However, the proportions of European-educated and Japanese-educated persons are much higher in the 1942 list.[2] Certification was self-selected, and persons with these credentials may have been more motivated than others to seek certification. Certainly the 1942 roster does not suggest that our 40 percent estimate is too large. It does imply that our lists of students studying in Europe are less nearly complete than the lists of students in the United States.[3]

The chapters which follow provide detailed information on the roles of western-educated economists in the Christian colleges and in three major Chinese universities—Beida, Qinghua, and Nankai.

Only about one fifth of the Chinese who studied Economics at the graduate level in the United States in 1906–50 returned to teach Economics in Chinese universities. The true proportion was undoubtedly higher, since our faculty lists are incomplete. However, it is instructive to examine the time patterns of student movements. Table 6-3 matches students returning to teach Economics with the total student population by time periods.

Table 6-3. Students Returning from the U.S. to Teach Economics in China Compared with Total Chinese Studying Economics at Graduate Level in the U.S.

Time period	All students	Returned to teach*	%
1906–19	98	27	28
1920–29	303	89	29
1930–39	287	84	29
1940–49	474**	47	10
Total***	1,162	247	21

* Persons teaching Economics up to 1949. Excludes persons whose U.S. study came after their teaching.
** Li Peien (PhD 1950) was included under his MA year 1921.
*** Students with unknown dates are excluded.

There is a striking contrast between the higher proportion—almost one third—of students of the 1920s and 1930s returning to faculty positions, and the very low proportion from the 1940s. Wartime conditions boosted the total number of students coming to the United States, and reduced the number returning to teach in China by the end of our time period. However, a substantial number of students (we counted 45) who completed their overseas studies in the 1940s returned to take faculty positions subsequent to 1949.

It is also instructive to examine the proportions of the various degree categories who returned to faculty positions, as shown in Table 6-4.

Table 6-4. Persons Returning from the U.S. to Teach Economics in China, by Degree Categories

Degree	Total students*	Returned to teach	%	Total 1920–39	Returning	%
GS	414	62	15	144	33	23
MA	542**	107**	20	327	73	22
ABD	72	19	26	38	14	37
PhD	134**	64**	48	82	53	65
Total	1,162	252	22	591	173	29

* Persons teaching Economics up to 1949. Excludes persons whose U.S. study came after their teaching.
** Li Paien entered as MA 1921.

As one might expect, the proportion returning to teach was higher for persons with more advanced degree status. Two thirds of the persons receiving American doctorates in the 1920s and 1930s returned to teaching situations. Included in this distinguished group were Chen Daisun, He Lian, Fang Xianting, and Zhao Naituan, who returned to head the Economics programs in Qinghua, Nankai, and Beida. These programs, which sent so many subsequent students overseas, are examined at length in subsequent chapters.

Table 6-5 provides similar information on Chinese who studied Economics in Europe. There is a strong central tendency in the neighborhood of one third. Slightly under one third of the students returning from the United States up to 1939 taught Economics. Slightly over one third of the students returning from Europe through 1939 taught Economics. There is a reassuring consistency in the cross-country data. The apparent higher percentage of European students returning to teach, in comparison with those from the United States, is probably a reflection of source bias. Much of our information on European students is derived from Chinese university records. Students who did not complete a continental doctorate or a British thesis degree are underrepresented.

The number of Chinese Economics students in Europe was particularly large in the 1930s, with a correspondingly large flow back into Chinese

Table 6-5. Chinese Returning from Europe to Teach Compared with Total Studying in Europe

Period	Total students	Returning	%
1900–19	28	10	36
1920–29	71	26	37
1930–39	184	63	34
1940–50	71	16	23
Total*	354	115	32
NB: Students with unknown dates are excluded, as are duplicate entries.			
Country*			
Britain	162	69	43
France	113	41	36
Germany	122	46	38
Other European countries	21	8	38

* Some persons studied in more than one country. Data exclude 1950.

universities. In contrast, during the 1940s both the number of students and the proportion returning to teach were much smaller—partly because we did not try to analyze faculty subsequent to 1949.

A postscript is provided by data from a directory of Chinese university full-time professors published in 1990. Of the 646 Economics professors listed, 333 received at least one degree by 1950 or earlier. Of these 333, 100 listed study abroad. Table 6-6 lists their study locations. This set is supplemented by 32 additional part-time professors listed in *Biographies of Contemporary Chinese Economists* (1987).

The *Directory* lists persons holding professorships as of 1987. By then, of course, many pre-1951 professors had died, left China, or withdrawn from teaching. For all that, more than one-fourth of the pre-1951 cohort had studied abroad, and 19 percent of them had studied in the United States.[4] It is surprising to observe the very low proportion of German- and French-educated economists in the recent tabulations. The role of western-educated economists after 1949 is further examined in the final chapter.

Occupations

Our chief concern has been with students who returned to teach Economics in China. However, the majority of them did not. It is useful to have an idea of what they did.

Table 6-6. Foreign Study by Older Chinese Economics Professors Listed in 1987 and 1990 Directories

	1987	1990	Total	%
Total listed	33	333	366	100
No foreign study	7	233	240	66
U.S.:				
GS	3	25	28	8
MA	2	25	27	7
ABD	0	4	4	1
PhD	3	9	12	3
Others (not economics)	0	3	3	1
Britain	10	12	22	6
France	0	6	6	2
Germany	2	3	5	1
Japan	9	10	19	5
USSR	2	3	5	1
Total foreign	28*	100	128*	35

* After deducting duplicates.

Source: Calculated from listings in *Biographical Directory of Professors in Chinese Universities and Colleges*, 1990; *Biographies of Contemporary Chinese Economists* (1987), removing duplicates.

Extensive lists were published in 1917 and 1925 showing "returned students" from the United States (Chao 1917; *Who's Who in China* 1925). These identified the U.S. schools attended, degrees, and employment on returning to China. A total of 924 returned students were listed, of which 32 specialized in Economics and 60 more combined Economics with another field. Table 6-7 summarizes their degrees and their subsequent occupations. (We used additional occupational information from the other sources noted in this chapter.)

Qinghua archival material contains information about the employment of the alumni in 1935. We supplemented this with other biographical material to produce data for 114 preparatory students who studied Economics at the graduate level in the United States, including the 83 covered by Table 6-10 below. Their occupations are surveyed in Table 6-8.

Over 40 percent entered university teaching or economic research (three in the list were on the research staff of the National Economic Council in 1935). One fourth took government positions. And about 40 percent were in business positions.

Table 6-7. Chinese Students Returning from Economics Study in the U.S., 1917, 1925

	Highest degree in the U.S.				
Specializing in:	None	BA	MA	PhD	Total
Economics only	7	10	13	2	32
Economics plus other	9	16	23	12	60
Total	16	26	36	14	92

	Employment after Returning to China			
	Econ. only	Econ. plus others	Total	Advanced deg.
Universities	10	24	34	22
Government	12	21	33	17
Banking	5	18	23	14
Other business	8	12	20	10
Others	6	9	15	10
(–) Duplicates	–9	–24	–33	–23
Total people	32	60	92*	50

* Many people are in more than one category.

Sources: Chao 1917; *Who's Who in China* 1925.

Table 6-8. Occupations of 114 Qinghua Preparatory Students Returning from the U.S., 1935

Occupation	Number	% of Reported
Universities	46	40
Research Organizations	7	6
Government	32	28
Banking	18	16
Other business	23	20
Others or none	22	19
(–) Duplicates	–34	–
Total	114	–

Sources: Calculated from data from Qinghua archives and other biographical sources. Components add to more than 100 percent because some persons are in more than one category.

These data are very consistent with those examined earlier in this chapter. More than half of the Chinese who studied Economics at the graduate level in the West took positions in government or in business. One third or less became university teachers of Economics. A substantial number who took government positions produced economic research and publications. We return to this topic in Chapter 14.

Government Positions

We have noted such prominent political figures as T. V. Soong, Sun Fo, and Chen Gongbo among the western-educated economists. Our biographical sources identified 209 of our western-educated economics students who obtained government positions. About half of these (105) also taught Economics in Chinese universities. Since the various issues of *Who's Who in China* focus mainly on political leaders, particularly those in civilian branches, it is not likely we have overlooked major figures. However, a vast number of lower-ranked government workers did not register in these sources. Multiple office-holding was quite common, and it is often difficult to determine which positions were important and responsible and which were honorific sinecures.

Table 6-9 shows our estimates of five major areas of government which attracted the largest number of our subjects. These were local and provincial government, foreign affairs, finance and taxation, railways and communications, and the various yuans established under the Kuomintang.

One fourth of our American PhDs held (high) government positions, and the proportions were similar for German-trained (26 percent) and British-trained (25 percent) economists. Of the 209 in the sample, 87 (42 percent) did their western study in the 1920s. This reflects the rapid expansion of government positions after the KMT triumph in 1927, as well as the normal time lapse between study and prominence. Our tabulations reflect only government positions held prior to the Communist take-over; only 13 students from the 1940s are among the 209.

In Table 6-10, we have attempted to list some of the most prominent government officials who studied Economics in the West. One resource was a biographical directory prepared by the Chinese Communist Party in 1945, identifying 460 of the most important Kuomintang leaders.[5] Sixteen of their subjects are in our student lists; 15 of these held government positions.

Table 6-9. Western-educated Economists Holding Various Types of Government Positions after Returning from their Studies, 1906–1950

Provincial and local government	49
Finance, taxation*	41
Foreign affairs and diplomacy	40
Any Yuan	26
Railways, communications**	24
Others	54
(–) Duplications	–25
Total	209***

* Includes Salt Administration, a major revenue source.
** Excludes substantial number directly involved in railway operation and management.
*** Excludes research positions in government research units.
Sources: Chiefly *Who's Who in China*; *Biographies of Kuomintang Leaders*, 1948; Boorman, *Biographical Dictionary of Republican China*, 1967–71; Qinghua Archives.

Table 6-10. Western-trained Economists in Prominent Government Positions, 1905–1949

Name	Western University	Major Positions
Chang Ping-chun (G, F)	LSE	Staff, Ministries of Interior, Industry, Foreign Affairs; Sec., Councillor, Executive Yuan
Chang Tien-tse (F)	Leyden, Penn	Dep. Dir., Min. Ec. Aff.; Dir., Salt Administration
Chen Chang-heng (F)	Harvard	Staff, Leg. Yuan; Dir., Budget Bur.
Chen Chin-tao (F)	Yale	Minister of Finance
Chen Kung-po (F)	Columbia	Minister of Industry
Cheng Chung-hsing (G, F)	Cambridge	Nat. Mil. Council; Leg. Yuan; Sec.-Gen., Control Yuan
Chien Chang-chao (G)	LSE	Staff, Ministries of For. Aff., Ed.; Vice-chair, Nat. Res. Comm.
Ho Lien (F)	Yale	Vice-Min. Ec. Aff.; Exec. Yuan
Ho Hao-jo (G, F)	Wisconsin	Mil. Off.; Hunan Prov.; Nat. Mil. Council
Ho Ssu-yuan (G, F)	Chicago, Berlin, Paris	Col., Nat. Mil. Coun.; Shandong Province
Hsiao Cheng (G, F)	Berlin	Head, Land Adm. Bureau

Name	Western University	Major Positions
Huang Han-liang	Columbia	Dep. Minister Rwys.; Minister of Finance
Kan Nai-kuang (G, F)	Chicago	Staff, Ministries of Interior, For. Aff.; Asst. Sec.-Gen., Central Planning Board
Ku Meng-yu (G, F)	Berlin	Minister of Railways
Liu Ching-shan (F)	Penn	Director of Railways; Nat. Ec. Council
Liu Ssu-yeh (G, F)	LSE	Minister of Finance
Lo Mei-huan (G)	Southern California	Ningsia Prov. Gov.
Lou Tung-sun (G)	Paris	Chek. Prov.; Legislative Yuan
Ma Yin-chu	Yale	Legislative Yuan
Sun Fo (G)	Columbia	Mayor, Canton; Minister of Rwys.; President, Legislative Yuan
Soong Tze-ven (G)	Columbia	Minister of Finance; Minister of Foreign Affairs
Wang Kuo-hua	Chicago	Staff, Nat. Ec. Co.; Chek. Prov.; Ministry of Railways
Wu Ching-chao (F)	Chicago	Staff, Min. Ec. Aff.; Sr. Sec., Executive Yuan
Yang Tuan-lu (G, F)	LSE	Nat. Ec. Co.; Nat. Mil. Council
Yu Chin-tang (G)	Iowa	Vice-minister of Education

G: Listed in *Biographies of Kuomintang Leaders*, 1948.
F: Faculty in Chinese universities.
Sources: Same as Table 6-9.

It would be comforting to demonstrate that the presence of so many western-trained economists had a salutary effect on the economic policies of the Chinese government. However, one must remember that the national government prior to 1927 was relatively impotent and, under the KMT after 1927, only slightly less so. It was primarily a military dictatorship and the dominant figures were, with few exceptions, military figures or wealthy gentry.

Western-trained economists tried in the earlier years to put China on the gold standard, but the country would probably have suffered more from the Great Depression had this been done. Most Chinese economists supported variants of Sun Yat-sen's proposals for state-dominated development undertakings. However, the extension of government-owned industry after 1937 disillusioned many, such as Ho Lien and H. D. Fong.

Western commentators have faulted the KMT government for failing to deal more effectively with rural distress. But this criticism loses much of its bite when one considers the limited success of the rural programs of the Communist regime. More fundamental were the government's failures to extend infrastructure (including schooling), establish and secure property rights, and achieve domestic peace and order.

The presence of western-trained economists probably contributed to the large output of surveys and other research by government bodies, especially after 1927. And one productive offshoot of Sun Yat-sen's program was the brief but significant success during the 1930s in attracting foreign capital and promoting joint ventures in transportation, communication, and electric power.[6] Disillusion with the process has been particularly associated with Soong, whose career began with so much promise, only to lapse into a quagmire of family-centered corruption (Wang Y. C. 1966; Seagrave 1985).

Origins

Out of our approximately 1,600 students, we have identified undergraduate backgrounds for about 1,200, or three-fourths. The proportion is highest for students going to the United States (82%), then Britain (75%), and Germany (61%). For students going to France and other European countries, only 34% are identified. Table 6-11 presents data on the undergraduate schools of these students.

Table 6-12 shows the time pattern for those who studied in the United States. In the early years, virtually all students completed an undergraduate degree in the United States. After 1930, most students completed undergraduate studies in China.

This time pattern can be interpreted in the following way. The first generation of Chinese who studied Economics at the graduate level in the United States had also done their undergraduate study there, though many were Qinghua preparatory students. They spent a long time in the United States and were highly fluent in English. That generation became in turn the teachers of the second generation, most of whom studied in China as undergraduates. By the decade of the 1940s, 80 percent of the students coming to the United States had undergraduate degrees in China. Among this second generation, those who returned to China had spent less time in

Table 6-11. Undergraduate Backgrounds of Chinese who Studied Economics in the West, 1900–1950

	Students going to		
	U.S.	Europe	Total*
Christian College:			
St. John's	63	4	67
Nanjing	62	3	64
Yanjing	53	7	60
Lingnan	25	0	25
13 others	72	10	81
Total	275	24	297
Chinese University:			
National Peking (Beida)	37	29	65
National Central (NCU)	42	12	54
Qinghua (a)	37	12	47
Jiaotong (b)	39	6	45
Nankai	35	11	45
Fudan	33	3	36
Southwest Associated (c)	25	2	27
49 others	137	51	188
(–) Duplications	–11	–4	–15
Total	374	122	492
Foreign:			
U.S.	343	11	352
Britain	3	37	40
Japan	9	16	24
Others—duplicates	0	12	12
Total	355	76	428
Summary:			
Christian colleges	275	24	297
Chinese universities	374	122	492
Foreign	355	76	428
Unidentified	224	169	390
Total	1,228	391	1,607

* Totals are sometimes less than components because of duplicates.

a: Qinghua tabulated after 1926 when it became a full-scale university.

b: Includes Peking, Shanghai, and Tangshan units.

c. Southwest Associated Universities included Nankai, Qinghua, and National Peking Universities 1938–45.

Table 6-12. Undergraduate Backgrounds by Time Period, Students in the U.S.

Date	Total No.	Undergraduate Background							
	Students*	Christian	%	Chinese	%	U.S.	%	Others	%
1906–19	98	9	10	3	3	77	77	9	9
1920–29	302	50	17	47	16	173	57	32	11
1930–39	287	84	29	99	34	56	20	48	17
1940–50	534	131	25	226	42	36	7	141	26

* This is a non-duplicating total. Each student is entered for one date, typically when the degree was conferred. Students with unknown dates are excluded.

the United States. But many, especially from 1945–50, did not return to China (see Chapter 15).

Three special channels by which Chinese students entered into graduate study of Economics in the West deserve attention. The first is the Christian colleges. Of the 788 reporting undergraduate degrees in China, 38 percent attended Christian colleges. Christian college graduates went overwhelmingly to the United States, which received 92 percent of those tabulated. Of the 652 going to the United States with undergraduate degrees received in China, 42 percent were from Christian colleges.[7] It is unlikely that their share in total enrollment came close to 42 percent.

The second special channel for Chinese students coming to the United States was Qinghua College. Qinghua opened in 1911 primarily as a secondary school and junior college, sending students to complete undergraduate degrees in the United States. Table 6-13 presents data on 187 preparatory students from Qinghua who came to the United States to study Economics in 1911–29.

A striking feature is the very high proportion of these students who continued into graduate study. Of the 187 students tabulated, only 40 stopped with undergraduate study. Of the other 147, 114 proceeded to graduate study in Economics.[8] Of the 187, 53 returned to teach Economics in China.

The third channel we wish to stress involved people who received undergraduate degrees in Economics in China and went to work for research organizations which subsequently sponsored their study abroad. This was important particularly for the Institute of Social Sciences under Academia Sinica and is described further in Chapter 14. This channel brought a

Table 6-13. Preparatory Students from Qinghua College who Studied Economics in the U.S., 1911–1929

Qinghua year (a)	UG only	GS	MA	ABD	PhD	Total Ec. Grad. st.	Other Grad. st.	Total
1911–15	9	5	7	3	2	17	5	31
1916–20	12	17	16	6	6	45	12	69
1921–25	9	9	21	3	8	41	11	61
1926–29	10	5	4	0	2	11	5	26
Total	40	36	48	12	18	114	33	187

a: Year student completed Qinghua preparatory study and came to the U.S.
Source: Qinghua University Archives; added names from student files used for Chapter 5, particularly the 1921 *Who's Who of the Chinese Students in America.*

number of noteworthy scholars, such as Wu Baosan, Luo Zhiru, and Zhang Peigang.

Still another selective channel was furnished by the master's degree programs conducted by some of the major universities in the 1930s and 1940s. We identified 25 students in the Nankai graduate program 1939–43 (during wartime) under the direction of Li Zhuomin. Of these, 15 went abroad to study Economics further in the West, with 5 receiving doctorates.

Research Topics

Data on research topics for students in U.S. universities have been collected for all PhD students, all ABD students, and 324 MA theses. Their topics are summarized in Table 6-14. Fourteen PhD or ABD students appear twice, where the student did an MA thesis on a different topic at a different university.

Relatively few of the studies dealt directly with economic development. Topics which drew a lot of attention involved international economic affairs, money and finance, government finance, and agriculture. In each of these categories, a large proportion were China-related. Many studies concentrated on contemporary issues of Chinese economic policy. China was regaining tariff autonomy in the 1920s, and undertook important changes in money and banking arrangements in the 1930s.

Research topics for Economics graduate students in Britain and the European Continent are summarized in Table 6-15. For Britain, these include all reported theses, including some which were not completed.[9] For

Table 6-14. Research Topics of Chinese Studying Economics at Graduate Level in the U.S., 1906–1950

Topic	MA	ABD	PhD	Total	China Topics
Agriculture	47	10	22	79	44
Development	8	3	11	22	12
International econ. & finance	69	13	23	105	78
Labor and human resources	27	5	7	39	17
Money, finance	76	19	21	116	58
Public finance	46	16	20	82	37
Transportation	20	7	22	49	9
Others	31	15	23	69	28
Total	324	88	149	561	283

Source: Student data bases.

Table 6-15. Research Topics of Chinese Graduate Economics Students in Britain and Other European Countries, 1900–1950

	Britain		France		Germany		Others		Total (net)	
Topic	#	China	#	China	#	China	#	China	#	China
Agriculture	5	2	16	16	11	11	1	1	33	30
Development	4	2	1	1	8	8	2	2	15	13
Int. econ. & fin.	14	7	15	14	16	12	3	3	47	36
Labor	5	2	8	4	5	3	3	3	21	12
Money, finance	16	9	17	15	21	20	3	2	56	45
Public finance	2	2	9	9	3	3	0	0	14	14
Transportation	2	1	4	4	10	9	1	1	16	14
Others	5	1	13	12	5	14	3	1	33	26
Total	53	26	83	75	86	78	16	13	235	190

# = Total number of graduates.
China = Those studying China-related topics.

continental countries, tabulations are primarily doctoral dissertations, supplemented by a few other publications in the relevant European language.

Table 6-16 shows the proportional division of topics in each country. No country devoted a lot of studies to economic development, but the continental countries had a higher proportion than the United States. In Britain, attention was heavily concentrated on topics relating to international economics and to money and finance, each representing nearly one fourth of the total. Both of these categories also received much attention in all

Table 6-16. Percentage (%) Distribution of Research Topics

Topic	U.S.	Britain	France	Germany	Others	Total
Agriculture	13	11	17	13	8	13
Development	4	6	5	7	8	6
International economics & finance	18	25	21	17	17	20
Labor & human resources	7	8	13	7	25	10
Money, finance	20	25	17	19	17	19
Public finance	13	9	13	8	0	10
Transportation	9	4	5	11	8	7
Others	16	13	10	19	17	14

countries. In France, relatively more attention went to agriculture and to labor and human resources, at the expense of transportation and the unclassified group. Germany had surprisingly few on public finance, considering the creative contributions German economists had made to this field.

A striking feature is the very high proportion of China-related topics in France, Germany, and the other continental countries. It appears that the various faculties of Economics relied on their Chinese doctoral students to provide them with information about China, information particularly from Chinese-language sources. Nine-tenths of the research studies in continental countries were China-related.

In contrast, only about half of the studies done in the United States were China-related, and the proportion was even lower in Britain. Undoubtedly many of the students felt the same as Ma Yinchu, that studying the institutions and practices of the West could help them point out things which China might beneficially imitate (or, in a few cases, avoid).

Besides information from thesis topics, we should add that 82 of the students tabulated in the GS and MA categories in the United States were explicitly enrolled in programs in agricultural economics. Of these, 36 came from John Buck's program at Nanjing University, which is described in Chapter 10. Of the 82, 26 enrolled at Wisconsin and 18 at Cornell; and 48 of them came during the period 1945–50, mostly sponsored by the U.S. Department of Agriculture.

Our chief purpose in analyzing these research topics is to give an idea of the topics students (and their advisers!) were interested in. Most theses and dissertations were student exercises, completed to earn a degree. They have seldom been cited in more recent scholarly studies of China's economy.

A distinguished dissertation dealing with economic development was

Zhang Peigang's "Agriculture and Industrialization", completed at Harvard in 1946. It won the Wells Prize and was published in 1949. We examine it more closely in Chapter 14. Here we merely note that it deals only tangentially with China, and its analytical framework does not seem well adapted to provide insight into China's development.

In all fairness, some of the Chinese dissertations have permanent scholarly value. Dwight Perkins cited Ji Chaoding with approval. Qiu Kaiming's study of Chinese rural surveys has been useful in our Chapter 14, though it displays no evidence of adviser John Black's innovating work on production functions. Shao Bingkun's review of the literature on China's agricultural economy is still valuable. Wu Yuanli's LSE dissertation is a useful survey of China's economy in the last years of the KMT, but has of course been eclipsed by his extensive subsequent publications.

In Chapter 14 we examine the contribution of western-trained Chinese economists in the production of published scholarly studies of China's economy. One important conclusion is that there was a large output of such studies, particularly in the 1920s and 1930s. The most prolific authors were predominantly western-trained economists. However, most of the authors were not western-trained. The dominant role of western-trained economists in universities was not replicated in authorship. Clearly the presence of the western-trained contingent did not inhibit development of a large and diverse research output by indigenous Chinese scholars.

Overview

A large part of the introduction of western economics into China between 1900 and 1950 involved the massive flow of Chinese to the West for graduate study and back to China to teach. We have identified about 1,600 students involved in this process, with approximately 1,200 studying in the United States. Excluding students abroad in the 1940s, about one third of these students returned to faculty positions, often in their former undergraduate schools. In the chapters which follow, we examine this process in more detail with reference to major Chinese universities. These schools—Nanjing, Yanjing, Beida, Qinghua, and Nankai—played major roles in sending Economics students overseas and engaging them to teach Economics. We begin with the Christian colleges, since their documentation is more complete. The foregoing has documented their major role in preparing students for graduate study in Economics in the West and providing many of them with faculty employment.

Appendix

Occupations

Surveying our entire student population, we have data on occupations for slightly over one half. Because of the nature of our sources, the unknown persons are unlikely to have the same occupational distribution as the known. We have intensively researched university faculty data. And the who's-who types of references cover major government positions. Missing are a large number of persons active in family businesses, persons in lower-level government positions, and others deceased, disabled, or not working. The data cited in Table 6-8, based on Qinghua surveys, are probably much closer to an unbiased sample, except they are limited to persons who studied in the United States.

Table 6-17 gives a summary of the categories of occupations most relevant for the introduction of western economic ideas into China. This include teaching (all kinds, not just Economics), Chinese government service, working for research organizations in China, and journalism and editorial work. Here we include positions held after 1949 as well as before.

Differences between U.S.-based and European-based students arise because there were so many students in the United States in the 1940s. Quite a few did not return; of those who did return, there was not enough time for them to obtain recorded employment. Our coverage of non-degree students is much more complete for U.S.-based students, and these were more likely to leave no recorded employment.

Table 6-17. Some Occupations of Western-trained Economists

Category	#	Teach.*	Govt.**	Research	Edit.	Total***	No Info.
U.S.	1,228	315	135	58	11	533	695
Europe (net)	391	152	78	22	14	217	174
Total (net)	1,607	460	209	80	24	738	869

Some persons are listed for more than one country or category. Not all categories are shown (e.g. business).

= Total number of persons in our student files.

* Includes some teaching subjects other than Economics.

** Excludes research workers in government research units.

*** Number of persons for whom we have some occupational identification.

7

Economics in China's Christian Colleges: Overview

By 1900, several missionary schools had extended their scope to the college and university level. Lutz 1971 estimated the total college-level enrollment of the Christian colleges to be 164 in 1900 (p. 78). Over the next twenty years their number and enrollment expanded rapidly, although the indigenous Chinese universities grew even faster. According to William Fenn, "By 1910 there were eighteen [Protestant] institutions with a combined enrolment of one thousand. By 1920 some thirty institutions had achieved at least a junior college standing, [and] sixteen, with a total of sixteen hundred students, were functioning as four-year colleges." (Fenn 1976, pp. 43–44) Their operations were based primarily on financial support from the United States (Trescott 1997). A major step was the creation of Yenching (Yanjing) University in 1917 by a merger of several institutions in the Peking area. Other major Protestant institutions included Nanjing University, St. John's (Shanghai), and Lingnan (Canton Christian College). In 1903 a Roman Catholic college, Aurora (Zhendan) was established in Shanghai, and two additional Catholic universities developed in the 1920s.

During the first quarter of the twentieth century, the missionary colleges played a major role in Chinese higher education. Our estimates (Chapter 10) indicate that Christian colleges accounted for more than 40 percent of university level students in 1900–10, about one third in the next decade, and about one fourth by the mid-1920s. We have already noted their major role in preparing students for Economics study in the West. Of the 1,228 students we have identified as studying Economics at the graduate level in the United States, 275—almost one-fourth, were Christian college graduates. They constituted over 40 percent of the students in our sample completing undergraduate study in China. One reason for this high percentage was that the missionary colleges developed a high level of English-language competence among their students, who were exposed to numerous western teachers, principally Americans. And the students came from well-to-do families who could subsidize overseas study.

Because of their financial dependence on donations from western countries, the Protestant missionary colleges produced a large volume of catalogues and other documents in English. So our coverage of their faculty is less incomplete than for the indigenous Chinese universities. Table 7-1 shows for the leading missionary colleges the number of Economics faculty in our file and the number of students we have recorded as going on to Economics study in western countries.[1]

Table 7-1. Christian Colleges: Economics Faculty and Students Going to the West for Economics Study, 1900–1950

School	City#	Faculty			Students going to the West
		Western	Western-educated Chinese	Total Faculty	
Nanjing	Nanjing	19	49	114	65
Yanjing*	Peking	7	42	85	61
Hangzhou	Hangzhou	4	23	48	8
Sh./Suzhou**	Sh./Suzhou	4	24	43	35
Lingnan	Canton	8	26	42	25
West China	Chengtu	6	14	41	4
St. John's	Shanghai	7	2	32	67
Fujian Ch.	Fuzhou	3	11	29	7
11 others		33	32	100	26
Gross total		91	233	534	298
(–) Duplicates		–2	–27	–37	–1
Net total		89	206	497	297

* Includes predecessors.
** Includes wartime Shanghai/Soochow.
# Most had different locations in 1941–45.
Sources: See Appendix. Faculty lists exclude persons whose western study came after faculty service.

Nanjing's top ranking in both lists reflects the presence of two programs. One was "regular" Economics, the other the agricultural economics program in the College of Agriculture and Forestry (CAF). CAF accounted for about half of the listed faculty (including most of the westerners) and most of the students going overseas. Yanjing ranked second in numbers of faculty and overseas students, and offered an Economics program that ranked high in intellectual quality and in activism. Beyond those, the numbers diverged. St. John's sent a large number of students, but we have a relatively small number of faculty. There was not much turnover, and individual faculty taught heavy loads. Other schools for which we have a lot of faculty had high turnover, with many short-time and part-time teachers.

Early Times

Prior to 1915, instruction in Economics (in common with most other subjects) was conducted mainly by western missionaries with little formal academic preparation in the subject field. One individual might be called on to instruct in many fields. When North China College (a predecessor of Yanjing) graduated its first class (of six) in 1892, they had studied political economy as well as numerous other subjects. All of their instruction had been in the Chinese language, aided presumably by the political economy textbook composed (in Chinese) by the school's president, Davello Z. Sheffield.[2] Around 1902, Mr. Elmer L. Mattox of Hangzhou College was teaching: "plan of salvation; organic, inorganic, and analytical chemistry; general history; arithmetic; and English. Another year he taught Leviticus, Numbers, Acts, Deuteronomy, chemistry, political economy, history, and English." (Lutz 1971, pp. 61–62)

At Canton Christian College (Lingnan), President Oscar F. Wisner taught the three semesters of political economy offered around 1900. Presumably he composed the remarkable course description for the elementary course which included the following:[3]

> The Chinese are not excelled in frugality in their private life by any people in the world. Yet they are not a wealthy nation. The causes of their poverty are public ones: failure to develope [sic] the natural resources of the country, lack of facilities for the speedy and easy distribution of products, wasteful political methods, a reluctance to enter into full commercial relations of reciprocity with other nations, the stagnation of capital through fear of official oppression or lack of proper protection of industries etc. From a secular standpoint no list of subjects is of higher value to the Chinese as a people than those that may be grouped under the heading of Social and Political Science.

From fragmentary data we have identified 32 people who taught Economics at China's Christian colleges prior to 1920. Of these, 25 were westerners, including 19 Americans and 3 Frenchmen (at Aurora). Very few had any graduate training in Economics, and virtually all of them taught other subjects as well. We have included two men who successively headed the Peking School of Commerce and Finance, an institution sponsored by the YMCA. Ray Ovid Hall, who headed it in 1915–16, had a master's degree from Columbia. After his return to the United States he completed a PhD and pursued an academic career. Walter Young, who headed the school in 1919, had a master's degree from Princeton. His China experience was later overshadowed by his two brothers, Arthur and John Parke Young, both of whom were part of Edwin Kemmerer's 1929 commission of financial experts.

Aurora University, the Roman Catholic institution in Shanghai, relied predominantly on French Jesuits as instructors.[4] As in France, Economics offerings were included in the School of Law. In 1920, Aurora began to offer a doctorate in law, similar to those we described in Chapter 5 for the French universities, comparable to an American master's degree. Besides writing a thesis, doctoral students took advanced study in history of economic thought, finance legislation, and economic geography of China. One of the first doctorates went to Hou Wenping, who subsequently studied in Paris and returned to join the Aurora faculty.[5]

Several of the early Chinese faculty achieved distinguished academic careers. Li Binghua, who joined Fujian Christian College (FCU) in 1919 with an undergraduate degree from Ohio Wesleyan, later obtained a doctorate from Wisconsin and taught Economics at Yanjing and at various Shanghai missionary institutions well into the 1940s. Kwok Yam-tong (Guo Yintang) joined Lingnan in 1911 with a master's degree from NYU and remained on that faculty into the 1930s. His colleague Wu Kai-in (Jixian) joined in 1915 after graduate study at Columbia. After an interlude in business, he rejoined the faculty and remained until the 1940s.[6]

As more courses came to be taught in English, opportunities expanded for Americans schooled in Economics but not fluent in Chinese. The missionary colleges attracted many students who were eager to learn English, often in hopes of finding careers in western-dominated firms in the treaty ports. Many of these were interested in Economics for the same reasons. However, some schools were slow to expand their course offerings in Economics (Lutz 1971, p. 189).

In 1922 a blue-ribbon international study of Christian education in China urged the colleges to give increased attention to economic and social problems. The study recommended three related goals for China's Christian education:

a. The systematic development of a Christian public opinion, leading to the formulation and wide diffusion of a Christian ethic on vital economic, social and political issues.
b. The careful organization of economic and sociological research that will provide the data necessary for this Christian ethic to find expression in a concrete and constructive policy of economic and social reform . . .
c. The training of Christian leaders for those professions or services—which exert the greatest influence on public opinion or which most materially affect the evolution of the nation's social, industrial, and political life.[7]

In the second decade of the twentieth century, the Christian colleges began to attract noteworthy western figures in their Economics departments. Most had somewhat more academic preparation in Economics, and several were distinguished for expanding their interests well beyond the traditional role of classroom instructor. Four major personalities were Kenneth Duncan, Charles ("Carl") Remer, John Lossing Buck, and John Tayler. Buck and Tayler are discussed in detail in the two subsequent chapters.

Kenneth Duncan became professor of Economics and Dean of the faculty of Canton Christian College (Lingnan) in 1911 after completing his bachelor's degree at Wabash College. He interrupted his teaching to complete a master's degree at Wisconsin in 1915. Recognizing the need for teaching materials, he prepared two books for this purpose, *Essentials of Economics* (Shanghai, 1914) and *Exercises in Elementary Economics* (Canton, 1918). *Essentials* was a 150-page work primarily devoted to mainstream western neo-classical economics (Duncan 1930). It gave a full account of the determination of competitive price by supply and demand and also sketched the marginal productivity theory for the determination of wages, interest, and rents. Duncan stressed the functional value of free competitive markets and private property. Chapters on socialism and on Henry George's single-tax proposal both ended with unfavorable judgments. Chinese-language equivalents were given for 245 English terms. But Duncan made no effort to provide readers with systematic description or analysis of Chinese economic conditions. The book was used in other schools as well as Lingnan and was in its eleventh printing in 1930. Duncan returned to the United States to complete a PhD (Michigan, 1923) and subsequently became professor of Economics at Claremont Men's College, California.[8]

Remer's career in China displayed many parallels. He came to St. John's in 1913 as head of the Economics department after completing a bachelor's degree at Minnesota. He also prepared a book for classroom use: *Readings in Economics for Chinese* (Remer 1924). The book, nearly

700 pages in length, went through several printings in China and was reprinted in the United States in 1981. Remer assembled 61 readings, of which 39 dealt with China. A number of these came from the *Chinese Social and Political Science Review*, which had begun publication in 1916. The readings demonstrated a concern for economic development and for the social environment of economic activity (Remer 1924). Remer returned to the United States and completed a PhD at Harvard in 1923. In his long teaching career at the University of Michigan, he became a leading authority on China's international economic relations. His books dealt with China's foreign trade (his dissertation), Chinese boycotts, and China's foreign indebtedness. He returned to China to work on the latter project, and taught again at St. John's in 1930–31. He also participated in famine relief activities in North China.[9]

A survey of enrollments in the Protestant colleges for 1925–26 indicated they had about 3,500 students and that Economics constituted about three percent of course offerings and student semester hours. There was wide variation across the institutions. Nanjing, St. John's, and Yanjing reported large numbers of Economics courses and enrollments (Cressy 1926).

In 1928 Yoshi S. Kuno, an education researcher at Berkeley, produced a ranking of Chinese universities as a guide to admissions officers in American universities. China's top universities, such as Qinghua and Beida, were in the A and B categories. Kuno ranked Nanjing's CAF in the A group, and Nanjing's overall program in the B group with Yanjing. Eight of the mission colleges were in the C category, matching the average of indigenous Chinese universities (Kuno 1928, pp. 55–62).

In Table 7-2 we examine the evolution over 1915–30 of numbers of Economics courses and faculty listed in catalogues for the six missionary colleges with the most substantial Economics listings.[10]

Kenneth Duncan's influence is evident in the significant number of courses at Lingnan as early as 1915. John Tayler's appointment to head the Economics department at Yanjing was quickly followed by a grandiose catalogue listing—sixteen courses in 1920. The Yanjing Economics faculty grew steadily from the mid-1920s, reaching the remarkable total of fourteen persons by 1930. Of course, here as elsewhere, some of these were part-time people recruited from neighboring schools or from local business and government. Many schools listed more courses than they could staff, and offerings were spaced out over a two-year cycle.

The Economics program also showed impressive growth at Nanjing University. Leadership in "regular" Economics was provided by Guy Sarvis,

Table 7-2. Semester Courses (C) and Faculty (F): Economics Catalogue Listings, Selected Protestant Colleges, 1915–1930

Year	Lingnan		Nanjing (a)		St. John's		Suzhou		W. China		Yanjing	
	C	F	C	F	C	F	C	F	C	F	C	F
1915	7	2	3						1	0	1	1
1920	10	1	12	2	8	2	2*	0*	2	1	16	1
1924		11	8		4	1	4	2		4		
1925	15			15	4		8	1				
1930	16	5	27**	13**	16	3	11	1	11**	0**	17#	14

* 1919
** Fall, 1931
# 1929
(a) Nanjing data include agricultural economics.
Sources: Cressy, "Christian Higher Education in China; A Study for the Year 1925–1926", 1926; China Christian Educational Association, Bulletins 26, 27, 28 (YDS).

who was primarily a sociologist. He came to China after finishing graduate study at Chicago in 1911. The breadth of his interests and social concerns is evident in the creation of courses in "The Economic Resources and Problems of China" (introduced 1917) and "The Economics of War" (1919). His influence probably also accounts for the fact that Nanjing offered relatively few courses in mainline business administration prior to his departure in 1927 for a position at Hiram College.[11]

Courses in agricultural economics began to appear in the Nanjing catalogue in 1917, but the program really took off with the appointment of John Lossing Buck in 1920. His research attracted grant funding and enabled the department to develop much of the expansion in course listings and in personnel evident in the 1931 figures.

St. John's University in Shanghai also developed a large menu of course offerings, but with far fewer listed faculty than Yanjing or Nanjing. After Remer's departure, the department was headed by Philip Beach Sullivan, who joined in 1922. Sullivan had completed a bachelor's degree at Michigan and returned there for a master's degree in the late 1920s. He served as department chair until 1942.[12] His principal Chinese colleague was Chao Shao-ting (Zhao Shaoding), a St. John's alumnus (1922). Zhao joined the faculty after completing a master's degree at Chicago in 1925 and remained until the university was dissolved, becoming department chair after Sullivan's departure.[13]

Courses and Textbooks: Elementary Economics

In their early years, most of the Christian colleges simply offered a one- or two-semester course entitled "Introduction to Economics" or "Principles of Economics" or simply "Political Economy". When advanced courses were added, the earlier course remained as an introduction. Sometimes the college catalogues identified the textbooks, or at least those in English. Most were American. One author whose writings were extensively used in China was Richard T. Ely, whom we met in Chapter 4. Ely had studied in Germany and was a strong advocate of a Christian viewpoint which challenged the validity of laissez-faire and supported many types of government intervention designed to reduce inequality and curb the excessive power of large firms. He argued that "men must learn to own their property for the good of society, or society will own it for them. The right of private property . . . is ever on trial." (Ely 1893, p. 233) Since most of the western economists teaching in China's Christian colleges were supporters of the Social Gospel, it is not surprising that Ely's *Outlines of Economics*, first published in 1893, was widely used.[14] It was listed for "Introductory Economics" at Nanjing (1912–14, 1919–31), at Suzhou (1915 and 1934), St. John's (1920–21, 1925), Lingnan (1915–30), and Fujian (1934). In addition, Hangzhou (1924) used *Elementary Principles of Economics* by Ely and George R. Wicker (initially published in 1904). Ely was also co-author of *Foundations of National Prosperity* (1917), which stressed problems relating to natural resources. During the 1930s this was the text at St. John's for a course in "Principles of National Economy". Lingnan assigned it for a course on "Conservation of Economic Resources" (1918–26).

In both *Outlines* and *Elementary Principles*, Ely developed at some length the marginal utility approach to product value. But he did not use the (logically parallel) marginal productivity theory to analyze wages. His wage explanations left much more scope for "bargaining" and, by implication, were less pessimistic about the possibilities of raising wages through union activity or government intervention.

Another frequently-found textbook author was Thomas Nixon Carver, noted in Chapter 4 as a prominent early member of Harvard's Economics department. Carver's *Principles of Political Economy* (1919) was used at six of the missionary colleges in the early 1920s. His *Principles of National Economy* was assigned at Cheeloo in 1928, and Fujian assigned his *Principles of Rural Economics* in 1934. Carver's 1919 book contained a great deal of descriptive information about the sectors of a modern economy, useful in analyzing their contributions to national economic welfare and productivity. But it was much more rooted in neo-classical theory than were Ely's books. Carver was a strong devotee of the marginal productivity theory of demand for factor services. His work stressed the importance of entrepreneurs and inventors and warned against economic interventions which would hamper their productive activities.[15]

Other elementary texts used at more than one college were those by Henry Seager (Nanjing 1910 and 1920, Suzhou 1923 and 1929), and by Fred Fairchild, Edgar Furniss, and Norman Buck. Nankai faculty translated Fairchild into Chinese. During the war, a special reprint of the English-language version was prepared for Chinese readers.

All of the elementary texts cited in the catalogues we have examined were from the United States except three. Aurora in 1916 was using *Notion d'Economie Politique* by Julien Boitel and Rene Foignet. Some protestant schools used Charles Gide's *Principles* (translated from the original French) and (Englishman) Henry Clay's *Economics for the General Reader*.[16]

Advanced Courses

During the 1920s, emergence of a "consensus curriculum" in Economics was facilitated by periodic meetings among the faculty from the various colleges.[17] Table 7-3 shows the frequency with which nine major subject areas appeared as course listings in the catalogues of the eleven Protestant colleges with Economics programs. These are arranged from the left by frequency, a ranking which also reflects the rapidity with which they were adopted. As the right-hand column indicates, not all colleges were represented by catalogues in all four time periods.

As time passed, some colleges offered more than one course per subject area, as well as adding additional areas. To be sure, not every course was actually available every year.

As Table 7-3 indicates, courses in public finance and money and banking were the most widely offered, and the earliest. Both involved policy issues which were receiving a lot of attention in China—and both represented sectors where there were good jobs in China for educated people. The most commonly cited textbooks were from the United States.

By examining all our catalogues up to 1937, we were able to find authors and titles for 109 textbooks and assigned readings in Economics courses. These included 75 books from the United States, 18 from Britain and 3 from France, including English translations of Charles Gide's

Table 7-3. Catalogue Listings of Various Economics Courses, Christian Colleges, 1915–1937

Date	Number of Schools Reporting:									
	Public Finance	Money & Banking	Inter-national	Labor	Stat-istics	Western Ec. Hist.	Hist. of Ec. Th.	Agricul-tural Ec.	Advanced Theory	No. of schools documented
1915–19	3	2	1	1	1	1	1	1	0	7
1920–24	5	5	5	4	2	3	3	3	4	10
1925–29	6	5	3	5	4	3	4	3	2	8
1930–37	10	10	7	7	9	8	7	7	6	11

Note: As far as possible, only Economics courses are tabulated, not Business Administration.

Dates for individual colleges are as follows:

Cheeloo:	1918, 1923, 1925, 1928, 1931
Fujian:	1916, 1920, 1934
Ginling:	1919–20, 1928, 1931, 1933
Hangzhou:	1921–22, 1924, 1934
Huazhong:	1932, 1934–36
Lingnan:	1915, 1917–24, 1926, 1934, 1937
Nanjing:	1910, 1912, 1914–15, 1917, 1919–20, 1922, 1924, 1931–33
St. John's:	1920–21, 1925, 1928–30, 1932–37
Suzhou:	1915, 1919, 1923–25, 1929, 1934
West China:	1920, 1922–26, 1929, 1931, 1933–37
Yanjing:	1914–16, 1920, 1923–24, 1927, 1932, 1936

Principles, and the familiar text by Gide and Rist in the history of economic thought. Ten books are best classified as Chinese—either published in China, by Chinese authors, or about China. However, the Fujian catalogue of 1934 noted that "The textbooks used are mainly in Chinese, but only the English texts are listed." (p. 43) As Hu Jichuang (1982) has pointed out, Chinese-language textbooks in Economics were produced in significant numbers beginning in the 1920s. We should assume that these were often used even in the Christian colleges.

Several of the colleges developed courses in agricultural economics. Nanjing University created its College of Agriculture and Forestry (CAF) in 1915, and began to list courses in agricultural economics in 1917. In 1920 John Lossing Buck joined the faculty, and he soon developed this area into a major enterprise, to be described below. Lingnan also entered this area at about the same time. In 1918 their introductory course was modified to give "special attention to agricultural economics" centered around Edwin Nourse's textbook. At Yanjing, John Tayler's interest in cooperatives was reflected in a course in that topic listed from 1920. In 1927 this was supplemented by one in rural economics. That title was also used at West China Union, first appearing in 1929 and taught by sociologist Lewis Havermale. WCUU added a course in cooperatives in 1936. Cheeloo was also offering rural economics by 1931.

In the early 1930s, interest increased in the general topic of rural reconstruction, spurred by attention from the Chinese government and also by the availability of funding from the Rockefeller Foundation. Ultimately the funding went primarily to Yanjing, Nanjing, and Nankai for a joint program to be described in the next chapter. A similar emphasis was developed at Fujian, built around the appointment to the faculty in 1934 of Chen Hsi-ching (Francis Chen—Chen Xicheng).[18] This brought courses in rural economics, rural survey, and rural cooperation. In 1936 FCU was reorganized to create a College of Rural Reconstruction.[19] Although Francis Chen left FCU to head the local government's Bureau of Cooperatives, FCU maintained the focus on rural reconstruction through the remainder of its existence.

Several of the colleges experimented with courses dealing with socialism and social reform proposals. In 1915 Lingnan listed "Population and Labor Problems, Socialism". In 1921 this became simply "Socialism", with "special attention given to Marxian philosophy, to modern evolutionary socialism, and to present-day radical movements, Socialism in China." (p. 76) In 1924, Yanjing listed "Radical economic theories: State and Guild socialism, syndicalism, collectivism, communism, etc." In 1927 the title became "Socialism and Social Reform" and in 1932 simply "Socialism". By then Yanjing also listed a course on the Soviet economy. At West China in 1922, the combined department of Sociology and Economics listed "Current Social Movements: A consideration of the various phases of the class struggle as developed in Socialism, Bolshevism and Syndicalism with a view to evaluating these and other related movements in their relations to the New China." (p. 30) In 1929 St. John's listed "Social-Economic Reform Movements and Programs: A Study of anarchism, syndicalism, socialism and communism (including bolshevism) and of other reform programs of a less radical nature." In 1931 Nanjing listed "Capitalism and Socialism", and Hangzhou in 1934 showed "Socialism and Socialistic Movements". One may infer from the widespread commitment of faculty to the Social Gospel that the treatments were often sympathetic to (at least the non-violent) reform proposals.

During the 1930s and 1940s the KMT government made sporadic attacks on leftists in the Chinese universities. It does not appear that this ever extended to the missionary colleges, or that it was concerned with much more than extra-curricular political activity. For whatever reason, however, the courses on socialism and social reform largely disappeared from the missionary college menu during the 1940s.

China Material

While the textbook listings were primarily American titles, the catalogues promised that topics related to China would not be neglected. Lingnan set the tone early on. In 1915 their course in commercial geography included "an intensive study of the resources of China and China's place in the world's commerce. An investigation into the methods which should be used to develop China into a world power." (p. 35) Their listings for economic history, public finance, and international economics also promised China-relevance. In 1918 Lingnan's new course on Conservation of Economic Resources included "a survey of the natural resources and products of China of economic significance" (p. 48).

Hangzhou promised in 1921 that its introductory course "studies [the] economic condition of China . . ." (p. 32) Cheeloo used a similar phrasing (1923, p. 32; 1925, p. 54). By 1935, Huazhong's principles course included "the background of the economic struggle, economic history, population problems and natural environment of China" (p. 34). Suzhou promised in

1915 that, in its introductory course, "special effort is made to relate the work to Chinese conditions" (p. 17). In 1923 they listed a separate course in Chinese Economic Problems. West China was very explicit in 1920: Introductory Economics would involve "special reference to China. The class visits places of special economic interest in the city [Chengdu] and the vicinity. Each student is required to carry on an investigation of some phase of economic life in Szechwan . . ." In Advanced Economics, "the emphasis will be on the relations between the State and economic conditions, especially in China, on China's public finance, her economic resources, and the efforts which are being made to develop them" (pp. 23–24). However, these ambitious goals disappeared by the mid-1920s.

Peking University (Yanjing's immediate predecessor) in 1920 listed a course on China in Economics. By 1923, the (Yanjing) title had become Chinese Economics, and by 1927 it was Present-day Economic Problems in China. Chinese material was also promised for courses in money and banking, public finance, business administration, and foreign and domestic trade (pp. 28–30). By 1936, Yanjing listed Modern Economic Development in China, Chinese Economic Problems, Chinese National Economy, Chinese Cooperatives, and also promised China material in nine other specialized courses. Aurora created a Political Economy section in its School of Law in 1932, with emphasis on political economy, history of economic thought, economic geography, and finance. The 1935 catalogue remarked that "In spite of the fact that it is extremely difficult to gather together documents in all these subjects, the Professors have always striven to develop phases all concerning China." (p. 68)

Besides the foregoing, courses titled History of Chinese Economic Thought were listed by Lingnan (1923–24), Nanjing (1931–33), and West China (1936–37). And courses titled Economic History of China were offered by Hangzhou (1934), Lingnan (1934–37), and Suzhou (1934).

Both St. John's (1921) and Yanjing (1923) extended their programs to offer master's degrees in Economics. There was not an extensive menu of graduate courses. Master's candidates were typically required to take one or two courses in advanced economic theory, prepare a graduate thesis, and participate in a thesis seminar. Nanjing created a master's degree program in agricultural economics in 1935 (Buck 1970, pp. 178, 232).

Table 7-4 shows available estimates of the number and proportion of students majoring in Economics in 1930–36. The recorded numbers show a pronounced upward trend, from 225 in 1930 to 485 in 1936. The median percentage of (Arts and Sciences) students was ten percent.[20]

Table 7-4. Economics Majors in China's Christian Colleges, 1930–1936

	1930		1931		1932		1933		1936	
	#	%	#	%	#	%	#	%	#	%
Cheeloo (a)	0		0		23	(6)	29	(7)	73	(14)
Fujian (b)	21	(26)	41	(24)	32	(17)	24	(14)	12	(7)
Ginling	1	(1)	3	(2)	13	(12)	13	(9)	0	
Hangzhou	22	(16)	49	(23)	74	(21)	86	(22)	121	(23)
Huazhong	0		0		3	(3)	9	(8)	25	(12)
Lingnan	0		0		12	(3)	0		0	
Nanjing (c)	33	(16)	27	(13)	51	(9)	62	(11)	81	(10)
St. John's	9	(16)	21	(18)	27	(15)	37	(15)	nd	
Suzhou	27	(7)	37	(12)	30	(5)	31	(5)	75	(16)
Yanjing	112	(16)	n.d.		86	(11)	95	(13)	98	(13)

n.d.: no data
Omitted: Hwanan, Shanghai, and West China, which record zero or no data.
Percentages for 1928–31 are Arts and Sciences only; 1932–36 are all majors.
Undeclared students omitted in calculating percentage.
(a) Cheeloo includes Sociology 1932, 1933, and Political Science 1936.
(b) Fujian includes Political Science 1932, 1933, 1936.
(c) Nanjing data exclude Agricultural Economics.
Sources: Christian College Educational Association, Bulletins 26, 27, 28, 29, 30, 33, 36, 41 (YDS).

Business

The early leaders of the missionary colleges did not see training for business as a major part of their mission, but by 1920 such training was becoming important. The 1922 report on Christian Education in China observed that "Because of economic pressure and social structure of China almost every student attends college primarily from a desire to increase his earning capacity." (Committee on Relation of the Church to China's Industrial and Economic Problems 1922, p. 112) Children from business families were much more likely to attend the relatively unprestigious missionary institutions than were children of officials and professionals.

The 1922 report argued that:

> There are at least three outstanding reasons why commercial and industrial training should have a place in any scheme of Christian education in China. First, there is the Christian duty of doing all that is possible in the relief of poverty . . . there is a large possibility of relief of poverty in China by better utilization of the human resources . . . [Second] is the possibility of a better

> utilization of the human resources of the country by giving to promising youths a chance to fit themselves for larger responsibilities than they can assume if they are deprived of educational opportunity . . . [Third] is the duty of Christianizing the commercial and industrial order. (pp. 235–237)

In many of the colleges Economics and Business were combined in one department. Lingnan and St. John's developed extensive business programs at an early date. By 1923, Lingnan had absorbed Economics into a Department of Business Administration. Similarly, at Hangzhou, Economics was in the College of Commerce by the 1930s. Nanjing, Yanjing, and Cheeloo introduced numerous business courses during the 1920s. Only a few of the smaller colleges resisted this trend. At West China, Economics was linked with sociology, and there was no significant business program. In both Aurora and Suzhou, Economics was an adjunct to the study of law.

At most of the major colleges, roughly equal numbers of Economics and Business courses were offered. The often-understaffed departments usually found available faculty teaching both Economics and Business. The overlap is evident in the professional biographies of major economists in the missionary colleges. Professor Hu Jiyuan was a member of the Hangzhou faculty from 1929 until 1950. After graduating from Hangzhou, he completed another bachelor's degree at George Washington and a master's degree in foreign studies at Georgetown. After returning to teach at Hangzhou, he published college textbooks in marine transport and marine insurance which were the only significant works of their kind in Chinese. When Hangzhou was disrupted by the war, Hu moved to Peiping where he was a visiting professor at Yanjing and Dean and Professor of Economics at China University.[21]

The President of Hangzhou University from 1929 until 1950 was Lee Baen (Elmer Lee), the son of a Chinese Episcopal minister. Also a Hangzhou graduate, Lee did graduate work in Business and Economics at Chicago and Columbia. Returning to China, he taught at the Government College of Business and the National Jinan University, and chaired the Department of Business at the University of Shanghai. He also worked as English Editor and Director of the correspondence school program in business for the Commercial Press in Shanghai, for which he wrote textbooks in advertising, salesmanship, and office management. During his presidency at Hangzhou he taught courses in both Economics and Business. When he was forced to resign after the Communist take-over, Lee was able to complete his doctorate at Columbia in 1950 with a dissertation on banking reform in China.[22]

Economics Faculty in 1934

We have relatively comprehensive data for 1934 on the Economics faculty of the Christian colleges. Our listings include a total of 86 individuals, of whom almost half (42) were on the staff of the College of Agriculture and Forestry at Nanking. Table 7-5 gives data on their foreign study.

Table 7-5. Foreign Study by 1934 Teachers of Economics, Christian Colleges

	Chinese	Foreign	Total
Study in the U.S.:			
PhD	3	3	6
MA	17	4	21
Others	3	1	4
Subtotal	23	8	31
Other Foreign Study:			
PhD	0	3	3
MA	1	2	3
Others	4	3	7
Subtotal	5	8	13
None or unknown	42	0	42
Total	70	16	86

The 86 faculty include 16 westerners, equally divided between Americans and others (including 4 Frenchmen at Aurora). Of the 86, 31 had studied in the United States. Of the 28 Chinese who had studied abroad, 23 had gone to the United States.

War and Disruption, 1937–1946

The missionary colleges had experienced many upheavals even prior to 1937. Aurora had been rent by schism in 1905, and the heretics had founded Fudan University. A similar process took place at St. John's, leading to the creation of Guanghua University in 1925. A bout of anti-Christian agitation led to interruption of activities at several colleges in the 1920s. Revolutionary violence in 1927 was also a source of interruption, particularly at Nanjing, where a university official was killed and the university closed for a year. Several institutions in the Shanghai area experienced temporary interruptions attending the fighting with Japanese troops in 1932.

The outbreak of war with Japan in the summer of 1937 disrupted most of China's universities. Patriotic anti-Japanese feeling was very intense among most students and many faculty. When Peiping came under Japanese control in 1937, the principal national universities moved their operations to the interior. Yanjing was able to keep operating until the Japanese attack on Pearl Harbor in December, 1941, then transferred operations to far-away Chengdu. Furen was able to continue operating throughout the war, masquerading as a German-dominated institution. Aurora and Hautes Etudes also maintained their operations at their pre-war locations. In 1937, most of the missionary colleges in the Shanghai area moved operations into the International Settlement. By 1940 there were over 3,000 students enrolled with this group (Lutz 1971, pp. 364–365).

In 1938, Fujian Christian University moved inland to Shaowu. After Pearl Harbor, Hangzhou University moved from Shanghai to share this location. As Japanese forces moved inland, Nanjing and Ginling moved by stages to Chengdu, the home base of West China Union University, where they resumed operations in 1938. After Yanjing arrived in 1942, enrollment in the missionary colleges of Chengdu reached an estimated 2,800 (Lutz 1971, p. 380).

The migrations were very arduous; many faculty and students traveled hundreds of miles on foot. Living conditions were strained, and the academic resources were often primitive. Most of the western faculty members left China after Pearl Harbor, although John Tayler and J. L. Buck stayed longer. Academic standards inevitably declined in the face of all the interruptions and dislocations. Textbooks and other supplies were very scarce and library facilities very limited. Admission standards were lowered.

After Pearl Harbor, Shanghai University closed for the remainder of the war period. St. John's continued to operate in Shanghai, but drew heavy criticism from patriotic Chinese. Faculty left behind from the various Shanghai institutions continued to offer courses through somewhat informal organizations called Shanghai Institute and East China University.

The missionary colleges played a major role in the movement to create industrial cooperatives, which began in 1938 as a patriotic gesture to furnish war materials to the government and to provide jobs for people in the interior. The movement drew heavily on the efforts of economists at Yanjing and Nanjing and will be examined in more detail in the following chapters.

After 1945: Inflation and Civil War

The war's end in the summer of 1945 was almost as disruptive as its coming. Because of transportation limitations, most schools continued some or all of their operations in their hinterland locations for another year. During the interim, work was started to rehabilitate their earlier physical plants, which had in all cases become seriously damaged and depleted.

Most of the colleges found themselves besieged with applications and felt obligated to accept higher enrollment than they would have done a decade earlier. In consequence, "the Christian colleges, which had about 6,000 students in 1936, had almost doubled in size by 1947" (Lutz 1971, p. 405). The pipeline of secondary students with good training in western languages had been severely impaired by the war, and academic standards therefore continued to suffer. Relatively few western teachers were willing to come to teach Economics.

The status of Economics programs varied from school to school. Table 7-6 summarizes available data on Economics majors in the Protestant colleges. Several schools recorded majors numbering in the hundreds; our data for 1947 and 1948 suggest that the Protestant colleges as a group had well over

Table 7-6. Economics Majors (Fall Term), 1946–1949

	1946		1947		1948		1949	
	#	%	#	%	#	%	#	%
Cheeloo (a)			99	(16)			10	(10)
Fujian (b)	38	(6)	160	(37)	120	(26)		
Hangzhou	0		0		0		12	(1)
Huazhong	130	(29)	169	(31)	160	(28)	89	(24)
Lingnan			215**	(22)				
Nanjing	166**	(15)			124*	(13)	84*	(13)
St. John's					475*	(32)		
Suzhou			198	(15)				
West China	297	(14)	205	(11)	145	(9)	158	(10)
Yanjing			97	(12)	101	(11)	132 (c)	(11)

* Includes Agricultural Economics.
** Spring 1947.
(a) Includes Political Science.
(b) All Agricultural Economics.
(c) Fall 1950.
Sources: College reports to United Board; see Appendix.

a thousand Economics majors. (Of course, these totals were drawn from three or four classes, so the annual flow of Economics graduates would have been only a third or a fourth as large.)

Ginling and Hangzhou were exceptions. At Ginling, only elementary Economics was taught in this period. At Hangzhou, no Economics majors were available until 1949, with emphasis being given to business courses. At Fujian, the program was entirely focused on agricultural economics, a circumstance which elicited this wry comment in 1947:[23]

> For a long time Agricultural Economics drew the largest number of students, as the best training for "bank jobs" and some government experiment station jobs. Then with the bad financial conditions, this outlet stopped and Economics enrollment slowed down. But now it is said that "the demand in Formosa [Taiwan] exceeds the supply" and Agricultural Economics has become popular again . . .

Course registration data for St. John's show the signs of a school stretched tight with large enrollment and limited staff. In Spring 1948 only six Economics courses were offered, but most of these had multiple sections. A total of 18 sections were available, with an average of 47 students in each. In Fall 1948 eight courses were offered, spread over 19 sections with an average enrollment of 63 students.[24]

Yanjing was also struggling to provide a minimum course menu with a sparse faculty. Besides a core of eight full-year courses required for majors, Yanjing offered in 1947 only Chinese economic history and courses in cooperatives, rural economics, and advanced money and banking.[25]

One of the few printed catalogues for the period is a Lingnan pamphlet giving "Information and Curriculum 1946–48" with a much longer and more diverse menu. This offered 23 different course titles in Economics, including economic history of China, Chinese reconstruction problems ("including Sun Yat-sen's Program of Reconstruction"), socialism, planned economy, agricultural economics, and land problems.[26]

Nanjing's course offerings for 1947–48 fell somewhere between these two extremes. Nanjing offered ten courses each semester beyond the elementary level. Their menu included economic policy and Chinese as well as western economic history.[27]

Economics Faculty Members, 1947

Although printed catalogues are virtually non-existent for the post-war period, the Protestant colleges did supply the United Board with personnel rosters each semester, many of which survive. From these and other sources we have assembled data for 1947 (or adjacent years). These show a total of 90 Economics faculty. We have included data (quite incomplete) for the Catholic colleges. The disproportionate representation of Nanjing's CAF no longer existed; that unit reported ten faculty in 1947. Only three foreign teachers were found in this sample. Nine persons from the 1934 survey also appeared on the 1947 rosters.[28]

Table 7-7 presents data on the overseas study by the 87 Chinese in the 1947 tabulations.

Table 7-7. Foreign Study by Chinese Teaching Economics in Christian Colleges, 1947

	Chinese	Study in the U.S.			Other Foreign Study		
College	Faculty	Verified PhD	Verified Master's	Others	Verified Doctorate	Verified Master's	Others
Aurora	1						
Cheeloo '46	5						1
Fujian '46	5	1	1	1			
Furen	7	1			1	1	
Hangzhou '46	6		1	1			
Huazhong '46	5			1	1		
Lingnan	8	1		2			1
Nanjing '46	15		1	3	2		2
St. John's	7	1	1	1			
Suzhou '48	7			1			2
West China	9			2			1
Yanjing	12	1	3	1	2		1
Total	87	5	7	13	6	1	8

Note: Data for some schools are from 1946 or 1948 as indicated.
For discussion of verified degrees, see Chapter 5.

Of the 87 Chinese teaching Economics in 1947, 25 had studied in the United States and 15 in other foreign countries. Eleven held verified doctoral degrees. Thus the relative importance of foreign graduate degrees was smaller in 1947 than in 1934. Further, the predominance of American graduate degrees was not as pronounced in 1947 as in 1934 (we could not identify the academic credentials of any of the three westerners).

The 1947 reports give data on the age distribution of the Economics teachers. For the 70 people reporting, the median age was in the low 40s, and only nine teachers were 50 or over. Of the 80 teachers reporting length of service with their school, 40 had been with their current employer for two years or less. However, the ten faculty reported for Nanjing's CAF had served there for an average of 12 years.

In the late 1940s, civil war disrupted academic conditions in all Chinese universities. The frequency of student demonstrations and the decline in university discipline contributed to further erosion of academic standards.

During 1948 it became evident that the Communists would be successful. During the first two years of the new regime, most of the colleges continued to function normally. To be sure, there were more meetings for political study. Most faculty and students took time off in 1950–51 to participate in the land reform program. A few Marxist courses and teachers were added. With the intensification of the Aid-Korea-Hate-America campaign in 1951, however, the government moved swiftly to close the missionary institutions. Their physical facilities and faculty were assigned to government universities. Most of their Economics faculty members remained in the country and continued to teach in their new assignments.

Christian College Economics Faculty: Overview

For the entire period of our study, we have identified a total of 498 persons who taught Economics in the Christian colleges. Of these, 89 were foreign visitors and 206 were Chinese who studied in the West. These two categories, constituting three-fifths of the total, represented the chief potential channel for the introduction of western economic ideas through the missionary colleges.

Nineteen of the visiting foreign economists had American doctorates. However, 10 of the 19 were in agricultural economics, all but one in the CAF program at Nanjing University. Second, of the remaining nine doctorates, five were outside Economics, reflecting the frequency with which Economics courses were taught by people from other academic backgrounds. Three of the doctorates (John Lossing Buck, Kenneth Duncan, and Yanjing's Augusta Wagner), were obtained quite a few years after the individual began teaching in China.[29]

The largest number of foreign visitors went to Nanjing—a total of 18. Aurora University, which received a significant inflow of French Jesuits, ranked second in number of foreign visitors with thirteen. Close behind came three schools where significant leadership came from abroad: Lingnan (8), St. John's (7), and Yanjing (7). The predominance of the United States was very pronounced, particularly in the Protestant colleges.

The same predominance is displayed among the Chinese teachers of Economics who pursued graduate study overseas, as we reported in Table 7-1. Of the 233 with some foreign study, 121 studied Economics at the graduate level in the United States, and an additional 50 studied in the United States in another category or subsequent to their teaching. Twenty-six studied in Britain and an equal number in France plus Germany. The time profile of the western-educated Chinese indicates an overwhelming preponderance of U.S.-trained people except for the decade of the 1930s, when European-trained people accounted for about one third of the total. Over the entire period, three-fourths of the Chinese Economics teachers in Christian colleges with recorded overseas graduate study did that study in the United States.

To evaluate research and publication by Chinese faculty, we assembled a file of the names of authors of about 2,600 items dealing with China's economy published in the period ending in 1950. Details appear in Chapter 14. Of the 409 Christian college Chinese faculty, only 89 appeared among the authors. The 22 percent representation is substantially below the average for indigenous Chinese universities (28%) reported in Chapter 10. However, Nanjing (with 35%) and Yanjing (with 29%) scored above that average. Between them, the two accounted for 55 of the 89 names. Thus the other Christian colleges did not publish much on China's economy.

Overview

China's Protestant colleges provided a platform for a number of dedicated and energetic western missionary economists, notably Kenneth Duncan, Charles Remer, John B. Tayler, and John L. Buck. They shared a devotion to the Social Gospel and a conviction that the study of Economics could bring about improvement in the lives of the Chinese people. Many mainstream Economics courses used American textbooks and described American economic institutions and policies. They did not apparently devote much attention to the economy of Japan, which might have represented a more appropriate model. Tayler, Buck, and other western teachers did work hard to develop teaching materials and courses which applied economic principles to Chinese conditions. They tried to overcome the emphasis on rote learning and on the stereotype of a remote and detached faculty member. In the following two chapters, we describe in detail the activist propensities of Tayler and Buck which carried their influence well outside the classroom. The only indigenous Chinese university with comparable activities was Nankai.

Many Christian college graduates were invited to stay on as instructors. A large number went abroad to study Economics in the West and returned to take senior faculty positions. In Chapter 7, we noted that more than 100 of the Economics faculty in Christian colleges also taught in indigenous Chinese universities, including a high proportion of the PhDs. Surprisingly, the proportion of western-trained Chinese economists in the Christian colleges was not higher than in the indigenous universities.

As we indicated in Chapter 6, the Christian colleges contributed a sizeable share of total university education in China prior to the anti-Christian campaigns of the mid-1920s. And they consistently accounted for a disproportionately large share of the Chinese going to the West for further study of Economics.

After 1949, the Communists wasted little time in closing the Christian colleges in 1951–52 and expelling their few remaining western faculty. They have to the present day consistently disparaged the China activities of western missionaries; thus it is unlikely that Chinese scholars will do justice to the productive contributions of the Christian colleges. An eloquent testimonial, however, has been furnished by their large and enthusiastic alumni associations. In 1992, the Yanjing Alumni Association was headed by two high-ranking government dignitaries, Han Xu (former ambassador to the United States) and Huang Hua, who held numerous positions in foreign affairs. In 1988 Lingnan University was reconstituted as a unit within Zhongshan University in Guangzhou.

Appendix

Sources for the Christian Colleges

Most of the detailed information in this chapter comes from the catalogues and other documentary materials held principally in the Archives of the United Board for Christian Higher Education in Asia (UBCHEA) (Record Group 11) in the library of Yale Divinity School (YDS). These were supplemented with materials in the Burke Library of Union Theological Seminary (UTS, New York City), the Harvard-Yenching library (HY, Cambridge MA), the Rockefeller Archive (RA, Tarrytown, NY), the archives of Peking University, Shanghai Municipal Archives, and the library of the Shanghai Academy of Social Sciences.

Aurora: The Shanghai Archive holds a large collection of Aurora documents in Chinese, French, and English, many untitled; their file number is Q242. 1935 catalogue (National Library, Beijing). L'Université d'Aurore *Bulletin*, a journal of scholarly articles, identifies a few faculty. Issues for 1933–44 were examined in the British Museum, London. Likewise *Annee Scholaire*, issues for 1933–45.

Cheeloo (Shantung Christian University): Catalogues available for 1917, 1918, 1922, 1923~~, 1925~~, and 1931 in boxes 262 and 263 YDS. Additional faculty information in box 42, folder 1071 (hereafter 42/1071) and 266/ 4265. Enrollment information in 266/4268.

Fujian Christian: Catalogues available for 1916, 1919, 1920, 1922, 1924–26, 1934, in 109/2397 YDS. Additional faculty information in Scott 1954, pp. 39–43, 61; 42/1072, 108/2391, 109/2405, 2406, 2407, 2410, 122/2568. Enrollment data 109/2409 and 2410.

Furen: Interview with Lu Chung-tai; William Liu dissertation.

Ginling: Catalogues available for 1919, 1920, 1928, 1931, 1933, in 128/ 2632–4 YDS. Additional faculty information in 128/2632–4 and Thurston and Chester, pp. 152–160. Enrollment information in 128/2637 and course information 128/2635.

Hangzhou: Catalogues available for 1921, 1922, 1925, 1934, in 160/3023. Combined catalogues with other Shanghai institutions for 1938 (128/2635, 160/3024) and 1940 (448/6004). Additional faculty information in 42/ 1073; 160/3026–8. Enrollment data in 160/3026, 3028; course information in 160/3024, 3026.

Hautes Etudes: information from student theses in Peking University Library; 1929–30 catalogue furnished by William Malatesta.

Huazhong: Catalogues available for 1932, 1934–36 in 165/3076–7 YDS. Additional faculty information in Coe, 1962; 165/3080, 3081; 174/3172. Enrollment information in 42/1073; 165/3079, 3081.

Lingnan (Canton Christian): Catalogues available for 1900, 1903, 1906, 1909, 1915, 1917–26, 1928–30, 1934, 1937, in 181/3246–51 YDS. Additional faculty information from Corbett 1959 and 42/1074. Course information 181/3251.

Nanjing: Catalogues available for 1910, 1912, 1914, 1915, 1917, 1918, 1919, 1920, 1922, 1924, 1931, 1936 in boxes 197 and 198 YDS. Chinese-language faculty and course lists are in 201/3434 YDS (1931) and HY (1932–34). Additional faculty information, Buck, 1970, pp. 175–178, 324–325; Lamberton 1955; 198/3396, 3398, 3406; 42/1075; *Social Sciences in Nanjing*. Enrollment data in 42/1075; 197/3392; 198/3398; 201/3434. Course information in 197/3389A. CAF reports are in RG 1, Box 1, Folder 11, RA.

St. John's: Catalogues available for 1920, 1921, 1925, 1928–30, 1932–39 in UTS. Additional faculty information from *The Johannean* (yearbook) 1934–41 and 1946, in library, Shanghai Academy of Social Science; 42/1076 and 239/3940 YDS. Enrollment data 239/3938–9. Faculty and course data in memoranda in Shanghai City Archives, obtained by Yin Hong.

Shanghai: Hipps 1964; faculty and courses in combined lists for 1938 and 1940 in 128/2635, 160/3024, 448/6004; 1943 in 269/4293.

Suzhou: Catalogues are available for 1909, 1910, 1912, 1915, 1919, 1921, 1923, 1924, 1926, 1929, 1934 in UTS. Additional faculty information in 42/1076; 269/4287, 4293 YDS; Nance 1956. Enrollment data in 42/1076, 129/4291 YDS and President's report, 1940 in UTS.

West China Union: Catalogues available for 1915, 1920, 1922–26, 1929, 1931, 1933–37 in 278/4397, 4399, 4400–1 YDS; UTS (1923–26) and HY (1935–36). Additional faculty information in 42/1077 and 279/4406–7. Enrollment data in 42/1077–8; 279/4403, 4406.

Yanjing: Catalogues available for 1914–16 (North China Union College) and 1919 (North China Union Women's College) in UTS; 1920, 1923, 1924, 1927, 1932, 1936, 1938 in 308/4744–5, 4747 YDS; 1932 and 1936 in RA, Series 601, Box 41, Folder 342. Additional faculty information from 42/1079, 308/4748–9, 4750–3; Edwards 1959; archival research by Peking University library staff; Hong Jun-yan interview. HY has Chinese language directory 1932 and announcement of courses 1940–41. Additional course data in 308/4747. More detail accompanies Chapter 8.

8

Economics at Yanjing University (Peking)

During the period 1917–50, Yanjing University in Peking was the most important of the Christian colleges in China and an important element in the entire system of Chinese higher education (Lutz 1971; West 1976; Edwards 1959; Yeh 1990; Israel and Klein 1976). Between the mid-1920s and the university's forced termination in 1951–52, Economics was the largest department in the university in terms of major students. While this popularity reflected in part the presence of business training courses, the Economics Department consistently provided students with information concerning the Chinese economy and demonstrated the relevance of western economic analysis to China's problems. Further, the Economics Department displayed notable leadership in developing activist programs to encourage grass-roots improvement in Chinese economic conditions.

John Bernard Tayler

The character of the Economics Department was shaped by its long-time chairman, John Bernard Tayler (1878–1951).[1] Trained as a chemist in his native Liverpool, Tayler worked briefly in industry, then came to China in 1906 as a missionary, sponsored by the London Missionary Society. After working as a teacher and administrator in a secondary school for boys, he was recruited in 1917 to become associate professor and chair of the Economics Department (and its only member until 1922) at (Christian) Peking University, soon to become Yanjing. In preparation, Tayler spent the year 1919–20 at the London School of Economics (LSE), studying with A. L. Bowley, L. T. Hobhouse, L. C. Knowles, and C. M. Lloyd.[2]

At Yanjing, Tayler quickly created an academic program with extensive materials relating to China. The 1920–21 catalogue listed "China in Economics", including "geographical situation . . . ; mineral resources . . . ; agriculture; transportation; conservancy, afforestation, and colonization; industrial organization, modern industries; trade, currency, banking, and credit; public finance; labor problems; standard of living, betterment."[3]

Tayler was never content to be a mere academic. His missionary spirit impelled him to seek out pragmatic programs to improve the economic condition of the ordinary Chinese people. He was active in the work of the China International Famine Relief Commission (CIFRC), which began operations in November, 1921. Here he displayed his concern with organizing and promoting cooperatives, a concern which was ultimately to become his occupation.

To provide information for this work, Tayler undertook in June, 1922, a survey of rural economic conditions. Sixty-nine Chinese students from nine colleges conducted the survey in 240 villages of five eastern provinces. Results were published in the *Chinese Social and Political Science Review* in 1923–24 (Malone and Tayler). This work closely paralleled that of John Lossing Buck at Nanjing University, also active in CIFRC.

In 1920 Tayler was instrumental in bringing Agatha Harrison, who had been training welfare workers at LSE, to China, where she worked diligently during 1921–24 on such problems as child labor, workers' health and safety, and hours of work (Porter 1977, pp. 68–80). Tayler wrote several pamphlets for the National Christian Council (NCC) in 1923 trying to interest "the various Christian colleges . . . in the industrial question" (Porter, p. 46).

Tayler's influence was also evident in the 1922 NCC report on "The Church and the Economic and Industrial Problems of China" (Committee on Relation of the Church to China's Industrial and Economic Problems 1923). The report sensibly identified the major causes of Chinese poverty as overpopulation and the lack of economic development. Some of the recommendations involved moral exhortation directed toward landowners and entrepreneurs, but the report also endorsed government programs to set labor standards in such areas as work hours and apprenticeships.

In 1923, the CIFRC Committee on Credit and Rural Improvement developed a model constitution for credit cooperatives and began granting funds to aid in forming them (Nathan 1965, pp. 29–31). By 1927, the number of cooperative credit societies in Hebei Province (around Peking) had increased to 561, with 13,000 members, largely through CIFRC efforts.

Beginning in 1925, CIFRC was instrumental in developing a training program for cooperative leaders involving staff from Yanjing and Qinghua universities (CIFRC 1930; Mallory 1931, p. 490).

In various committees of the National Christian Council, Tayler steadily pushed to stimulate interest in grass-roots programs to develop rural industry and cooperatives. He was a prolific writer on topics relating to the poverty of China's common people. Low productivity could be traced to lack of capital and enterprise, which were in turn aggravated by the "insecurity of property and life . . ." (Tayler and Zung 1923, p. 3).

Tayler was impressed with the work of American institutional economists, particularly Wesley Mitchell (Trescott 1992; Rutherford 2000). At a time when economic growth and economic development were not stressed in mainstream western economics, these topics received much attention from Tayler and his colleagues. Tayler believed that in China "the institutions and the influence of earlier stages of development persist with quite unusual strength into modern times" (1923, p. 337). Instead of deploring this, as many western observers did, Tayler advocated drawing on the strengths embodied in the family, the village community, and the gild.[4]

In a 1926 presentation to the Chinese Economic Association, of which he had been a founding member in 1923, Tayler urged the group to promote and coordinate studies of comparative institutions, East and West, particularly those aimed at understanding and assisting "the economic development of China", and especially "raising the standard of living in China" (1926, p. 851). Not only should real incomes be increased, but "by various cooperative arrangements and forms of collective consumption, [Chinese people might be able to] secure a very large measure of satisfaction from the wealth they possessed" (1926, p. 853). Tayler's humanitarian concerns were balanced by his economist's recognition that "higher wages will be impossible unless the output per worker can be increased" (1926, p. 855). Tayler had high hopes for "scientific management" being promoted in the West by Frederick Taylor and Frank and Lilian Gilbreth (Tayler 1928, pp. 87–89). Higher productivity would require the development of an effective class of business leaders and organizers, which might involve "the creation of new institutions and new moral sanctions to make them workable" (1926, p. 856). To Tayler, the most promising of such innovations lay in the development of cooperatives.

Much of Tayler's energy went into Christian grass-roots development activities. He chaired the commission on social research of the International

Institute of Social and Religious Research in 1924–25. When NCC formed a Committee on Christianizing Economic Relations in 1929, Tayler became its secretary. His efforts came to focus on promoting rural industrial cooperatives, efforts which are reviewed later.

Faculty Expansion

Yanjing's Economics department faculty and course offerings expanded steadily during the 1920s. An important addition was Li Binghua, who joined Yanjing in 1922. Li, a graduate of Ohio Wesleyan, returned to the United States to complete a Chicago MBA in 1926 and a PhD at Wisconsin in 1931, writing his dissertation on China's transportation system. He remained at Yanjing until 1933. Like Tayler, Li developed an enthusiasm for institutional economics, based on his study with John Maurice Clark at Chicago and John R. Commons at Wisconsin (Trescott 1992, pp. 1233–1234). Li introduced a course in institutional economics in 1932.

Augusta Wagner (1896–1976) joined Yanjing in 1925, shortly after her graduation from Wellesley College. Her college years came later in life than for most students, because she spent several years working for the National Board of the Young Women's Christian Association and for the International Ladies Garment Workers Union (Wagner 1938a, p. 302). Although her undergraduate major was philosophy, she used furlough years to study Economics at Columbia, receiving an MA in 1930 and PhD in 1938.

Her doctoral dissertation, directed by Leo Wolman, was "Labor Legislation in China" (1938a). The work received the Seligman prize "for the best PhD thesis in a five year period in the departments of Economics, Sociology, History, Political Science, International Affairs and Law" and was reprinted in 1981. She was able to draw on the research of several Yanjing colleagues: sociologist Leonard Hsu (Xu Shilian), historian Jefferson Lamb (Lin Donghai), and social economist Maxwell Stewart.[5] Wagner viewed with moral outrage the low wages, long hours, unsafe and unsanitary working conditions, and mistreatment of Chinese women and children. But she recognized that the productivity of labor set limits on what intervention could achieve (1938a, pp. 107–108, 121–123, 137, 261–262). She was optimistic that shorter hours might make workers more efficient, and that a minimum wage law might encourage employers to adopt more efficient techniques (pp. 122, 127, 261–262).

Wagner also prepared a textbook in elementary economics for use at

Yanjing: *An Introduction to Economics for Chinese Students* (1938b).[6] Written in simple, concise English, the book presented the Chinese language equivalents for about 500 technical terms.[7] The structure of the exposition drew heavily on Raymond Bye's *Principles of Economics* (1936). Bye's textbook was definitely a neo-classical work, but Wagner modified the presentation at many points to give it a more institutional cast. She added substantial sections presenting Chinese data and discussions of Chinese institutions, particularly in chapters dealing with labor, capital, and enterprise. Three valuable chapters explored the relationship between population and resources in China. Wagner devoted several chapters to institutional aspects of economic growth and development, often in the vein of "obstacles to development". Although her discussions of market failures sometimes indicated a large potential role for the government, she often depicted the Chinese government as an obstacle to economic growth (1938, pp. 50–51, 68–70).

Wagner's text removed much of the formal theorizing which formed the backbone of Bye's book. She used only one diagram, and omitted almost all references to marginal productivity. She also supplemented Bye by drawing on Sumner Slichter's *Modern Economic Society* (1931), a relatively institutionalist text.[8] She expressed numerous moral judgments critical of market economy: income distribution is unfair, so resource allocation is biased by the disproportionate influence of the rich; profit-seeking firms exploit workers and consumers because the victims lack information and bargaining power, and competition leads to waste, instability, and monopoly. Her perceptions of market failure led her to support many "reforms" of the New Deal sort—progressive taxation, labor unions, minimum wage laws, child labor limitations, and social insurance. However, she also noted many examples of "government failure" in China (pp. 50–51, 68–70, 95–96). She consistently emphasized that China's basic economic problem was overpopulation relative to resources and technology. The main remedy had to be sought through economic growth. But the reader was not left optimistic that free markets and existing government would bring much improvement (p. 234).

Surprisingly, Wagner took a relatively negative stance on centralized economic planning. She bluntly argued that central planning means central control, with "a large amount of arbitrary decision" and "final authority over the lives of individuals [relying on] compulsion" (p. 250). A centrally controlled system lacks price-profit pressures toward efficiency—her discussion suggests familiarity with the Mises-Hayek critique of socialism.

Central economic control can mean "the individual may easily be sacrificed to the system", in which "a small powerful group . . . might hold the great mass of people in complete subjection to their own purposes" (p. 251). Considering how thoroughly these conditions were realized after 1949, it is noteworthy that pre-1949 economic commentaries in China rarely sounded these warnings.

Other Faculty

The first PhD economist at Yanjing was a Chinese, Huang Hsien-ju (Xianru). He graduated from Oberlin in 1923 and completed a doctorate at Columbia in 1928 with a dissertation on state taxation of U.S. railways. He taught at Yanjing 1928–32.

Also arriving in 1928 was Gideon Chen (Zhen Qitian), a mainstay of the faculty until 1942, serving at times as Department Chair and Dean of the College of Public Affairs. Chen had attended Yanjing and studied in Japan. In 1923 he became a staff member of the Industrial Commission of the National Christian Council, working closely with J. B. Tayler. He studied in England for two years beginning in 1925, then returned to work for the NCC Committee on Christianizing Economic Relations until 1929, when Tayler persuaded him to join the Yanjing faculty (Porter 1977, pp. 129–130, 137, 145–146).

In his remarks to the 1927 Conference on Christianizing Economic Relations, Chen strongly urged the Chinese to study more systematically the processes of economic development in the West (1927, pp. 64–65). In 1929, he warned that China's situation was generating dangerous tensions. He felt the goals of development and social justice called for "regulated social development" with a major role for government economic planning and control, not merely in providing infrastructure, but as potential owner and operator of heavy industrial facilities (1929, pp. 101–105). Chen had confidence that the newly formed Nationalist government under Chiang Kai-shek would be able to carry out the kind of program he envisioned. However, "economic planning in China tends to lay emphasis on what is needed to be done, and to neglect the organizational side, how to do it" (1934, pp. 357–358). Considering "the question of economic organization . . . neither Russian Communism nor Italian Fascism would be immediately introduced into China, for both presume a strong political party and an effective administration, which are not in existence in China just now".[9] Chen was also not optimistic that a capitalist system would be developed in China, and he endorsed the cooperative movement as the most promising prospect. Even so, he expressed his support for "one big central plan" that would be "the antithesis of competition" (1934, p. 377).

Chen's preoccupation with economic development and economic planning is evident in the courses he (as department chair) offered under his name in the 1936–37 Yanjing catalogue. They included a year's sequence in modern economic development in Asia, Chinese national economy, history of socialism, and economics of industry ("with special reference to present day problems in China") (*Yenching University Bulletin* 1936–37, pp. 97–100).

Rural Reconstruction

In 1928 J. B. Tayler's activist propensities led him to propose the formation of a Yenching School of Applied Economics. A promotional brochure outlined his thinking as follows:

> [In the proposed program] all postgraduate studies and research will be directed . . . not so much to learn Western economic theory and practice, but rather in the direction of actually uncovering the economic conditions of China and determining appropriate remedial measures. Experimental undertakings will be emphasized. In these, the unit for experimentation will generally be the single village or group of villages, and the objective will be to develop improved methods of production both agricultural and industrial, better roads and means of transports, elementary sanitation, practical village schools, credit facilities, cooperative harvesting, purchasing of supplies and sale of products . . .[10]

Tayler was able to move in this direction even with Yanjing's existing resources, as the following newspaper description of 1929 illustrates:[11]

> The major emphasis of the department of economics, beyond the teaching of economic theory, is research in the effects of modern conditions on Chinese trade and industries, and the modifications of them which may be found possible without the substitution of Western methods of organization. This study has been done most thoroughly in the pottery industry . . .
>
> Such research is done almost entirely . . . by graduate students. The department of economics had more graduate students last year than all the departments of the college of arts and letters combined . . . The rural marketing study is dealing at present with the marketing of grain, seeking to find out especially how far the farmer is getting his due and how he might be benefitted by cooperative organizations.

> The division in local industries is making a study of the coal industry. Here is available for study in one small area mines using quite primitive methods, others with some use of machinery, and a third group that are quite modern. Research into the weaving industry is seeking to find out how much it is a full-time work of those engaged and how much it is supplementary to the agricultural work of the villagers.

Tayler was impressed by the work of Sam Dean, a Presbyterian missionary with engineering training who had initially come to China in 1915 and had been briefly connected with Yanjing. Dean had long cultivated an interest in what we would now call "appropriate technology", and Tayler sought to extend this type of work as a basis for small scale industrial development.

In February, 1931, Tayler, acting through the NCC Committee on Christianizing Economic Relations, organized a conference on People's Livelihood (Sun Yat-sen's expression). He presented results of his own studies of rural industries, concluding that "China can apply modern science and modern methods of organisation to village and local industry [without] . . . undue reliance on the urbanisation of industry." (1931, p. 53) He was convinced that "most industries do not demand a large scale productive unit", and that individual small firms would imitate improved methods of production if those were introduced by government-sponsored demonstration organizations. He was certain that "by organising [producers] in guilds or cooperative societies for the satisfaction of their credit needs, for the supply of materials from a distance, of power and equipment, an industry of this kind can be modernised as well on the basis of federation of small independent producers as it can on that of a large corporation." (p. 54)

In 1932 Tayler organized the North China Industrial Service Union. A fund-raising letter described the project as follows:[12]

> We are wishing to continue and expand the quite important work that Mr. Sam Dean is doing in designing appliances suitable for village use in the textile industries. He has already been successful in working out such appliances for wool. The problems before us are to extend that to the improvement of village appliances for cotton . . .

Similar specific goals were described for iron smelting in Shansi Province and for pottery making in North China.

Assisting Tayler with the Service Union was Lu Kuang-mian (Guangmian). While a student at Beida in 1923–24, Lu had been very impressed with the ideas of Liang Shuming concerning rural reconstruction

(Alitto 1979; van Slyke 1959). Lu had studied agricultural economics and cooperatives in Aberdeen, Scotland, and at LSE. Returning to China in 1931, he found a position at Yanjing as secretary of the Student Public Welfare Committee. Beginning in September, 1932, he helped organize a marketing cooperative among cotton farmers. The project grew into the Hebei Cotton Improvement Commission. According to Douglas Reynolds, "By 1937, this organization had a staff of 240 persons working in 52 counties of Hopei, with an annual budget of CNC $500,000 and marketing some CNC $10 million worth of cotton annually."[13]

Significantly, the cotton program extended beyond cooperative marketing to embrace also the industrial processes of ginning and baling (Tayler 1934, pp. 56–57). Tayler's activities involved a significant element of extension service similar to the work of American land-grant colleges. He worked at Yanjing village field stations in Qinghe and Dingxian.

Tayler left the Yanjing campus briefly in 1934 for a position with the newly formed National Agricultural Research Bureau (NARB) in Nanjing. However, he soon returned. The chief reason was that some of his ideas had become embodied in an inter-institutional program with substantial funding from the Rockefeller Foundation. In 1934 Yanjing established an Institute of Rural Reconstruction, stressing hands-on grass roots development efforts like those Tayler had been emphasizing. To aid in teaching and field work, Tayler recruited two new faculty from NARB. One was Yu Yung-tzu (Yongzi), a graduate of Japan's Imperial University, who had worked with CIFRC. The other was Cheng Lin-chuang (Zheng Linzhuang), a Yanjing graduate with a master's degree from Columbia, who became a mainstay of Yanjing's Economics Department for the remainder of its existence.[14]

The Rockefeller-sponsored program was formalized in 1936 as the North China Council for Rural Reconstruction. It involved a number of academic disciplines at Yanjing, Nankai, and other institutions (Chiang 2001, pp. 63–71, 124–128; Thomson 1969). Scarcely had this ambitious program been initiated, however, than the outbreak of war with Japan forced its discontinuation.

This program, and other related experiments in "rural reconstruction" associated with Yen Yang-chu (Yan Yangchu) and Liang Shuming, have received mixed reviews. Skeptics argued that China's rural social structure was dominated by a parasitic gentry class which did not favor improvements in productivity and in the living conditions of the mass of farmers.[15] While low productivity was the root cause of rural poverty, improvements in productivity might not bring much benefit to the majority of farmers, given the constraints of the social structure. However, the Yanjing program had important carry-over into the wartime industrial cooperatives program and the post-war Joint Commission on Rural Reconstruction.

The Yanjing Program after 1927

By the late 1920s, enrollment in Economics courses had reached the proportional level which it was to maintain thereafter. In Spring, 1927, Economics majors numbered 72 out of a total enrollment of 502. A 1928 memo characterized Economics as "the most popular department in the university".[16] In the fall of 1929, Economics courses constituted 442 course enrollments out of a total of 4,048 in the entire university. These and subsequent enrollment data are summarized in Table 8-1. Correspondingly, the department's instructional faculty expanded rapidly in the late 1920s. The department began to employ its recent graduates as assistants for teaching and research.

The Economics curriculum continued to make an effort to give students information about their own country. An entry-level course in Chinese Economics in the early 1920s was replaced by 1927–28 with an upper-level course, "Present Day Economic Problems in China". In addition, several courses expressly promised to include China-relevant material: business administration, money and banking, public finance, and foreign and domestic trade.[17]

Table 8-1 shows Economics majors to have been consistently more than 10 percent of the University total enrollment. These year-by-tabulations are confirmed by summary totals for longer periods. The University Alumni Bureau reported in 1937 that over the entire 1917–36 period Yanjing had graduated 1,782 people. "Economics seems to have been the most popular subject of study here as there have been 228 graduated from that department." The department awarded 6 master's degrees before suspending graduate work in 1931.[18]

The popularity of economic study reflected its being the closest thing in the curriculum to preparation for business. A review of alumni careers as of 1936 covered 212 Economics graduates of 1926–35. Of these, 13% were in banking, 14% in other business, 15% in government positions, and 20% in teaching (*Quarterly News*, February 1936).

Beginning in 1923, most Yanjing Economics students wrote a senior thesis. Virtually all of these thesis documents are preserved intact (along

Table 8-1. Economics Enrollments at Yanjing, 1927–1950

Date*	Male	Female	Total Economics	Total Univ.
1926S			62	
1927S			72	502
1930S	89**	14	103**	747
1934F	76	20	96	
1935F	91	17	108	885
1936F	86	15	101	823
1937F	80	12	92	500
1938S	99	12	111	588
1938F	180	22	202	942
1939F	157	21	178	981
1940F			138	1,085
1941F	115	22	137	1,089
1947S	83	14	97	781
1948F	89	12	101	942
1950F	94	38	132	1,148

* S and F denote spring and fall terms.

** Includes 11 graduate students.

Sources: 1927, 1930, 1941, 1947–50 from Archives of the United Board for Christian Higher Education in Asia (Record Group 11, Yale Divinity School) as follows: Dora Bent Circular, Jan. 21, 1930, Box 314, Folder 4813. Memoranda for individual years in Folder 4762, Box 308; "Enrollment", Spring 1947, Box 42, Folder 1079; "Yenching University, 10/31/48". Box 42, Folder 1079.

Printed: Yanjing College of Public Affairs newsletter sequentially titled *Public Affairs* (1934–35), *Quarterly News* (1935–37), *News Bulletin* (1937–40), Folder 5674, Box 370. 1940 data are from *Princeton-Yenching News*, June, 1941, p. 2 (Box 22, Folder 208, RG 1, Series 601, Rockefeller Archive). 1926: *Yenching Yearbook*, 1928 (Chinese language), Box 371, Folder 5691, YDS.

Enrollments at Chengdu

Date*	Male	Female	Total Economics	Total Univ.
1942F	74	17	91	392
1943F	70	17	87	
1944F	68	13	81	

Sources: "College of Public Affairs . . . Report of the Work of Three Years 1942–1945" (mimeo), RG 1, Series 601, Box 22, Folder 207, RA. The 392 total is from another mimeo—may refer to 1943.

with the rest of the Yanjing library) in the library of Peking University. They are reviewed below.

Two Yanjing graduates joined the faculty in 1929, Huang Cho (Zhuo) and Hou Shu-tung (Shutong). Hou spent the three years 1932–35 at Liverpool, where he received a PhD with specialization in monetary economics. Both he and Huang left together in 1937 to join the newly formed Institute of Economic Research under the Ministry of Railways (*News Bulletin*, November 1937, p. 5).

A noteworthy American "China hand" joined the faculty in 1932 in the person of Harry B. Price. He was born into a China missionary family. Soon after beginning graduate study of Economics at Princeton, he became a junior member of Edwin Kemmerer's Commission of Financial Experts which spent most of 1929 in China. He completed a master's degree at Yale in 1932.

After beginning teaching at Yanjing, Price soon became distressed by the inadequacy of teaching materials, and assembled reading materials he felt dealt well with China's economy, including writings of R. H. Tawney, John Lossing Buck, and J. B. Condliffe. Soon he was using these as a basis for a course called Chinese economic problems, explicitly designated as "a non-technical course designed especially for non-majors . . . Special attention is given to questions of natural resources, population, rural development, transportation, and industrialization". His course in European economic history was described as providing "a basis for comparison which will be useful in later study of Chinese economic conditions" (*Yenching University Bulletin 1936–37*, pp. 97–98).

Harry Price was particularly aware of China's problem with over-population and, with his students, began to assemble Chinese writings on the subject. He reviewed the issue in a simple but powerful essay (Price 1937a) in the second issue of *Democracy*, a magazine which he, along with Helen and Edgar Snow, helped establish in 1937.

In 1937 the Price family were in the United States on furloughs when war with Japan broke out, and they did not return. Harry became executive secretary of the American Committee for Non-Participation in Japanese Aggression, which lobbied to restrict American exports to Japan (Friedman 1968). In 1941 he became an executive of China Defense Supplies Inc., a China-financed firm involved in procurement of Lend-Lease products for China. In December, 1944, he returned to China to spend four years as Deputy Director of the Chinese operations of the United Nations Relief and Rehabilitation Administration (UNRRA). His final assignment was to prepare the China sections of the monumental history of UNRRA published in 1950 (Woodbridge 1950, v. 2, pp. 371–453).

Industrial Cooperatives

The Japanese invasion which began in 1937 brought about the collapse of the joint rural reconstruction program into which so much money and effort had been put. However, J. B. Tayler, Lu Guangmian, and other Yanjing people played a large role in the program to develop industrial cooperatives (Reynolds 1975; Trescott 1992). The program originated in 1938 as an effort to help develop industry in the sections of China not occupied by the Japanese, especially industry which could supply military needs. Beginning with a blacksmiths' cooperative in Shanghai, the movement soon enlisted support from the national government and spread rapidly.

J. B. Tayler, who had been on furlough in Britain when he learned of the movement, hastened to return to China to participate. He became one of the directors of the training program, dealing with both technological and organizational elements. The program also attracted some of Tayler's students and former associates at Yanjing. Lu Guangmian became the director of the Northwest Region, aided by his wife Chiang (Jiang) Shuhuan, a Yanjing graduate. Another top official was Meng Yung-chien (Yongjian), who had received bachelor and master's degrees in Economics from Yanjing in 1924 and 1925. Yu Yongzi, whom Tayler had recruited to the Yanjing faculty, was also a participant, as were J. L. Buck and several other Nanjing staff.

By the end of 1941, the program had apparently reached its peak, with 1,737 societies and 23,000 members. Adverse influence from the national government was a major factor in the subsequent gradual decline. In September, 1942, Tayler sadly reflected that "the movement is being destroyed . . . by methods analogous to those . . . in Germany and Italy . . . Cooperation has been sacrificed to create taxable capacity in rural areas or to provide funds for friends of magistrates or the [KMT] Party."[19]

Douglas Reynolds estimated that the industrial cooperatives program probably added about one percent to China's national product, and three percent to industrial production, during the wartime period. They contributed important products to military procurement and provided jobs and training for refugees and rural residents.

After the war's end, the program stabilized again with about 300 societies, some of which remained highly productive.[20] The leadership were optimistic with the Communist take-over in 1949, since there had been a number of industrial cooperatives in Communist territory. Meng Yongjian became head of the national cooperative organization in the new government. However, within a couple of years the new government transformed the former cooperatives into parts of a centralized and bureaucratic system. In 1982, after the post-Mao thaw, Lu Guangmian was one of a number who helped revive the industrial cooperative program.

Under Occupation 1937–1941

Yanjing and Catholic Furen University were, because of their foreign sponsorship, able to continue operating in Peking after 1937, but most other universities in Peking were closed. One result was a boom in enrollments at Yanjing. Another was that Yanjing took on faculty members displaced from other schools. Professor Yuen Wen-pu (Wenbo) joined the Economics Department in 1937, after teaching at Nankai for six years. He held a doctorate from NYU with a major research interest in the history of economic thought. Yanjing was also able to hire Kuo Jui-chang (Guo Ruizhang), who held an MA from Boston University (1926) and had taught at several Peking institutions before becoming Dean of the YMCA Commercial College. Hu Jiyuan, professor and department chair at Hangchow Christian College, served as visiting professor 1938–40 (*News Bulletin*, November 1937; October 1939).

The Economics program appeared relatively strong during most of the period 1937–41. In 1938 the University began to publish a journal, the *Yenching Journal of Social Studies*, to which Economics faculty contributed. The department began in 1939 calculating and publishing price indexes for Peking, reflecting escalating inflation (*News Bulletin*, April, October 1939). In 1940 the department began to publish their own journal, *The Economic Annual* (in Chinese).

In 1937, Yanjing received a grant from the British Boxer Indemnity Fund to develop a program of tutorial instruction similar to Oxford. Two British instructors were engaged, George E. Taylor and Michael Lindsay.[21] Lindsay had graduated from Oxford and spent a year as a research student at Cambridge, where he attended lectures by J. M. Keynes and picked up some of the excitement associated with Keynes's work (Lindsay 1938). Arriving at Yanjing early in 1938, he began by offering a tutorial in monetary theory with emphasis on Keynes.

Soon after his arrival, Lindsay, George Taylor, and another colleague visited the communist-led guerilla forces about 200 miles south of Peking. Lindsay observed "I was impressed with the Chinese Communists and compared them very favorably with the Communists I had known in England, who were extremely doctrinaire . . . Here the Communists seemed reasonable people and what they were doing was obviously helping the ordinary people."[22] On his return to Yanjing, Lindsay became actively involved in the anti-Japanese underground, particularly buying needed supplies and conveying them outside Peking. In June, 1941, Lindsay married Li Hsiao-li (Xiaoli) , who had been one of his tutorial students and had aided him in his underground work.[23]

Yanjing's "Indian Summer" interlude of 1937–41 ended dramatically with the Pearl Harbor attack in December, 1941. Many faculty and staff, including Gideon Chen, Yuan Wenbo, and Augusta Wagner were arrested or interned. Yanjing's activities in Peking were shut down. Chen was released after about six months and joined a Japanese-connected research institute.[24] Augusta Wagner and other internees were held for 18 months and then repatriated on the Gripsholm.[25]

When word of Pearl Harbor reached them, Lindsay and his wife escaped into communist-held territory (Band 1948; Lindsay 1975). Ultimately the Lindsays made their way to Yenan and worked with the Communists until the end of the war, chiefly assisting with radio technology and translation.[26] After leaving China, Lindsay held faculty positions in England and Australia before becoming Professor of Far Eastern Studies at the American University in Washington in 1959. He became an outspoken critic of the Communist regime and particularly of the ideological dogmatism which he felt brought much harm to the Chinese people.[27]

Some Yanjing faculty were able to make their way to Chengdu in West China, where a Yanjing program was reconstituted in 1942. As Table 8-1 indicates, Economics continued to attract a large proportion of the student enrollment—15 to 20 percent (see John Fairbank 1982, p. 232). Zheng Linzhuang made his way from Peking in 1942 to head the department. A major addition to the department was Professor Chao Jen-tsun (Zhao Renjun), formerly of Qinghua, who had received his doctorate from Harvard in 1929. His specialty was monetary economics. He also gave courses for the other Christian colleges domiciled in Chengdu and wrote on topics relating to the monetary situation and inflation.

The Department also reacquired Jao Yu-su (Rao Yusu), who had graduated from Yanjing in 1934, worked for Harry Price and others as a research assistant, and taken a master's degree at Smith College in 1940.

She became a central figure in the university's international trade specialty, for which a grant was received in 1943 from the Foreign Trade Commission of the national government. A Rockefeller Foundation observer noted in 1943 that the Public Affairs program in Chengdu "is certainly weak", and compared with its halcyon days in the 1930s this was undoubtedly true.[28] Considering the logistical obstacles and economic hardships, it was quite an achievement to maintain any kind of university instruction at all.

Post-war Developments

After the war ended in late summer, 1945, operations in Chengdu were continued for an additional year, but the main campus was able to resume activities in October, 1945. In March, 1947, acting Dean Chao Cheng-hsin (Zhao Chengxin) reported that:

> Professor Cheng Lin-chuang is the Chairman of the Department [of Economics] and is the only full-time member. We have to depend upon seven part-time members from Tsinghua, Peita, and Fu-jen universities to carry the academic program of the department.
>
> In research, no systematic work has been planned so far because the University is in a very bad financial situation this year. Economics is doing some work on price index for the United Service to China.[29]

Rockefeller Foundation representative Roger Evans visited Yanjing in May, 1947. He noted that Economics was (as usual) attracting the largest number of students (100 out of 780), and that Zheng Linzhuang "is literally worn to a skeleton" from overwork.[30] Zheng was able to escape to another year of study at Columbia in 1947–48. The department received brief service from three western-educated Chinese who went on to distinguished careers elsewhere. He Guoliang (Alfred K. Ho), a Yanjing graduate of 1941, completed a PhD in political science at Princeton and returned to teach Economics in 1946–48. He subsequently served for many years as a professor at Western Michigan University and published an important book on joint ventures in 1991. Jiang Shuojie (PhD LSE 1944) taught part time at Yanjing while on the faculty at Beida in 1946–47. Xu Yunan (PhD Cambridge 1940) taught part-time at Yanjing in 1946–47 while on the Qinghua faculty.

For all the turmoil, Yanjing enrollment in general and Economics in particular, remained strong in the late 1940s. However, "normal" operations lasted only briefly. In December, 1948, the area containing the Yanjing campus came under control of the advancing Communist forces. By fall, 1949, the program began to reflect the new regime, through the appointment of Shen Zhiyuan, a Marxist. He had studied in the USSR and written a textbook entitled *Outline of New Economics* (originally 1934) which he used in his large lecture course in elementary economics. He also taught at Beida and Qinghua and was very popular with the students.[31]

In 1951–52 Yanjing's official existence came to an end. Peking University moved from its downtown location to the Yanjing campus. In 1952 most of the Yanjing economists were assigned to the newly formed People's University, only a short distance from Yanjing's location. Zheng Linzhuang went as Professor of Agricultural Economics (died 1987). Chao Ching (Zhao Jing) went to Beida where he was teaching history of Chinese economic thought in 1992.

Some Reflections

There can be no doubt that the Yanjing program was a vehicle for the introduction of "western" economic ideas. As I have shown elsewhere, Yanjing's Economics faculty could be classed predominantly as institutionalist (Trescott 1992). Institutional economics stressed the study of the social institutions within which economic activity takes place. This included trying to incorporate relevant findings from sociology and psychology. Institutional economics was generally critical of the market system, and institutionalists were generally proponents of social reform programs. For Christians like J. B. Tayler, the foregoing were all blended with a strong adherence to the Social Gospel. Several Yanjing faculty members, including Li Binghua, Augusta Wagner, Harry Price, and Zheng Linzhuang had studied with such prominent American institutionalists as John R. Commons, John Maurice Clark, and Wesley Mitchell.

At the same time, J. B. Tayler consistently worked to make the course work relevant to China. And his field work directed toward appropriate technology and the cooperative movement led to highly productive results, particularly in the Hebei cotton program and the industrial cooperatives system.

Foreign Study by Alumni

As we noted in the previous chapter, 61 Yanjing alumni went on to study Economics in the West. Fourteen Yanjing alumni are known to have received doctoral degrees in Economics in the United States and Great Britain. By far the best known was Fei Ching-han (Jinghan), who as John Fei became one of the leaders of development economics in the United States. He had graduated from Yanjing in 1945 with a senior thesis on the marginal productivity theory of wages. He became the first Chinese to receive a doctorate in Economics from MIT, writing on general equilibrium theory. He became a professor at Yale and was co-author in 1964 of an influential book, *Development of the Labor Surplus Economy* (with Gustav Ranis). He was a long-time adviser to the government of Taiwan.[32]

The earliest Yanjing-alumnus doctorate was Wei Wen-pin (Wenbin), who graduated from Yanjing predecessor Peking Methodist University in 1908 and completed a doctorate at Columbia in 1914. He then entered China's diplomatic service. Chen Xicheng (Francis Chen) received two graduate degrees from Yanjing after graduating from Fujian Christian College (FCU). After completing a doctorate at Yale, he returned to help establish the rural economics program at FCU, noted in Chapter 6. Hou Shutong, noted above, earned a doctorate from Liverpool while on the Yanjing faculty. Ms. Kuan Shu-chuang (Guan Shuzhuang, Mrs. Ting) received a doctorate from Radcliffe and worked for the United Nations. She then returned to China to join the staff of the Chinese Academy of Social Sciences.

Hsia Hsiu-yung (Xia Xiuyong, Ronald Hsia, Yanjing 1941) received a doctorate from Southern California in 1950. He joined the faculty of the University of Hong Kong in 1956 and was professor and chair by 1965 (AEA Handbook 1969, p. 204). Chou Shun-hsin (Zhou Shunxin, Yanjing 1945) completed a doctorate at Columbia and went on to a long career on the faculty of the University of Pittsburgh.

Foreign Study by Faculty

Over the entire span of Yanjing's lifetime, we have identified 85 faculty members, not including teaching assistants and research assistants. Seven of these were foreign, and we have noted all but one, namely Matt Taylor, a Princeton BA who taught for one year 1930–31. John Tayler was connected with Yanjing, off and on, for 26 years, and Augusta Wagner for 17. Tayler did not have a lot of formal graduate study in Economics, but his writings showed evidence of an effort to keep up with the literature. After his departure in 1943, Yanjing had no foreign teachers in Economics.

Of the 78 Chinese faculty, 43 were full-time. Of these, 28, almost two-thirds, had studied abroad. Half of the 35 part-time Chinese faculty had studied overseas. These proportions were much higher than the average for the other Christian colleges. The share of foreign-educated faculty was particularly high around 1929–31 (when the faculty reached its maximum absolute size) and just after World War II (when numerous visiting faculty were engaged).

Of the 46 Chinese faculty members who had studied abroad, 17 held doctoral degrees. Out of the 46, 33 had studied in the United States: 12 at Columbia. Only 7 of the 46 had studied in Britain: 4 at LSE.

A common criticism of western teachers and western-oriented institutions was that they did not use materials directly relevant to China. The western teachers we have described at Yanjing do not deserve this criticism. J. B. Tayler worked hard to generate data about Chinese conditions and to make these data useful for teaching purposes. Both Harry Price and Augusta Wagner assembled teaching materials appropriate for Chinese students.

Chinese universities were criticized as being remote from the everyday life of Chinese people, and particularly from the vast rural population (Yeh 1990; Chan and Dirlik 1991). The Yanjing economists were anything but remote from Chinese life. This was especially true of Tayler's work to promote appropriate technology and the cooperative movement. Augusta Wagner participated actively in the work of the Yanjing Relief Committee, "which," she wrote, "with the exception of the Chinese Congregational Church in a nearby village . . . is the only organized association for the relief of the thousands of desperately needy people in the surrounding villages."[33]

J. B. Tayler was also a dedicated researcher, and inspired his students and colleagues in the same direction. We have examined the titles of 461 Yanjing student theses in Economics for the period 1924–49. Of these, 339 (about three-fourths) dealt with China-related topics.[34]

Another dimension of Yanjing activism was exemplified by the Economics student who changed his name from Wang Ju-mei (Rumei, b. 1913) to Huang Hua. In his Yanjing student days, 1932–36, he was a friend of Harry Price and the Snows. He left Yanjing shortly before graduation to join the Communist forces. He helped establish the Foreign Affairs Office of the new regime in 1949. Ultimately he rose to a leading position, serving as ambassador to Ghana, Egypt, Canada, and the UN. In 1974 he became Minister of Foreign Affairs (Huang 1990, p. 32; Klein and Clark 1971, pp. 393–395). He was still active in public affairs in 1992, and was one of the leaders of the Yanjing alumni association. Indeed, the size and vigor of the Yanjing alumni association was itself a strong testimonial to the institution's quality.

9

John Lossing Buck and Agricultural Economics at Nanjing University

Among the missionary colleges, the University of Nanjing was unusual in possessing two separate departments of Economics. The orthodox department, which we mentioned in Chapter 7, was generally quite undistinguished. In contrast the program in agricultural economics, developed by John Lossing Buck, was the most distinguished in Chinese universities.[1] When Buck began his academic career at Nanjing in 1920, there was virtually no agricultural economics as such taught in China's educational system. Buck's work over the subsequent twenty-five years as a researcher, teacher, grantsman, and program developer helped make this an important field of academic research and teaching. As much as any part of the Economics curriculum, agricultural economics was heavily focused on economic growth and development.

Buck's Early Career

J. L. Buck was born and raised on a farm in New York State. He graduated in 1915 from the New York State Agricultural College at Cornell University, where he was active in Christian groups. In 1916 he accepted a position as an agricultural missionary to China, beginning with an experimental farm in Northern Anhui Province. On his way to this assignment, he met Pearl Sydenstricker, the American-educated daughter of an American missionary couple long resident in China. They were married in 1917 and became a highly effective team. J. L. Buck spent much of his first year learning the Chinese language, in which his new bride had already achieved exceptional fluency. She often accompanied him on visits to Chinese farm families and was able to win the trust of many of the farm women. This experience provided her with much of the raw material out of which she was able to fashion *The Good Earth* and many other China-related writings which were to win for her the Nobel and Pulitzer prizes and international fame and fortune.[2]

In 1920 J. L. Buck joined Nanjing University at the invitation of Dean John Reisner, a schoolmate and fellow Christian from Cornell. Through their efforts, the College of Agriculture and Forestry (CAF) became virtually a branch campus of Cornell. In 1920–21 CAF enrolled only 21 undergraduate students. Rapid growth followed for the next decade, and by 1929–30 it had 169 undergraduates.[3]

Reisner wanted Buck to develop a program in agricultural economics. Buck had majored in agronomy and had no significant background in Economics. In 1924–25 he addressed this deficiency by spending an academic year back at Cornell to obtain an MS. Initially, however, he simply plunged into teaching from his Cornell mentor George Warren's *Farm Management*. Buck's vision of the subject essentially followed Warren's model.

Agricultural Economics

Agricultural economics as an academic specialty had emerged in the United States around 1900.[4] Cornell offered a course in economics of agriculture in 1901, and Wisconsin followed a year later. In 1906 Thomas Nixon Carver introduced his course in agricultural economics at Harvard. George Warren's text, *Farm Management*, appeared in 1913.

These pioneers were typically men who had been raised on farms. Their presentations undertook to explain to prospective farmers how to maximize their profits, and (somewhat less extensively) what the economic consequences of such maximization would be (Taylor 1905, p. 40; Warren 1913, p. v). Carver and Taylor both discussed at length the Law of Diminishing Returns and economies of scale, and explained optimal input and output choices in terms of marginal analysis. These early presentations relied primarily on verbal exposition, supplemented with descriptive statistics and an occasional graph or numerical illustration.

According to George Warren, "the best way to find out what methods of farm organization and management are most successful is to study the methods now used and the profits secured in large numbers of farms, and determine how the more successful ones differ from the less successful

. . . " (pp. v–vi, 134–140, 535). Thus survey research was central to Warren's research.

Warren stressed the calculation of implicit factor rewards for the farm family's labor and capital. Unpaid labor of family members needs to be valued at what it would cost to hire comparable workers, and those implicit costs should be included in expenses. Warren was confident that men could expect to progress from hired hand to tenant to owner—climbing the "agricultural ladder" (p. 27). He stressed the importance of finding productive work all year.

On the whole, Warren's books had very little explicit economics. There was no attention given to how supply and demand for individual agricultural products explained output and prices. The marginal principle, clearly stated by Taylor and by Carver, did not appear. Emphasis was on calculating labor income, and its relation to farm size and labor utilization.

China Surveys

As Buck later recalled, he was quickly dismayed by the lack of basic information on Chinese agricultural conditions. Furthermore, "the students were mostly not the sons of farmers—they had little experience with farmers, and actually looked down on farmers" (Buck 1962, pp. 9–10). He obtained permission to conduct on-the-spot surveys of individual Chinese farmers, using CAF students. He expected that the data would be valuable for teaching purposes, and that the survey experience would bring the students into more direct familiarity with rural China. They would also learn survey methodology—following Warren's analytical scheme very closely.

The first actual survey work began in April, 1921, as Liu Tung-hsin (Dongxin) began work with farmers in the Chinhei district of Zhejiang Province (Buck 1930a, p. 5). The CAF *Annual Report* for 1922–23 presented preliminary findings for 102 farms near Wuhu in Anhui Province, giving data on tenure, incomes, size of farm and family, and inputs and outputs (pp. 12–16). From this modest beginning, the survey project took on massive proportions: "data had been obtained from 2,866 farms in 17 localities of 7 provinces during the summers of 1922–25" (Buck 1973, p. 15). After interruption by the civil war in 1927, Buck completed the write-up in 1928 (with considerable help from his wife, by her accounts). With support from economist J. B. Condliffe and the Institute of Pacific Relations, the work was published in 1930 as *Chinese Farm Economy*

(CFE). It served as Buck's dissertation for a PhD awarded in 1933 after another year at Cornell. The work was soon translated into Chinese. We discuss it in detail below.

In 1922–23 Buck was teaching courses in agricultural economics, rural organization and credit, and farm management. The following year he added courses in rural sociology and marketing (Buck 1973, p. 14). He was quick to recruit graduates of his program to aid in teaching and research. Paul Hsu (Xu Cheng) joined the staff in 1922, and Swen Wen-yuh (Sun Wenyuh) and Chiao Chi-ming (Qiao Qiming) were appointed in 1924 (Buck 1973, p. 13).

In the early 1920s, Buck became a member of the Committee on Credit and Economic Improvement of the China International Famine Relief Commission (CIFRC), along with J. B. Tayler of Yanjing. From this connection Buck's program became committed to helping the development of cooperatives. Direct grass-roots work was done by Paul Hsu, who organized his first cooperative among Nanjing vegetable growers in 1923.[5] By 1927 the CAF program had promoted the formation of 20 credit cooperatives.

During the 1920s, Buck published numerous articles in Christian periodicals urging church support for agricultural development and agricultural education (Buck 1923, 1927a). He was active in the Committee on Christianizing the Economic Order, which published in 1927 his striking article on farm ownership and tenancy (Buck 1927b). After noting that "the extent of farm tenancy in China compares very favorably with that of other countries" (p. 3), he pointed out marked increases in tenancy in several areas. "There is no agricultural ladder in the sense often referred to in the United States . . ." (p. 17) Farmers were hampered in purchasing land by lack of credit facilities. He noted examples of tenants treated as virtual serfs and of oppressive conditions for tenants imprisoned for non-payment of rent. His striking conclusion was "Probably a law should be passed and enforced looking forward to the elimination of all large land holdings. European history is full of instances of the breaking up of large estates, and it seems that China must do likewise." (p. 26)

In 1927 the Nanjing area was torn by civil war associated with the Communist element of the Kuomintang. Westerners were killed or threatened, and the Bucks evacuated to Japan for several months. The experience undoubtedly helped strengthen their anti-communist convictions.

In 1930–31 economic historian Richard Tawney of LSE spent several weeks with CAF, staying at the Buck home, lecturing on European agrarian conditions, and working on his influential book *Land and Labour in China*, which appeared in 1932. The book included numerous citations of Buck and other CAF staff members, as well as Yanjing's John Tayler.[6]

During the discussion of *Chinese Farm Economy*, J. B. Condliffe urged Buck to submit a proposal for a grant to study land utilization in China. With support from the Social Science Research Council, the project swung into operation in 1928–29. The project brought boom times to the Nanjing campus.

Buck's description of the program in 1931 stressed that CAF's "Department of Agricultural Economics is the only training center for students of agricultural economics in China". Courses offered included the following:

Agricultural Economics
Farm Management
Farm Accounting
Humanistic Geography
Regional and Economic Geography
History of Chinese Agriculture
Rural Sociology
Rural Organization
Agricultural Statistics
Rural Problems
Rural Finance
Marketing Farm Products
History of Land Tenure in China
Agricultural Policy
Research Methods in Agricultural Economics

There were 19 major students and 16 minor students.[7] In 1931 Kenyon Butterfield, president of the Massachusetts State College of Agriculture, came to China to review mission work. His 1931 report praised the CAF program lavishly:

> This institution is the greatest contribution to China from the West in the field of agricultural education; indeed, in no land of the so-called missionary areas is there a college of agriculture of the same scope of service or extent of achievement. It is probably at the present time the most influential institution of its kind in China. (Butterfield 1931, p. 35)

The availability of grant funds clearly enabled Buck's program to maintain a large and diverse faculty and a wide variety of course offerings.

In 1934 the Department of Agricultural Economics reported 43 staff members—faculty and research staff.[8]

Land Utilization

Whereas *Chinese Farm Economy* appeared to be the work of a single master and a large number of servants, the land utilization project enlisted numerous major researchers from the West.

George Warren's son Stanley (Cornell PhD 1931) spent the year 1931–32 assisting in tabulations and training staff. Dr. David Weeks, Professor of Agricultural Economics at Berkeley, served as visiting professor in spring, 1932. When Buck returned to Nanjing after completing his doctorate in 1933, he brought with him Ardron B. Lewis, who had also just completed his doctorate at Cornell and who worked at Nanjing until 1936. John Raeburn, Glenn Hedlund, and Marshall Curtiss, all Cornell doctorates, came for one-year stints in 1936–38. Yang Wei, a Nanjing graduate who joined the CAF faculty in 1930, received his Cornell PhD in 1935.

The reputations of Buck and the Nanjing department led to numerous advisory and consulting activities. For the national government (now headquartered in Nanjing), Buck directed surveys of damage from the 1931 flood and from the Japanese hostilities in Shanghai in 1932 (Stross 1986, p. 181). In early 1934 the department agreed to conduct surveys in the area from which the Communists had recently been ousted, to determine the need for bank loans and other assistance. And beginning in 1934 Buck served for several years as a special advisor to the U.S. Treasury in matters relating to silver—discussed further below.

Throughout this time, work on the extremely ambitious land utilization project was proceeding. Tabulation of survey results began in 1931, involving as many as 100 clerks working with the abacus.[9] Ultimately in 1937 *Land Utilization in China* was published. In addition to a massive volume of text, there was a second containing statistical tabulations and a third comprising an atlas. Of the fifteen chapters in the text, Buck was listed as author of eight, the topics of which corresponded fairly closely to those of *Chinese Farm Economy*. Of the nine other authors, only two were Chinese: Chiao Chi-ming (Qiao Qiming), co-author with Frank Notestein of the chapter on population, and Swen Wenyuh, who wrote the nutrition chapter in collaboration with Leonard Maynard. Ardron Lewis wrote the chapter on prices and taxation. The work was soon translated into Chinese. We analyze it below.

The first footnote in *Land Utilization* cited *The Good Earth*, which Pearl had published in 1931 and for which she had received the Pulitzer Prize in 1932. But soon after their return to China in 1933, she indicated her desire to end the marriage, and in 1935 she divorced Lossing, giving him a generous financial settlement.[10]

In 1937–38 Buck collaborated with W. Marshall ("Charlie") Curtiss in preparing a book on farm management for Chinese readers. They composed a version in simplified English (completed in 1942) which was translated into Chinese by Nanjing staff members Ko Fuh-ting (Ge Fuding) and Wang Yin-yuan (Yinyuan) (published 1946). This book, *Farm Management in China*, was largely a description and evaluation of Chinese farm practices summarized from Buck's previous works.[11] In September, 1936, CAF (which had been publishing research bulletins throughout its existence) began a monthly periodical entitled *Economic Facts*. Buck became a frequent contributor in the 1940s.[12]

When hostilities with Japan escalated in 1937, Nanjing University moved west to Chengdu. Several other Christian colleges moved there as the war progressed. Buck spent much of his time in Chongqing, the wartime capital, where he held an advisory position to the Chinese government in 1939–40. He resumed his active involvement with CAF in 1940. He participated in a survey of Sichuan province in 1940–41, directed by Qiao Qiming (Buck, 1943). In 1941 he married his Chinese secretary, a decision which cost him his missionary status. At the end of the war, he served for about two years as chief economist for the National Agricultural Engineering Corporation, a spin-off from UNRRA. Buck subsequently became head of the Land and Water Use Branch of the Food and Agriculture Organization of the United Nations. In 1954 he helped establish the Rockefeller-sponsored Council on Economic and Cultural Affairs, which later became the Agricultural Development Council.

Buck continued to write extensively on matters relating to Chinese agriculture. In a 1966 study, he used the data from *Land Utilization* to diagnose deficiencies in agricultural data published by the Chinese Communists. In the following sections, we deal analytically with Buck's major research and other elements of his professional career.

Chinese Farm Economy

The work was based on survey data covering 2,866 farms involving a total of 17,000 persons (Buck 1970, p. 174). The survey instrument itself was a questionnaire printed out over nine pages, one which must have taken the typical respondent several hours to complete. The final book was heavily quantitative, containing 251 numbered tables and 69 diagrams. Buck followed George Warren's model very closely. Each farm reported its output (quantity and value, marketed and consumed at home). Inputs were measured, and imputed market values were attached to the labor of the farmer and his family and to owned land and capital. The resulting data on economic profit and returns to farmers' labor were compared with such determinants as size of farm, size of family, and tenancy status. The end result, though analytically justifiable, provided the reader with a rather bewildering array of measures of farm effectiveness. The opportunity cost approach was a reminder that a farm operation represented an efficient use of resources only if the various inputs all received rewards equivalent to what they could earn in other activities. However, the results depended on how these input values were estimated (not clearly explained). And for many farm families, good alternatives were not so readily available (Martin 1991, pp. 130–131).

The text was often enriched with penetrating direct observations, supported by 39 photographs. Buck was quick to praise the farmers for their diligence and shrewdness, but his commentary constantly noted areas for improvement. As mere factual exposition, the book contained much striking information. In Buck's sample, ninety percent of the farm land had been inherited. The typical farm occupied about five acres and usually consisted of a number of non-contiguous plots.[13] Crop production was overwhelmingly directed toward direct human use for food, fiber, and fuel (there was little deliberate production of animal forage) (Buck 1930, pp. 167–168). More than half of each farm family's consumption was produced on their farm, but more than half of their output was marketed (p. 196). Of the effective land input, 92 percent was directed toward grains (chiefly rice and wheat) and seeds, while fruits and vegetables received only negligible amounts (pp. 182–187). Land taxes in China were higher per acre than in the United States.

Larger farms were more successful, because on very small farms, there was simply no opportunity to use the productive potential of the human resources over the entire year (Buck 1930a, p. 231). Underlying the problem of small farm size was the fundamental fact of China's overpopulation, a theme to which Buck referred repeatedly. He also stressed the urgency of developing non-farm production, particularly in rural areas. The urgent needs for improvements in transportation, credit facilities and education were often cited (pp. 406–408). By frequent comparisons with conditions in developed countries, Buck reminded readers of the shockingly low levels of labor productivity and consumption prevalent in China. While consolidation of land holdings might increase efficiency, the real problem was what to do with the abundant labor (Buck 1930, p. 143). Similarly, mechanization could not be recommended: there was little to be gained by substituting costly capital for cheap labor.[14]

Although he did not spell out his analytical framework, Buck clearly understood that in an area where labor was abundant relative to land and capital, labor incomes would be very low per worker and the rewards to ownership of property would be high per unit. Social injustice was inherent in the structure of the situation.

Buck's study was being prepared during the same period that Sun Yat-sen's slogan "All land to the tillers" was drawing great attention. Although Sun had died in 1925, the Kuomintang had gained national power in China in 1927 and proclaimed its dedication to Sun's ideals. And the Communist insurgents were even stronger in their commitment to radical redistribution of land.

In *Chinese Farm Economy* and other publications, Buck and his Nanjing colleagues devoted considerable attention to issues related to land tenure and tenancy.[15] Buck's China survey design focused on the individual farm unit and did not systematically deal with a landlord class as such. Of the 2,866 farms surveyed, 63 percent were owner-operated, 17 percent involved part ownership, and 20 percent were tenants (Buck 1930a, p. 145). For a sub-sample of 641 farms involving tenants and a few part owners, Buck found that rents averaged about 40 percent of the crop, but with substantial variations (pp. 148–149). Family earnings (adjusted for family size) were about twenty percent lower for tenant farm families than for farm owner families (pp. 151–155). Buck estimated that landlords were receiving an average of 8.5 percent as a rate of return on the rented property—not a very high rate for a less-developed country. Even so, he concluded that rents were "too high" in many localities and recommended a simple formula to determine "fair" rents, using a technique for valuing the farm land based on its net receipts (pp. 159–166). Buck thus implicitly aligned himself with the KMT Land Law of 1930 which set a limit on rents (but was never enforced).

Buck did not attempt to determine the distribution of farm acreage occupied by tenants, although his survey design generated the data for this. His survey did not deal directly with landlords who did not farm themselves.

And landless hired farm workers appeared in the survey only as they were reported by farm operators. Measures of dispersion and distribution of income and wealth did not figure much in Buck's reporting scheme. And he gave very little data on physical volume of production.

Buck argued that "farmers usually are growing the crops best suited to the locality. By the trial and error method they have found out which are the most profitable." (Buck 1930a, p. 183) However, he did not present any estimates of the relative profitability of the various crops. A tantalizing brief tabulation gives output per man-hour for five major products, from which we can get a rough idea of the average revenue product of labor, which we show in Table 9-l.

Table 9-1. Buck's Estimates of Labor Productivity

Crop	Output per man-hour (kilograms)	Price (CNC$)	Ave. rev. prod. of labor (CNC$)
Corn	1.1	0.0464	0.051
Wheat	1.6	0.0673	0.108
Rice	2.2	0.0555	0.122
Soybeans	1.3	0.0611	0.079
Kaoliang	1.6	0.0445	0.071

Source: Buck 1930, pp. 214, 313. Prices in the source are per quintal of 100 kilograms and are adjusted to kilograms here.

The high values shown for the average revenue product of labor for wheat and rice help explain the fact that 91 percent of the farmers in North China grew wheat and 92 percent in South China grew rice. Buck urged the farmers to devote more effort to fruits, vegetables, and animal products.

The book concluded with a lengthy analysis of data relating to farm consumption and living conditions. These of course demonstrated the extreme poverty of most families. Buck estimated annual per capita consumption to be $38.44 in Chinese currency, equivalent to US$20.56, "a startlingly low figure upon which to maintain existence" (pp. 387–390). Buck expressed his concern that poor education led farmers to wasteful decisions. His missionary convictions were supported by data showing that farmers with a Christian orientation were more likely to avoid gambling, alcohol, tobacco, and superstitious indulgences.[16]

Viewed in its totality, *Chinese Farm Economy* is an exercise in descriptive statistics supplemented by a wealth of descriptive detail about farm life and practices. Sampling errors and correlation coefficients were given for many of the data. Buck's survey was so rich that in fact the text discussed only a small proportion of the interesting relationships among the data. The analytical framework was primarily that of farm management rather than economic analysis.

In 1933, Alfred Chiu (Qiu Kaiming) reviewed the Nanjing agricultural surveys published to that date. His judgment was not enthusiastic. The early survey instruments were unsatisfactory and the samples were not representative.[17] However, his chief criticisms were directed at the earlier (and smaller) surveys rather than at CFE. And they were equally applicable to most of the other contemporary surveys, such as those of Chen Hansheng.

Land Utilization in China

A new and vastly expanded survey operation underlay the land utilization study. During 1929–33, a vast team of Chinese investigators surveyed 16,786 farms and 38,256 farm families in 22 Chinese provinces. Whereas the earlier project had used a single survey instrument, the later involved ten separate surveys (four of which, however, involved a single schedule each for each locality). Farm surveys and population surveys were the most extensive, while smaller numbers were surveyed regarding prices, farm practices, food, and standard of living (Buck 1937, pp. viii–x).

There was similarity in topics with *Chinese Farm Economy*. Eight chapters in *Land Utilization* had identical or similar titles and reported survey responses to similar inquiries. Strangely, Buck did not in general compare the 1929–33 survey results with those for 1921–25.[18] New chapters dealt with topography, climate, soils, agricultural regions, prices and taxation, and marketing. The tedious and sometimes confusing details on various measures of farm income, family income, labor income, etc., were not repeated in *Land Utilization* (LU).

Buck did do a bit more cautious aggregating in LU. He compared the implications of his own survey results with other data to get an idea of the total cultivated area of China's farms (pp. 162–167). He estimated that, for the entire area surveyed, 28.7 percent of farm land was rented (p. 194) but as in CFE, very little data were given to specify the concentration of ownership. The population chapter compared various ways of estimating China's total farm population (pp. 361–363). There were still no presentations from which one could easily estimate the total output of different products by the sample (and even less than in CFE on the money value of different outputs). However, Buck did experiment with an aggregate measure called the "grain equivalent". Output of each product was converted to grain equivalent either on the basis of its food value or its market value. This provided a useful index to be applied to output per worker, per farm, etc. (pp. 278–288). China's farmers produced the equivalent of 1,393 kilograms per man compared with about 20,000 for the United States (p. 282). On the input side, he formed an aggregate termed "man-equivalent", weighting women's labor as 0.8 of a man's, and children's labor as 0.5, and adjusting each downward for idle time (LU p. 475).

Land Utilization directed somewhat more attention to changes over time. One striking finding was that the "well-informed" respondents to the locality survey overwhelmingly indicated that the "plane of living" had improved in recent years.[19]

Like *Chinese Farm Economy*, much of *Land Utilization* gave the appearance of raw material rather than finished product. In the pre-computer age, the data processing tasks were too great to produce all the possible interesting statistics. The statistical volume was printed in China, and had to be completed in haste when the war broke out in 1937. The original data were soon lost as the university had to evacuate. As before, LU provided much vivid descriptive detail. Farm size and idle time continued to be a preoccupation with Buck. But he had many recommendations to improve operations and many policy suggestions to create infrastructure relating to transport, credit, and education. Although the data in *Land Utilization* indicated slightly smaller incidence of tenancy than had *Chinese Farm Economy*, Buck acknowledged that tenancy problems were "of great importance in certain sections, and here a national policy must be developed to meet the needs of the farmers working the land". Without mentioning Sun Yat-sen, Buck cautiously endorsed the idea of "land to the tillers".[20] But he urged that "any attempt at major changes in agricultural economic organization such as collective farming or other large scale farming enterprises should for the present be undertaken only on an experimental basis and on a very limited scale." (p. 21) The basic problems remained those of population growth and low labor productivity.

Reviewing LU in the *New York Times*, geographer George Cressey (1938) stated "This is unquestionably the most detailed study ever made of any aspect of Chinese life." Its materials have become raw material utilized in most scholarly studies of China's agricultural economy, particularly the wealth of cross-sectional data in the statistical appendix. Over the period 1970–91, Buck's China writings received 168 citations in the scholarly journals surveyed for the *Social Science Citation Index*, most of them to LU.

Buck's research results, chiefly those in LU, have been utilized in four categories of scholarship on China's economy. The first involves simple descriptions: China's regions, soil and climate, farm size, patterns of production, and peasant living conditions. Examples are Pelzer (1941), Feuerwerker (1977), Buchanan (1970), Gray (1980), Hughes and Luard (1959), Donnithorne (1967), Bray (1984), Shen (1951), and Eckstein (1975). Second, Buck's data have been used in efforts to estimate China's total output of food and farm products. The pioneering studies of China's national income by Wu Baosan (1965) and by Liu and Yeh (1965; Liu, Twanmo, and Yeh 1964) relied heavily on Buck's data. In many such studies, comparison of pre-1949 and post-1949 conditions added elements of ideology and drama. Perkins (1969) took a rather skeptical view of Buck's data and relied primarily on other materials in estimating long-run growth trends in China's farm output.

The third major application of Buck's data involved such sensitive matters as tenancy, concentration of land ownership, and income distribution. Many commentators have seen the greatest flaw in China's traditional rural economy as the inequality and resulting exploitation of poor peasants by wealthy landowners, middlemen, and moneylenders. These views were being advanced during Buck's career by R. H. Tawney, Sun Yat-sen, Chen Hansheng, and many other writers. Buck's own data certainly did not paint a rosy picture of Chinese farm conditions. But they were criticized for sample bias which tended to overrepresent better-off farm families. Schran (1969) and Arrigo (1986) are monographic studies which focus strongly on the Buck data, and Hou (1979) compares Buck's tenancy estimates with a number of others. The lively controversies in this area were reviewed in Myers (1991), Martin (1991), and Fleischer and Liu (1992).

Items in the fourth category looked more overtly at the relevance of neo-classical economic analysis and the virtues and defects of free competitive markets for China, past and present. Wiens (1982), a dissertation written under Dwight Perkins, subjected the Buck data on inputs and outputs to elaborate scrutiny in determining competitive equilibrium values for prices of factors of production. Liang (1982) was a dissertation in geography which juxtaposed Buck's data on farm conditions in individual areas with data on railway development to assess the latter's impact. Other neo-classical studies dealing with Buck's data were Faure (1989) and Rawski (1989). The genre drew criticism in Huang (1990, 1991).

Demography, Money, Cooperatives, etc.

While Buck's surveys had their origins in issues relating to farm management and rural sociology, the chapter titles from LU reflect the broadening of his program to make major contributions to two subject areas extending well beyond traditional agricultural economics. The first of these was demography. Buck was unrelenting in dramatizing the underlying problem of China's overpopulation. He devoted a chapter to the subject in CFE. Qiao Qiming became Nanjing's resident expert on the subject.[21] Buck was able to bring a number of authorities to Nanjing to lecture and advise. He began with his wife's brother, Edgar Sydenstricker, director of research with the Milbank Memorial Fund (1930). Two of America's top demographers followed: Walter Willcox of Cornell (1930) and Warren Thompson (Scripps Foundation) October 1930–April 1931, and October 1934–April 1935. The data underlying the rather brief LU chapter on population by Notestein and Qiao were given an extensive reassessment in Barclay et al. (1976).[22]

The Nanjing program became heavily involved with analysis of money and prices in the 1930s. Ardron Lewis, who came to Nanjing in 1933, had been greatly influenced by the monetary theories of Cornell professors George Warren and Frank Pearson, who were credited with influencing President Roosevelt to devalue the dollar in 1933. In 1933 Lewis and Chang (Zhang) Luluan published a research bulletin blaming China's severe agricultural depression on the link between the Chinese monetary unit and silver. The Ministry of Industries responded by appointing in February 1934 a committee to study silver values and commodity prices, including Lewis, Zhang, and Buck. The committee's book-length report was largely drafted by Lewis.[23] The report was influential in persuading Finance Minister H. H. Kung to cut the Chinese yuan loose from silver and link it with the (then floating) British pound.

China's monetary situation was being harmed by the efforts of the U.S. government to raise the market price of silver. In 1934 Treasury Secretary Henry Morgenthau Jr. appointed Buck as a special adviser to the Treasury department on matters relating to silver. Buck spent several months in Washington, then continued in this advisory role after returning to China. He was technically on leave from teaching at Nanjing from late 1934 to early 1939, but continued work on drafting LU.[24] In the 1940s he frequently wrote on topics relating to money and prices in *Economic Facts*.

As noted, the Nanjing program was actively involved in promoting the development of cooperatives. Much of this effort focused on the town of Wujiang, where Nanjing had a multi-faceted extension program. When the area was badly damaged by flood in 1931, the University administered substantial flood relief money in the area and used the opportunity to expand cooperatives. These included an irrigation society formed in 1930 and 31 rural credit societies in 1931–32 (Buck 1973, pp. 51–52). In 1933 a cotton ginning and marketing cooperative enlisted over 400 members. It was oriented toward quality control and related to the production of improved cotton fiber. By 1934 the Wujiang program had been brought to the stage of comprehensive rural development, with attention to health and education as well as farm management.

In 1932 the CAF created a separate division of Rural Finance and Cooperation. Qiao Qiming, a major organizer of credit cooperatives, left CAF in 1940 to become general manager of the farm loan section of the Farmers Bank of China.[25]

By 1934 Nanjing staff members had promoted the formation of 50 cooperative societies with membership of 1,272 persons. A grant in 1933 from the Shanghai Commercial and Savings Bank supported two teaching positions and student scholarships relating to the study of cooperatives. The funds were used to bring in C. F. Strickland (who served a year in 1934–35), an Englishman with extensive experience with cooperatives in India, and W. Mackenzie Stevens (1934–36 and again in 1942), an expert in cooperative marketing. They were followed by Dr. Glenn Hedlund from Cornell (1936–37). Fang Xianting credited them with developing "the first more or less satisfactory class for the training of cooperative staff . . ." (Fong 1937, p. 137)

When the outbreak of war with Japan led to the transfer of the Nanjing program to Chengdu, a number of Nanjing staff became involved in the promotion of industrial cooperatives. Buck and sociologist Lewis Smythe became members of Indusco's International Committee.[26]

Graham Peck, an American journalist, visited Chengdu in 1942. While his impression of the Christian colleges at that time was rather negative, he reported that "the Nanking University School of Agriculture . . . was [regarded as] the only department of any mission college in Chengtu with a first-rate academic reputation." (Peck 1950, pp. 362–363) In 1940–41 enrollment in agricultural economics averaged 118 students, about one-fourth of the total enrollment in CAF (Buck 1973, p. 58).

Nanjing University, like the other Christian colleges, was closed by the

Communist authorities in 1951–52. The CAF program was merged with a similar program at near-neighbor National Central University to form Nanjing Agricultural University.

Reviewing his program many years later, Buck noted that between 1920 and 1945, 194 students received bachelor's degrees in agricultural economics from Nanjing. Master's degrees were authorized in 1935, and 17 of these had been awarded by 1945 (Buck 1970, pp. 178, 323). The department hired many of its graduates to aid in instruction. Virtually all the western teaching faculty were Cornell PhDs.

Buck's program generated a large flow of students to graduate study in agricultural economics in the West. Our files show 43 students going to the United States from this program.[27] Six received doctorates (four from Cornell).[28] Sixteen CAF graduates received master's degrees, eight of these from Cornell. Twenty-one were non-degree graduate students, of which twenty were sent in 1945–46 by the U.S. Department of Agriculture, twelve of them going to Wisconsin.

We have identified 42 Chinese faculty teaching agricultural economics in CAF.[29] Of 31 whose undergraduate backgrounds are identified, 27 were CAF graduates. Twenty-two of the 42 studied in the West (although 6 of these went abroad subsequent to their faculty service). Of the 22, nine attended Cornell and three went to Wisconsin in the special USDA program of 1945–46.[30]

Research and publication were stressed. Nanjing ranked first among the Christian colleges in the proportion of faculty publishing items on China's economy. An *Agricultural Index*, published by CAF in December 1933, identified some 30,000 Chinese language items and 6,000 English-language items in some 350 periodicals, covering the period 1858–1931.[31] Buck's program maintained close ties with the National Agricultural Research Bureau, created in Nanjing in 1933. Chang Hsin-yi (C. C. Chang—Zhang Xinyi), who joined CAF in 1927 after completing a master's degree at Cornell, also worked for NARB in pioneering estimates of crop output and acreage in China. Shen Hsien-yao (Xianyao) graduated from Buck's program in 1928, was recruited into the faculty, finished a master's degree at Cornell in 1938, then became head of the agricultural economics program in NARB.

Randall Stross (1986) published the most thorough description of Buck's Nanking career, but took a strongly sarcastic and condescending tone.[32] Stross misleadingly argued as if Buck's work dominated Chinese studies in agricultural economics. On the contrary, after the mid-1920s there was a flood of publications, particularly on issues relating to land tenure and rural income and wealth distribution (Chiu 1933; Fong 1935). Many of these were highly critical of the existing order.[33]

It is also misleading to portray Buck as a complacent supporter of the status quo. Although he was strongly anti-communist, his writings gave much attention to the poverty and injustice in rural China and the attendant dangers of violent upheaval. He had numerous recommendations for improvements through public policy, notably in the development of transportation, water control, credit, and education. But he rejected radical measures and recognized that neither debt nor tenancy was intrinsically bad. Experience since 1949 with both collectivization and "land to the tillers" has demonstrated that neither is a true remedy for overpopulation and low labor productivity. China's economy in the twentieth century is still struggling with the problems of finding non-farm employment for hundreds of millions of persons who are not really needed for farm production.

Buck's achievements were not limited to his research. He was an extremely effective institution builder. Former students and colleagues praised his leadership, noting that he treated his Chinese staff well and inspired them to good work.[34] They noted the large number of Nanjing graduates in agricultural economics who subsequently played important roles on the mainland and in Taiwan. Qiao Qiming became a dean at Taiyuan Agricultural University. Prominent in Taiwan were Yu Tsuo-yi (Zuoyi) and Qian (Chen) Shian, the latter at the Chinese Cultural University; several others went to Tunghai University in Taiwan. On the mainland, prominent Nanjing people included Yin Liangen (chair, agricultural economics, Beijing Agricultural University); Jiang Jie (chair, agricultural economics, Southwest Agricultural University); Wang Gangshen (chair, agricultural economics, Northwest Agricultural University); Yang Xishan (Dean, Management College, Jiaotong University); and professors Ding Zhugui and Ouyang Ping (Central China Agricultural College, Wuhan); Yang Jiaju (Shenyang Agricultural University); Xie Hu (Shanghai Agricultural Institute); Chen Dao (Beijing Agricultural University); Huang Yisun and Wang Youzhu (Southwest Agricultural University); Zhu Dianyu (Xinjiang August First Agricultural College); Sun Zuyin, Li Huiqian, and of course, Wang Xixian and Wang Yinyuan, all at Nanjing Agricultural University.[35] Buck himself noted several of his former students who came to work for FAO, including W. Y. Yang and Chang Chi-wen (Zhang Qiyun) (Buck 1962, pp. 48, 58).

10

Economics in Chinese Universities: Overview

Recognizable modern universities along western lines arose in China around 1900. A strong impetus came from China's defeat by Japan in 1894–95, bringing a renewed commitment to modernization. The first modern Chinese university established outside the missionary program was Beiyang ("North Sea") University. It began operations in Tianjin, China's third largest city, in 1895.

Although Beiyang was planned to stress science and technology, it also had a law school in which Economics was taught.[1] In 1895–1900, 183 students attended Beiyang. In 1916–17 the law program was transferred to Beida, and Beiyang became exclusively a technical school.[2]

A sister institution, Nanyang ("South Sea") University, opened in Shanghai in 1896. It was successively a teacher training institution and a school of economics and political science.[3] One of the first Economics instructors was Kojo Teikichi, a Japanese. In 1896, he published a Chinese version of the Japanese translation of Adam Smith's *The Wealth of Nations* (Reynolds 1993, p. 111). Then in 1902 Nanyang published Yan Fu's translation.

Nanyang employed probably the first social-science PhD to teach Economics in China. This was Clement Moore Lacey Sites, who completed a doctorate in political science at Columbia in 1899.[4] For his Economics course at Nanyang, Sites published in 1904 a 67-page English-language mini-textbook. In the first section he explained the roles of capital, labor, natural forces, and economic organization in the determination of production. The second section gave a simplified explanation of the determination of competitive price by the interaction of demand (based on marginal utility) and cost. The opening comments give us a view of his teaching technique:

> The plan of work that has been found most satisfactory is to take the latter part of a recitation period for developing the new topic. The text is presented and explained, and one or two illustrative examples are drawn out from the class. At the next lesson each student brings in a paper on which he has written, in his own words, the principles of the topic, with examples based on his own observation or previous knowledge. This hour is spent in criticising, reciting, comparing, and blackboard work on definitions, classification and outline. On the third day, the students bring in their notebooks in which the whole lesson has been rewritten in accordance with the corrections and suggestions made on the second day.
>
> The aim [of the text] is to furnish the student with the terminology of the subject and with accurate statements of essential notions, leaving explanations to be supplied by the teacher orally and examples to be elicited chiefly from the students themselves.[5]

If Sites followed this admirable model in the classroom, his approach was far removed from rote learning. And it represented a commitment to make the material relevant to China.

Another technical college opened in Tangshan in 1905, and established a branch in Peking in 1907. After numerous administrative changes, the Peking, Tangshan, and Shanghai institutions were combined as Jiaotong ("Communications") University under the Ministry of Railways.[6] They stressed scientific and technical study, but a program in railway management had a significant economic component and engaged some high-quality economists, including Ma Yinchu and Mai Chien-tseng (Jianzeng—Columbia PhD 1930).[7] In 1931 the program was expanded to a College of Administration, covering railways, finance, industry, and government. Beginning in 1929, Juwan Usang Ly (Li Zhaohuan), who was ABD in Economics at Penn, became president of Jiaotong, a position he held until 1949.

The Jiaotong catalogue for 1931–32 listed the following courses and textbooks for Economics:

Elementary Economics	Ely and Wicker, *Elementary Economics*
Principles	Seager, *Principles of Economics*
Econ. and Pol. Geography	Lecture notes
Co-operative Principles	Webb, *Industrial Co-operation*
History of Econ. Thought	Lecture notes
Economic Theories	Lee Kan, Selected Papers
Valuation	Vanderblue, *Railroad Valuation*

Land Economics	Ely and Morehouse, *Elements of Land Economics*

Related departments offered the following:

Money and Banking*	Holdsworth, *Money and Banking*
Domestic and For. Ex.*	Whitaker, *Foreign Exchange*
Public Finance	Hunter, *Outline of Public Finance*/lecture notes
Economic History	no listing
History of Railway Dev.*	Lecture notes

* Course descriptions explicitly specified China-related material.

Other courses (for which we lack details) included Economic Legislation, Railway Operating Economics, Labor Problems, Industrial History, Standard of Living, Program for Social Reorganization, Dynamic Economics, Current Economic Problems, Business Cycles, and Social Insurance (Jiaotong University, 1931–32, pp. 57–75, 126–132).

All of the textbooks just enumerated were from the United States. As noted in Chapter 6, Jiaotong furnished a large number of students who studied Economics in U.S. graduate schools, especially those studying transportation at the University of Pennsylvania. The 1931–32 Catalogue lists 26 faculty teaching Economics and related subjects (professors and lecturers). Of these, 24 had studied in the United States.

Early Universities

Beida

Peking University, ultimately to become China's pre-eminent university, opened in 1898 as part of the short-lived reform movement of that year. Because of disruptions accompanying the Boxer Rebellion, between 1903 and 1911 only about one thousand individual students attended, of whom about 300 completed a degree. In its early years, it was academically undistinguished and its students were often accused of misconduct.

All this changed when Cai Yuanpei became president in 1916. Conventional Economics was presented by dignitaries such as Ku (Gu) Mengyu, who had studied in Germany, and Ma Yinchu, whose Columbia doctorate was awarded in 1914. Economic topics were also discussed dramatically by such strong personalities as Chen Hansheng, Li Dazhao,

Liang Shuming, and L. K. Tao (Tao Menghe). These matters are described in detail in Chapter 12.

Fudan

After Aurora University opened in Shanghai in 1903, its chief benefactor, Ma Hsiang-po (Ma Liang) soon became dissatisfied with the authoritarian atmosphere. He led a schism in 1905 which took numerous students with him to a newly formed secular (and private) institution, Fudan University. Sparse enrollment and irregular operation were characteristic of its early years. There were only 62 graduates in 1912–21 (Hayhoe 1983, pp. 332–338). Most courses were taught in English with American textbooks. One of the first instructors in Economics was U.S.- and German-trained Hsueh Hsien-chou (Xue Xianzhou), who served as professor of German, Civics and Economics 1914–18. He left teaching to devote full attention to managing co-operative banks (Reynolds 1975, pp. 155–160; Lai Cheng-chung 1988).

Economics instruction at Fudan developed with the study of business administration. As late as 1926, the business school's only departments were banking and finance, industrial and business management, accounting, and international trade (Fudan University 1985, p. 350). Fudan established its Economics Department in 1930. The business-economics combination was exemplified by Li Chuan-shih (Quanshi), longtime professor and Dean of the School of Commerce from 1924. Li graduated from Beloit College, completed a master's degree at Chicago and a doctorate at Columbia, writing a dissertation on Chinese central and local finance. He was a prolific writer and produced a number of Chinese-language textbooks, particularly for elementary economics.[8] While at Fudan, Li also taught at several other universities, including Jiaotong, Suzhou, the Labor University, and the China Academy.[9] Li was a founder of the Chinese Economics Association and editor of its journal.

Li's economic analysis was marred by his belief that labor was "the determining force" of value. His scholarship was not highly respected among his peers, if this excerpt from a book review by Nankai's Yuan Wenbo is representative:

> To those who are familiar with Dr. Li's other works, it will not be a surprise to find that his *Contemporary Chinese Economic Thought* [1934] is like a second-hand bookstore where books of excellent quality are indiscriminately exposed for sale with the junk, which is selected . . . from the economic

> writings of Chinese merchants, politicians, propagandists, educators, etc., from the frivolous proposals of individuals and petty organizations, from government decrees on frugality, and from his own publications . . . Dr. Li lacks deplorably the sense of critical scholarship and fairness to his contemporaries, by giving undue weight to a number of frivolous writings, and by failing to give an original account of the main types of contemporary Chinese economic thought.[10]

The number of Economics majors graduating from Fudan each year is reported from 1930, when there were 9. In 1931 there were 27, but the total was between 10 and 20 annually in 1932–36 (Fudan University, 1985).

Qinghua, Nankai, and others

Qinghua College opened in 1911 with the purpose of preparing students for undergraduate study in the U.S. In 1926 it was transformed into a full-scale university. By the late 1920s Qinghua had one of the best Economics programs among Chinese universities (discussed in Chapter 13). It was also one staffed by a high proportion of American-trained economists.

When Nankai University was opened in 1919, the Economics program was heavily business-oriented, like that at Fudan. However, its orientation changed dramatically with the 1926 appointment of He Lian (Franklin Ho, PhD Yale) as department chair. Ho recruited his fellow Yale-PhD Fang Xianting, who became a prodigiously productive researcher (Trescott 2002). The Nankai program became very successful in obtaining grants from western sources to support Nankai research and Chinese-language textbooks aimed to "Chinafy" Economics. We examine the Nankai program in detail in Chapter 11.

In 1921, the government established the National Southeastern University in Nanking. It was built on the already-flourishing Government Teachers College (1915), and became the core of National Central University in 1927 (below). For a time, National Southeastern operated a commercial college in Shanghai in which Economics was taught. This last venture was initially shared with Chih-nan (Jinan) University, which had begun university-level programs in Nanjing in 1918, but moved to Shanghai. Jinan catered particularly to students from families of overseas Chinese (Chan and Dirlik 1991, pp. 144–145).

Beginning around 1920, "a group of professors who had left Russia founded the Harbin Law Faculty with Economical and Oriental sections, where Russian and Chinese youths of both sexes have received higher education in Economics and Law according to the regulations and syllabuses of the old Russian universities". The Chinese government took over in 1929. Harbin was essentially a Russian city, located in extreme northeast China, and swamped with Russian emigres fleeing the Revolution and civil war. Two of our "Chinese" students in the United States were from Harbin: Lazar Itzkovich and Andrei Grajdanzev.[11]

Zhongshan University

In Canton, the National Guangdong University (soon renamed National Sun Yatsen University, in Chinese "Zhongshan") was officially formed in 1924, absorbing the Guangdong Public Academy of Law and Politics, initiated in 1905. From 1912, the Academy had offered four-year courses in law and in political science and economics. The Economics Department reported only two graduating majors in 1926 and 1927, but then the numbers rapidly increased. A total of 215 students graduated in Economics in 1928–34.[12]

In 1931, Selskar Gunn of the Rockefeller Foundation visited Zhongshan and reported:

> I had an interview with Dr. Lo, an economist in the law faculty. He stated that there were eighteen men teaching economics and said they were all full-time. However, there was no evidence of research work. Dr. Lo said there was no money for research and if they had money there would be no data to work on. Apparently a lot of writing of textbooks in Chinese is in progress.[13]

Perhaps in response, the University established in 1931 a Bureau of Economic Research "entrusted with the work of investigating into the nature, structure, functions and evolution of Chinese economic societies".[14] They produced a series of research monographs in the ensuing years. By 1935, Robert Haas, visiting on behalf of the League of Nations, was very impressed with Zhongshan, particularly with the School of Agriculture.[15]

The Situation in the Mid-1920s

The *China Year Book* for 1925 published the available data on major Chinese universities, their faculty and enrollments. Some of these are shown in Table 10-1. The Table also incorporates information from Kuno 1928.

Table 10-1. Principal Chinese Universities Operating in 1923–1926

Name	Location	Type	Opened	Students	Faculty
Amoy University	Amoy	P	1921	435 (1931)	104
August Comte College	Peking	P	1917	(100)	n
Chaoyang University	Peking	P	1913	n	n
Chengdu University	Chengdu		1923 (K)	n	n
Chih-Tze University	Shanghai	P	1924	n	n
China Institute	Woosung	P	1922 (K)	n	n
China University	Peking	P	1912	n	n
Fudan University	Shanghai	P	1905	n	n
Great China University	Shanghai	P	1924	1,160 (1931)	151
Hebei University	Baoding	Pr	1921	390	39
Hunan University	Changsha	Pr	1926 (K)	n	n
Jiaotong University	Shanghai	N	1897	455	29
Jinan University	Shanghai	N	1919	623 (1928)	n
Nankai University	Tianjin	P	1919	350	31
Nat. Zhongshan	Guangzhou	N	1912	1,469 (1927)	n
Nat. Northeastern	Shenyang	N	1923 (K)	n	n
Nat. Southeastern	Nanjing	N	1915	2,671 (1923)	185
Nat. Peking University	Peking	N	1899	1,920	199
Northwestern Univ.	Xian	N	1924	300 (1923)	38
Peking Fah-chien	Peking	N	1923 (K)	n	n
People's College	Shanghai	P	1922–3	375	n
Shanghai Coll Law&PS	Shanghai	P	1924	n	n
Ta-tung ("Utopia") Univ.	Shanghai	P	1912	227 (1931)	52
Qinghua University	Peking	*	1911	252	51
Subtotal of 9 schools with data for 1923–24:				7,067	
Guess of other 9 excluding K:				5,591	
Approximate total (18)				12,658	
15 Christian colleges				3,714	645
5 Agricultural colleges				984	280
6 Technical colleges				1,634	220
2 Medical colleges				484	141
3 Teachers colleges				1,579	276

N: National P: Private Pr: Provincial

* Boxer Indemnity

Sources: *China Year Book* 1925, pp. 252–253; 1929, p. 529; "General Condition of All the Universities of the Country, 1931" (mimeo), in Archives of the United Board for Christian Higher Education in Asia, RG 51, Box 309, Folder 4762, library of YDS; Kuno 1928, pp. 47–49 (source for K items).

A survey of Chinese education in 1923 estimated there were 35 universities in operation, with a total of about 13,000 students. Because schools were constantly reorganizing, it is difficult to interpret or disaggregate these data.[16] Our rough approximations in Table 10-1 identify 33 universities, including the 15 missionary colleges. The 18 non-missionary schools alone account for about 13,000 students.

Considering the vast size of China's population (some 400 million), the true university population by 1923–24 was still very small. Its growth was constrained by the very meager development of primary and secondary education in China, combined with the extreme difficulty to learn the Chinese written language and apply it to western concepts.

The missionary colleges clearly played a relatively large role during this initial period. Enrollment estimates are shown in Table 10-2.

Table 10-2. Enrollment in Missionary and Other Chinese Universities, 1909, 1917, 1923, 1924, 1934

Year	Missionary	Others	Total	Missionary %
1909	667	749	1,416	47
1917	1,503	3,511	5,014	30
1923	3,262	13,098	16,360	20
1924	3,714	12,658	16,372	23 (from Table 10-1)
1934	4,629	23,126	27,755	17

Sources: Protestant colleges from Cressey 1928, pp. 26–27, minus theology and medicine; added Aurora enrollment of 117 (1909), 203 (1917) and 200 (1923). Catholic total for 1924 is one third of total enrollment, based on Li 1954, pp. 62, 67. Non-missionary totals from Hayhoe 1996, pp. 42, 47. Cameron 1931 gives 549 for 1909 (pp. 85–86). People's College data estimated from Yeh 1990, p. 145. All 1934 data are from Yeh (1990) citing Ministry of Education, pp. 282–283; many schools are omitted but proportions may be representative.

In the decade 1898–1908, missionary colleges probably accounted for about half of the university-level students. In the next decade the proportion was nearly one third, and by 1923, at least one fifth. During the 1930s, the missionary share was about 15 percent.

University Districts

An abortive attempt to centralize government control of the educational system after 1927 led to the creation of three "university districts", each with a comprehensive public university. From this emerged National Central University (NCU) in Nanjing, the new national capital. NCU absorbed and reorganized the former National Southeastern University and some other institutions in Nanjing. From the beginning, it was closely linked with the national administration and the Kuomintang (Hayhoe 1987, pp. 116–117; Chan and Dirlik 1991, pp. 227–230). It became immediately one of the largest and best-financed universities in China, reporting 2,146 students in 1931.[17] Many government officials taught at NCU.[18]

Tung Kuan-hsien (Dong Guanxian) became professor and dean of Economics at NCU in 1933, where he taught until 1943. He had studied in Japan, received a master's degree from Columbia, and did research in Berlin, London (LSE), Paris, and Brussels. He became a member of the central government's Control Yuan in 1936, a member of the People's Political Council in 1941, and supervisory commissioner of the Control Yuan for Shansi-Shensi area in 1944.[19] Ye Yuanlong was a member of the National Southeastern faculty who subsequently served as Economics Chair and Dean at NCU. Ye had done graduate work in Economics at Wisconsin and LSE in the early 1920s. He published a history of western economic thought in 1933 and was described as "a well-known Marshallian" by Yuan Wenbo in 1935. He was a member of the government committee on personnel selection and education. Subsequently he became education commissioner for Anhui and, later, Guizhou provinces.[20] Chao (Zhao) Lanping was another prominent NCU professor. Zhao had studied in Japan; he published two widely-used textbooks on economic principles (Hu Jichuang 1982).

The new government also created the Central Political Institute (CPI), a Nanjing-based KMT party school training people for government work. An important sub-unit was the Land Administration College, headed by German-trained Xiao Zheng and focused on the land proposals of Sun Yat-sen.

In Table 10-5 below, we note that about two-thirds of the Economics faculty members at NCU and CPI had studied abroad. More than half of these had studied in Europe, with a large German representation. And important members had studied in Japan.

The second university district produced a new National Zhejiang University in Hangzhou, combining several pre-existing institutions. It reported 614 students and 286 faculty in 1931. Although this school engaged some distinguished economists, notably Ma Yinchu, it never became very large.

The third district was to be located in Peking (renamed Peiping in 1928). While historic Peking University retained both its autonomy and its name, there emerged a newly-created Peiping University, a combination of other Peiping institutions, including a business school which subsequently engaged numerous economists. Peiping University also absorbed the Peking College of Agriculture, which was headed in 1928–33 by Dong Shijin.[21] Dong had received his PhD from Cornell in 1924 and published in 1933 a well-regarded textbook in agricultural economics. He subsequently headed agricultural colleges in Jiangxi and Sichuan provinces.[22] Peiping University reported 2,152 students by 1931 and remained one of the largest universities, though of very uneven quality.

Wuhan

National Wuhan University was established in 1927, absorbing the previous Wuchang Normal College. Its program in Economics was (and still is) well-regarded. In the 1930s it was noteworthy for having a core of British-trained economists.[23] The university reported 571 students in 1931.[24] Among the leading economists was Yang Tuan-lu (Duanliu), credited with introducing index numbers into China. After lengthy study in Japan and at LSE, he worked several years for the Commercial Press and briefly headed the social science institute under Academia Sinica. He joined Wuhan in 1930 and remained until his death in 1966. The 1936 catalogue listing for his course in monetary economics included an impressive supplementary reading list including items by Irving Fisher, Gustav Cassel, and J. M. Keynes. He also assigned the major western writings on China's monetary system.[25] Also at Wuhan was Liu Binglin, who had studied at LSE and Berlin in the early 1920s. His textbook *Economics*, initially published in 1925, went through at least ten editions and was widely used.[26] A distinguished graduate was Pan Yuan-lai (Yuanlai), who taught at Wuhan for five years after graduating in 1930. In 1935 he went off to LSE. After his return, he taught at National Northeastern University 1938–49.[27]

The Wuhan catalogues for 1933 and 1936 listed 29 western textbooks for seven Economics courses. Of these 29, 14 were British, 11 American, 3 German, and 1 French.

The Labor University

One of China's most unusual experiments in higher education was the

Labor University ("Laoda"), which opened in Shanghai in September, 1927. It was in some degree a successor to the short-lived Communist-dominated People's College of Shanghai (1922–27).[28]

The Labor University was largely the work of people dedicated to non-violent pursuit of philosophical anarchism through education. The university developed a number of factories and experimental farms in which the students and others participated. In explicating the school's purpose in 1930, Cai Yuanpei, a major supporter, remarked that:

> Since China began to adopt the education systems of foreign countries, there has been many a special school of agriculture or industry, or industrial and agricultural departments in universities. Such schools were originally intended to combine learning with practice; but once in China, their nature changed. Those who attended them wanted just to read books without any practice, and quickly became learned gentlemen. The children of peasants who went to school returned home to look down on their parents; the same with workers. (Quoted Chan and Dirlik 1991, p. 60.)

Economics was an important field of study. In 1929, when Laoda had 289 students, a Department of Economics was formed, which by spring 1930 had enrolled 93 students (Chan and Dirlik 1991, pp. 77, 281). The university offered courses in history of socialism, history of international labor movement, Chinese social problems, social insurance, labor legislation, and unemployment economics. But most of the Economics courses were similar to those in more conventional universities (ibid., pp. 84–95). All students were required to participate in an annual social survey, involving "investigative research on labor conditions and labor enterprises in China . . ."[29] Like most Shanghai universities, the Labor University relied extensively on part-time teachers, persons holding positions with other universities, government, or business. Several Laoda economists were attached to Fudan: Li Quanshi (discussed above), Sun Han-ping (Hanbing—MBA Washington State), Tang Ching-tseng (Qingzeng—MA Harvard), and Chu Tung-chiu (Zhu Tongjiu—MBA University of Washington). Tso (Zhu) Shikang (Sheldon Tso—PhD Indiana) also taught at Jiaotong and held various government positions. Wan Chung-hsin (Zhongxin), Chang (Zhang) Yunfu, and Zhu Tongjiu taught at Jinan.[30] The francophone emphasis was reflected in the presence of Teng Han-chung (Deng Hanzhong), Chang Yuan-ju (Zhang Yuanruo), and Chen Luzhen, all of whom had studied in Paris, and Koung Shien-ming (Gong Xianming), whose doctorate was from French-speaking Louvain (Belgium) (Chan and Dirlik, pp. 136–144).

Caught in the political turbulence of the early 1930s, Laoda was forced to close in 1932. Among its distinguished alumni were two leftist economists, Feng Hefa and Hsu Ti-hsin (Xu Dixin) (ibid., pp. 156–157).

Also in Shanghai was China Academy, "founded in 1905 by Chinese students who withdrew from Japanese universities and returned to China to protest both Japanese discrimination against Chinese students and Japanese aggression in China" (ibid., p. 150). Shanghai gained a new private university in 1924 with the creation of Ta-hsia (Daxia—"Great China") University. It arose from a schism within fledgling Amoy University (started 1921 in Fuzhou—Yeh 1990, p. 103). Both schools drew from the same pool of commuter faculty which served Fudan and Laoda.

University Conditions around 1930

A useful perspective on Chinese university conditions was furnished in Yoshi Kuno (1928), a study prepared to assist American universities in evaluating the qualifications of Chinese applicants (pp. 56–64). He gave top rankings to Beida, Jiaotong, Nanjing, National Central, Qinghua, and Yanjing. Of the 13 principal schools in the next class, eight were Christian colleges. The other five were Zhongshan, Fudan, Nankai, Peking Fah-chien (Fahjian), and Peking Normal. Lower ranks included 5 Christian colleges and 30 others. Kuno also attempted to guide readers through the vast welter of consolidations and name changes. His data identify 39 relatively reputable universities and an additional 47 of dubious repute. This testifies to the rapid proliferation of institutions in the late 1920s.

According to official estimates, the number of students in colleges and universities was roughly 29,000 in 1930, three-fifths of them located in Shanghai or Peking. The student total increased only slowly in the 1930s, reaching 31,000 by 1937.[31]

In 1931 the League of Nations sent an education mission of four experts (one of them R. H. Tawney of LSE) who reported their impressions from a three-months' visit. They deplored the widespread imitation of American educational practice. In university instruction, they criticized the heavy reliance on lectures, western-language textbooks, and "materials and illustrations drawn principally from countries other than China".[32]

Selskar Gunn of the Rockefeller Foundation, who visited China also in 1931, also reached unflattering conclusions. "It is dubious," he remarked, "if the time has yet come when the National Universities can develop research work in the Social Sciences. [Their difficulties include] inadequate funds, political interference, and insubordination of the students." Gunn felt that "the best centers for research in the Social Sciences seem to be Nankai, Yenching and Nanking Universities" (Gunn 1931, p. 17). On a return visit in 1932, Gunn recorded the following remarks by L. K. Tao:

> Teaching of s[ocial] s[ciences] in the National and provincial universities is very poor. The instruction is all lectures and essentially concerned with theory and western problems. There are some pretty good men at Peita [Beida], TsingHua and WuHan . . . Undoubtedly Nankai is best institution in China for the ss.[33]

There is no doubt that Chinese students of Economics were often assigned western textbooks and given information about western economic conditions. Within limits, this could be defended on two grounds:

First, economic theory attempted to formulate *principles* which would be valid under many possible social and political conditions. Economic resources are always scarce and always have alternative uses. Free competitive markets are one way to allocate scarce resources effectively. Market-based incomes reflect productivity and relative supplies of land, labor and capital. Societies which neglect the basic truths of mainstream economics suffer serious adverse consequences, as the regimes of Stalin and Mao Zedong amply demonstrated.

Second, Chinese students studied the economic *policies* of western countries to get a better idea of what China ought to do. What was culture-bound, however, was the implicit assumption that the Chinese government could do the things which western governments were doing.[34]

Chinese universities embodied some deep-seated Chinese traditions. One of these was rote learning, required by the nature of the Chinese language and reinforced by the tradition of the civil-service examinations. Another was the role-playing associated with the student and scholar. Education remained a means to qualify for government employment. Despite the efforts of John Lossing Buck and Liang Shuming, China had no counterpart of the American land-grant college, located in a small town, educating children from farm families in agriculture, engineering, and home economics.

However, there were numerous efforts to incorporate China-related materials into the teaching of Economics, already documented for the Christian colleges. Nankai University staff prepared Chinese-language Economics textbooks with significant China emphasis. Even before 1927, Beida offered history of Chinese economy (Li Shiheng) and history of

Chinese finance (Luo Ding). In 1934 Great China offered history of Chinese economic thought, economic problems in China, Chinese economic history, and China's fiscal problems. Their course in agricultural economics was "based on the economic situation in China", while courses in public finance and money and banking promised China-related materials (Da-hsia University 1935). National Wuhan University (1936) listed history of Chinese economy (Li Chien-nung, Jiannong) and modern Chinese finance (Liu Binglin). Similarly, National Zhongshan University (1935) listed Chinese monetary theory and history of Chinese economy. Sichuan University (1936) reported history of Chinese finance, taught by Chen Shaowu. They also offered history of Chinese economy. Jiaotong in 1935 offered history of railway development in Asia. Their course descriptions promised China-related content for money and banking and for domestic and foreign exchange (Jiaotong University 1935, pp. 128–132). Fudan (1937) listed courses in history of Chinese economic thought, history of Chinese public finance, China's fiscal problems, China's tariff, and China's finance.

With the exception of Qinghua, the non-missionary Chinese universities experienced chronic financial stringency. Uncertainty about being paid was a common excuse for multiple job-holding. Government universities were notoriously subject to political intervention. Anyone suspected of Communist involvement could be dismissed or persecuted. An extreme case was the summary execution of Li Dazhao by the Peking warlord government in 1927. Journalist Edgar Snow and his wife Helen were very close to the student activists in the mid-1930s. She reported: "Li Ta, prof. of Economics at Chungkuo [China University] was dismissed for Marxist views; students demanded return; he's back now [1935]. Chen Chi-hsu, professor of economics Peita, dismissed 1934, dismissed for Marxist views, but was 'no good Marxist.' Lin Ting-yu, Chungkuo, Economics Dept., also for his views." (Snow 1961, p. 196) The Snows were particularly critical of Professor Chou (Zhou) Ping-lin of the Beida Economics Department, whom they labeled a "Fascist" eager to persecute radicals among students and faculty (pp. 93–95).

The KMT was militantly anti-Communist but not anti-socialist, in view of their dedication to the socialistic proposals of Sun Yat-sen. So it is not surprising that in the mid-1930s we find courses entitled "Socialism" or something similar listed by Great China (1934), Szechuan (1936), Fudan (1937), Wuhan (1936), and Beida (1935). Jiaotong's 1936 course in economic systems dealt with socialism and communism. Beida also offered

"Research on Marx's Theory", taught by Chen Chi-hsiu (Qixiu) in 1933 and Chin Tsan (Qin Zan) in 1935. Zhongshan and Sichuan offered "Social Problems and Social Policy"; Jiaotong listed "Program for Social Reorganization" (1931), and Qinghua offered "Economic Policy and Strategy for Social Reform" (1935), taught by Xiao Chu. We have already denoted the frequency of similar courses in the Christian colleges.

Despite—or in response to—the criticisms of Chinese universities, the output of research on China's economy expanded rapidly between 1927 and 1937. We examine this product and its producers in Chapter 14.

We noted in Chapters 4 and 5 that most Chinese who studied Economics in the West did not receive a heavy dose of sophisticated and mathematized microeconomic theory in their western studies. If anything, Chinese universities (Christian and other) gave even less attention to theory, at least until the 1940s. One might have expected more of this at Jiaotong, with its engineering orientation. But their course in engineering economics was based on a 1923 American textbook by John C. L. Fish, which gave only a rambling treatment of managerial economics. Emphasis was on estimating costs and revenues. Despite references to Fisher and Marshall, the book presented no marginal analysis, no calculus, and no systematic development of present value or internal rate of return.

Impact of the Japanese War

The outbreak of open war with Japan in 1937 disrupted China's universities severely. The principal universities moved their operations west, outside the areas of Japanese occupation. Thousands of students and faculty migrated, many on foot, to the interior to remain with their institutions (Fenn 1940). Nankai, Qinghua, and Beida ultimately gravitated to Kunming, in the far southerly Yunnan Province, where they operated as Southwest Associated Universities ("Lianda"). Despite the adversities, John Israel (1983) was able to argue that Lianda was "where liberal education in China reached its pinnacle".[35] The pragmatic side of Lianda was reflected in the fact that "close to a third [of the students] graduated in economics" (p. 93). Lianda is discussed further in the chapters on its constituent universities.

Some universities continued to operate in the Japanese-controlled areas, even after 1941. In Peking, Furen University presented itself as German-controlled. China University continued to operate. There was a Japanese-controlled Peking University (Fu 1993, p. 97). In Tianjin, an interesting relict of the Nankai Institute of Economics was the Adam Smith Institute.

It was directed by Yuan Wenbo of Nankai. The puppet government which administered Japanese-occupied territory boasted in 1944 that "some 17 private colleges and universities have been restored or are under restoration . . .", most notably St. John's. Approved government institutions included a sanitized Peking University, National Central, and Shanghai University.[36] But clearly the Japanese did not encourage higher education for Chinese (Fenn, p. 18).

New universities were created by the Chinese national government. National Chung-cheng (Chiang Kai-shek) University opened in Nanchang. From 1944 to 1949 it was headed by Xiao Chu, who was ABD in Economics at Harvard in the early 1920s and had taught at Nankai and Qinghua.[37]

Not surprisingly, the wartime disturbances had an adverse effect on educational quality.[38] The rampant inflation greatly reduced the purchasing power of faculty salaries. The government provided financial support for many students, but at a level which left many of them seriously undernourished. The war did bring higher education into many regions where it had been lacking. And the total number of students in higher education increased from about 42,000 in 1936 to 79,000 in 1944.[39] But publication of research about China's economy was drastically reduced.

Controls and Guidelines

Beginning in 1938, the national Ministry of Education, working with numerous academic advisers, developed a number of guidelines for universities. These included identifying required courses (within each major field and across fields), preparing syllabi for some required courses, and sponsoring the preparation of Chinese-language textbooks. These guidelines were optional for individual universities.

In 1939 the suggested list of required courses for Economics was presented.[40] They were as follows:

[Elementary] Economics
Accounting
Statistics
Banking and Monetary Theory
Economic Geography
History of Western Economy
Finance Theory and Policy
International Trade and Finance

History of Chinese Economy
Economic Policy
History of Economic Thought

The list does not differ much from what an American university might have required. However, the American school would probably have required at least one course in intermediate microeconomic theory (while probably omitting economic geography).

The course list was assembled by seven economists (Sun 1987, p. 321). It is worth examining their credentials, since they were among those most highly esteemed (at least among the politically correct).[41] They are shown in Table 10-3.

Table 10-3. Compilers of Suggested Courses in Economics, 1938

Name	Foreign study	Faculty positions	1942?	Gov.?
Zhao Lanping	Japan	CPI, NCU, Nanjing, Jinan	yes	
Chen Changheng	U.S.: GS Harvard	(prob. NCU, CPI)	no	yes
Chen Daisun	U.S.: PhD Harvard	Qinghua, SWAU	yes	no
Zhu Xie	Ger: doc. Berlin	NCU, CPI	no	yes
Fang Xianting	U.S.: PhD Yale	Nankai, SWAU	no	later
Pi Zongshi		Beida, Wuhan	no	
Yang Duanliu	Japan, GB (LSE)	Wuhan	no	yes

1942? indicates whether the individual was included in the 1942 roster of certified professors.

All but one had studied overseas, three in the U.S., two in Japan, one in Germany, and one in Britain. Three had doctorates. Three were associated with the politically favored universities in Nanjing/Chongqing. At least three held government positions.

In 1940 the Ministry issued regulations providing for the certification of college faculty members. Faculty who achieved certification gained access to reappointment, sabbatical leave, and research grants. Faculty ranks consisted of professor, associate professor, instructor, and teaching assistant. The regulations indicated the qualifications in terms of education, teaching effectiveness, publications and length of service (Ou 1977, p. 110).

In 1942 the Ministry published lists of faculty certified to that date. There were 101 professors and other teachers of Economics, representing 40 different institutions. There were nine from National Central and ten from the Central Political Institute, both of which were close to the national government and to the KMT. The Southwest Associated Universities (Beida, Qinghua, Nankai) recorded only six. The Christian colleges placed ten on the list, from six schools. So the sample was not a large proportion of Economics faculty—perhaps one-fifth. And the institutional coverage was far from random.[42]

Nevertheless, it is instructive to look at the foreign study reported by the 101 respondents. Table 10-4 reports their foreign study, cross-classified by age groups.

Table 10-4. Certified Economics Faculty 1942: Age and Foreign Study

Age	U.S.	Britain	France	Germany	Japan	Others	No For.	Total
20–29	0	0	0	0	0	0	5	5
30–34	3	2	0	0	2	0	3	10
35–39	7	5	5	2	6	3	2	30
40–44	12	3	5	2	3	2	8	35
45–49	5	1	1	4	4	0	0	15
50+	7	1	1	1	1	0	1	12
Not id.	1	0	0	0	0	0	0	1
Total	35	12	12	9	16	5*	19	108
(–) Duplicates								–7
Net total								101

* Includes 3 Swiss, 1 Philippines, 1 USSR.
Source: Ministry of Education 1942.

About one-third of the certified faculty had studied in the United States, and nearly two-fifths in Europe. The latter seems too large to be representative of Chinese Economics faculty in general. It is striking that the five youngest faculty reported no foreign study, while of the 27 faculty aged 45 and over, all but one had studied abroad. One-sixth of those reporting had studied in Japan.

More Faculty Analysis

In Chapter 6 we briefly examined the foreign-study experiences of Chinese Economics faculty. Here we look more closely at four universities discussed in this chapter: Jiaotong, Fudan, Central Political Institute, and National Central. Table 10-5 gives the same categories used in Table 6-1.

Table 10-5. Foreign Study by Economics Professors in Four Major Chinese Universities before 1950

	Jiaotong	Fudan	CPI	NCU	Pooled
U.S. Graduate Economics	36	25	12	28	81
PhD	12	6	4	11	26
ABD	5	1	0	0	6
MA	12	9	2	6	27
GS	7	9	6	11	22
U.S. later	3	1	0	0	4
Other U.S.	14	2	2	3	19
Total U.S.	53	27	14	31	104
G.B. & W. Europe					
Britain	1	14	3	14	27
France	1	5	5	7	14
Germany	5	7	7	10	20
Others	0	1	2	1	3
Later	2	0	0	0	2
Net W. Europe	9	20	14	28	53
USSR	0	1	0	0	1
Japan	0	7	6	3	13
(–) Duplicates	–1	–7	–7	–4	–17
Net western*	57	47	27	57	148
% Western	86	52	59	70	62
No foreign study	5	37	13	24	72
Total	66	91	46	81	237

* Excludes "later": foreign study after faculty service.
Sources: See Appendix.

Because many of the faculty taught in more than one of these institutions, there are 237 separate individuals represented. They constitute about one fourth of our ALLFAC category in Table 6-1, and more than one third of the CHINFAC component.[43] CPI and NCU were in Nanjing and shared quite a few professors, many of whom also held government positions. Both Fudan and Jiaotong were located in Shanghai, but Fudan's emphasis was on business, while Jiaotong was a highly technical engineering school closely linked with the railway sector.

Jiaotong's faculty composition was unusual. Almost all of the reported faculty had studied overseas, 80 percent in the United States (though many of these were outside graduate Economics). Fudan had the lowest western-study component of the four. The two Nanjing institutions combined recorded about two-thirds of their Economics faculty with western study, evenly divided between European-trained and American-trained professors. Britain and Germany were strongly represented, as they were also at Fudan. Only seven percent reported study in Japan, none at Jiaotong.

Despite the dislocations and hardships of the war with Japan, the Chinese universities expanded their enrollments and faculties. Standards for admission and retention were less stringent than before the War. By 1945 there were 141 institutions of higher learning, with about 83,000 students (Hayhoe 1996, p. 56).

In January 1942, the U.S. State Department created a China program within its Department of Cultural Relations. Some of its activities aided Economics programs in Chinese universities. The program sent microfilm copies of American professional journals and other materials. The two microfilm machines at National Central University were in constant use. "Nearly all the persons using the projectors were faculty members . . . Studies on post-war planning have been most in demand." The program also arranged for printing in China, and free distribution to students, of textbooks, including the widely used principles text of Fairchild, Furniss, and Buck.[44]

Post-war Chaos

With the end of the war in mid-1945, most of the universities made arrangements to return to their previous locations, where physical facilities and libraries had often been destroyed. By 1947 the number of institutions of higher education had grown to 207, with 155,000 students (Hayhoe 1996, p. 56). The 16 missionary universities, with about 16,000 students, now represented slightly over ten percent (Li 1954, pp. xii–xvii).

Economic and financial conditions remained chaotic. Wartime inflation gave way to post-war hyperinflation. Real incomes of university faculty remained low, and multiple jobs continued to be a necessity for survival. War with Japan gave way to civil war between KMT and Communists, with violence particularly concentrated in Manchuria. The Communists sponsored new universities in the areas they controlled. Noteworthy was the United University of Northern China, the nominal precursor of People's University. University life was frequently disrupted with protest demonstrations against the political and ideological repression and inflationary policies of the KMT government.

In the spring of 1947, Roger Evans of the Rockefeller Foundation made a reconnaissance of Chinese universities, looking for people worthy of financial support. Evans judged Peking University to have the best Economics department in China (p. 63). In his opinion, "Shanghai's leading universities are St. Johns, U of Sha[ngha]i, Fuhtan and Aurora [Jesuit] none first class." (p. 12) He noted the success of National Central University in developing research in scientific fields, but felt that social sciences were not well developed (p. 88).

Textbook Authors

In his landmark 1982 review, Hu Jichuang identified 35 Chinese authors of Economics textbooks or related writings. Of these, 15 appear in our listings as having studied in the West. Of these, seven studied in the United States, eight in Britain, and three in Germany (three studied in two countries). All 15 also appear in our listings as teaching Economics in Chinese universities. Of the remaining 20, three had studied in Japan; those three held university positions. Of the remaining 17, only four were faculty and one held government positions.[45] The Beida catalogue for 1933 lists 13 authors of assigned Chinese-language texts. Of these, four studied Economics in the West, two had western business degrees, and one studied in Japan. Six were unidentified.

Visiting Westerners

Unlike the missionary colleges, the indigenous Chinese universities did not normally engage westerners to teach economic subjects. Besides Sites at Nanyang, the Germans Friedrich Otte and E. Erde were on the early Beida faculty. At Qinghua, Economics began with an American, Clarence Dittmer. In the early 1930s, John K. Fairbank, on his way to prominence as a sinologist, taught economic history at Qinghua, using notes borrowed from Yanjing's Harry Price.

About the same time, there was a brief and ill-documented experiment with an American-run college in Peking. This was California College in China, conducted in collaboration with the College of Chinese Studies.[46] In 1933–34 Dr. Arthur Coons of Occidental College spent a year there teaching Economics. Coons had received his doctorate from Penn in 1927 with a dissertation on foreign loans to the Chinese government.[47] We also know that universities were established in the communist-dominated areas of Northeast China during the civil-war period, including the putative predecessors of People's University.

Otto van der Sprenkel, who studied and taught at LSE, came to Nankai in 1948 as a visiting professor attached to the Institute of Economic Research. He observed directly the change-over when the Communists came to power in 1949 (van der Sprenkel 1951).

Summary

As the twentieth century opened, China began to establish recognizable universities along western lines. It took another twenty years before Economics had emerged as an academic specialty. From that time on, however, the field attracted a large proportion of students. The indigenous Chinese universities relied heavily on western-educated Chinese to teach Economics. More precise information on this topic is presented in the chapters on Beida, Nankai, and Qinghua, and in the concluding chapter. Similarly, the Chinese universities relied heavily on western textbooks, although the proportion of Chinese-language works increased steadily.

Nankai was the only indigenous university which consistently stressed research by faculty. However, Chinese professors published a lot. Much of their writing was not exactly research in the western sense but it provided useful commentary on current events and popularized renditions of economic ideas.

The Chinese universities inherited a tradition emphasizing rote learning. Chinese professors tended to see economic analysis as a set of free-standing Great Truths rather than as a set of tools. And a great majority of Chinese economists seem to have accepted rather uncritically the utility of a large role for the national government in owning and managing industry and other economic activities.

Our roster of Economics faculty identifies teachers at 99 non-missionary schools, and identifies students from 36 of these who studied Economics in the West. Table 10-6 identifies the schools with the largest numbers of these.

There was a rough correspondence between the number of faculty identified for each school and the number of students studying in the West, but it was far from perfect. None of the schools not recorded on the list sent more than seven students to the West.

All the universities we have described had a lot of western-educated faculty. The preponderance of U.S. backgrounds was particularly pronounced at Jiaotong, Nankai, and Qinghua. The German-Japanese

Table 10-6. Major Chinese Universities: Number of Faculty and Students in our Listings

University	City	Economics Faculty#	Econ. Students to West	1934 Enrollment
Fudan	Shanghai	91	36	1,364
Nankai*	Tianjin	88	53	406
Beida*	Peking	82	78	1,001
National Central	Nanjing	81	54	932
Jiaotong	**	66	45	687***
Qinghua*	Peking	47	55	1,141
Cent. Pol. Institute	Nanjing	46	15	n.d.
Zhongshan	Guangzhou	45	13	2,284
Jinan	Shanghai	38	14	434
National Wuhan	Wuhan	27	22	563

* Faculty (8) and students (27) at Southwest Associated Universities were prorated.
** Includes Shanghai, Peking, and Tangshan.
*** Shanghai only.
# Includes foreign nationals.
Sources: See Chapter 6. Enrollment data are from Yeh 1990, pp. 282–283.

influence was most substantial at Zhongshan, National Central, and Central Political—schools very close to the government and to the KMT. British influence was most evident at Wuhan.

To assess the level of scholarship of the Chinese universities, we have assembled a file of about 2,600 names of Chinese authors of publications about China's economy published in the period ending in 1950.[48] Table 10-7 shows the number and proportion of authors among the Chinese economics faculty of the principal universities shown in Table 10-6.

The data in Table 10-7 confirm the emphasis given by Nankai to research and publication. The KMT favorites, National Central and Central Political, also scored very high. Across our total listing of Economics faculty in the Chinese universities, there were 182 authors out of 656 faculty, a 28 percent showing. Considering that many faculty were part-time, holding positions in government or in business, the proportion of authors is quite impressive. One should add that many publication outlets are not covered—*Ta Kung Pao* newspaper, for example. And of course many Chinese economists published studies of topics other than China's economy.

Table 10-7. University Faculty who Published Materials on China's Economy, 1910–1950

University	Number of Chinese Economics Faculty	Number of Authors	%
Nankai	84	37	44
National Central	81	34	42
Central Political Institute	46	19	41
Qinghua	45	16	36
Beida	76	25	33
Jinan	38	12	32
Zhongshan	45	14	31
Fudan	91	25	27
Wuhan	27	7	26
Jiaotong	64	15	23
All Chinese universities	656	182	28

Christian colleges were tabulated separately; see Chapter 7.
Sources: See Appendix; Chapter 14 for publications.

Appendix

Sources for Names of Economics Faculty

Information on Nankai, Beida, Qinghua, and Southwest Associated Universities is presented in the subsequent chapters. Much information for the other Chinese universities came from biographical references: numerous general who's who publications, and the specific biographical references itemized in the appendix to Chapter 4. Faculty lists without dates for NCU and CPI are presented in *History of Social Sciences in Nanjing*. Professor Zhou Guowei, who wrote the relevant section, provided additional information in an interview in 1999, kindly arranged by Zhou Shudong. The 1942 roster of certified professors gives current and past employment: Ministry of Education 1942. Chan and Dirlik (1991) identifies numerous Shanghai economists.

Catalogues and other reference materials for China Academy, Fudan, Zhongshan, Wuhan, Daxia, Jiaotong, Peiping, and Sichuan Universities are listed under the institutional names in the reference list.

11

Economics at Nankai University

Nankai University, established in 1919 in the northeastern Chinese port city of Tianjin, became within a few years one of the leading universities in China.[1] By vigorous recruiting and through a personnel policy which encouraged research and publication, Nankai had developed by the 1930s one of the leading Economics departments in China. The Nankai economists (and particularly Fang Xianting) searched very hard to find in western economics some guidance for China's economy.

Nankai University was the outgrowth of a private school created by Zhang Poling. At first the Economics program was heavily business-oriented, like that at Fudan. One of the earliest Economics faculty was Chou Hsien-sung (Zhou Xiansong), who had completed a master's degree at Penn in 1923. But he left for business positions after a short time (*Who's Who in China* 1925). Another early faculty member was Li Pao-liu who received master's degrees from both Wisconsin and Harvard; he became Dean of Commerce at Nankai, but soon moved to Qinghua (ibid. 1925). He was followed as Dean by Tang Wen-kai (Wenkai), who was ABD at Chicago. He left in 1928 for a position with the Chinese Bankers Institute in Shanghai (*CYB* 1935). In 1925, Xiao Chu (ABD Harvard) was appointed head of the Economics and Literature Departments. However, in 1928 he was lured away to Qinghua.

In his influential study, *Chinese Intellectuals and the West*, Wang Yi-Chu quoted from a 1924 article by a Nankai student which included the following:

> The university teachers teach American politics, American economy, American commerce, American railways, American this, American that . . . The student, when he graduates, also goes to the United States and somehow manages to

> secure a master's or doctoral degree. After he returns to China, he steps into the shoes of his teachers and perpetuates the revolving educational system. (Wang 1966, p. 371)

If this was a fair representation of Nankai Economics in 1924, it did not stay that way. Nankai soon began an upgrade of its own, beginning with the 1926 appointment of He Lian (Franklin Ho), who had completed a Yale PhD with a dissertation on income tax administration in western countries. More importantly, he had worked closely for three years with Irving Fisher, concentrating on index numbers.[2] At Nankai He Lian was quick to establish a program for compiling and publishing index numbers on major economic magnitudes.[3]

He Lian was strongly oriented toward research and grant funding. He helped organize a Nankai Committee on Social and Economic Research in 1927. That same year he obtained a grant from the China Foundation to study family budgets of workers in Tianjin. He presented some of his index numbers at a conference sponsored by the Institute of Pacific Relations (IPR) in 1929 (Ho 1930). In 1928–29, He was awarded grants from IPR to study population movement to Manchuria and industrialization in Tianjin. He made a strong impression on IPR research director J. B. Condliffe, a New Zealand economist, who ranked He among the five best economists in China. He also impressed Roger Greene of the Rockefeller Foundation in 1928 (Chiang 2001, pp. 87–92).

In preparation for his teaching, He Lian visited a dozen major Chinese universities. He reported, "I did not find any college which offered a course on the economic development and organization of China or on rural economics in China."[4] (Ho 1967, p. 72) In 1929, He successfully recruited his Yale schoolmate Fang Xianting to join Nankai.[5] Fang had written a doctoral dissertation on "The Triumph of Factory System in England".[6] Franklin Ho believed that the study of economic history had prepared Fang to analyze economic development (Ho 1967, p. 73). However, there was little in the dissertation to support this view. While it described in detail the organizational forms prevailing in 1840, there was little historical context, no significant economic analysis, no real discussions of public policy, and no references to China or developing countries in general.

At Nankai, Fang became a prolific writer of research studies, beginning with the analysis of Tianjin's industries. The work focused primarily on carpets, hosiery, rayon, and cotton. While the motivation for the study was concern for industrial modernization, only the cotton industry met this criterion, the others being mainly handicraft activities chosen because of data availability (Chiang 2001, p. 98). In December, 1930, Nankai was visited by the distinguished British economic historian R. H. Tawney, who spent nearly a month there working on his IPR-supported study of China's economy, *Land and Labour in China* (1932).

Nankai offered faculty much lower teaching loads than most Chinese universities, but with a very modern expectation about their corresponding commitment to research (Fong 1975, pp. 40, 44). Faculty were forbidden to hold other employment. Following heavy faculty defections to national universities in the late 1920s, He Lian persuaded President Zhang to give strong emphasis to business and economics.[7]

In 1931, He formally organized the Nankai Institute of Economics, with an organizational structure and agenda crafted toward fund-raising. Its prospectus promised to teach Economics in a manner relevant to Chinese conditions and to conduct research on China's economy in a way that would enrich teaching and provide textbook materials.[8] The prospectus warned that the Chinese student of Economics, lacking China-relevant materials, "seizes with avidity the generalizations of western economics, without realizing the conditions which limit their application in his own country. His thought becomes abstract and dogmatic . . . His time and energy are spent in producing rhetorical essays on subjects such as 'economic interpretation of history,' 'land nationalization,' 'government ownership and control of industry,' and similar topics."[9] The document gave priority to China's need for "trained men to undertake the huge task of public administration". It questioned whether China's development "will be effected haphazard [sic] as a result of the activities of reactionary interests or of revolutionary enthusiasts, . . . or whether they will be to some extent guided by scientific knowledge and by men of trained intelligence, who look at the problem as one of social engineering for the common good." (p. 3) Eight research areas were proposed: "surveys of agricultural economy, industries, fatigue and efficiency in industries, commodity production and distribution, currency and inflation, usury, local government finance, and the administration of the land tax" (Chiang 2001, p. 106).

In December, 1931, the Rockefeller Foundation agreed to grant the Institute US$75,000 over the five-year period beginning in 1932. And IPR agreed to fund a study of district government in North China.

The policy emphasis in the Institute prospectus paralleled political developments in China. Since 1927 the new KMT government had pledged itself to carry out Sun Yat-sen's ambitious program for China's economic development. By 1929, teams of foreign experts were advising on economic policies, and a new National Economic Council was formed to try to implement their recommendations (Eastman 1974, pp. 216–220, 237–238; Kirby 1983; Fong 1936b). Another influence came from Yanjing Economics professor John Bernard Tayler, who organized the North China Industrial Service Union in 1931 to study and improve rural industries. His vision was to combine training of development workers with participation in village development. Tayler persuaded Franklin Ho to be a member of the board of directors of the Service Union. The Rockefeller Foundation staff were also impressed with Tayler's work (Chiang 2001, pp. 120–121, 235–236; Thomson 1969, pp. 135–139).

The Nankai program began to give much more attention to rural and agricultural concerns. Courses in agricultural economics were introduced in 1933, when they hired Shison Lee (Li Qinglin) who had just completed a PhD at Illinois. Field research on district government and local organizations had begun in 1932, directed by political scientist Zhang Chunming.[10] In January, 1933, they began case studies of rural industries, under the direction of Fang Xianting, concentrating on handloom weaving in Gaoyang and Lihsien (Chiang 2001, pp. 111–119; see also Fong 1933). In addition, an ambitious but vaguely defined survey of farm families was projected.[11] Looking ahead, an Institute report of May, 1933 promised that "the collection of mere figures . . . will be reduced to a minimum, while the observation and recording of facts from an analytical viewpoint . . . will be given greater attention."[12]

With the inflow of grant support, the Institute rapidly enlarged its staff, reaching a peak of 32 members in 1933–35 (Chiang 1986, p. 192). Eleven of these were professors. The staff included sociologists and political scientists as well as economists. Among the economists who joined the staff in 1932 were two from other Chinese universities—Jen Tsung-chi (Ren Zongji—MA Columbia 1924) from Yanjing, and Yuan Wenbo (PhD NYU 1930) from Fudan. Three others were hired as they completed graduate degrees in the United States—Li Qinglin (above); Leonard Ting (Ding Ji—MBA Harvard 1932); and K. C. Wong (Wong Guozhong—MS Columbia 1931).[13] The Institute employed several Nankai graduates as instructors and research fellows. Two of these became mainstays of the program—Li Jui (Rui) and Wu Ta-yeh (Daye). Both went abroad for graduate study under RF fellowships.[14] By 1937 both were professors. Wu Baosan spent a year teaching at Nankai in 1932 before leaving for a distinguished career which included a Harvard PhD and authorship of the first major study of China's national income.[15]

A master's level graduate program was instituted. Thirteen students were admitted in the fall of 1933, focusing primarily on banking and agricultural economics, for which field work was provided.[16] The initial conception indicated confidence that professional economists needed little formal study beyond the undergraduate level, provided they served a kind of apprenticeship in research.

The Institute also became a prolific source of published output. Besides a large number of monographs, they produced the *Monthly Bulletin on Economic China* (in English) which evolved into the *Nankai Social and Economic Quarterly* (*NSEQ*) with a wealth of articles, book reviews, and bibliographies dealing with China's economy. In Chinese, there were the *Quarterly Journal of Economics and Statistics* and the *Economic Weekly*, a newspaper supplement. Their index numbers were updated and published every month. The Institute issued in 1931 its own standardized Chinese economic terminology, and He Lian was a major participant in the national program to do the same thing in 1936 (Ho 1967, p. 88). He's textbook on public finance was published in 1935 (with Li Jui as joint author).[17]

The Rockefeller Program

In December, 1934, the Rockefeller Foundation approved a million-dollar grant for an experimental program to deal with Chinese rural reconstruction. The program envisioned cooperation among the Nankai Institute and several other institutions, including Yanjing University and the Mass Education program of James Yen (Thomson 1969, pp. 135–140). In April, 1936, the member institutions formed the North China Council for Rural Reconstruction. The focus was to be on training administrators for government programs to promote rural development at the grass roots, with Nankai given responsibility for the areas of economics (supplemented by J. B. Tayler's Yanjing program) and local government. Two rural field stations were provided, one at Dingxian, headquarters of the Mass Education program.

For this program, Nankai initiated a new two-year graduate program with emphasis on cooperatives, land problems, and local government and finance. Students were to take a year of course work, then spend about half a year in field research and another half year in a kind of internship in rural development programs. Ten graduate students were dispatched in three groups on extensive programs of field research.[18] At this point, the graduate program contained no course work specifically on economic theory.[19]

The evolution of the Nankai program from 1931 to 1936 showed a large element of creative opportunism. Neither He Lian nor Fang Xianting was, by temperament or training, drawn directly toward grass-roots local development. That impulse came from J. B. Tayler and from James Yen, filtered through the incentive system of the Rockefeller Foundation. The most original contribution of the Nankai component was the concern with local government, and that mainly involved political scientists. Nevertheless, both Franklin Ho and Fang Xianting assumed major roles in the new programs, teaching and writing in areas related to rural problems.

As the Nankai staff adapted to the focus of the Rockefeller program, their research orientation also shifted. They became painfully aware of the limitations of efforts to do broad surveys based on questionnaires and interviews, and came to emphasize intensive case studies of particular localities and activities.

Policy Views

To this point, the prolific published output from the Nankai program consisted primarily of descriptive materials, typically incorporating whatever statistical data could be obtained. He Lian and Fang touched on major obstacles to economic growth. Some related to government—absence of educational programs and infrastructure (especially transportation), abusive taxation, and unfair treaties giving advantages to foreign products and firms. Others involved deficiencies of Chinese market economy. Rural industries lacked information, standardization, and quality control, all of which required some degree of collective action, for which Fang particularly recommended cooperatives.[20] These writings were consistent with the grass-roots character of the Rockefeller program and reflected the influence of Tawney and Tayler.

Indeed, the difficulties of the Chinese people in developing effective forms of collective action, both public and private, had received a lot of attention from earlier Chinese scholars, notably Liang Qichao. The student of economic history might have seen this problem lurking behind the absence, in China, of the vigorous development of town life which was significant in Europe by the fourteenth or fifteenth century.[21] In Anglo-American development, effective collective action was central to the emergence of the factory system (focus of Fang's dissertation) and the corporation. But western mainstream economics did not help He, Fang, and their colleagues to analyze this question (see Schrader 1993).

In 1936, both He and Fang presented comprehensive visions of China's development problems and appropriate policies, visions quite different from the articles just cited.[22] Both affirmed the general merits of Sun Yat-sen's approach to development. He's endorsement was more thorough. He supported Sun's emphasis on "equalization of land ownership" and "all land to the tillers", and, like Sun, neglected programmatic detail. He also reiterated Sun's recommendations for promoting farm consolidation and mechanization and for encouraging population movement to sparsely settled areas. Regarding industry, He endorsed tariff protection, as Sun had done.[23] Whereas Sun had urged a vast program of government investment, ownership and operation in industry and trade, He envisioned government planning and control without so much outright ownership. Like Sun, He urged the government to extend highways and railways. In the area of his own special interest, He recommended that the government develop income and inheritance taxation to provide it with the financial resources for a more activist policy (Ho 1936a).

Fang's thoughts on the same topics showed many parallels, particularly the commitment to a comprehensive, non-socialist (and vaguely articulated) system of government planning and control.[24] He urged that the system should include extensive trade unions for workers and trade associations for firms. Fang did not strongly endorse Sun's slogans regarding land policy nor his mercantilistic views on tariff protection.[25] Instead, Fang suggested export restrictions on natural resource products such as iron ore and tungsten. Fang also recognized that China's factor endowments dictated labor-intensive production, rather than the high capital intensity implied by Sun Yat-sen and implicitly endorsed by He.

Conspicuously absent from the writings of He and Fang was any concern about China's population growth as a source of low incomes and a possible focus for policy actions. This, too, was consistent with Sun Yat-sen's outlook, and in sharp contrast to Tawney.

Fang's 1936 monograph, entitled *Toward Economic Control in China*, strongly implied the desirability of strong central control (Fong 1936b, especially pp. 1–4, 74–83). There was not a sensitive awareness of the government's shortcomings in providing a basic framework of law and order, nor of the potential hazards, both in terms of inefficiency and in terms of freedom and fairness, of an extended role for government.

In 1936 He went on leave to become head of the Political Department of the national government's Executive Yuan in Nanjing.[26] Fang became the operating head of the Institute. In 1932–37, the majority of faculty were performing conventional academic activities of teaching and research. Enrollments in Economics increased rapidly. In 1931–32, there were fifteen students above the freshman level. By 1936–37 the number had grown to 117 (Nankai Institute of Economics 1937, p. 17). Nankai aggressively continued to recruit newly returned students with western degrees to join the faculty, but many left quickly for positions in the business world. Among the important new recruits who stayed longer were Pao Chueh-min (Bao Juemin) and Li Choh-ming (Zhuomin). Bao was hired as lecturer in economic geography after his graduation from National Central University in 1933. In 1937 he went to London and completed a PhD in that field at LSE in 1940. He remained a member of the department for the next half-century and was still involved in the program in 1992.[27] Li joined Nankai after completing a PhD at Berkeley in 1936.[28]

Chen Chen-han (Zhenhan) was initially appointed to the faculty in 1935, but soon left to study for a PhD at Harvard, which he completed in 1941. He then returned to Nankai along with his wife Tsui Shu-hsiang (Cui Shuxiang), who had done graduate work at Wisconsin and Radcliffe. Both were Nankai graduates.[29] Rockwood Chin (Chin Quock-ping—Chen Guoping)) joined the faculty after completing his doctorate at Yale in 1937.

The Economics curriculum was heavily descriptive, with only one 3-hour course in value and distribution (and perhaps the one in theory of credit) devoted to contemporary economic theory.[30] The descriptive material was strongly oriented toward Chinese conditions.

Looking back over the early years of the Nankai program, it appears that initially He, Fang, and their recruits did not hold strong analytical or ideological views relating to China's economy. Their studies, whether at Yale or other respected graduate programs, were largely descriptive. Microeconomic theory did not constitute a major part of their graduate study. Courses generally presumed the existence of a market economy, but it was either taken for granted or criticized—seldom praised. Nor was much attention given to its cultural and legal underpinnings, nor to ways of making it work better.[31] As time passed, however, stronger views on policy emerged. By 1936, both He and Fang were endorsing ambitious programs for government economic planning and control which were totally out of scale with the Chinese government's competence and capacity to command resources.

In March, 1933, the Nankai program began a valuable and significant activity. Every week they produced a supplement for publication with the *Ta Kung Pao* ("The Impartial"), a major daily newspaper. "The Supplement has for its chief function the presentation and interpretation of facts about current economic problems for the Chinese reading public in popular language."[32] We examined the authorship of 152 of these items published over the period 1933–37.[33] There were 61 different authors. Nine of these were not in Economics. Of the remaining 52, only 15 had studied Economics in the West. Many were junior faculty or graduate students. However, the western-returned students were the most prolific publishers. This matches a pattern we will develop much more fully in Chapter 14. The overwhelming majority of Chinese authors of publications about China's economy had not studied Economics in the West. But the most prolific publishers, and the leaders of organizations sponsoring publication, were generally western-trained.

Impact of the Japanese War

The outbreak of war with Japan in 1937 was devastating for Nankai. The campus was a major target for some of the first Japanese air raids. Nankai, along with the government universities, evacuated. After a short period in Changsha, Nankai's undergraduate activities were moved to Kunming in the extreme south of China, where they were merged with Peking University and Qinghua to form the Southwestern Associated Universities. The research and graduate teaching of the Nankai program went to Chongqing, the wartime capital.[34] The graduate program was resumed in 1939, when the department boasted of having "the largest graduate class in economics in the country".[35] The program received a substantial infusion of theory, primarily from Li Zhuomin. We identified 25 students who participated in the Nankai graduate program in 1939–43. Of these, 15 went on for graduate study in the United States or Britain.

The faculty was cut from 20 members to 12. Fang Xianting left temporarily to head the revived activities of the North China Council for Rural Reconstruction in Guizhou Province.[36] A major addition was Lin Weiying, who had worked briefly with the National Economic Council after completing a doctorate at Columbia in 1936.

He Lian remained in high-level government service during most of the war, being reputedly Chiang Kai-shek's most trusted economic adviser. In December, 1943, He became Deputy Secretary-General of the Central Planning Board.[37]

Fang Xianting spent most of the period 1941–43 in the United States, first in study at Harvard and then working for the U.S. Board of Economic Warfare in Washington (Fong 1975, pp. 77–83). Fang came under the influence of Alvin Hansen at Harvard and became interested in Keynes. He reported that he "managed to dispatch the first and probably the only shipment of Keynesian and related literature via the Burma Road to Chungking . . ."[38]

Study of Keynes was incorporated into Nankai's graduate theory courses. Soon graduate students began to publish articles with strong Keynesian tones. The first-year graduate course in economic theory came to focus chiefly on Marshall, Robinson, Chamberlain, Hicks, and Keynes.[39] Clearly the Nankai program maintained close intellectual connections with major Economics programs in principal western countries. However, one may entertain reservations about just how much benefit to China's economic policy resulted from this affinity.

Fang returned to China in early 1944 to assist He as research director of the Central Planning Board (Fong 1975, pp. 64–66). Not surprisingly, a major focus of Nankai research and publication was on China's wartime economy (particularly the inflation problem) and plans for post-war reconstruction. By 1945 eight of the 17 Nankai Institute staff in Chongqing were also working with the Central Planning Board or Ministry of Economics.[40]

Post-war Developments

When the War ended in 1945, Nankai University was reconstructed in Tianjin, reopening in 1946 with new status as a national government university. Roger Evans, visiting on behalf of RF, was told in May 1947, that "10 young Ph.D.s from Columbia, Harvard, Yale, etc. are [coming] in the fall to constitute the remaining staff of the Institute."[41] But the leading economists soon dispersed, particularly as the threat of communist take-over became an actuality in 1949. Rockwood Chin left in 1945, joining the U.S. Department of Commerce.[42] Li Zhuomin spent two years in the United States in 1943–45 as part of the Ministry of Foreign Affairs Post-war Study Group. He then became Deputy Director of China National Relief and Rehabilitation Administration (CNRRA), closely linked with UNRRA.[43] Chen Zhenhan and Cui Shuxiang transferred to other universities in Peking. Fang moved to Shanghai in 1946 as the Acting Director of the newly formed China Institute of Economics.[44] In 1948 he joined the staff of the Economic Commission for Asia and the Far East (ECAFE) under the UN, where he remained until 1968. Wu Daye also joined ECAFE, becoming chief of the Statistics Section (Fong 1975, p. 42). He Lian returned with the Nankai faculty to Tianjin and even served briefly as President of the University. However, the imminent Communist take-over led him to move to New York where he joined Columbia University (Fong 1975, pp. 86–91).

Most of Nankai's permanent faculty acquisitions in the late 1940s were persons who had not studied abroad. Some became quite distinguished: Teng Wei-tsao (Weizao), with an MA from Nankai in 1944, joined the staff in 1946, went on to translate Hayek's *Road to Serfdom* in the early 1960s and became Nankai's president 1981–86 (*Nankai University Doctoral Programs*, pp. 75–79).

The Communists took over control of Tianjin in early 1949. Initially the University was not much affected. Fang reported in June, 1949, that "the most significant changes introduced are the addition of two courses, one each on Marx's idea of capital and on socialism".[45] Evidence of a relatively protected atmosphere was the ability of Nankai to continue to recruit returned students from overseas. Yang Jingnian (Oxford PhD), Chien (Qian) Rongkun (Nankai MA, graduate study at LSE), and Chen Yinfang (Delaware MA) all joined Nankai in 1951. All three of these were still active in the Nankai program in 1992.[46] But after 1951, recruiting was of necessity restricted to persons who had not studied abroad—except perhaps in the USSR.[47] Ji Taoda, who had studied at Moscow's Sun Yat-sen University, was brought in from Shanxi University to become Chair (*Biographies of Contemporary Chinese Economists*, 1987).

The turbulent developments in Chinese academic affairs after 1950 did not permit any university to maintain an international standard in teaching and research in Economics or much of anything else (see especially Lieberthal 1980, pp. 154–157). Graduate study in Economics was concentrated in the newly formed People's University in Beijing. Chinese higher education was largely shut down during the Cultural Revolution (1966–76). Universities reopened in 1976 and became relatively international in their program orientations. The Nankai program did maintain good staff and institutional cohesiveness which enabled it to resume a position of prominence.[48]

Some Assessments

We have recorded 82 Chinese who taught Economics at Nankai down through 1949. Of these, 58 had some foreign study (including four who went abroad after their faculty service). Of these 58, 32 took some graduate Economics study in the United States, including 13 with doctorates. A dozen had studied in Europe, seven of them in Britain. Germany and Japan only accounted for six.

We have identified 45 Nankai students who proceeded to graduate study in Economics in the West, including several from the MA program. There were 35 going to the United States and ten to Britain and Europe. Ten completed PhD degrees, some outside Economics, some after 1950. Eight of the 45 returned to the Nankai faculty, and an additional nine became faculty at other Chinese universities.

The Economics program at Nankai developed in a relatively few years into one of the best in China. Admittedly, it displayed some of the less attractive features of grantsmanship, promising grandiose and unattainable programs in research and textbook composition. The graduate program shifted rapidly from one focus to another, partly for opportunistic reasons. But the program maintained a sincere commitment to "Chinafy" Economics. The Nankai index numbers were a valuable component of data on current economic conditions. Several useful textbooks were produced dealing with Chinese conditions in Chinese language.[49] A very large volume of material was published describing conditions in Chinese industry and trade. The value of these studies was affirmed when the Japanese had the entire set translated into Japanese in 1936 (Ho 1967, p. 100). In 1947, one resident westerner told RF's Roger Evans that "The only really good economic work in China was done by Nankai, but the staff dispersed to the States to avoid political entanglements."[50]

Compared to other Chinese university programs, Nankai was relatively free from political interference or student unrest. Morale was obviously good, and impressive institutional continuity was maintained. He, Fang, and other Nankai staff were appointed to government positions on the basis of merit and worked hard (if in vain) for sensible policies.

The leaders of the Nankai program were groping to develop a point of view concerning China's economic policy. Initially, they displayed a faith in radical empiricism: enough index numbers and industry case studies would form a pattern. In the next stage, He and Fang were swept up in the grass-roots-development rural-reconstruction focus derived from J. B. Tayler. Then their outlook swung strongly toward the state-dominated industrialization advocated by Sun Yat-sen. Their 1936 writings display an uncritical acceptance for a major role for government as owner and operator of productive facilities.[51] In 1939, Fang supported state-driven industrial development in the unoccupied regions of China in order to resist Japan's aggression. He wrote:

> China under present war conditions must hasten to industrialize the best she can, just as Soviet Russia had to industrialize under the NEP in 1921, through the exercise of the strictest economy over the national life. The capital needed must be derived, as in Soviet Russia, from the forced savings on the one hand, and through the exportation of agricultural and mineral products on the other. (Fong 1939, p. 303)

By 1936, the role of capital had become a central element in Fang's writings on industrialization (Fong 1936c). "Industrialization begins with the possession of capital", he wrote in 1942, placing natural resources second and human resources third (1942b, p. 45). His time at Harvard encouraged him to try to fit Keynesian ideas into his approach to development.

Learning about the shortcomings of Chinese government from the inside, He Lian backed away from endorsing a large role for the government. Writing in 1941 at a low point in his government service (he had just been dismissed from the Agricultural Credit Administration as a scapegoat for inflation and corruption), he stated:[52]

> There are many in the government . . . who are in favor of a controlled economy; but I and others feel that this is not a realistic attitude . . . China, with no census as to production or population, and with a political machinery which cannot function from top to bottom, presents difficulties of a nature that are not similar to any in foreign countries. At a time of stress and strain, a thorough policy of control, without a full realization of its consequences, is also fraught with danger.

When Roger Evans of the Rockefeller Foundation visited with Fang in China in 1947, he too had modified his outlook:[53]

> HDFong may have been rendered irresponsible by repeated *gambeis* ["bottoms-up"] with *maotai* [a Chinese strong drink] but it still may prove worth while to follow up some of his references: e.g., that China is fascist, that bureaucracy is consuming the country . . . HDF[ong], on the way home, renounces all interest in the 5-year plan of industrialization in which he earlier played such an enthusiastic and prominent part, but it is not clear whether this is due to disillusionment with planning or with the present regime.

He and Fang did not get much help from the intellectual centers of western economics in this painful and conscientious search. The Nankai program was constantly being freshened by recruiting staff from those centers. During the period under examination, graduate study in Economics in western universities involved substantial amounts of descriptive information about taxation, banking, transportation, and industrial organization, intermingled with criticisms of the inefficiencies and injustices of market economies.

The Nankai experience is a sobering reflection of the condition of academic economics in the West between 1920 and 1950.

12

Beida: Western Economics at Peking University

China's pre-eminent university, Peking University (often abbreviated "Beida"), was initially created by the Emperor as part of the short-lived reform movement of 1898. It absorbed the Tongwenguan, the translators' college, which had been operating since 1862. The noted American missionary William A. P. Martin, who had been an official of the Tongwenguan, became the first dean of the western faculty at Beida, initially known as the University at the Capital and occasionally, the Imperial University (Sun 1987, p. 82).

The new university began with fewer than 300 students, mainly studying foreign languages. Its operations were totally disrupted by the Boxer Rebellion in 1900, in which two professors were killed. Soon after, Martin and the other western teachers were dismissed and were replaced by Japanese. The University officially reopened in January, 1903, with about 140 students. Between 1903 and 1911, only about one thousand individual students attended, of which about 300 completed a degree. The earliest reported course in Economics was taught by a Japanese, Sugi Eizaburo (Sun, p. 84). From 1903, economic topics were offered as part of the Division of Law and Politics, and Economics remained close to the law school. In 1912, Economics became a separate department with emphasis on economic policies and business practices. Economics and commerce were merged in 1917 (Chen 1993, pp. 67–68, 109–115).

The University suspended operations again with the overthrow of the monarchy in 1911, and its name was changed to the National University of Peking.[1] Yan Fu served briefly as its president in 1912, long enough to begin recruitment of like-minded scholars committed to modernization and westernization.

In 1916, Cai Yuanpei became president. Under his leadership Beida became distinguished as a center for intellectual innovation, often overlapping with political radicalism. Cai had studied in Germany and returned full of excitement about the intellectual spirit of German universities.[2] Beida became a center of the "New Culture" movement to transform Chinese language and literature. It became a hotbed of student political activism and radicalism, exemplified by the May 4th (1919) uprising to protest the terms of the Versailles Peace Treaty (Schwarcz 1986).

The period of Cai's presidency was one of great intellectual excitement. Liang Qichao joined the faculty. John Dewey and Bertrand Russell came for extended periods as visiting lecturers.[3] Four of Cai's appointments involving Economics exemplified his ideal type of professor. One was Liang Shuming, hired to teach philosophy, who was developing highly original ideas about reforming rural social organization. A second was Chen Hansheng, who had just completed a history doctorate in Germany after previous study in the United States. Chen became one of the most diligent and critical researchers into Chinese agricultural conditions. The third was Li Dazhao, hired mainly as a librarian, but involved in teaching history and economics.[4] In 1921, Li and humanities dean Chen Tu-hsiu (Zhen Duxiu) were among the founders of the Chinese Communist Party. And it was Li who brought to Beida a young assistant librarian named Mao Zedong. Fourth was Tao Menghe (L. K. Tao), educated in London, nominally teaching sociology, but largely concerned with economic questions.[5] None of these four had training in conventional western economics.

In 1921 Liang Shuming published a book entitled *Eastern and Western Cultures* which became widely read and helped draw overflow crowds of students to his lectures.[6] Liang presented an original indigenous Chinese approach to economic development. The book stressed the uniqueness, durability, and unity of Chinese culture, and raised strong doubts about the ease with which western cultural traits could be incorporated into China. Liang questioned whether all nations pass through similar "stages" in the process of economic development:

> [I]f Western culture had not made contact with us, . . . China would have gone another three hundred years . . . or even another thousand years, and absolutely would not have produced steamboats, railroads, airplanes, scientific method, and democratic spirit . . . The Chinese have not been traveling on the same path as the Westerners. (Quoted Alitto 1979, p. 87.)

As early as 1923, Liang began to urge agrarian reform as a solution to China's problems (Alitto, p. 147). He was highly critical of the western influence on Chinese schooling, emphasizing instead programs to promote student development, practical learning, and moral responsibility. He found the atmosphere at Beida stultifying, with too much emphasis on lectures and memorization, on the study of western ideas. In 1924 he resigned and entered a long period of personal search and exploration which culminated in forming his own center for rural development. Liang was a charismatic lecturer and writer, and attracted many disciples. One of these was Lu Guangmian (then a chemistry student at Beida), whom we described in Chapter 8, working closely with John B. Tayler at Yanjing in promoting grassroots rural development.

Chen Hansheng joined the Beida faculty in 1924, as Professor of History. He soon became close to Li Dazhao. Chen applied for membership in the Communist Party, but was persuaded to join the related Comintern in 1926 instead, beginning a long career as a secret agent.[7] Although his studies had dealt mainly with international relations, he soon turned his interest to China's peasants. In 1927–28 he spent a year studying in Moscow, in part to keep a safe distance from the warlords who killed Li. He worked in the International Agrarian Institute where he encountered the principal Soviet authority on Chinese peasants, the Hungarian Louis Magyar. Chen did not return to Beida but taught at Peiping University and held a series of research positions which are discussed below.

In contrast to Chen's scholarly demeanor, Li Dazhao devoted his time at Beida to organizing and propagandizing for radical political change—even violent revolution. He joined the faculty in February, 1918, just as he was learning about the Russian Revolution. "For Li in 1918 the primary appeal of the October Revolution lay in the belief that the 'spirit of Russia' was uniquely qualified to 'harmonize Eastern and Western civilizations' because Russia bordered on both Europe and Asia and had therefore been influenced by both Eastern and Western civilizations." Li believed that "the very backwardness of nations like China and Russia held the seeds of youth and progress—whereas the material maturity of the West was a prelude to decline and decay." (Meisner 1967, pp. 64–65) Li believed that "ethical ideas, such as mutual aid and universal love, have always been present in the human mind but the economic structure [of capitalism] is such that it destroys every possibility of their realization." (Huang 1965, p. 28)

Li became a Marxist and expressed his views in an influential article which appeared in 1919, just days before the historic May 4th events. He recognized the weakness of the labor theory of value. The relevance of class struggle to China was found not so much in internal divisions, but rather the sense that Chinese people as a whole were "proletariat", victimized by western exploiters. In 1924 he completed a book titled *The Essentials of Historical Study*, which dealt not only with Marx but also Turgot, Condorcet, Saint-Simon, and Comte, particularly with their views on the role of economic forces in historical evolution. But Li's classroom lectures on Chinese history showed little evidence of a Marxist approach (Meisner, p. 170). Li's 1925 article "Land and the Peasants" assessed the disappointing degree to which Sun Yat-sen's proposals for equalizing land ownership had been achieved.

Gu and Ma

Other strong personalities were more central to the Beida Economics Department. Ku (Gu) Mengyu was one of the first Chinese to graduate from Beida (1906), where he specialized in German. A government subsidy enabled him to study Economics at Leipzig and Berlin universities in 1906–11. He returned to a professorship at Beida in 1911 and became Economics Department Chair in 1918. In the early 1920s he was listed as teaching socialist theory and systems. He joined the Kuomintang in 1924, when it still presented a liberal and reformist appearance, and left Beida the following year for a political career.[8] Li Tang, who had studied at Berlin University, taught financial subjects at Beida until 1923; he later held prominent positions in the Ministry of Finance.[9] Two German nationals, Friedrich Otte and E. Erde, taught briefly.[10] Otte's 1922 dissertation for the University of Jena dealt with foreign control of China's finances (*Jahresverzeichnis* v. 38 [1922], p. 478). E. Erde taught "private economics" and various business courses in the early 1920s.

Ma Yinchu, who joined the Beida faculty in 1915, was also highly energetic, outspoken, and committed to using Economics to influence policy. He had completed a doctorate at Columbia with a dissertation on New York City's finances. While at Beida, Ma also joined the Bank of China, first in research, and then in helping manage the note-issue department. At Beida he taught courses in money and banking and published numerous commentaries on China's money and banking conditions. He took a year's leave in 1920 "to investigate industrial and commercial activities in Shanghai".[11]

In 1923 Ma collaborated with Liu Dajun in establishing the Chinese Economic Association and became its first president. He was a prolific writer on matters of economic policy, producing volumes of collected lectures in 1923, 1925, 1926, and 1928. He was highly critical of Marxism.[12] China's central problem, he believed, was lack of capital. He felt that the most useful economic ideas for China were those of Friedrich List and Othmar Spann. Ma favored high import tariffs to stimulate industrial development in China. Like Sun Yat-sen, Ma condemned the dominant influence of foreign countries on Chinese government financial policies, and favored an active government role in promoting China's economic development.

Ma's schoolmate Chen Shao-kwan (Zhen Shaokun) joined the Beida faculty in 1916. His Columbia dissertation (1914) reviewed the history of taxation in China. He held various positions in the Ministry of Finance and taught history of economics, principles of political science, and municipal administration at Beida up to 1933. Like Gu, he had been a Beida student, graduating in 1908 (Chao 1917).

Another early Beida economist was Chen Chi-hsiu (Qixiu), who had studied at Tokyo's Imperial University. He came to Beida in 1919 and taught statistics. Both he and Ma were members of an early Marxist study group. Chen spent two years studying in Moscow in 1923–25 and returned to Beida to teach about Marx.[13]

Wang Chi-chang (C. Z. Waung—Wang Qichang) taught economic history at Beida 1913–19 while on the staff of the Ministry of Finance. Wang had completed an honors degree at LSE in 1911. He later entered the banking business.[14]

Many of the Beida faculty of the 1920s do not appear in our lists of those who studied in the West. Pei (Bai) Pengfei (economic geography, finance) had studied in Japan. He was an authority on labor law (*Who's Who in China* 1936, p. 198). Yu Wen-tsan (Wencan), who taught international finance and some business courses, had an undergraduate degree from Chicago and a law degree from Harvard.[15]

Ma Yinchu left Beida in 1927, moving to Zhejiang University when it was established in that year and then in 1928 to Jiaotong University in Shanghai. After the Communist revolution, he served as President of Beida from 1951 to 1960.

Ma's departure was representative of a general downturn in the condition of Beida, mainly associated with the chaotic political climate of the warlord years and with Cai Yuanpei's departure in 1926. Liang Shuming left in

1924, ultimately creating his own center for rural reconstruction. Li Dazhao was seized and executed in 1927 by the warlord government for his pro-communist activities. Chen Hansheng was later dismissed for his leftist views. So was Chen Qixiu.[16] Beida's finances were periodically straitened and faculty often went unpaid for months.[17] Many took second jobs. After 1928, the national government moved to Nanjing. The universities in Peking could no longer make use of government officials as part-time teachers. And, as Li Dazhao's execution made clear, the warlord presence was a potentially threatening one.[18]

Although Beida's Economics during Cai's presidency contained many disparate elements, it still reflected predominantly the German-Japanese orientation toward active state economic leadership, a perspective consistent with the views of Sun Yat-sen. Both Gu Mengyu and Ma Yinchu left Beida in part to be more involved in the hoped-for modernizing activities of the KMT.

Data on the number of students graduating with a major in Economics show dramatically the extreme swings in the excitement level of the Beida program. These are shown in Table 12-1.

Table 12-1. Students Graduating with Major in Economics, National Peking University, 1913–1948

Year	Number	Year	Number
1913–19	34	1931	36
1920	30	1932	67
1921	32	1933	21
1922	37	1934	24
1923	66	1935	37
1924	54	1936	19
1925	125	1937	77
1926	107	1938–45*	75
1927	39	1946	1
1928	16	1947	49
1929	17	1948	1
1930	15	no date	25
Total			1,004

* Period when Beida was part of Southwest Associated Universities in Kunming.
Source: Derived from *Peking University Graduates, 1911–1948* (Chinese language), Peking University, 1948.

In 1931, Selskar Gunn of the Rockefeller Foundation visited Beida and reported that:

> Political Science and Economics have more students than any other branch [of Social Sciences] and the immature minds of the students, according to the President, have been incapable in the past of evaluating information which they have obtained in the University. The result has been a good deal of communism.[19]

Beginning in 1931, Beida Economics came under the direction of Chao (Zhao) Naituan, himself a Beida alumnus. Zhao had completed a PhD at Columbia in 1930, working (as did so many Chinese students) under the supervision of E. R. A. Seligman. Zhao's dissertation concerned Richard Jones, an early British economist who could be viewed as one of the creators of institutional economics. Like many of his contemporaries, Zhao believed that institutional economics was better adapted to Chinese needs than the abstractions of mainstream neo-classical economic theory.[20] Zhao had the opportunity to embody these notions in his teaching, which extended to the introductory course, advanced economics, economic theory, and economics readings in English. However, Zhao's temperament was more like that of a traditional Chinese scholar. He looked the part, with a long beard. His institutionalism lacked the activism of Gu and Ma, or the Yanjing faculty.

Beginning in 1932, Zhao received financial assistance for his research on the history of economic thought from the China Foundation for the Promotion of Education and Culture. In the 1930s, Beida created a journal entitled *Social Science*, to which Zhao contributed several substantial articles. One surveyed business-cycle theory, another surveyed price theory. He explored the origins of Adam Smith's ideas, and summarized several books on the recovery program in the U.S. In 1938 he presented an overview of the major developments in economics over the previous 40 years. He continued to study the history of economic thought and after the War published books on both western and Chinese contributions.[21]

Chao Jen-tsun (Zhao Renjun), a member of the Qinghua faculty, sometimes came to Beida to teach statistics. He had received his PhD from Harvard in 1928. Chin Tsan (Qin Zan), who taught courses in finance in 1927–37, was ABD at Columbia.[22] Another distinguished part-time visitor was Dong Shijin, teaching agricultural economics. He had obtained a PhD from Cornell in 1924 and was Dean of the National College of Agriculture in Peking 1928–33.

Although Economics enrollments revived somewhat after 1930, they never regained the high levels earlier attained. Israel and Klein (1976, p. 23) commented that by 1935, Beida:

> had lost its political vitality. As a government school situated inside Peking's city walls, it easily succumbed to pressures of local and national authorities . . . Gone were the excited and dissonant voices of the New Culture period.

To be sure, excitement and dissonance were not synonymous with scholarly originality and rigor. But the Beida economists did not manifest much of those either.[23]

The 1933 Program

An unusually detailed rationale and description for the Beida program was published in 1933.[24] The prospectus identified several goals which embodied Zhao Naituan's institutionalist perspective. Students were urged to pay attention to economic change, and to place the study of any society in a context based on its historical and social situation. "It is wrong to regard economic rules and social orders as immutable." Analysis should be based on statistical data. Moral considerations should be factored into policy analysis.

Zhao's elementary course recommended the following English-language textbooks, all by American authors:[25]

> Lionel Edie, *Economics, Principles and Problems*, 1933 ed.
> Richard T. Ely, *Outlines of Economics*, 5th ed.
> Sumner Slichter, *Modern Economic Society*, 1931
> Henry R. Seager, *Principles of Economics*, 3rd ed., 1923
> Frank Taussig, *Principles of Economics*, 3rd ed., 1921

These books represented a wide variety of viewpoints, ranging from the very neo-classical approach of Taussig to the institutionalism of Slichter.

Zhao's sophomore course in advanced economics focused on Alfred Marshall's *Principles*, using the 1920 edition to develop "neo-classical basic theories to make preparation for contemporary ideas". This was supplemented by *Memorials of Alfred Marshall* (1925), and John Maynard Keynes's *Essays in Biography* (1933), as well as Paul Homan's *Contemporary Economic Thought* (1928) and Langford L. F. R. Price's *Short History of Political Economy in England* (14th ed., 1931). In this list, all were British except Homan (who visited China about this time).

Most of the course listings identified Chinese as well as western readings. Chou Tso-jen's (Zhou Zuoren) money and banking course suggested three western items plus the following:

Chang Chia-hsiang (Zhang Jiaxiang), *History of Chinese Currency*
Ma Yinchu, *Theory of Chinese Banking*
Yang Yinpu, *Theory of Chinese Finance*

The course in general finance theory by Qin Zan was described in a detailed outline covering government expenditures, taxation in theory and practice, and public debts. His reading list was also lengthy, with eight western items and the following:

Chia (Jia) Shiyi, *Fiscal History of the National Republic of China*, and *Sequel to Fiscal History*
Luo Chieh-fu (Jiefu), *Problems of Chinese Finance*
Chin Kuo-chen (Jin Guozhen), *Theories of Chinese Finance*

Zhou Zuoren's course in history of economic thought enumerated a standard list of major western topics: mercantilism, physiocracy, and classical economics, then added communism, historicism, and "psychologism". The reading list included:

Lu Ping, *History of Economic Thought*
Arthur E. Monroe, *Early Economic Thought*, 1924
Theo Suranyi-Unger, *Economics in the Twentieth Century*, 1931
Samuel H. Patterson, *Readings in the History of Economic Thought*, 1932
Othmar Spann, *Types of Economic Theory*, 1930
Charles Gide and Charles Rist, *History of Economic Doctrines*, 1915

This list displayed more diversity of national origins, with Austrian Spann and French Gide and Rist—both available in English and Chinese translations.

The course in banking systems taught by Zhou Zuoren recommended students read these items:

Ma Yinchu, *Theory of Chinese Banking*
Hsu Chi-ching (Xu Zhijing), *Contemporary Financial History of Shanghai*
Studies of management of major Chinese banks published by the Economic Research Department of the Bank of China
H. Parker Willis and Benjamin H. Beckhart, eds., *Foreign Banking Systems*, 1930
Willis, *The Federal Reserve System*, 1923
Edwin Kemmerer, *ABC of the Federal Reserve System*, 9th ed., 1932

Kemmerer had spent most of 1929 in China with a large supporting cast of financial experts. They produced a number of detailed studies of Chinese money and finance, but these did not appear in any of the course reading lists. However, some of these ideas may have been covered in Zhou's course in currency problems, which recommended the following:

Chuan Kuo-bao (Quan Guobao), *The Chinese Currency System*
Peng Hsueh-pai (Xuepei), *Chinese and Foreign Currency Policies*
Ministry of Finance, *Drafts and Explanations for China's Gradual Adoption of a Gold Standard Currency System*
Irving Fisher, *Stabilizing the Dollar*, 1920
J. M. Keynes, *Monetary Reform* (1923); *Treatise on Money* (1930)
Ralph Hawtrey, *Monetary Reconstruction* (2nd ed., 1926); *Gold Standard in Theory and Practice* (3rd ed., 1933)
Robert A. Lehfeldt, *Restoration of the World's Currencies*, 1923
Gustav Cassel, *Money and Foreign Exchange after 1914* (1922); *Post-war Monetary Stabilization* (1928)

The longest course outline (almost three printed pages) was for Qin Zan's Topics in Public Finance. (Many of the topics and readings were also included in his more advanced course in Public Debt and the Budget, which I have not abstracted.) The course explored in detail the shifting and incidence of taxation and the taxation of land. There was also a lot of attention to budget principles and practices. Suggested readings were correspondingly numerous (and mostly western), but included:

Jia Shiyi, *Fiscal History of the National Republic, Sequel*
Wang Hsien-chiang (Xianqiang), *Problems of China's Land-Value Tax*

The course in international trade offered by Zhou Binglin stressed theories of international trade and international prices, but dealt also with foreign exchange markets. Reading suggestions were as follows:

Alfred Marshall, *Money, Credit and Commerce*, 1923
Frank Taussig, *International Trade*, 1928
James W. Angell, *The Theory of International Prices*, 1926

Zhou Binglin also offered economic development of major western countries. Besides country studies, the course explored "agricultural revolution, industrial revolution, commercial revolution, mechanical transportation, evolution of commercial policies in various countries". Suggested readings were by John Clapham and Lilian Knowles.

Hu Chuan-chih (Qianzhi) offered a course in history of Chinese [government] finance. He urged the students to pay attention to three points:

1. "In Chinese fiscal history, irregular measures were common, and people suffered. However, they also had strong points: the earliest forms of accounting, the simplicity and stability of taxes."
2. "Sages' thoughts evolved into reality."
3. "Finance should stress science today and fit the theories to the world . . . Today's students of finance will be tomorrow's fiscal officials. Their responsibility is great."

The recommended readings, all in Chinese, were as follows:

Huan Kuan, *Theory of Supervision*
Li Hsi-sheng (Xisheng), *Records of Accounting during the Kung-hsu Period*
Wu Hsiang-chi (Xiangzhi), *Tsing Dynasty Fiscal Records*
Jia Shiyi, *History of Finance in the National Republic*
Yang Ju-mei (Rumei), *Theories of Finance in the National Republic*
Sun Yi-chang (Yirang), *Chou-Li-Cheng-Yi* (specific periods and leaders)

Dong Shijin, Dean of the Peking College of Agriculture, offered the course in agricultural economics. He was preparing his own textbook, which appeared in 1934, and undoubtedly presented it in the lectures. His prospectus promised to develop the most important principles of agricultural economics and to analyze China's agricultural economy. However, the recommended readings were all western, as follows:

James E. Boyle, *Agricultural Economics*, 3rd ed., 1928
Thomas Nixon Carver, *Principles of Rural Economics*, 2nd ed., 1932
Edwin G. Nourse, *Agricultural Economics*, 1923
Henry C. Taylor, *Agricultural Economics*, 1921

The course in labor problems was presented by Li Kuang-chung (Guangzhong). His brief course outline has an institutional cast, with topics such as "machines and labor problems", "psychological aspects of labor problems", the labor movement [trade unionism, presumably], employer-worker relations, methods to secure industrial peace, and international labor standards. Besides five western items, the reading suggestions included:

Chen Da, *Chinese Labor Problems*
Bai Pengfei, *Outline of Comparative Labor Laws*
Ku Ping-yuan (Gu Bingyuan), *Collection of Chinese Labor Law Regulations*

Chen Qixiu offered a course about Karl Marx. The ten topics listed include such central parts of Marx's economic analysis as the theory of value and the analysis of wages and capital. There were sections on accumulation and crises, imperialism, and transition, but no explicit attention to Marx's analysis of history. Students were urged to read Marx's *Capital* and *Critique of Political Economy*. The other reference was Rexenberg's (Rosenberg?) *Annotation of Das Kapital.*

The reading lists (not all described here) were relatively ambitious. The English-language listings resembled—and may have been—reading lists for graduate-level courses in the United States. Very likely most students did not read them, but relied on lecture notes and on Chinese-language references. The latter were a distinct minority. It is fair to say that this entire document illustrates Beida's commitment to the introduction of western economic ideas into China. At the same time, there was a conscientious effort to present materials relating to China.

The 1935 Program

In 1935 a similarly detailed program description was published.[26] As one would expect, many of the items were relatively unchanged. But greater attention seems to have been given to China's economy.

Zhou Binglin offered a new course on the theory of industry and trade, based on Alfred Marshall's *Industry and Trade* (4th ed., 1923). The course description indicated an emphasis on "industrial technology and the evolution of commercial organization . . . Though there is some analysis, the main point is to describe in order to provide historical and practical knowledge which can hardly be obtained from theoretical economics."

Another new course dealt with the history of socialism and social movements, taught by French-trained Lu Yuwen. The reading list was quite extensive (and all in English), as follows:

Harry W. Laidler, *History of Socialist Thought*, 1927; *Socialism in Thought and Action*, 1920
Werner Sombart, *Socialism and the Social Movement in the Nineteenth Century*, 1909
Max Beer, *General History of Socialism and Social Struggles*, 1930; *Fifty Years of International Socialism*, 1935
Friedrich Engels, *Socialism, Utopian and Scientific*, 1892
Karl Marx and Engels, *Communist Manifesto,* [1848]
Bertrand Russell, *Proposed Roads to Freedom: Socialism, Anarchism and Syndicalism*, 1919

Sidney and Beatrice Webb, *History of Trade Unionism* (rev. ed., 1920); *Industrial Democracy*, 1920
Rajani Palme Dutt, *The Two Internationals*, 1920
D. Ryazanov [David B. Goldenbach], *Karl Marx and Friedrich Engels*, 1927

It is significant that this course could be offered. This suggests that the dismissal of Chen Qixiu occurred because of his overt leftist political activism, and that the KMT authorities were less zealous in persecuting the mere presentation of leftist ideas in the classroom.

The course in modern economic theory was now given by Li Nailu, with a distinct Austrian tilt. The course offered "Pre-war economic thought (1871–1914) with emphasis on neo-historicism and the Austrian-German School", represented by Gustav Schmoller, Eugen Bohm-Bawerk, Georg F. Knapp, and Beatrice and Sidney Webb. For the post-war period emphasis was given to Othmar Spann, Joseph Schumpeter, Robert Liefman, and Werner Sombart. Reading suggestions were as follows:

Eugen Böhm-Bawerk, *Positive Theory of Capital* (1925 trans.)
John Neville Keynes, *Scope and Method of Political Economy*, 1904
Friedrich von Wieser, "The Austrian School and the Theory of Value", *Economic Journal*, 1891
Allyn Young, "Jevons's Theory of Political Economy", *Economic Problems New and Old*, 1927
Thorstein Veblen, *The Place of Science in Civilization*, 1919

Zhou Binglin and Tao Hsi-shen (Xisheng) offered a course on research in Chinese economic history and another on the history of China's economy. These seemed to have been particularly directed toward graduate students. Students were required to contact the Chinese Economic History Office, "which is set up for the purpose of this course" to use its materials. This Office was especially collecting materials on the Song and Tang dynasties.

Chen Huishen presented a new course on current economic problems in China. Thirteen different instructors were listed, covering such topics as Chinese banking and currency, land tax, income and inheritance tax, local finance, dumping of Japanese goods into the Chinese market, land use, and coal and textile industries.

Zhao Naituan's course in economic theory showed substantial updating, adding the following readings:

Herbert J. Davenport, *Value and Distribution*, 1908; *Economics of Enterprise*, 1913
James Bonar, *Philosophy and Political Economy*, 3rd ed., 1922

Oswald Fred Boucke, *The Development of Economics*, 1933
William A. Scott, *Development of Economics*, 1933
John A. Hobson, *Work and Wealth*, 1914
Frank A. Fetter, *Economics*, 1927
Thorstein Veblen, *Theory of Business Enterprise*, 1904
John R. Commons, *Institutional Economics*, 1934

While Fetter's book was strongly Austrian-marginal-utility neo-classical in approach, many of the others had a strong institutionalist cast.

Zhao also introduced a course on business cycle theory, listing 13 assigned titles. All were western items, including such notables as Alvin Hansen, J. M. Clark, Wesley Mitchell, Irving Fisher, Arthur Pigou, and Frank Knight. Zhao's efforts to direct students' attention to the problems of the Great Depression were admirable. Unfortunately, the analysis of business cycles at the time was seriously muddled. Not until the publication and digestion of Keynes's *General Theory* (1936) did the economics profession succeed in focusing attention on the behavior of aggregate demand. The absence of such a focus prior to 1936 contributed to the muddled policies adopted by many western countries in the 1930s. Here, as in other subject areas, the efforts of Chinese economists to transmit valuable insights from western analysis were thwarted when those "insights" were deficient.[27]

These Beida documents list a total of 153 separate publications assigned to students. We identified the national origins of the authors as shown in Table 12-2 below.

Table 12-2. National Origins of Beida Recommended Readings in Economics, 1933 and 1935

Country	Number	Percentage %
China	22	14
U.S.	72	47
Great Britain	39	25
Germany	8	5
France	5	3
Others	7	5
Total	153	100*

* Rounded to the nearest whole number.

Items by American authors made up about half of the total, while Britons contributed another one fourth. About one out of seven readings was of Chinese origin. Books from non-Anglo western authors were represented by English translations.

Readings Collections

Beida's Economics Department also compiled during the 1930s sets of notes and readings relevant to particular courses. One of these, a two-volume undated set entitled *Readings in Economics*,[28] consisted of English-language materials by western authors. Volume 1 contained items dated 1935 and earlier. The selections were an odd mix. The first, probably lifted from a western introductory text, reviewed "Fundamentals of the Science of Economics", such as wants and utility, wealth, property, income, value, exchange, money, and prices. The second was a detailed description of planned Chinese policies for the cotton and silk industries. There followed three American pieces on securities and acceptances. The next three dealt with China's foreign trade. Next was an American study of colonization possibilities in China's northwest. Nankai's Leonard Ting reviewed the role of Chinese banks, and Dorothy Orchard assessed China's manpower.

Volume 2 apparently appeared soon after the outbreak of the War in 1937. Its main section, "The Problem of Economic Organization for War", included selections from 11 western authors, including Adam Smith, Veblen, Clarence Ayres, and Harold Moulton. Other sections dealt with "The Consumer's Dilemma" (in wartime), "Getting Out of War", "Keeping Production Up", and "The Fetish of Reconstruction".

Library inventories indicate that Beida produced at least four other sets of readings: "Notes on Political Economy", "Principles of Economics", "Economic History", and "Money".[29]

The innovations seem to have been relatively successful. By 1937 the Economics Department reported 77 majors (p. 228). The atmosphere under Zhao was more scholarly than before, but lacked the social activism demonstrated at Nankai and Nanjing, and to a lesser degree, at Yanjing.

Wartime and Post-war Conditions 1937–1950

When the War broke out in 1937, Beida moved its operations to Changsha and then to Kunming. There the Southwest Associated Universities (SWAU) began operations in May, 1938, combining resources of Beida, Qinghua, and Nankai universities. This combination produced a faculty of high quality, but faculty and students experienced extreme hardships during much of the War. Library facilities were scant and textbooks scarce. Teaching was very uneven and research virtually ceased.[30] Zhao Naituan did manage to publish a number of short articles in newspapers. One bibliography cites two in 1943, three in 1944, and nine in 1945. These ranged over such diverse topics as "economic freedom versus economic equality", the economic significance of scientific inventions, prospects for China's industrialization, and demobilization at the war's end (*Biographies of Contemporary Chinese Social Scientists*, 1982, pp. 268–270).

Beida's representation in SWAU was smaller than those of Qinghua and Nankai. Zhao Naituan, Zhou Zuoren, Qin Zan, Zhou Binglin, and Yang Hsi-meng (Ximeng—Simon Yang) remained the core of the Beida contingent. The same group continued in this role after the University returned to Peking.

In 1947, Roger Evans, representing the Rockefeller Foundation, visited Beida. He reported that the University now had 3,500 students, of whom 300 were in Economics and another 80 in agricultural economics. He noted that there were "9 professors in economics and their quality makes [Beida's] Department the strongest in China". However, he warned that "The English of Chinese students so declined during the war years that American visiting lecturers . . . will find it hard to communicate successfully here."[31]

Beida did indeed add some impressive new talent. Jiang Shuojie had studied under Friedrich Hayek at the London School of Economics. He came to Peking in 1946, teaching at Yanjing as well as Beida. He left China in 1948 for Taiwan, International Monetary Fund, and Cornell. Known later as S. C. Tsiang, he became a major contributor to analysis of money and international finance and an important advisor to Taiwan.

At the other political extreme was Fan Hong, who had graduated from Beida in 1925. He worked for several years in the Shanghai Institute of Social Sciences, publishing in 1929 a study of the development of wage theory and in 1930 a translation of *Progress and Poverty*, by Henry George. Under sponsorship by the China Foundation for the Promotion of Education and Culture, he went to England in 1935 to study at Cambridge, where he worked mainly with Maurice Dobb and Michael Kalecki. His Marxian leanings were evident in a 1939 article in the *Review of Economic Studies* comparing "Keynes and Marx on the Theory of Capital Accumulation, Money and Interest".[32] He taught at Fudan during the War and joined Beida in 1946. In 1947 he published a short textbook entitled *Modern Monetary Theory*. This incorporated elementary Keynesian analysis of saving and investment with more traditional discussion of money's usefulness, determination of the money supply, and the value of money.[33]

Another distinguished addition was Chen Zhenhan. He had taught at Nankai after finishing his studies there in 1935, then went to Harvard for a PhD with a dissertation on the location of the cotton manufacturing industry in the U.S.

Beida also briefly enjoyed the services of Hu Jichuang, who had completed a master's degree at LSE in 1938. Tai Shiguang, whose master's study at Michigan had concentrated on statistics, visited from his regular position at Qinghua. Tung Kuan-hsien (Dong Guanxian) had a master's degree from Columbia, and Yen Jen-keng (Yan Rengeng) had studied at both Columbia and Harvard. Beida thus managed in the late 1940s to attract more western-trained economists than those that had joined between 1933 and 1945.

Zhao Naituan became a very prolific writer. His bibliography lists 46 items published in newspapers in this period.[34] Most of these were commentaries on current events and policies. But he also managed to write about "ups and downs of classical economics" and to reflect on the Communist Manifesto on its 100th anniversary in 1948. Much of this reflection was captured in another of his titles: "Hotbed of Communism: Hunger and Inflation". In 1948 he published a monumental history of western economic thought, a book which went through several subsequent editions.

After the Revolution

For a time after 1949, Beida ceased to be the flagship university in the Chinese national system. The focus shifted to the newly-created People's University (Renda). Marxian social-science thinking and teaching were to be concentrated at Renda, which for a time had a near-monopoly on graduate instruction in Economics.

Chen Daisun, longtime head of the Qinghua program, was brought in to head Beida's Economics Department, a position he held into the 1980s. When Yanjing University was closed down in 1952–53, Beida moved from its grubby downtown location out to the northwest corner of Beijing, occupying the beautiful campus built for Yanjing in the 1920s. Some of the Yanjing economists were transferred to Beida. Zhao Jing and Hong Junyan (Junyan), who completed their Yanjing studies in the late 1940s, became key members of the Beida faculty.

Beida soon added some top-grade U.S.-trained economists with mathematical and econometric sophistication. Luo Zhiru (PhD Harvard 1937) had been teaching at National Central and working in government statistical agencies. Du Du completed a doctorate at Illinois in 1950 with a dissertation on "The Pricing System in a Planned Economy". Zhou Huazhang received his PhD from Chicago in 1952, where he studied with Tjalling Koopmans.[35]

Zhao Naituan wisely directed his scholarly attention to collecting a vast array of materials on the history of Chinese economic thought. Chen Zhenhan was one of a number of western-trained economists who were denounced as "rightists" during the intense political campaign of 1958, with Fan Hong and Zhao Jing among the denouncers.

The Beida Faculty and Alumni

From numerous faculty lists and from biographical records of individuals, we have identified 76 Beida Economics faculty. (This tabulation does not include Chen Hansheng, L. K. Tao, or Liang Shuming, whose appointments did not officially include Economics.) Among the 76 were 44 with foreign study. Twenty-two studied in U.S. graduate programs, with 7 holding doctorates. Sixteen studied in Europe, eight of them in Britain, and ten in Japan. The balance of national representation was quite different than in Nankai and Qinghua, where U.S.-trained faculty predominated. For most of our period, the department was chaired by Gu Mengyu (German-trained) and Zhao Naituan (PhD Columbia).

Beida alumni contributed significantly to the flow of persons going to the West to study Economics. Thirty-seven studied in the United States and 28 in Britain and Europe—a more cosmopolitan division than in many other schools. Seventeen Beida alumni received western doctorates, including five in the United States and ten in Germany.[36] Ten of these alumni returned to join the Beida faculty, and an additional twenty became faculty members at other Chinese universities. Xiao Zheng returned from Germany to direct the Institute of Land Research at the Central Political Institute and later transferred this expertise to Taiwan. Zhu Xie built on his German doctoral research to head the Economics Department at National Central University and to publish extensively on government finance and related topics (*Who's Who in China* 1950, p. 60).

Down through the time of Cai Yuanpei's presidency, the Beida Economics Department had a strong international quality. Nineteen of the earliest 23 faculty members had studied abroad, eleven in Germany or Japan. Subsequently, the foreign-trained component was only about half, as Beida, like the other universities, hired its own good students.

Among the universities we are surveying, the Beida faculty contained the largest number of Marxists, beginning of course with Li Dazhao and Chen Hansheng. An early convert was Li Chi, who graduated from Beida in 1918 and studied political economy at Frankfurt. He taught sociology at "Red" Shanghai College (noted in Chapter 10), wrote about Marx and translated portions of *Das Kapital* (Chiang 2001, p. 142). Chen Qixiu was apparently on the faculty from 1919 to 1934; Chow Tse-tung described him as a "pioneering translator of a part of *Das Kapital* and a famous economic writer" (1960, p. 244). Chien Chia-chu (Qian Jiaju) was hired at Beida after he graduated in 1930. According to Douw, Qian had been a Communist since 1925 (1991, pp. 154–155). He left in 1935, perhaps as part of the process that led to Chen's dismissal. Fan Hong arrived in 1946. On the other side, Zhou Binglin was (according to Helen Snow) a leader of anti-Communist activities in Beida (pp. 94–95).

Evidence of a Marxist element is certainly supported by the career of Chen Chung-ching (Zhongjing). He entered Beida in 1934 and became a student activist during the mass protest of December 9, 1935. He became a leader of the Communist-linked National Liberation Vanguard of China. After military service he became an official in the San-min Chu-I Youth Corps created by the KMT. They assigned him to Kunming where he studied at SWAU. After completing his studies there, he proceeded to study Economics at Columbia University, in 1946–49. Returning to China after the Communist take-over, he rapidly moved into a series of prominent positions in diplomatic service, particularly those involved with cultural relations with foreign countries. His career was temporarily derailed during the Cultural Revolution, but he was rehabilitated and ultimately became a member of the Beida faculty.[37]

Another important Marxist was Wang Sihua (Beida 1926), who studied in France and England in 1926–30. He then joined the Beida faculty and also taught at the Franco-Chinese University. In the late 1930s he moved to Yanan, taught at the Communist Central Party School, and was Director of Japanese research for their Central Academy. In 1952 he became Director of the state office of statistics in the new Communist government (*Biographies of Contemporary Chinese Social Scientists*, IX).

Graduates of SWAU are discussed in the next chapter. Beida's post-1949 development figures prominently in our final chapter.

13

Qinghua College and Qinghua University

Qinghua College opened in 1911 with the specific mission of helping prepare Chinese students for university study in the United States. The U.S. government remitted to China $12 million from its share of the Boxer Indemnity. These funds subsidized the students while at Qinghua and provided scholarships to support their subsequent study in the United States.

Preparatory Phase

Qinghua began operations in 1911 primarily as a secondary school, admitting students for a program lasting as long as eight years. It is clear, however, that many entered with advanced standing. In 1921 there were 210 students in the "Middle School" section and 346 in the "High School" section (Soothill 1925, p. 203). Courses equivalent to the college freshman and sophomore level were in place by 1917, including Economics. The first Economics teacher was Clarence G. Dittmer, a doctoral student at the University of Wisconsin. He spent three years at Qinghua while preparing his dissertation on living standards in China (Dittmer 1918). His textbook was Richard T. Ely's *Outlines of Economics*, which was used in a number of Chinese universities at that time and had already been translated into Chinese.

Liu Dajun joined Qinghua in 1916, initially as an English teacher, but soon moved into Economics as well.[1] He had completed a bachelor's degree in Economics at Michigan in 1915 and had traveled extensively in the United States to study the economic impact of the War. He left Qinghua in 1919 to begin a highly productive career as one of the national government's principal statisticians. His Michigan schoolmate Carroll Malone, who taught history at Qinghua, collaborated with Professor John B. Tayler of Yanjing on pioneering surveys of rural economic conditions.[2] A Qinghua transcript in use around 1920 indicates two one-semester courses in Economics: economic theory and economic problems. However, a student who graduated in 1921 took an additional year of Economics which included a course in public finance.[3]

In 1922 Qinghua hired Tsai Chin-pin Tsen (Cai Jingping), who had completed his preparatory study at Qinghua in 1915 (Q15), studied at Columbia and left ABD in 1920. Cai, who specialized in labor economics, taught at Fudan and other Shanghai schools in 1920–22. He left Qinghua in 1928 to join the new KMT government, helping organize the Bureau of Inspection and Testing of Commercial Commodities (*Who's Who in China* 1931, p. 381).

Chen Ta (Da, Q16) joined Qinghua in 1923. He had completed his bachelor's degree at Reed College and received a Columbia doctorate in sociology/demography with a dissertation on Chinese migrations which was published by the U.S. Department of Labor in 1923. Chen had met American birth-control advocate Margaret Sanger just before her 1922 visit to China. In his teaching, he alerted students to the problems of China's overpopulation. He was trying to overcome the strongly anti-Malthusian views of Sun Yat-sen, who argued that China's population was, if anything, too small, and that China was in danger of being swamped by "other races". As late as 1944, a prominent economist noted that, because of Sun's influence, "it is very difficult to advocate birth control just at the present" (MacNair 1944, p. xxxii, quoting Wu Jingchao).[4]

In 1924 Chu (Zhu) Binyuan (Q16) joined the Qinghua faculty to teach Economics and Business. He had completed a master's degree at Columbia in 1920 and worked in banking. After the new KMT government was formed, Zhu moved to Nanjing in 1928, joining the Bureau of Statistics of the Legislative Yuan and teaching at National Central University.[5] Li Pao-liu (Baoliu—Q12) also taught briefly at Qinghua. He had master's degrees from Wisconsin and Harvard and had been Dean of Commerce at Nankai.[6] All of the six persons whom we have identified as teaching Economics at Qinghua prior to 1925 had studied in the United States and four had been Qinghua preparatory students. The most prominent returning preparatory students came to Qinghua after it attained full university status—Chen Daisun (Q20), Zhao Renjun (Q21), and Huang Xianru (Q21). They are discussed below.

Between 1914 and 1929, 1,268 Qinghua preparatory students came to study in the United States (Wang 1966, pp. 111–112). Of these, 187 were Economics students. We examined this group in Chapter 6. All of these began their overseas studies as undergraduates, but 114 proceeded on into graduate-level Economics. The Qinghua preparatory group constituted about 30 percent of the graduate-level Chinese Economics students we have recorded for 1915–29.

These Qinghua students completed their baccalaureate studies in 48 different U.S. colleges and universities. The largest number (25) went to Wisconsin, perhaps reflecting the influence of Dittmer (and Ely). Pennsylvania ranked second with 21. Relatively few attended Harvard or Columbia as undergraduates.

The preparatory students contributed to the introduction of western economic ideas through university teaching and through research. Table 13-1 summarizes data on the occupations of the 144 of them who continued into graduate programs.[7]

Table 13-1. Subsequent Occupations of Qinghua Preparatory Students in Economics who Entered U.S. Graduate Study

Occupation	G	MA	ABD	PhD	MBA	Other Graduate	Total
Economics faculty	7	15	5	14	4	3	48
Economics research	3	2	1	3	5	1	15
Government	8	7	3	7	3	5	33
Banking	2	9	2	1	5	1	20
Other business	7	8	2	0	5	2	24
Others, unknown	10	13	1	1	0	4	29
Total students	34	47	11	18	20	14	144

Some persons appear in more than one category. Rows add up to totals shown; columns do not.
Sources: See note 5.

Of our 144 preparatory students, 48—one third—taught Economics in Chinese colleges and universities. Eleven of these returned to Qinghua, and we will discuss them further below. In all, the 48 worked in 35 different institutions, several in three or more. The 18 who received doctoral degrees are enumerated in Table 13-2. Many have been discussed above.

Combining undergraduate and graduate study in the United States, many of the preparatory students were away from China for a long time.

Table 13-2. Qinghua Preparatory Students who Received Economics Doctorates in the U.S.

Name	Q year	Graduate school	PhD year	Teaching
Chen Da	1916	Columbia	1923	Q, Yanjing, SWAU
Chen Daisun	1920	Harvard	1926	Q, SWAU
Duan Maolan	1921	Columbia	1928	(Nankai)
He Haoruo	1922	Wisconsin	1926	(Nanjing, Nat. Cent.)
Huang Fenghua	1914	Columbia	1919	
Huang Xianru	1921	Columbia	1928	Yanjing, Beida, Q,
Ji Chaoding	1924	Columbia	1936	(St. John's)
Li Gan	1920	Harvard	1927	(Nat. Cent., Jiaotong)
Li Quanshi	1918	Columbia	1922	Fudan, Suzhou
Liang Zhuzhang	1927	Penn	1933	Guangzhou, Jiao., NE
Lin Weiying	1928	Columbia	1936	Nankai, SWAU
Liu Tingmian	1918	Columbia	1924	(Nanjing, Nat. Cent., Northeast, Yanjing, Fudan)
Mai Jianzeng	1923	Columbia	1930	Q, Jiaotong
Pan Guanghui	1925	NYU	1929	
Tang Chongci	1919	California	1927	
Zhao Renjun	1921	Harvard	1928	Q, Yanjing, Guanghua, Sichuan
Zhu Baoxun	1922	Columbia	1929	(Yanjing)
Zhu Zhongdao, Tahmy	1914	Harvard	1920	

Parentheses indicate persons primarily employed outside universities, chiefly in government.

Sources: Qinghua University Archives; Yuan 1961; Boorman 1967–71; *Who's Who of the Chinese Students in America* 1921; other student files.

The median time between arrival in the United States and completion of studies ranged from 4 years for MA students to 5 for ABDs, and 7 for PhDs. Though many of them wrote theses and dissertations on China-related topics, their environment and studies were focused on the United States and other western countries.[8] Between their time at Qinghua and their lengthy time in the United States, they became extremely fluent in English and strongly geared to academic achievement—thus the high percentage who proceeded into graduate study.

The returned students brought back to China the various activities and concepts relevant to quantitative research. The most important of these were survey research and index numbers. As we noted, Qinghua entered early into survey research through the work of Malone and Tayler. Numerous government agencies and banks developed research and statistical departments. After the mid-1920s, there was a vast outpouring of statistical data on China's economy. Of our 144 returned preparatory students reviewed in Table 13-1, 15 were identified with research organizations (9 of these also did university teaching). Chang Hsin-yi (C. C. Chang, Zhang Xinyi, Q22) was one of the first researchers with the National Agricultural Research Bureau, producing pioneering estimates of China's farm land area and crop output. Liu Tingmian (Q18) headed the post-1927 Nanjing government's national statistical office, and staff members included Chen Huan-yin (Q22), Tseng Chao-cheng (Zeng Zhaocheng, Q20), and Wu Ta-chun (Dajun, Q23). Associated with the National Economic Council (NEC) were Huang Xianru (Q21), Lin Weiying (Q28), and Yu Hsiang-ling (Xiangling, Q24). The NEC was part of the government's effort to attract foreign investment in the transport and industrial projects associated with Sun Yat-sen.

Of the returned students associated with the Central Bank, the most interesting was Ji Chaoding (Q24). He apparently joined the Communist Party secretly in the mid-1920s during his student days at Chicago. His Columbia dissertation dealt with the long-term evolution of water-control projects—a study noted favorably by Dwight Perkins (1968). Ji worked for several years as a researcher for the New-York-based Institute of Pacific Relations, writing on China-related topics. Aided by personal connections with H. H. Kung, he returned to China to a high position with the Currency Stabilization Board in 1941, and held other government positions during the War. After the War he taught at St. John's University, became research director for the Central Bank, and moved into a comparable position with the newly formed People's Bank after the Communist take-over in 1949 (Boorman 1967, I, pp. 293–297).

Another prominent figure linked to both teaching and research was He Haoruo (Q22, PhD Wisconsin). A government official and high military officer, He became a lieutenant general in 1945. He served as Chief of the Fiscal Department of Hunan Province, where he founded the Hunan Economic Investigation Bureau ("A Survey of Recent Studies on Chinese Economy, 1927–1947"). During the War he was successively Director of Commodity Administration in the Ministry of Economic Affairs (1942); Deputy Secretary-General of the National General Mobilization Council

(1943–44), and member of the National Military Council. While in Nanjing, he taught at National Central and Nanjing Universities.[9]

Duan Maolan joined the Ministry of Foreign Affairs and ultimately held diplomatic staff positions in Australia, the Philippines, and England in 1941–49 (*Who's Who in China* 1940; *Who's Who in Modern China* 1954, p. 221). Li Gan held numerous government positions. In 1935 he was with the Shanghai Tax Regulation Committee. During the War he was Commercial Councillor in the Chinese Embassy in Washington D.C. He subsequently served on the Supreme Economic Council and Import Export Board. He moved to Taiwan in 1949 (*Who's Who in Modern China* 1954, p. 125).

A Real University

In 1925 Qinghua became a full-scale university, with Zhu Binyuan as first Chair of the Economics Department. In 1928 it became a national university. The explicit aim of preparing students for study in the United States was phased out, and the preparatory department closed in 1929. As late as 1928–29 the total enrollment was only about 500 students (*China Year Book* 1931–32, p. 452). Economics offerings expanded rapidly. Economics majors numbered only eight in 1926, but the number shot up to 95 by 1928.[10] In 1927 Qinghua hired Liu Ssu-yeh (Siye), who had just completed a PhD at the London School of Economics.[11]

John Israel commented as follows about Qinghua at this time:

> Tsinghua became China's most Americanized national university—in some ways every bit as Americanized as its privately established neighbor, Yenching. Like most Chinese universities, Tsinghua hired its own [graduates], and its administration and teaching staff soon became dominated by an old boy network of Tsinghua graduates with American Ph.Ds.
>
> Tsinghua's American-plan curriculum emphasized a broad liberal education in the first two years followed by specialization in a major. Regulations and procedures, examinations, grading, etc., were likewise based on the American model . . .
>
> By the mid-1930s Tsinghua was not only China's outstanding higher educational institution for the sciences and engineering, but also among the nation's preeminent universities in the social sciences and humanities.[12]

Qinghua's funding arrangements were much more generous than other Chinese universities, making possible a very high ratio of faculty to students, and reducing faculty turnover (Israel 1982–83, pp. 29–30).

The Chen Daisun Era

One of Dittmer's best students was Chen Tsong, later known as Chen Daisun. Dittmer persuaded Chen to enroll at Wisconsin, where he completed his undergraduate studies in 1920. He then proceeded to Harvard where he obtained his PhD in 1926 with a dissertation on the relation between local government expenditures and population density in Massachusetts. After traveling extensively in Europe, he returned to China to join Qinghua where he became Economics Chair in 1928 and Dean of the Law School in 1929.[13]

Chen continued his research into public finance, assembling a large body of material on financial systems of various countries. Unfortunately, these were lost during the War and never published. However, he did publish frequent commentaries on current economic events and conditions.[14]

Chen's main task, however, was to staff a rapidly expanding department. By 1932 he had assembled an impressive group with American graduate degrees in Economics. These included two of his Harvard schoolmates, Xiao Chu and Zhao Renjun. Xiao had studied at Missouri and Cornell before moving to Harvard in 1922. He worked with the Economic Research Institute there and began (but did not complete) a dissertation on the theory of business profits. In 1925 he joined the Nankai faculty as Head of the Departments of Economics and Literature (!), moving to Qinghua in 1928. In 1932 he was teaching the introductory course, international trade theory, and general economic theory.[15]

Zhao Renjuan completed his doctorate at Harvard in 1928 with a dissertation on the relationship between real wages and the cost of living in Massachusetts. Before joining Qinghua, he worked as a statistician for the government Bureau of Markets, Ministry of Finance, preparing data for tariff schedules.[16] In 1932 Zhao was teaching mathematics of finance, statistics, railway economics, monetary theory, and business cycles.

In 1929 Qinghua hired Chen Jintao, the first Chinese to receive a PhD in Economics (Yale, 1906). By 1929 Chen was 59 years old. He had spent most of his time after 1906 in government positions, chiefly in the Ministry of Finance (Boorman 1967, pp. 170–172). He left Qinghua before 1932. Another senior appointment was Zhang Wei, who was in 1932 teaching history of Chinese finance. Zhang had received a bachelor's degree from Cambridge in 1910 and taught at the National Law College in Peking in 1911–16.[17]

Selskar Gunn of the Rockefeller Foundation (RF) visited Qinghua in

1931 as part of an extended reconnaissance of Chinese universities. He gave it very mixed reviews, as the following indicates:

> The Institution makes a generally good impression. However, this is the place where there has been much trouble with the students. As far as I could determine there is not very much [research] work going on in the Social Sciences, although Professor Chen [Da], whom I saw in Shanghai, is reputed to be one of the best men in the country. He is particularly interested in labor problems . . . I believe that there is no opportunity at the present time for any serious consideration of [RF] aid to Tsing Hua in either Natural or Social Sciences.[18]

The 1932 Qinghua faculty list showed two men with Columbia doctorates. Mai Jianzeng had obtained a Harvard MBA in 1926, then proceeded to Columbia where his doctoral research was on Albert Gallatin's fiscal policies. His principal appointment was at Peking's Jiaotong University where he taught business subjects. Huang Xianru had been a fellow Qinghua student with Chen Daisun and Zhao Renjun (see Table 13-2). Huang received his doctorate from Columbia in 1928, writing about state taxation of railways in the United States. He taught at Yanjing in 1929–32, then shifted to Qinghua. In 1932 he was teaching international economic policies, topics on taxation and rent, and history of economic thought.

John K. Fairbank, later to become one of America's premier sinologists, taught economic history at Qinghua in 1933–35 while working on his doctoral research.[19]

Operating on a spacious rural campus (which it still occupies) northwest of urban Peking, Qinghua flourished in the pre-war 1930s. The Economics program was highly popular. Over the period 1926–36, 259 students graduated with Economics majors, and there were 148 majors enrolled in 1936 alone. Qinghua introduced a graduate program in Economics, enrolling a total of 24 students, but the War disrupted the program and only two students finished master's degrees. One was Wang Binghou, who then joined the Qinghua faculty and ultimately went to Columbia for graduate study.[20]

Another former Qinghua preparatory student joined the Economics faculty by 1932: Tsai Ko-hsuan (Cai Kexuan, Q24). He had graduated from Wisconsin and received a master's degree from Columbia. In the mid-1930s he taught statistics, money and banking, and international economics. He also worked for the Ministry of Railways.

Western-trained economists who joined Qinghua after 1932 included a number of part-time professors from the faculties of other Peking universities. Qin Zan (ABD Columbia) taught for Qinghua beginning 1936. Qin was on the Beida faculty and had worked for the Institute of Social Research in 1929. Liu Tien-chen (William Liu) was professor and chair at Furen University. Liu had received a PhD from Northwestern in 1930 with a dissertation on John A. Hobson's welfare economics. He taught economic theory and history of economic thought in the mid-1930s.

A course list for 1935 indicates that the introductory course, taught by Chen Daisun, used the familiar American textbook by Fairchild, Furniss, and Buck. Other courses included economic history of Europe, statistics, accounting, money and banking, public finance, history of economic thought, international trade and finance, railway economics, and economic theory. Xiao Zhu offered a course in economic policy and strategy for social reform. This course encouraged students to discuss the feasibility of various reform policies for China.

Wartime Operations

When the War broke out in 1937, Qinghua moved its operations to Changsha and then to Kunming, combining with Beida and Nankai to form Southwest Associated University (SWAU). In Changsha, 1,452 students enrolled in November 1937, of which 631 were from Qinghua. After the move to Kunming, classes began in May, 1938, with about 1,000 students. Ultimately enrollment reached about 3,000 students, but attrition was very high. The combined Economics teaching staff in Kunming was of high quality. But the faculty and students lived under conditions of extreme hardship. Teaching was uneven and research virtually ceased (Fenn 1940; Fairbank 1982, pp. 192–232).

However, Qinghua was able to recruit talented economists with western degrees. The biggest impact was made by Xu Yunan, a Qinghua graduate of 1935. Xu had received a doctorate from Cambridge in 1940 with a dissertation on the impact of the depression on China's cotton industry. Cambridge in the 1930s and 1940s had been in the forefront of innovation in western economics, spearheaded by Joan Robinson and John Maynard Keynes. Xu had studied with Keynes and Robinson, and incorporated their ideas into his courses in economic theory. These were received with great enthusiasm by the students. Xu played a major role in bringing Keynes's ideas into China (Trescott 1996).

Wu Qiyuan came to Kunming in 1938 after completing a doctorate at

LSE on the history of the theory of international price relationships. He published a number of articles on wartime economic problems, including an excellent analysis of the inflationary impact of Chinese wartime monetary policy.[21] Throughout the SWAU period, European economic history was taught by Chang Teh-chang (Dechang), who had studied in England.

Lee Shu-ching (Li Shuqing) had graduated from Qinghua in 1935. After completing a master's degree in agricultural economics at Wisconsin in 1938, he returned to teach this field at SWAU in 1939–44. After the War he returned to the United States and received a PhD in 1950 from Chicago.[22] Another Qinghua graduate was Tai Shih-kuang (Dai Shiguang 1931), who completed a master's degree in Statistics at Michigan. He returned to teach at SWAU in 1938.[23]

One of the most ambitious research enterprises of the wartime period involved population research by Chen Da. Beginning in 1938 he organized and directed an Institute for Census Research. Over the next few years this institute was involved in a number of local enumerations. Chen produced a major book on *Population in Modern China*, which presented a bibliography of 8,000 entries (through 1936) (*China Institute Bulletin*, November 1940, pp. 20–21).

Post-War

At the end of the War, Chen Daisun headed a committee to prepare the Peiping campus for Qinghua's return. It had been badly damaged by Japanese and KMT troops. Classes were resumed in November, 1946, with about 2,300 students. Hardship conditions continued for most students and faculty. Political instability and civil war brought constant turmoil. "In a two-year period there were thirteen boycotts of classes, adding up to nearly two months of classes." (Israel 1982–83, p. 159)

In May, 1947, Roger Evans of the Rockefeller Foundation met with Chen Daisun and other Qinghua notables. His discussion with Chen focused on research. According to Evans, Chen "stresses comparative, indigenous studies, proceeding from basic data to be collected from field studies . . ." Several such projects had been initiated at Kunming in 1944 using funds from the U.S. State Department. "Another interest of Chen's is Chinese finance during the war and post-war . . . Has substantial material, especially publications, interviews, etc., but access to official data is difficult and guarded."[24] However, Chen's reprinted publications did not represent the kind of extensive research of which he spoke to Evans.[25]

Evans also met with Wu Ching-chao (Jingchao). While nominally a member of the sociology department, Wu (ABD Chicago 1926) had been attached to the Ministry of Economic Affairs during the War and had written extensively about price controls and rationing. In 1947 he was studying the influence of local taxation on poverty.[26]

The most distinguished Economics appointment of this period was Liu Dazhong. Liu, who had an engineering background, received an Economics doctorate from Cornell in 1940 with a sophisticated mathematical analysis of optimizing behavior by an individual firm. He worked in the Chinese Embassy during the war, developing national-income estimates for China (see Liu 1965). He joined the Qinghua faculty in 1946, but left in 1948 as conditions deteriorated. He returned to a distinguished career as one of America's leading econometricians and a valued adviser to the government of Taiwan (*AEA Directory* 1964; Klein, Nerlove, and Tsiang 1980).

After 1949

The Qinghua campus came under Communist control in December, 1948. At first, the change of regime had no major effects on the Economics program. However, in 1952 Qinghua was reorganized to specialize completely in science and technology (Arkush 1981, pp. 221–228). The Economics Department was abolished and its faculty were transferred to other institutions. In the early 1980s, a program in business administration was introduced, and after a few years formal courses in Economics were again offered.

After the Qinghua Economics program was terminated in 1952, Chen Daisun served briefly as acting president of Central Finance and Banking College in Peking. In 1953 he was transferred to Peking University where he served for many years as Chair of the Economics Department. Ultimately he served on the National People's Consultative Committee and wrote influential articles on the advantages of market economy. He was able to familiarize many of his students with western analysis of market economy through his courses in the history of economic thought.[27]

Zhao Renjun went to Chengdu after 1937, teaching for Sichuan University and Yanjing. Returning to Qinghua after the War, he was subsequently transferred to the newly formed People's University, as was Dai Shiguang.

Xu Yunan joined the Beida faculty in 1952. He translated Keynes's *General Theory* into Chinese. He was persecuted as a "rightist" (along with

Wu Baosan, and other prominent economists) during the anti-rightist campaign of 1958. He died of lung cancer during this ordeal. Chen Da was also attacked as a rightist for his views on population.

Wu Qiyuan left Qinghua in 1947 and joined the United Nations Organization. He headed the Public Administration Division in the Department of Economic and Social Affairs (Fong 1975, p. 124). Wang Binghou also joined the UN in New York.

Overview

After becoming a full university, Qinghua continued to send students to the United States for graduate work in Economics. However, their impact on Chinese higher education was not as significant as the preparatory students enumerated in Tables 13-1 and 13-2. Subsequently to those, we have identified 47 Qinghua graduates studying Economics in the West, 37 in the United States. Of the 47, 14 received doctorates (including some after 1950 and outside Economics). Nineteen became faculty in Chinese universities, five of them at Qinghua.

The most prominent of Qinghua's returned students from the United States was undoubtedly Wu Baosan. After his Qinghua graduation in 1932, he joined the Nankai faculty. There he helped produce a Chinese-language textbook on economic principles based on the book by Fairchild, Furniss, and Buck, which Wu himself had studied at Qinghua. He then joined the Institute of Social Sciences under Academia Sinica, where he specialized in agricultural economics. He produced studies of marketing of foodstuffs in Fujian Province and of China's foreign trade in food products.

Wu then undertook graduate study at Harvard and was strongly influenced by the new Keynesian ideas which were being presented by Alvin Hansen and Seymour Harris. Returning to China in 1939 with a Harvard MA, he rejoined the Institute of Social Sciences, now operating in the interior, where he developed estimates of China's national income and its components. With five young collaborators, he began the work in 1941 and completed it in 1946. His estimates were published in a two-volume work. He then returned to Harvard where he used his estimates as the basis for his doctoral dissertation on capital formation and consumers' outlay in China.[28]

Both Huang Kailu (PhD Wisconsin) and Sang Hengkang (PhD Harvard) joined international organizations after the War. Huang worked with the International Labor Organization for a time, then ultimately came to the United States for academic positions. Sang worked for many years doing economic research for the United Nations Organization. In 1983 he organized and directed the Institute of Transport Economics at Nankai University.

Roger Evans met Xiang Jingyun (PhD Wisconsin) in 1947. After working with exchange-control programs, Xiang was then with UNRRA doing research on rehabilitation of land which was flooded when the KMT government destroyed dykes to deter the Japanese in 1938 (Evans Diary, pp. 15–16). He soon became a high-level administrator with UNRRA and its Chinese-government successor. Preparing to leave China as the Communists approached, he changed his mind in response to a fervent appeal from his secretary, a Communist agent. Under the Communist government he became the executive in charge of light industry for the region around Shanghai, but was persecuted during the Cultural Revolution (Antoinette Stepanek 1992, pp. 219–222).

An additional 27 students from SWAU studied Economics in the West, 25 in the United States. Seven of these completed PhD degrees. Yang Suehchang (Xuezhang) completed a Harvard doctorate in 1950 with a dissertation applying Keynesian income theory to China's depression experience in the 1930s. He ultimately joined the Shanghai Academy of Social Science (Hu 1984, p. 34). Five of the 27 returned to teach Economics in Chinese universities. Many of the 27 could not be traced.

We identified 47 persons who taught Economics at Qinghua up to 1947. Two were Americans, Dittmer and Fairbank. Of the 47, 20—nearly half—had studied in the United States. Table 13-3 provides more information about them.

Table 13-3. Western Study by Qinghua Chinese Economics Faculty up to 1947

Date appointed	to 1926	1927–36	1937–47	Total
U.S.:	5	18	4	27
PhD	1	7	1	9
ABD	1	3	0	4
MA	2	2	3*	7
GS	0	3	0	3
Other U.S.	1	3	0	4
GB & Western Europe	0	4	3	7
None or unknown	0	4	8	12
Total	5	26	14**	45**

* Includes Li Shuqing who completed PhD in 1950.

** Includes one who studied in both US and Western Europe.

Qinghua faculty composition displayed some noteworthy features. We did not find any faculty who had studied in Germany or Japan—in striking contrast with Beida. The faculty appointed before the war broke out in 1937 included a very high proportion of "Anglo"-educated Chinese—22 out of 26. Eighteen of the 45 Chinese faculty members had attended Qinghua, 11 as preparatory students and 7 in the university. Because of Qinghua's superior financial situation, the turnover was lower than in many other schools.

The Qinghua faculty displayed far less inclination toward Marxism than did Beida.[29] A rare Marxist among the Qinghua students was Yu Kuang-yuan (Guangyuan), who graduated in 1936 with a degree in physics. He moved into Communist territory and worked as an editor. After 1949 he became an official in the Scientific Planning Committee. He drafted a book in which he attempted to apply principles of optimization to a Marxist system, discussed in Chapter 15.

Wu Ching-chao (Jingchao), like Chen Da and Li Shuqing, bridged the gap between economics and sociology. After reaching the ABD stage in Economics in 1926, he shifted to completing a doctorate in Sociology at Chicago. Joining the Qinghua faculty, he wrote prolifically on economic topics. After 1935 he entered government service, primarily with the Ministry of Economic Affairs. He was an outspoken critic of most programs for "rural reconstruction" (Douw, pp. 122–126; McNair 1946, p. xxv). In 1940 Wu published three articles on wartime economic controls, and in 1945 wrote a pamphlet on industrial planning in China for the Institute of Pacific Relations. Roger Evans of RF met Wu in 1947 at Qinghua and reported approvingly of his research on the relation of local tax policies to rural poverty (Diary 1947, p. 69). He remained in China after 1949 and was targeted as a "Malthusian" in the anti-rightist campaign of 1957–58 (see Chapter 15).

To assess the level of scholarship of the Chinese universities, we have assembled a file of Chinese authors of publications about China's economy published in the period ending in 1950 (see Table 10-7). Table 13-4 shows the numbers of various Qinghua populations who appear in this list.

About one fifth of the preparatory students who studied Economics in the West, whether at graduate level or not, published something on China's economy. Once Qinghua became a university, alumni who undertook western graduate Economics study showed a higher proportion of authors. This is consistent with the view that the later generation, who studied longer in China and not as long overseas, were more inclined to such

Table 13-4. Publications on China's Economy by Qinghua Students and Faculty, 1911–1950

	Number in group	Number who published	Percentage %
Preparatory students, economics	187	39	21
Preparatory students grad. economics	114	30	26
Qinghua graduate economics	47	15	32
Qinghua faculty*	45	16	36

* Chinese persons teaching Economics.

publication. The Qinghua faculty scored an impressive 36 percent. Although not quite so high as research-oriented Nankai University (44 percent), Qinghua scored higher than Beida (32 percent). Qinghua people dominated the important research areas of demography (Chen Da) and national-income measurement (Wu Baosan and Liu Dazhong). Wu Jingchao and Wu Qiyuan published extensively during the War.

14

The Role of Western Economics in Economic Research in China 1900–1950: Techniques, Ideas, and Personnel

We have touched at many points on the research activities of western-educated Chinese economists. In Chapters 4 to 6 we examined the research involved in doctoral dissertations and master's theses. Most of these did not represent particularly creative or distinguished work.[1] The Chinese university environment was also a very uneven basis for economic research. Among the Chinese universities, for many years only Nankai specified that research and publication were expected of faculty members.[2] Among the missionary colleges, Nanjing's College of Agriculture and Forestry provided much of the best research into China's agricultural economy. However, a number of Chinese universities created economic research units in the 1930s. And our commentaries on individual economists have identified many who published prolifically. Indeed, the traditional Chinese image of the intellectual, which so strongly influenced the behavior of Chinese academics, stressed the role of writing.

We examine western economic ideas in relation to economic research in China prior to 1950 in terms of principal research organizations and principal research techniques. From either perspective, there was little economic research prior to 1920. The first Chinese economist with a strong research impulse was D. K. Lieu (Liu Dajun). He graduated from Michigan in 1915 with a bachelor's degree in Economics. He taught English and Economics at Qinghua for a couple of years, but quickly began writing about China's economy. He became active in the newly formed Chinese Social and Political Science Association and contributed frequently to its English-language journal, the *Chinese Social and Political Science Review* (*CSPSR*). In 1921 he helped organize the Peking national government's Bureau of Economic Information and served as its research director until

1928. Liu was a founder of the Chinese Economic Association in 1923 and was for the following 30 years one of China's most prolific producers of empirical economic research.[3]

Liu's most important work was his *Growth and Industrialization of Shanghai* (Lieu 1936). This was a data collection without much economic analysis, based on surveys taken in 1931 and 1933. Reviewer Leonard Ting praised the work for presenting data on the value of output, costs of purchased inputs, and therefore an approximation to "value added by manufactures". These data became an important resource for Wu Baosan's pioneering national-income estimates, even though data were obtained for Chinese-owned factories only—a major limitation (Ting 1937, p. 1103).

By 1920 a number of government sources were gathering and publishing economic data. The Chinese customs service began under Sir Robert Hart to publish data on foreign trade and related magnitudes. The railway system was another source of economic data, reflecting the influence of Henry Carter Adams. Within the Ministry of Finance, the Bureau of Markets published data on wholesale prices, and began in 1919 to present index numbers of prices. The government's Bureau of Economic Information began in 1923 to publish the *Chinese Economic Monthly* which became (1927) the *Chinese Economic Journal*. These presented numerous data from surveys and other studies (Chiu 1933, pp. 7–17, 71–72).

By the 1930s scholars with western training in statistical methods held a number of positions with government statistical agencies. Wu Ta-chun (Dajun) headed the national government's Bureau of Statistics 1932–47. He received a BA (Economics) and an MBA from Penn, finishing in 1926 (*China Handbook* 1950; *China Year Book* 1931). Lin Wei (Peter Wei Lin) was by 1931 a division chief in that agency (Lin 1931, p. 135). Lin was ABD in Economics at Columbia, where he had completed a master's degree in 1922. Chu Chun-yi (Jennings P. Chu—Zhu Junyi) had received a doctorate in education and statistics from Columbia in 1922. In 1933 he became Co-director of the National Bureau of Statistics (*Who's Who in China* 1936, pp. 62–63). Chen Chung-shen (Zhongshen) had written a doctoral dissertation on the Chinese census (Columbia 1925) and in 1928 became an official in the Ministry of Industry, Commerce and Labor.[4] Liu Tingmian (Columbia PhD in Economics, 1924) held a high post in the Statistical Section, Legislative Yuan by 1933.[5] However, the actual data gathering and data processing in government agencies was largely done by young people with a Chinese bachelor's degree (or less).

The principal research techniques were survey research, based on interviews and questionnaires, and the creation of index numbers of economic magnitudes. Both of these were unquestionably imported from the West. Both were extensively practiced in the principal research universities—Nankai, Nanjing, Yanjing—under the direction of westerners such as John B. Tayler and John Lossing Buck or western-trained economists such as Nankai's Fang Xianting and He Lian.

Survey Research

As described by Chiang Yung-chen (1986, 2001), social survey research in China began with the work of American sociologist John Stewart Burgess, who directed some students in interviewing (1912) and subsequently surveying (1914–15) Peking rickshaw pullers. Social surveys were experiencing a great upsurge in the United States at the time, arising from the Christian concern with poverty and social justice.[6] In 1917 Burgess enlisted the aid of Procter and Gamble heir Sidney Gamble. Gamble had received a master's degree in Economics from the University of California, where he had studied with Jessica Peixotto, one of the pioneers in household budget studies analysis. Burgess and Gamble undertook a vast survey of Peking, for which field work extended over 1913–19. Results were published in Gamble and Burgess, 1921.

Gamble produced a major article on "Prices, Wages and the Standard of Living in Peking, 1900–1924" (with Meng Tien-pei; *CSPSR* July 1926). He then directed a more rigorous household survey for which a number of families maintained and reported daily receipts and expenditures. He was able to obtain reportable data from 283 families covering the year ending November, 1927. The survey yielded data on wages and occupations as well as consumption.[7] According to Chiang 1986, "in the late 1910s and early 1920s, [Gamble] was the center of social research in Peking, where he supervised his own Gamble Institute, offered fellowships to students at the Yenching Sociology Department, and financed his own social surveys." (Chiang 1986, p. 269)

Clarence Dittmer, who taught Economics at Qinghua, conducted a household survey using student assistants for his Wisconsin doctoral dissertation. Data were collected over 1914–17 for 195 families, each of which was interviewed (Dittmer 1918; Chiu 1933, p. 216). Qinghua demographer Chen Da (PhD Columbia) undertook several surveys in the early 1920s. His survey of two villages published in 1924 reached the families of school children by having each child escort an investigator to the child's home.[8]

Survey work soon spread to rural China. One stimulus was the formation in November, 1921, of the China International Famine Relief Commission (CIFRC). Both John B. Tayler (Yanjing) and John Lossing Buck (Nanjing) were actively involved with CIFRC, and this involvement led both to begin work on rural surveys. Tayler's project began in June, 1922. Sixty-nine Chinese students from nine colleges conducted the survey in 240 villages of five eastern provinces. Results were published in three installments in the *CSPSR* in 1923–24.[9] Buck's first survey of 102 farms near Wuhu was published in 1923–24. During 1922–23 he surveyed 150 farms in Yenshan county (published 1926).[10] Farm surveys became a central focus of the CAF program, with a heavy emphasis on interviewing individual farm families, as we noted in Chapter 9.

A German agricultural economist, Wilhelm Wagner, published in 1926 a book entitled *Chinesische Landwirtschaft* (Chinese Agricultural Economy). Wagner first came to China in 1911 and taught German in a Shandong middle school, then joined the staff of an agricultural experiment station. Among other data, he relied on intensive budget studies for a small number of farms (Myers 1970, pp. 22–23). A Chinese translation was published in 1935 (Bauer and Hwang 1982, p. 254).

Other universities undertook surveys about the same time. The College of Agriculture at National Southeastern University in Nanjing used students to survey southern Jiangsu Province in 1921–22. Zhongshan University in Guangzhou introduced a course in Rural Survey in 1920 and began actual survey work soon after. They published surveys of silk and sugar industries, using data from 1921–22 (Chiu, pp. 200–204). The missionary Shanghai Baptist College developed a survey program around 1923, aided by sociology professors from Brown University.[11]

Sidney Gamble turned his attention to rural surveys in 1926 when he became affiliated with James Yen's Mass Education Movement. In collaboration with Lee Jinghan, he organized a series of surveys in the rural areas of Dingxian, near Peking. Economic results were published in 1933 and 1936 in Chinese, but the English-language version, with much more detail, did not appear until 1954 (Gamble 1954). Results were reported for a larger sample of 5,255 families and a smaller sample of 515.

By the mid-1920s China was witnessing an explosion of social and economic surveys. "According to one estimate, there were over nine thousand surveys conducted between 1927 and 1935 . . ." (Chiang 2001,

p. 58). This process was advanced by the creation of the two parallel (later intersecting) research institutes for social sciences (below). One chronic problem in these studies was a lack of attention to sampling error. How representative of the larger population were the survey results?[12] A more mundane problem was that a large proportion of the raw data collected could not be properly processed and published.

Index Numbers

The story of index numbers is shorter and simpler. In 1919 the government established the Bureau of Markets, Ministry of Finance, in Shanghai to collect data on wholesale prices as a basis for tariff revision. Under the direction of T. Sheng (Sheng Jun), they began to produce ongoing index numbers for wholesale prices in September, 1919. A major purpose was to sort out the impact of inflation on various participants in the economy. Sheng wrote in 1925, "the system of indexing was unknown until some ten years ago when Mr. Yang Tuan Loh [Lu] introduced it to this land . . ."[13] A good review of the evolution of index numbers in China is given by Lin Wei-ying 1935, pp. 96–103.

In 1924 Sheng sent inquiries to many western experts asking for advice on the choice of price quotations. Replies were received from Walter Stewart of the Federal Reserve Board, Walter Layton of the London *Economist*, Arthur Bowley of LSE, and other representatives of periodicals and official agencies (1925, pp. 34–55). Separate indexes for import and export prices began in 1926, with cost of living added in 1930.

During his time at Yale, He Lian (Franklin Ho) had worked closely with Irving Fisher in developing index numbers.[14] When He left Yale in 1926, Fisher gave him $500, which He used to buy a set of the annual reports of the Chinese Customs Service. He used these to derive historical indexes covering 60 years for the prices and quantities of imports and exports, and for China's barter terms of trade. Soon Nankai was publishing a wide variety of index numbers for Northeast China. Zhongshan University's newly formed (1931) Bureau of Economic Research published wholesale price indexes for the Guangzhou area. The Institute of Social Research, China Foundation, began publishing in 1929 a monthly index of the cost of living in Peiping (Simon Yang 1928; Fong 1935, pp. 163, 168). A number of the universities, including Nanjing and Yanjing, developed price indexes for their localities.

Like social surveys, price index calculations became very numerous after 1930. In 1944, Li Zhuomin commented:

> There is now practically no city of any importance in the interior that does not claim at least one series of wholesale or retail price indexes, compiled by the Central Government agencies, the Government Banks, or the Provincial Governments. Not a few of these series, however, are of questionable value. This widespread interest in price indexes has really grown out of the need of finding some basis on which to adjust the scale of payment for the government employees. (Li Choh-ming 1944, pp. 214–215)

We must also mention national-income analysis, although it did not take shape even in the West until the 1930s, and did not materialize in China until the 1940s. The pioneering national-income estimation in China was performed by Wu Baosan, while parallel estimation was being done in the United States by Liu Dazhong. These are further discussed below.

Developing statistical data on China's national economy was seriously impeded by internal disorder and particularly by the Japanese incursions from 1931 on. Loss of Manchuria disrupted the operations of the customs service and prevented calculation of accurate data on international trade and payments. Outright war from 1937 disrupted even more the collection and interpretation of national economic data.

Research Organizations

The China Foundation for the Promotion of Education and Culture was created in 1924 to administer the American Boxer Indemnity funds. In 1926 they established a Department of Social Research. It was renamed the Institute of Social Research in 1929 and was long headed by L. K. Tao (Chiang 1986, p. 258; Sun 1987, pp.115–116). The Institute employed its own research staff who produced a number of monographs as well as a journal, *The Quarterly Review of Social Sciences.*

Tao's preface to one of the earliest monographs provides a poignant insight into the environment for social surveys:

> Circumstances . . . were unfavourable for conducting a survey of this kind when this Department first commenced its operations some two years ago. The country was then divided into a number of administrative areas under various militarist leaders and it was extremely difficult to obtain permission from them for any kind of serious study of labour. Except for districts under the jurisdiction of the Nationalist Government where a liberal policy toward labour was pursued, labour unions were all banned and any intercourse between

> an educated person and a labourer might entail danger to both . . . In fact, labour was then a tabooed subject. Even a strictly theoretical discussion of it was hardly considered proper, as it was apprehended that it might be propaganda of socialistic ideas in disguise.[15]

One of the earliest monographs, "An Index of the Cost of Living in Peiping", by Simon Yang (Yang Ximeng), illustrates the combination of social survey and index number calculation. Yang worked with 48 working families, each keeping household accounts for the period November, 1926 to April 1927. These provided base-period quantities which he used to calculate a Laspeyres index, following Fisher.[16]

Yang's study and six other Institute monographs were reprinted in 1982, edited by Ramon Myers. Of the ten authors identified, only two had studied Economics at the graduate level in the West. Selskar Gunn of the Rockefeller Foundation, who visited the Institute in 1931, noted that "most of [the] research workers . . . have had all of their training in China".[17]

In 1928 the newly formed KMT government established the Academia Sinica to conduct and promote scientific research. It was initially headed by Cai Yuanpei. By 1931 it had organized nine institutes, including an Institute of Social Sciences. In 1929 Cai appointed Chen Hansheng to head the sociology program. Chen had left his post at Beida to study in Moscow at the International Agrarian Institute. He directed several studies relating to land tenure and social relationships in agriculture.[18] Among members of his research staff were several of his former Beida students, chiefly Chang Hsi-chang (Zhang Xichang) and Wang Yinsheng (Douw 1991, pp. 145–151; Chiang 2001, pp. 162–165). The now-best-known members of the group were Xue Muqiao and Sun Yefang, who became prominent after 1949. A major concern for Chen was to determine China's "stage of development according to the [Marxian] universal pattern of development".[19]

In 1933 Chen and associates formed the Society for the Study of China's Agrarian Economy. Their periodical *Rural China* published much of their research. In 1933, Chen was appointed a member of the newly formed Commission for Rural Rehabilitation, and was able to design large-scale rural surveys of four major provinces. Chen used these to support his view that "China's agrarian economy would not by itself move toward capitalism" (Chiang, p. 188). Chen's surveys, like those of J. L. Buck, did not measure land owned by absentee landlords. Even so, they convincingly documented the concentration of land ownership and the extreme poverty of many of the farmers.

Chen's own research activities, however, were frequently interrupted by his role as a secret agent working for the Comintern, with attendant evasive maneuvers. These took him to Japan and Moscow for much of 1934–35. He moved to New York and worked for the Institute of Pacific Relations from 1935 to 1939 (Chiang 2001, pp. 179–221).

In 1929 the Economics Program at Academia Sinica (AS) was headed by Yang Chien, who conducted research into income taxation and into land economics in China. He was assisted in the latter by Kao Chung-hsia (Gao Zhongxia—MA Columbia 1925). Yang Duanliu studied China's foreign trade over the previous 65 years.[20] Yang Duanliu subsequently headed the Economics program before moving to his long-term position teaching at Wuhan University.

Another early member of the Institute of Social Sciences was Yen Jen-keng (Yan Rengeng), who joined in 1933 when he graduated from Nankai. The Institute sponsored him to come to the United States to study at Harvard and California. After 1946 he taught at National Central University (Evans Diary, p. 88).

In 1934 the two research organizations were combined as the Institute of Social Sciences, still under Academia Sinica (Chiang, pp. 182–183). This Institute maintained offices in Peiping and Nanjing. Economic research was divided into ten divisions: modern economic history, industrial economics, agricultural economics, money and banking, public finance, international trade, population, labor problems, statistics, and public utilities. L. K. Tao became director of the reorganized institution. By the end of 1935 the combined staff had produced research dealing with eight topics, including the "likin" (trade tax), the impact of drought, Peiping municipal finance, Japan's foreign-exchange rate, cooperatives, and wages in China's cotton mills. Research was under way on 19 topics.[21]

From bibliographic sources noted later in this chapter, we assembled names of 32 researchers, authors or editors of Institute publications.[22] In combination with those already discussed, they display a striking pattern. Only three had studied graduate-level Economics in the West before joining the Institute—Chu Chi-sheng (Zhu Jisheng—Wisconsin), Yang Duanliu (LSE), and Qin Zan (Columbia). But at least 14 were able to go abroad for graduate study after serving a research apprenticeship with the Institute. These are identified in Table 14-1.

We have a list of 26 research fellows in Economics attached to the Nanjing office of the Institute.[23] The most prominent was Luo Zhiru, who had completed a PhD in Economics at Harvard in 1937. Liang Qingchun

Table 14-1. Chinese Economists who Moved from Academia Sinica and Predecessors to Graduate Study in the West

Name	Date at AS*	Graduate school	Degree
Cheng Yu-kuei (Zheng Youkui)	(1936)	Brookings 1945	none
Liang Ching-chun (Qingchun)	1927–29	Harvard 1934	PhD
Liang Fang-chung (Fangzhong)	1934–43	Har., LSE 1943–47	none
Luo Zhiru	(1932)	Harvard 1937	PhD
Tang Hsiang-lung (Xianglong)	1929–36	(GB, FR, GE) 1936–39	none
Tiao Pei-chan (Diao Peiran)	(1929)	Har., Il. 1930–33	MA
Wu Pun-nung (Bannong—Leonard)	(1932)	Columbia 1936	MA
Wu Baosan	1932–36**	Harvard 1949	PhD
Yan Rengeng	1932–42	Har., Col. 1942–45	none
Yang Ximeng (Simon)	(1926–35)	Michigan 1936	MA
Yao Tseng-yin (Zengyin)	(1943)	Minnesota 1947	none
Yen Chung-ping (Yan Zhongping)	(1943)	(England) 1947–50	none
Zhang Peigang	(1938)	Harvard 1946	PhD

* Parentheses indicate person was in the organization at that date.

** Returned after Harvard MA 1938 and again after PhD.

Sources: *Contemporary Chinese Social Scientists*; *Brief Biographies of Contemporary Chinese Social Scientists*; *Social Science Biographical Directory*; Wu Baosan interview; publication data in sources noted later in this chapter; "Academia Sinica with its Research Institutes".

joined the Nanjing office after graduating from National Southeastern University in 1927. He then went to Harvard in 1929 and completed a PhD in agricultural economics in 1934, returning to positions with National Zhejiang University (1935–41) and the Farmers Bank (1941–46).[24] Two other fellows had done prior Economics graduate work in the United States: Chen Changheng (GS 1916) and Tiao Pei-chan (Diao Peiran—MA 1933).[25] However, 22 of the 26 are not recorded in our data as having studied in the West or holding Economics faculty posts in Chinese universities.

The most prominent economic researcher with the Institute was Wu Baosan. He joined the Institute in 1932 upon graduating from Nankai. Wu went to Harvard for graduate study, received a master's degree in 1938, and studied in Britain and Germany. Returning to China, he rejoined the Institute in 1939, after it had moved west into Sichuan Province. Wu collaborated with Chun Tsi-yi (Zhun Ziyi) to produce a book on food marketing in Fujian Province and also prepared a statistical analysis of China's foreign trade in foodstuffs (see Ou 1942).

In 1941, Wu became the first Chinese scholar to attempt to prepare national-income data for China. This became a major project for the Institute. Wu had five young assistants, all recent university graduates.[26] Ultimately a two-volume work summarized Wu's estimates in Chinese, while several English-language articles appeared in major western journals (Ou 1946a, 1946b, 1946c). About the same time, national-income estimates were also published by Liu Dazhong (PhD Cornell), working at the Brookings Institution (Liu 1946).[27] Liu's estimates for 1933 were 40 percent higher than Wu's, a difference arising from agricultural estimates (Feuerwerker 1968, pp. 6–9).

Wu's most prominent colleague was Zhang Peigang, who joined the Institute staff after graduating from Wuhan University in 1934. He entered the Harvard graduate program in 1941 and completed his doctorate in 1946 (discussed below).

Rockefeller Foundation's Roger Evans visited the Peiping office of the Institute in 1947. They had six staff, 14 "compilers", and nine translators. They were studying wartime economic conditions using Japanese materials. He felt that director Tao was "a 'good' man, but neither forceful nor imaginative" (Evans Diary 1947, pp. 29, 48).

After 1949, the Institute of Social Sciences became the Institute of Economics under the Chinese Academy of Science. According to Wu Baosan, the staff in 1949 were disgusted with Chiang Kai-shek and all remained in China when the Communists came into power. L. K. Tao remained its head, and Wu Baosan served as deputy director until 1957, when he was victimized in the anti-rightist campaign (discussed in Chapter 15).

Bank Research Departments

In 1930 the Bank of China established the first research department among Chinese banks, and it was for some years regarded as the best ("Research Notes" *NSEQ* 8:2 [July 1935], pp. 395–396). In its prime, it was headed by the first prominent female economist in China, Chang Hsiao-mei (Zhang Xiaomei). She studied at NYU, Chicago, and LSE, and joined the Bank of China in the early 1930s.[28] By the 1940s, research leadership had passed to the Central Bank of China, where the research department came under the directorship of Ji Chaoding in 1946.[29] In 1947, Roger Evans described the research facilities of the Central Bank as follows:

> Chi has a staff of 120 in 4 sections: Statistics, Investigation, Publication . . . , General Administration, and 4 research groups of 19 experts within the Department on monetary matters, public finance, international economics and general economic problems. These experts include men like Chao Lin-pan [Lanpin] . . . formerly chairman of economics at National [Central] Political University . . . and author of the text book on money and banking used in civil service exams; D. K. Lieu, now at Washington, Chen Shao-te, in charge of the general economics work, formerly chairman of economics at [National] Central University, and Wu Chi-tao, Columbia graduate in charge of public finance section. The CB's library of 50,000 books is the largest of all the banks', especially good on Chinese, Japanese, and Western periodicals.[30]

By 1941 the Farmers Bank of China had developed a research department, headed by Liang Ching-chun (Qingchun). Liang had received a doctorate from Harvard in 1934 and had in 1935–41 headed the department of Agricultural Economics at National Zhejiang University (*AEA Directory* 1969).

Tawney's *Land and Labour in China*

R. H. Tawney's *Land and Labour in China*, published in 1932, was clearly the best brief overview of China's economy published to that date. Tawney spent his China visit drawing on the libraries and intellectual resources of Nankai, Yanjing, and Nanjing Universities. The major sections of the book, dealing with agriculture, largely reflect the research and ideas of John Lossing Buck and John Bernard Tayler. The sources cited are a good review of what materials were available by early 1931. Tawney cited 42 Chinese authors. Of these, 22 had studied in the West, 16 of them in U.S. graduate-level economics. Four had studied in Western Europe. His references included five Chinese doctoral dissertations. There are numerous references to D. K. Lieu and to researchers connected with Nanjing's CAF, L. K. Tao's Institute of Social Sciences, and government statistical sources.

Publications

In 1934, the Nankai Institute of Economics initiated a series of bibliographic articles which enable us to document the role of western-trained economists in economic publications. They published citations in both English and

Chinese for 2,235 books and pamphlets on China's economy held by the Institute Library, of which 1,232 were exclusively in Chinese language. Each quarter thereafter citations were published on additional books and pamphlets. In 1935 they added citations to periodical articles on China's economy. These were supplemented by bibliographies on special topics.

Since the Institute had been conscientious in acquiring publications since the early 1920s, their data give a good indication of the output of Chinese-language publications dealing with China's economy. Table 14-2 presents data on Chinese-language books and pamphlets 1922–35.[31]

Table 14-2. Books and Pamphlets on China's Economy in the Nankai Collection, 1922–1935

Year	Items by Chinese					No. Chinese
Published	All	Government	Railway	Banks	Others	authors
1922	33	15	2	0	16	11
1923	27	13	2	0	12	7
1924	36	15	4	0	17	13
1925	86	50	1	1	34	27
1926	33	10	2	0	21	18
1927	63	23	6	0	34	30
1928	85	31	3	0	51	37
1929	162	60	3	3	96	66
1930	219	76	9	4	130	91
1931	212	78	7	9	118	95
1932	161	58	4	12	87	64
1933	205	68	10	6	121	87
1934	243	86	9	19	129	120
1935	266	96	5	15	150	104

Sources: Compiled from *Monthly Bulletin on Economic China* [Nankai University] 1934; *Nankai Social and Economic Quarterly* 1935–40.

The data show a dramatic increase in books and pamphlets dealing with China's economy, particularly between 1927 and 1930 when the new government came into power. By 1935 the volume was ten times that of 1923, a pattern consistent with Table 1-2. The publications were extremely diverse. Government publications consistently represented about one third of the total. Some of these were the ordinary annual reports of agency operations. But many represented economic research. The Customs Service produced voluminous reports; those published in 1926 required over 2,700 pages.[32] Many provincial and local governments published economic research. The Hunan Economic Investigation Bureau, established by He Haoruo, published seven substantial monographs on various aspects of the Hunan economy in 1934–36, three by Zhang Renjia.[33] Most of the government items were published anonymously, but producing them required the services of a large number of research workers. The same was true for the economic research studies published by Chinese railways and banks, most of which came after 1929.

The number of items with identified Chinese authors remained below 30 per year until 1928, then increased rapidly. More than one hundred authors were involved in the output for 1934 and 1935. The time series pattern shown in Table 14-2 is replicated and extended by data we presented in Chapter 1, Table 1-2. These show the number of Chinese authors rising from an average of 16 per year in 1923–28 to a peak of 267 in 1936, then falling to 49 per year or less in 1938–49.

Comparing our list of authors with our rosters of Chinese who studied Economics in the West indicates that the latter constituted only 10–12 percent of the authors (See Table 14-4 below).

Periodicals

During the 1920s, the only periodicals which published much research on China's economy were the *Chinese Social and Political Science Review* and the *Chinese Economic Journal*. After 1930 the number of economic periodicals expanded rapidly. In 1930, the Chinese Economic Association initiated the *Quarterly Journal of Economics*. The Institute of Social Sciences began the *Quarterly Journal of Social Sciences*. Wuhan University created a journal with the same title in 1929. In 1935 both Zhongshan and Qinghua commenced journals entitled *Social Science*. Nankai produced several economic journals. The *Journal of Land Economics* was published by the Chinese Association of Land Economics, beginning in 1933.[34] The Chinese Economic Research Society began publication of *Chinese Economy* in 1933.[35]

In 1935, the Nankai bibliographers began a quarterly listing of periodical articles dealing with Economic China. Their 1935 listings included 61 different Chinese periodicals. Our analysis of the authorship of these articles is included in Table 14-3.[36]

Reviewing the articles published by the *Quarterly Journal of Economics* during its lifetime 1930–37, Sun Chung-hsing determined that "among the

301 articles, fifty-nine were related to the study of contemporary Chinese economic conditions; thirty-seven on money, twenty-seven on various kinds of economic theories; twenty-six on problems of taxes; sixteen on planned economy; fourteen on finance; and thirteen on economic thought." (Sun 1987, p. 139) The *QJE* presented a number of articles summarizing the important ideas of prominent figures in western Economics, including Gustav Cassel, John R. Commons, E. W. Kemmerer, J. M. Keynes, Malthus, Marx, and Adam Smith (p. 374).

Using tables of contents kindly provided by Professor Sun, we tabulated all the authors publishing in the *QJE* 1930–37.[37] The 272 items tabulated were produced by 155 authors. Of these, only 30 had studied Economics in the West, 26 in the United States. Thirty of the authors were economists with a connection with a Chinese university.

We also examined the authors listed in several specialized bibliographies. Fang Xianting presented a "Bibliography on Silver and China" (22 authors listed) in 1934 and another on China's land problem in 1935 (126 authors). Chinese who studied Economics in the West were represented in the Fang listings in about the same proportion as in the Nankai lists of books and of periodicals.

We examined the contents of seven issues of the *Economic Reconstruction Quarterly*, which began publication in 1942.[38] These are valuable for representing a later time period, for reflecting the concern with wartime conditions, and for discussions of recent developments in western economic theory. Of the 165 authors, 19 had studied Economics in the United States, 9 in Britain or Europe, and 22 had a university Economics connection.

In 1961 John Fairbank and Liu Kwang-ching published a bibliography of works on modern China acquired at the initiative of Alfred Chiu for the Harvard-Yenching Library. The listing is classified and quite selective. As a result the sections on Economics contain only 146 names. Of these, 17 had studied Economics in the United States and 5 in Britain and Europe.[39]

A striking contrast is provided by the monumental bibliographies published under the direction of G. William Skinner. The sections dealing with Economics are not as well focused as in Fairbank and Liu. We tabulated the stupefying total of 1,242 Chinese authors.[40] Surprisingly, 70 names from the Fairbank-Liu list do not appear in the Skinner lists. Of the names in the Skinner lists, only 62 had studied Economics in the United States and 37 in Britain and Europe.

We also tabulated the Chinese authors of items referenced in eight significant western studies dealing with China's economy 1900–50.[41] Of the (non-duplicating) total of 304 authors, 38 had studied Economics in the United States and 16 in Britain and Europe. A comparison of these tabulations appears in Table 14-3.

The results are remarkably consistent. Economists with graduate study in the United States accounted for about 10 percent of the publications, while those who studied in Britain and continental Europe were below 5 percent.[42] The totals in Table 14-3 exclude a non-trivial 60 persons who proceeded to study in the West subsequent to their economic publications in China. These were mostly members of Academia Sinica or similar research organizations, graduate students, and junior faculty. Some 15 to 20 percent had connections with university Economics programs.

Table 14-3. Chinese Authors of Books and Articles on China's Economy, 1900–1949

Name		Studied Economics in West					
	Total no. authors	U.S.	%	GB & Eur	%	Connect w/ Univ.	%
Nankai books: 1912–34	547	46	8	7	1	77	14*
1935–41	286	25	9	11	4	65	26**
Authors in both subsets	51	8	16	1	3	16	40
Nankai periodicals: 1934–35#	320	26	8	7	2	43	14
1935–41	636	59	9	27	4	78	14
Authors in both subsets	103	19	19	4	4	26	27
Quar. Jour. Econ. 1930–37	155	26	17	4	3	30	19
Econ. Recons. Quar. 1942–44	165	19	12	9	5	22	13
Fang: land	126	12	10	5	4	23	18
Fairbank-Liu	146	17	12	5	3	33	23
Skinner	1,242	62	5	37	3	134	11
8 Western studies	304	38	13	16	5	62	20

* For 1912–34, 55 in our list of Economics faculty, 22 others published by a university.

** For 1935–41, 51 in our list of Economics faculty, 14 others published by a university.

Items listed in April and July, 1935 issues of *Nankai Social and Economic Quarterly*.

Sources: See previous tables, text, and notes. Authors who studied in the West were included only if their publications came subsequent to their western study.

To judge sampling reliability, we subdivided our two Nankai data sets, books, and periodicals. In each case, the subsets are quite consistent. For each, we identified names of persons appearing in both the earlier and later subset—a rough measure of the more frequent publishers. As shown in Table 14-3, the people appearing in both subsets included significantly more U.S.-trained economists and more university economists.

It is evident that a large proportion of the flood of economics publications came from Chinese who did not study abroad and were not connected with universities. Much of the published material represented business and economic journalism. Some of the authors undoubtedly studied abroad as undergraduates (D. K. Lieu) or in fields other than Economics (Li Jinghan). Some of the Western-trained economists held positions in government agencies or banks and were the authors of anonymous publications.

An important implication of these data is that, while "returned students" from western study became a dominant element in teaching Economics, this domination did not extend to the realm of economic publishing. Rather, the explosion of publications reflected mostly the work of economists whose studies were limited to the Chinese universities. This was certainly true for the publications by the research organizations associated with Academia Sinica. Of course much of the research applied techniques learned from the West, notably survey research. The data describe a very vigorous and diverse literature dealing with economic topics.

Unfortunately, the outbreak of war in 1937 dramatically reduced the flow of economic publications, as Table 1-2 demonstrated. The *Quarterly Journal of Economics* and the *Nankai Social and Economic Quarterly* suspended operations. Government censorship became an obstacle to economic research, particularly when statistical data became "state secrets".

Western-trained Authors

From these bibliographic sources, we assembled all the names of Chinese authors of studies dealing with China's economy which appear in our lists of Chinese who studied Economics in the West. There were 203 of these, described in Table 14-4.

There were substantial national differences. Students from Germany and Britain scored relatively high—about one fifth of them published something on China's economy. The U.S. and France were relatively equal at about one out of eight. Some of these national differences arose from the

Table 14-4. Authors of Studies on China's Economy who Appear in our Student Lists

Country	Authors	All Students	Percentage %
United States	142	1,227	12
Britain	29	163	18
Germany	26	122	21
France	12	113	11
Other European countries	5	21	24

time pattern of the students. The 1940s students had little time to publish China research, and there was much less of it published in the 1940s. Because the United States received so many students in the 1940s, its proportion of authors was relatively low.[43]

We tested the hypothesis that Chinese receiving doctoral degrees provided a higher percentage of authors. This proved true for the United States and Britain (28 and 33 percent) but not for the continental countries. This may reflect the fact that the American and British doctorates were more demanding and more likely to transmit research skill and inclination.[44] No matter how we subdivide the student sample, the majority of western-educated Chinese economists did not publish any research on China's economy recorded in these references.

To pursue these matters further, we identified a small group with relatively numerous economic publications.[45] Since our source base is very incomplete, we cannot infer that these were the most prolific authors. They are listed in Table 14-5.

The overwhelming majority of this list studied in the West, although Chen Hansheng, Fei Xiaotong, and Li Jinghan were outside Economics (only publications dealing with Economics are tabulated). Names in our U.S. doctoral list include Zhang Peigang, Chen Da, Fang Xianting, He Lian, Li Quanshi, Ma Yinchu, and Wu Baosan. Wu Jingchao was ABD in Economics before finishing a doctorate in Sociology and wrote much on economic topics. Zhu Xie had a German doctorate. Zhu Tongjiu and Tang Qingzeng had American MAs, Jin Guobao and Dong Xiujia are in the GS list, Ting and Yang received American MBAs, and D. K. Lieu had an American undergraduate degree in Economics. Jia Shiyi was educated in Japan. He held positions in government financial agencies beginning in 1913 and published encyclopedic studies of fiscal policies (*Who's Who in China* 1950, p. 43; Fairbank and Liu 1961, pp. 321–322).

Table 14-5. Chinese with Numerous Economic Publications

	Number of items						
	Nankai list		Skinner			Study	
Name	Books	Per.	*QJE*	Ch.	Western	in West	Affiliation*
Chen Da	4	0	0	9	22	US: PhD	U
Chen Hansheng	5	4	0	10	17	(US/GE: His.)	U/R
Chin Kuo-pao (Jin Guobao)	6	2	6	3	0	US: GS	U
Ding Ji (Leonard)	0	7	0	0	6	US: MBA	U
Fei Hsiao-tung (Xiaotong)	1	0	0	10	8	(GB: PhD: an.)	U, R
Fang Xianting	18	21	1	11	28	US: PhD	U
He Lian	12	3	0	7	8	US: PhD	U, G
Ho Ping-yin (He Bingyin)	2	22	0	5	2		(G)
Jia Shiyi	7	2	7	7	0		G
Li Jinghan	2	6	0	24	3	(US: Soc.)	R/U
Li Quanshi	8	1	36	7	1	US: PhD	U
Li Tzu-hsiang (Zixiang)	1	0	0	14	0		
Liu Dajun	12	8	2	9	17	(US: BA)	U/G/R
Ma Yinchu	7	12	12	16	1	US: PhD	U, R
Sheng Chun	6	2	2	3	0		G
Tang Qingzeng	1	0	15	2	0	US: MA	U
Tung Hsiu-cha (Dong Xiujia)	2	2	5	6	0	US: GS	U
Wu Baosan	1	0	0	9	3***	US: PhD	U, R
Wu Jingchao	2	9	0	4	4**	US: ABD	U, G
Yang Yinpu	6	4	2	8	0	(US: MBA)	U
Zhang Peigang	1	3	0	7	0***	US: PhD	R, U
Zhu Xie	2	5	0	9	0	GE: doc.	U
Zhu Tongjiu	1	3	8	2	0	US: MA	

* Items in parentheses are uncertain. G = government; R = research organization; U = university.

** Wu subsequently received PhD in sociology.

*** Wu and Zhang received doctorates after much of their publication.

Some western-trained Chinese economists devoted their research efforts to topics other than China's economy—economic theory (Li Quanshi, Sang Hengkang, Jiang Shuojie), history of economic thought (Tang Qingzeng), institutions and policies of other countries (Zhang Decui, Xu Shilian, Ding Wenzhi). Further, our bibliographic sources do not list newspapers, and some western-educated economists wrote extensively for them.[46]

To provide a qualitative dimension, we return to the eight western studies mentioned above. Which Chinese authors were cited by most of these western authors? The answer is presented in Table 14-6.

Table 14-6. Chinese Authors of pre-1950 Studies Cited in Eight Western Studies

Name	Number of Citations
Wu Baosan	7
Fei Xiaotong	6
Fang Xianting	6
D. K. Lieu	5
Zhang Peigang	5
Chen Hansheng	5
He Lian	5
Zhang Xinyi	4
Chen Zhengmo	4
Qiao Qiming	4
Feng Hefa	4

Sources: See note 41.

Wu Baosan appeared in seven of the eight studies, reflecting the combination of useful research done for Academia Sinica and the uniqueness of his national-income estimates. Fei Xiaotong was an anthropologist who completed a doctorate at LSE in 1938 and published a number of impressive rural surveys. Zhang Xinyi (C. C. Chang) and Qiao Qiming both received master's degrees from Cornell and taught at Nanjing's CAF. Zhang also worked for the National Agricultural Research Bureau, publishing influential estimates of China's land and crop output. Chen Cheng-mo (Zhengmo) is a good example of a Chinese university graduate (Beida 1923) who did not study abroad but became a prolific author.[47]

More Research Organizations

During the War, the Institute of Pacific Relations was able to provide some financial aid to Chinese scholars by commissioning a series of monographs, including several on economic topics. The prospective authors included He Lian, Lin Weiying, Chen Da, Wu Qiyuan, Wu Jingchao, and Liang Qingchun. It is not clear if any of these were completed.[48]

When the War ended in 1945, He Lian and Fang Xianting organized the China Institute of Economics, located in Shanghai, and principally supported by the Kincheng Bank. The Institute began operations in March, 1947. They quickly presented a prospectus for an ambitious study of China's post-war economy, for which they had assembled an all-star cast of 17 potential contributors: Zhang Peigang, Chen Zhenhan, Zhou Shunxin, Fan Hong, Fang Xianting, Fang Shangui, Xu Yunan, Wu Baosan, Pu Shouchang, Shen Zuding, Ding Chen, Jiang Shuojie, Wan Guoding, Wang Nianzu (Samuel), Wu Bannong (Leonard), Wu Daye, and Wu Yuanli ("China Institute of Economics" 1947). This imposing roster included seven Harvard PhDs, three PhDs from LSE, and three members of the research staff of the Central Bank. Unfortunately, their projects were not completed.

The Institute set to work recruiting research staff, and by August, 1947, could list eleven besides He and Fang. These included Sang Hengkang (another Harvard PhD), Wu Yuanli, and Chu Pao-yi (Zhu Baiying) (MA LSE), Feng Huade (BS LSE), and seven recent graduates of Chinese universities, including four with MAs from Nankai. In the following year the Institute added five more recent Chinese university graduates. They published a weekly *Economic Review*. The Institute ceased operations in the spring of 1949.[49]

In the United States, the war's end witnessed the brief existence of the Sino-International Economic Research Center, with its headquarters in New York City. It was organized in 1944, sponsored by the National Academy of Peiping and the Agricultural and Industrial Bank of China. This provided support for a number of Chinese scholars located in the United States, and published a series of pamphlets on China's economy.[50]

An Overview

In his study of *Chinese Intellectuals and the West* (1966), Wang Yi-chu directed many criticisms at the returned students. He claimed that "Few Anglo-American-trained specialists wrote". If they did write, "they made no attempt to communicate their findings in simplified versions to the public" (pp. 374, 420). These claims seem ill-founded. During the huge upsurge of publications about China's economy, more than one fifth of all the returned students from western graduate Economics study were represented. Considering that the majority of these returned students found employment in business and government, this is a high proportion. We know that only a small proportion of American Economics PhDs published research after completing their degree. The fact that 28 percent of the Chinese receiving American Economics doctorates published items dealing with China's economy should be seen as quite high. Wang's assertion about "simplified versions" is also wide of the mark. In particular, the "returned students" who made up such a large proportion of the Economics faculties of Nankai and the CAF program at Nanking were prolific producers of items at all levels of readability. At Nanking, such items appeared in *Economic Facts*, while at Nankai, they were likely to appear in *Ta Kung Pao*.[51]

Considering the late start for economic research and publications in China, the volume of publications by the mid-1930s is impressive. Returned students from the West contributed to this in several ways. First, they provided many of the most prolific producers. Second, they helped create the two most research-oriented Economics programs in universities, Nankai and the Nanjing CAF. Third, much of the economic research in China involved survey research and/or index numbers, applying techniques from the West.

To be sure, the bulk of economic publications with identified Chinese authors were not the product of our western-trained group. It seems likely that a large proportion of this writing (as well as the anonymous publications) was by people in government, many of whom were graduates of universities in China.[52] Here we can find a "second-generation" group—the students of western-trained economists who played an important role in the major universities.

In the following sections we describe insights and attitudes in English-language publications by some major Chinese economists by the 1940s.

Fang Xianting

Fang's intellectual career provides a valuable case study in judging the contribution of western economic analysis to understanding China's economy and designing policy measures to deal with it.[53] Fang was not merely a prolific researcher; he was a researcher who tried to combine descriptive data on China's economy with western economic principles in a non-ideological manner. Initially, in the late 1920s and early 1930s, his approach was one of radical empiricism, accumulating a vast amount of descriptive information on China's industrialization. Then the influence of J. B. Tayler, R. H. Tawney, and the Rockefeller Foundation led him to the study of, and promotion of, grass-roots rural development (Fong 1937b). A third phase involved emphasis on the government-driven industrialization vision of Sun Yat-sen (Fong 1936b). In this phase, he stressed the critical role of capital as a constraint on China's growth, and endorsed "a planned economy", inspired by "Russian success in collectivist planned economy since the days of Lenin".[54]

Fang's 1942 pamphlet on "The Post-war Industrialization of China" recommended creating a government organization, the China Reconstruction Finance Corporation, as a center of a development program. Not merely a financing resource, the CRFC would play a major role in securing all types of inputs for the development projects. To supplement this, "a number of governmental or quasi-governmental corporations should be organized . . . to carry out the respective projects initiated by the CRFC." (Fong 1942b, pp. 80–81)

Fang took advantage of a sabbatical at Harvard in 1941 to search for China-relevance in Keynesian economics as presented by Alvin Hansen. In 1942, he suggested that:

> Under a unified fiscal policy, [China's] four government banks . . . can expand their credit, reduce the rate of interest, and thus encourage investment . . . Income from these investments when saved but not consumed will be available for further investments, and thus the process tends to become cumulative, and an expanding capital fund may be created for the purpose of financing China's postwar industrialization. (1942a, citing Keynes, *General Theory*)

Returning to China, Fang was recruited by his mentor, Franklin Ho, to head the research department of the government's Central Planning Board in 1944. In December, 1945, the Board completed the Draft Outline of the Post-war Five-year Plan, estimated to cost about US$6.6 billions (ECAFE 1950, p. 394). In the chaotic conditions of the post-war period, it could not be implemented. By 1947, Fang had turned his back on the whole planning approach (see above, p. 221). Soon after, Fang joined the research staff of the U.N. Economic Commission for the Far East (ECAFE), leaving China for another productive career.

Wu Jingchao

In 1944 and 1946, sinologist Harley MacNair produced two books of essays about China which included some excellent commentaries by western-trained Chinese economists, particularly Wu Jingchao, Qiu Kaiming, and Li Zhuomin.

Wu Jingchao studied Economics and Sociology at Chicago. He began a dissertation on China in the international economy, but then shifted fields to complete a doctorate in Sociology in 1928. He held teaching posts in that field at Nanjing and Qinghua, then joined the government and became in 1938 senior secretary in the Ministry of Economic Affairs (MacNair 1944, p. xiii). Wu was a leading critic of the rural reconstruction programs in the 1930s.[55] He rejected the idea that farm tenancy in itself was a major problem. "The central problem of our farmers is not that a part of them do not own their farms but that the average farm is too small to sustain a decent standard of living." (Wu 1944, p. 67) In his view, a major motive for industrialization was to enable workers to move out of farming into other activities. This would allow consolidation of farms and raise rural productivity. Wu was concerned with overpopulation and addressed the issue of birth control directly in discussion:

> It is very difficult to advocate birth control just at the present. The new Ministry of Social Affairs has formed a committee on social policy, and they invited all the professors of sociology . . . to serve as members . . . I think all of us [sociologists] advocate birth control, but the rest [i.e. "some members of the legislature and some other officials"] are against it. So we had a debate for two or three sessions—and, finally we came to this conclusion: that we are not going to use the words 'birth control,' but will use the words 'spacing of the family' . . . I think we got this idea over and they will allow this practice. If a person knows the methods of birth control, he is not going to have a large family. So as a result, I think we can achieve the same purpose.[56]

Wu described the process of wartime economic planning, but did not analyze the relative roles of government versus private ownership. He simply remarked that "The government wants to play a more important role in the field of heavy industries, leaving the consumer industries in the hands of the private enterprisers." (Quoted MacNair 1944, p. xxxv.)

Wu reiterated Sun Yat-sen's plea for foreign investment to aid China's development, stressing the possible physical removal of manufacturing facilities from the United States to China. He ended his 1944 essay on a shrewd cautionary note:

> If necessary we [China] may try to control the channels of international trade and resort to such devices as high tariffs, barter, the quota system, and

exchange control in order to get as much foreign exchange as possible into the hands of the government so that we may import the necessary instruments of production to build up our industry. This would bring hardships and sufferings to our own people, and its repercussions would be damaging to world economy and world peace."[57]

MacNair clearly had reservations about Wu's support for industrialization, which he characterized as manifesting "the determination of Chungking to industrialize China—be the cost what it may in human lives, human misery, human energy, and vastness of financial expenditures . . ." (1944, p. xxvi) Behind this hyperbole was the sensible suggestion that China should consider forms of modernization which did not stress industrialization so much (p. xxviii).

Qiu Kaiming

MacNair's 1946 volume also contained an excellent overview of Chinese agriculture by Qiu Kaiming. Like Wu, Qiu stressed "land limitations and population pressure" (1946, p. 466). While he mentioned "unequal distribution of landownership and oppressive systems of tenancy", he listed numerous other sources of rural distress, including soil depletion, poor transport, inequitable taxes, credit inadequacy, "an uneconomical system of farm layout, inadequate educational facilities, and lack of cooperation among farmers" (p. 467). Despite these, China had succeeded in significantly increasing agricultural output after 1937 (pp. 480–487).

Qiu echoed the emphasis of Wu Jingchao on population control and industrialization: "Industrialization is the best means for farm relief in China." (p. 491) He called for "the emergence of an unsentimental public opinion . . . since there is little hope of improving the standard of living of China's farmers until the size of farms is enlarged and the produce of farms per unit of labor as well as per unit of land is increased. Industrialization in the sense of application of science to agriculture as well as to industry seems to be the only way to achieve this objective." (p. 491)

The perspective of both Qiu and Wu was close to that of John Buck and the Nanjing staff. It was relatively free of class-war terminology and full of operational policy suggestions.

Li Zhuomin

The third of MacNair's high-quality essayists was Nankai's Li Zhuomin.

Li examined China's economic development from the perspective of her international trade and finance. He began with an almost obligatory litany:

> China has paid a high price for its economic transformation during the past century. Hand in hand with foreign trade came political institutions and practices which have hampered its development. In any evaluation of the influence of trade upon the country's economic development, recognition must be made of the struggle of foreign Powers for spheres of control and the abuses inherent in the interwoven Treaty Port and extraterritorial systems.[58]

Having said this, Li proceeded to point to the overwhelming economic advantages which China had derived from its opening to the rest of the world:

> The Treaty Ports grew into large commercial cities . . . Official efforts began to provide aids to navigation without which commerce could never have expanded as it did. (p. 493) [E]conomic development would have been much slower if foreign merchants had not begun to bring in investments as well as commerce. (Li 1946, p. 496)

> Practically all foreign investments, with the exception of railways and mining, were confined to Treaty Ports [of which there were 50 by 1915], where they were given protection by governing councils consisting of foreign residents . . . [F]oreign investments took the form of establishments directly managed and owned by foreigners; financing institutions, foreign trading concerns, and a labor force trained and developed by foreign enterprise grew in [these] ports . . . Ocean shipping brought raw materials to these ports [at low cost]. Consequently, these advantages encouraged Chinese private capital to seek safety and employment in the port cities. (p. 503)

> Under the system of extraterritoriality and Treaty Ports, . . . trade brought with it foreign investments which soon led to development of banking, communications, modern business methods, industry, and mining. Industrial growth accelerated under the impetus of the First World War and later of silver depreciation; in 1929 it received the added benefit of tariff protection. (p. 501)

With western standards of law and order and urban infrastructure, the Treaty Ports grew rapidly in the first half of the century. The environment was favorable for Chinese entrepreneurs, and workers flocked there to find employment. With the virtually "unlimited supplies of labor" from the impoverished countryside, wages were low and working conditions poor. Li felt the concentration of development in the Treaty Ports caused the rest of the country to lag, as capital was drawn to the ports.

And some traditional handicraft industries such as spinning and weaving were hard hit by competition from imports. "The force that brought suffering to artisans and peasants, however, eventually made possible the development of new handicraft industries for domestic and world markets, as well as commercialization of crops."[59]

Trade helped beget industry. "It was only when manufactured goods were imported in large quantities at prices low enough to reach the general public—which broke down old habits of consumption and created new demands—that industry could be profitably developed." (p. 494)

Li returned to ritual in endorsing a comprehensive national economic plan, but quickly qualified this to insist that "the interests of society must be safeguarded by encouraging full play of private initiative in all fields other than a few to be operated as government enterprises" (p. 505).

For all his reservations, Li's essay was a strong explication of the developmental benefits which China derived from opening to international trade and finance. There are many parallels with China's experience after 1978. The Special Economic Zones created around 1980 were mainly located in, and had many similarities to the Treaty Ports.

MacNair's essayists painted relatively positive pictures of China's economic conditions. They did not mention the problems of corruption and hyperinflation nor the incipient civil war.

Zhang Peigang

Zhang Peigang spent nearly a decade conducting economic research for the Institute of Social Sciences, Academia Sinica. He then proceeded to Harvard where he completed in 1947 a doctoral dissertation which was published under the title *Agriculture and Industrialization* (Chang 1949). It was awarded the Wells Prize as the outstanding Economics dissertation of the year. For our purposes, it is particularly interesting as a record of Zhang's search through all the tools provided to him in Harvard's graduate program for useful insights concerning economic development. The book was not primarily about China; rather, most of the descriptive data involved the United States and other highly developed economies.

Zhang's review of the tools is impressive. Microeconomic theory was represented by production functions, elasticities of demand and of substitution, and, regrettably, imperfect competition. However, there was no discussion of optimization in the design and use of capital goods—a critical issue in the Soviet system. Macro-economic theory was represented by business-cycle theory and Keynes's propensity to consume; and there were substantial segments of international trade theory, history of economic thought, and economic history.

The book is sub-titled "The Adjustments that Take Place as an Agricultural Country is Industrialized". Industrialization is perceived as a combination of capital formation and technological innovation. The farm sector shares in scientific improvements, provides surplus labor and raw materials to industry, and provides a market for consumer goods and for farm machinery.

Zhang, like Sun Yat-sen (whom he never mentioned), stressed the importance of developing internal transportation. But he had no discussion of the relative roles of public and private sectors, and no analysis of land tenure, farm credit, marketing, and research.

Read fifty years later, after a half-century which has seen so much experimentation and so much frustration in regard to development of low-income countries, Zhang's study seems more an academic exercise than a guide to policy. His conviction that "war is a stimulating factor for economic expansion" was hardly true for China, and his idea that war "helps wash away some of the institutional obstacles standing in the way of social reform" (p. 94) seems ironic in view of China's subsequent experience. Zhang witnessed this experience at first hand, returning to China to a long career at Wuhan University and Huazhong Institute of Technology.

Collectivism

Many Chinese economists besides Fang Xianting tried to analyze the proper economic role of government during the 1940s. The Kuomintang continued to express reverence for the grandiose statist development programs articulated by Sun Yat-sen. His son Sun Fo extended these in speeches and articles, even advocating close imitation of the coercive program of the Soviet Union.[60] Rather than focusing on economic growth and development, much of the Chinese discussion focused on industrialization. There was often a technocratic bias, neglecting issues of efficiency and resource allocation, and neglecting trade and service activities.

In January, 1938, the government created a Ministry of Economic Affairs, taking over from other agencies much of the ownership and operation of industrial facilities. The new ministry was headed by Dr. Wong Wenhao, a prominent geologist. The Chinese government extended its ownership and control of production during the war, and further enlarged it by seizures of businesses after 1945.[61]

In 1943, the Chinese government published, under the putative authorship of Chiang Kai-shek, two books entitled *China's Destiny* and *Chinese Economic Theory*. Both were essentially political propaganda designed to support elitist authoritarian government with a virtually unbounded (and certainly ill-defined) economic role. *Chinese Economic Theory* was reportedly composed chiefly by Tao Hsi-shen (Xisheng) and Chen Pao-ying (Baoying) and served as a required textbook in the Central Political Institute.[62] The book revealed that "The scope of Chinese economics is much broader than that of Western economics" because the former "is the study of how to make the nation rich and strong—to build a nation into a wealthy, powerful, healthy and contented state" (p. 243). The authors developed "Chinese economics" by a lengthy name-dropping exercise citing venerable sages throughout Chinese history who articulated cliches about the need for the state to do good things.[63] No sooner have we been told that "the basis of Chinese economic theory is man's rational nature—not his wants" than we learn that "Chinese economic theory does not base itself on the individual or single unit. It is based on the study of mankind and society as a whole." (pp. 244–245) There were brief references to Adam Smith, Friedrich List, Othmar Spann, Ricardo, Marshall, Hobson, Karl Marx, J. B. Clark, and Veblen. The authors were confident that "after the war, Western economists will abandon their selfish individualism and materialism and, starting from human nature and aiming at the people's livelihood, will strive to attain the same goal as that prescribed in the economic theories of ancient China" (p. 263).

Fang Xianting's 1942 pamphlet envisioned a very ambitious economic role for the Chinese government. For defense industries, "heavy industries, as well as large-scale public works and public utilities, state ownership and operation seems to offer the best solution" (Fong 1942b, p. 79). State influence would have been further expanded by Fang's proposed China Reconstruction Finance Corporation (Fong 1942b, pp. 79–82).

One of China's most prolific researchers, D. K. Lieu, offered his analysis of *China's Economic Stabilization and Reconstruction* in 1948. Reviewing proposals for government economic planning and control, Lieu urged a limited program of "key factor planning", involving government participation in (but not monopolization of) credit, transportation, and electric power (pp. 30–35). This was an insightful identification of critical infrastructure.

The most interesting of the Chinese discussions of collectivism was offered by Wu Yuanli. Wu had studied with Hayek at LSE and made a conscious effort to apply Hayek's principles in seeking "a fusion of free enterprise with a consciously planned over-all structure of the economy".[64] Wu was highly critical of Sun Yat-sen's statist proposals. He argued that the "savings of the agricultural population must be a decisive factor in domestic accumulation" (p. 20). These were largely being siphoned off by usury and taxes (p. 23). Industrial development was hindered by absence of "the rule of law, the first condition of a rational economic order" (p. 24). China's economic programs in the 1930s suffered from "the collectivist approach of the planners . . . They drew up grandiose schemes without any reference to external data, and stretched the hand of government intervention to many fields without being able either to make up their mind as to what was exactly wanted or to hold fast to what was well within its grasp." (p. 38) Wu noted that most proposals rested on inflow of foreign capital, but that the proposed government monopolies were likely to repel foreign investors (pp. 44–45).

Wu attacked collectivism in two propositions. "First, in all poor countries, the struggle for wealth and power . . . tends to be conducted unscrupulously . . . Secondly, a system of economic regimentation involving forced savings and the central direction of investments tends . . . to undermine political democracy."[65] He urged that the Chinese government pare down the scope of its nationalized enterprises, particularly those related to defense. Priority should go to measures to improve availability of credit and to upgrade human resources. Wu was also attracted to some sort of "model development scheme", perhaps along the lines of TVA, focused on electric power in the Yangzi valley (pp. 57–58). Ultimately, Wu's agenda was probably quite similar to that of D. K. Lieu.

In contrast to Wu Yuanli, many of the Chinese discussions of collectivism lacked familiarity with the extraordinary hardships associated with the Soviet experiments.[66] They shared with American institutionalists a faith in the wisdom and competence of government.

Inflation

Both the insights and limitations of western economics are well illustrated by the efforts of Chinese economists to analyze the inflation which raged with increasing severity through China from 1937 through 1949. Western economists had analyzed the European inflations during and after World War I with great clarity, exemplified by Keynes's *Tract on Monetary Reform* (1923). Government deficits were financed by central bank credit and by currency creation, driving up prices, which led in turn to an increase in the velocity of money and to foreign-exchange-rate depreciation. However, the discussions of Keynes's *General Theory* in the 1930s shifted attention away from the link between money and prices.[67]

Prices in China had begun to increase after the termination of the silver standard in 1935, but initially the increases were welcomed as relief from depression. Outbreak of war in July, 1937 accelerated price increases, which averaged 40 percent per year 1937–39, 90 percent 1939–41, 120 percent in 1941–45, and escalating to 300 percent 1945–48 and 1,750 percent 1948–49.[68]

Wu Yuanli (1956) remarked that "Although inflation was brought about by the war and the failure of the government's financial and fiscal policy, it in turn bred inefficiency and corruption, undermined the authority of the central government . . . , transformed the average citizen into a speculator, and created a mass despondence and moral vacuum that made the country ripe for the picking by the militant Communist Party."[69]

Data problems made it difficult for Chinese economists to draw close connections between money and prices. With transportation and internal trade disrupted, prices showed wide divergence from one locality to another. No simple and obvious data on the money supply were published, and the monetary situation was complicated by the fact that Japanese-sponsored banks created large amounts of notes and deposits in occupied areas. By most measures, the proportional increase in prices was much larger than the increase in money.[70]

Many of these issues were addressed by Lin Weiying in 1939. Lin, who had received a doctorate from Columbia with a monetary specialty, acknowledged expansion of legal-tender currency, but argued that much of it was replacing other types of money, and that the wide dispersion of different prices was evidence against a monetary explanation for the price increases (Lin 1939, p. 267).

In 1941, Ms. Cui Shuxiang published a survey of Chinese writings on causes of recent price increases. Five authors placed principal blame on "forestalling and engrossing": "Merchants and large producers store up and keep from sale large quantities of goods . . ."[71] Three others cited military procurement and population migration as sources of increased demand, combined with supply disruptions, downplaying the monetary factor. Several cited rising costs and exchange-rate depreciation.

Outside China, discussions of inflation among western economists went through a similar sorting-out. Ultimately, however, consensus emerged that, without increase in the money supply, increases in expenditures and in costs tend to be self-limiting, causing excess demand for money, which would halt the rise in incomes and prices.

Cui cited 25 authors. Among these, only she and her Nankai colleague Li Zhuomin put together a satisfactory analysis tracing causality from government deficits and monetary expansion to higher prices to higher costs and exchange-rate depreciation. Cui had done graduate study in Economics at Wisconsin and Radcliffe, while Li had completed a doctorate at California. She cited five other authors (including Lin Weiying) who had studied Economics in western graduate schools and who denied or neglected the monetary factor.[72] Their alternative "explanations" tended to play into the hands of the Communists by discrediting the private-enterprise system. The lack of monetary awareness among Chinese economists was matched by a lackadaisical attitude among bankers and government officials (Chang 1958, pp. 18–20, 39).

However, Wu Qiyuan (PhD LSE) published an excellent inflation review in the *Nankai Quarterly* in 1941. He wrote:

> Monetary disturbances, changes in the condition of transportation and in the condition of supply and demand, the existence of speculative dealings, and the Government's attempt to impose . . . price control, all combined to influence the prices of all commodities. Among them monetary changes were undoubtedly the most important . . . The increase in the velocity of circulation . . . was another important cause of the upwards movement in prices. (pp. 102–103)
>
> [T]he interrelationships between the volume of means of payment, prices, and exchanges in war-time China have been very close, conforming well to the phenomenon of inflation in the West, and . . . all these related changes . . . have been proved . . . to come within the expectations of theory." (p. 113)

We have no comparable subsequent literature survey, but it appears that recognition of the monetary factor became steadily more widespread. By 1948 top government officials recognized that "the root of the inflationary problem was . . . the budgetary deficit and the consequent need continually to create new money." (Eastman 1984, p. 179) Articles in western journals by Li Zhuomin (1945) and Andrew Chung Huang (1948) acknowledged this.[73] The Communists certainly recognized the monetary factor and wasted little time after 1949 in creating a new monetary system relatively free from inflationary influence (Wu 1956, pp. 64–87).

More Reflections

Our limited sketch of Chinese economic thinking by the 1940s reveals the difficulties for Chinese in deriving useful guidance from western economics.[74] The vast majority of Chinese economists appear to have accepted much of the collectivist model associated with Sun Yat-sen and lacked perspective on the negative aspects of real-world experience in the USSR. In 1956, Wu Yuanli commented that:

> Because the government had played an increasingly important role in the actual allocation and use of resources both before and after the war, and because inadequate attention had been given to the development of the economy through individual initiative within a well-ordered economy and established rule of law, there was not a broad and vigorous capitalistic economy in China at the time the Communists took over. The transition to a system of greater regimentation . . . was made all the easier both physically and ideologically." (Wu 1956, pp. 42–43)

Chinese economists almost unanimously supported protective tariffs. They accepted a greatly exaggerated view of the economic damage to China's economy from exposure to foreign products, investments, and business practices. These attitudes helped promote acceptance of the autarchic policies so often followed after 1949.

In discussing Chinese agriculture, most accepted populist folklore about the evils of middlemen, money-lenders, and landlords, not recognizing the neo-classical implication that high rents and interest rates were as much a manifestation of the factor imbalance among population, land, and capital as were the low returns to labor. Their negative stereotyping of merchants led some to blame inflation on "greedy speculators". With only a few exceptions, the Chinese economists did not present forthright defense of free markets. Their attitudes helped promote acceptance of the persecution and victimization of landlords, money-lenders, and entrepreneurs after 1949.

15

Epilogue and Overview

The focus of our study has been on the introduction of western economic ideas into China during the first half of the twentieth century. However, the events which followed 1949 helped put the previous developments into perspective. In particular, the vast number of western-educated Chinese represented a large stock of human capital. It is important to see what happened to them.

On October 1, 1949, Mao Zedong stood at the top of a great arch overlooking Tiananmen Square in Beijing and proclaimed the triumphant formation of the People's Republic of China. Chiang Kai-shek and the Kuomintang had fled to Taiwan.[1]

Within a few months the new regime embarked on two drastic activities which cost the lives of millions of their new subjects. The first was the land reform campaign. The Communists organized rural "struggle sessions" in which landlords and other bloodsuckers were denounced, humiliated, sometimes beaten, and occasionally killed.[2] Under careful management by Party leaders, land titles were rearranged.

Faculty members and students from the universities were mobilized to play an active role in the land reform process. As in the USSR, the farmers' new situation did not last long. By 1952 Party cadres were pushing farmers into mutual-aid teams and cooperatives, a process which culminated in the formation of the notorious communes in 1958.

The other drastic development was China's involvement in the Korean War, which broke out in the summer of 1950. By the time the heavy fighting had ended in 1953, there had been about 1 million Korean casualties and nearly as many Chinese.[3]

The Korean War helped draw China close to the Soviet Union. Russian capital and expertise increasingly flowed into China's economy and into the educational system. The Chinese government used the Korean War as a pretext for expelling virtually all other foreigners from China and harassing Chinese with western connections:

> "Posters began to appear . . . attacking members of Yenching University who had American connections. They were ordered to prepare statements of self-criticism. They had to confess as sins having gone to the United States, even having desired to go to the United States, having maintained American friendship, or having sent their scholarly articles to the United States for publication. Faculty members whose self-criticisms were found unacceptable were publicly castigated and removed from their positions." (Egan 1987, p. 199)

In the summer of 1951 a massive campaign was undertaken against domestic "counter-revolutionaries". The "Three-Anti" campaign of late 1951 brought labor unions under Party domination. The "Five-Anti" campaign of 1952 extended state ownership and Party control of business. Universities in general experienced what Kenneth Lieberthal described for Tianjin:

> During the Three Anti campaign, all of Tientsin's universities were closed, and the faculty suffered severe criticism at the hands of students and colleagues. As the campaign progressed, it increasingly focused on ridding the universities of bourgeois notions of education . . . and on removing or downgrading those professors who were least willing to accept the Communists' view of the university. By the end of the campaign . . . all graduates of Tientsin's higher education institutions in June 1952 became subject to unified assignment to jobs by the [government]. (Lieberthal 1980, p. 157)

The government adopted a system of economic policy much like that of the Soviet Union. Emphasis was placed on developing state-controlled heavy industry—a tendency already at work under the KMT and in line with Sun Yat-sen's doctrines. A beneficial change replaced the disastrous hyperinflation of the Kuomintang with moderate monetary growth.[4]

Diaspora

A significant proportion of western-educated Chinese economists left China in the 1940s or failed to return from overseas locations. Our biographical data for the roughly 1,600 students analyzed in Chapters 4–6 provide post-1949 information on 463 persons.[5] Of these, 139—30 percent—left China. Of the 463, 273 had studied in the United States; of these, 110—40 percent—left China. Table 15-1 provides further details comparing western-educated economists from our student lists who either remained in China or who left.

Table 15-1. Western-educated Economists who Left China or Remained in China after 1949

Category	Left	Remained	Total	% left
Studied in U.S.	110	163	273	40
PhD (to 1950)	34	30	64	53
ABD	11	12	23	48
MA	33	59	92	36
GS	32	62	94	34
Studied 1941–50	67	125	192	35
Post-50 PhD*	31	5	36	86
Studied in Europe	29	63	92	32
GB	13	40	53	25
Others	16	23	39	41
Studied 1941–50	4	11	15	27

* Includes only students in our file, in graduate Economics study by 1949. PhDs in Economics only.

Sources: Biographical sources cited in Chapters 4 and 5 and below; Tobin 1975; Thurston and Parker 1980; Reynolds 1981; Watson 1987; Hu 1984; Nairuenn Chen 1963; Li 1962; Lin 1981; Perkins 1966; Skinner 1965; Cheng 1957.

One factor influencing the decision to leave China was opportunity. Our file records 516 Chinese who studied graduate-level Economics in the United States in 1941–50. We have biographical information on 192 of these, of whom 67 remained in the United States. Many of these had not completed their graduate studies by 1950. No fewer than 31 of the 67 completed economics doctorates subsequent to 1950. In contrast, among the 125 who returned to China, only five completed post-1950 U.S. doctorates.

Another group with opportunity were the members of the diplomatic service stationed outside China. Several of these continued in diplomatic service for the Taiwan government. Among these were Duan Maolan (PhD Columbia), Yu Tsune-chi (Junji—DSc NYU), He Fengshan (doctorate from Munich), Dison Poe, Kan Nai-kuang (Gan Naiguang), Sun Pi-chi (Biqi), and Li Ti-tsun (Dijun).

Economists with close ties to the KMT government also emigrated. A significant number of the leaders of the Nankai Economics program had developed such ties during the War and departed subsequently. These included He Lian, Fang Xianting, Li Zhuomin, Li Shison, Wu Daye, Rockwood Chin, and Yang Shujin. Other departing economists with prominent KMT ties were He Haoruo (PhD Wisconsin), Li Gan (PhD Harvard), Lin Lin (PhD Ohio State), Leonard Hsu (GS Stanford), and Xiao Zheng, who had studied in Germany and went on to play an important part in Taiwan's land reform. Of course such high-placed political figures as Sun Fo and T. V. Soong left. Others included Lowe Chuan-hua (Zhuanhua) and Ma Yuen-cheung (Yuenzheung).

The three most significant destinations were the United States, Taiwan, and international agencies connected with the newly formed United Nations. Table 15-2 summarizes our information about the number going to each destination.

Table 15-2. Destinations of Chinese Economists Emigrating around 1949

Studied in:	Went to			Others or
	United States	Taiwan	International Agencies	unknown
United States	64	32	14	7
Britain	2	6	3	4
France	2	3	0	1
Germany	1	8	0	2
Other European	1	2	0	1
Total	70	49*	17	15

* Some persons are in more than one category.

When Chinese forces regained control of Taiwan upon the Japanese surrender in 1945, they soon transformed the former Taipei Imperial University into National Taiwan University (NTU). Numerous other universities formed on the island. We have faculty lists for NTU beginning in 1952. At that time the Chairperson was Lin Lin, who had received a PhD from the Ohio State University in 1934 and served briefly as Chair at Great China University in 1948. Lin had worked for the Chinese News Service and Ministry of Information, which involved close contact with KMT leadership (*AEA Directories* 1956, 1964).

Lin's successor as NTU Chair was Quan Hansheng, who had actually attended Taipei Imperial University and did graduate work at Harvard. He had taught at National Central and worked with Academia Sinica. Quan became one of Taiwan's premier economic historians.[6] Shih Chien-sheng (Shi Jiansheng), who studied at Harvard in 1944–45, also joined NTU, as did Wang Tso-yung (Zuoyong—MA Washington 1948, *AEA Directory* 1964). Shih produced an elementary textbook which was widely used in Taiwan. Jiang Shuojie taught at NTU for a year in 1948–49 before moving to the IMF.

Table 15-3 lists 15 prominent Chinese emigre economists.[7] Many of them have been discussed earlier. Quite a few of these were authors (marked *) of articles in a 1963 collection honoring He Lian.[8] Several in Table 15-3 contributed significant research after 1949 on China's economy: Chang Kia-ngau (Zhang Jiaao), H. D. Fong, Hou Chi-ming (Jiming), Li Zhuoming, Liu Dazhong, and Wu Yuanli. Alpha Chiang wrote a path-breaking textbook on mathematical economics. Jiang Shuojie contributed significantly to mainstream debates on monetary economics. Liu Dazhong

Table 15-3. Some Distinguished Chinese Emigre Economists

	Born	Study	Post-1949	Articles**	Books***
Chang Kia-ngau*	1888	Japan	Loyola (LA), res.	0	3
Cheng Pao-lun	1922	PhD Wis.	MI St.; Sim. Fraser	11	0
Alpha Chiang*	1927	PhD Col.	Denison, UConn	5	2
John Fei	1923	PhD MIT	Antioch, Cornell, Yale	22	3
H. D. Fong*	1902	PhD Yale	ECAFE	0	20
Ho Lien	1895	PhD Yale	Columbia	0	8
Hou Chi-ming*	1924	PhD Col.	Hobart, Colgate	5	4
Anthony Koo*	1918	PhD Har.	Michigan State	24	0
Li Choh-ming*	1912	PhD Cal.	Berkeley, CUHK	4	4
D. K. Lieu	1890	BA Mich.	Taiwan embassy	0	14
Liu Ta-chung*	1914	PhD Corn.	IMF, Cornell	20	6
Anthony Tang	1924	PhD Vand.	Vanderbilt	11	1
S. C. Tsiang*	1918	PhD LSE	IMF, Rochester	21	1
Wu Chi-yuen	1911	PhD LSE	UN, NYU	1	4
Wu Yuan-li*	1920	PhD LSE	Hofstra, Marq., USF	9	13

* Author in *TsingHua Journal*, 1963.

** Items listed in *Index to Economic Journals*, *Index to Economic Articles*, 1950–70.

*** English-language items listed in *National Union Catalogue*, pre-1956, 1958–62, 1963–67; non-duplicating.

advanced both the theory and practice of econometrics and collaborated with Jiang in giving valuable advice for Taiwan's financial policies. Cheng Pao-lun's contributions to financial economics earned him a place (along with Liu, Chiang, and Jiang) in Mark Blaug's *Who's Who in Economics* (2nd ed.). John Fei made path-breaking contributions to the analysis of economic development and advised the government of Taiwan. Most of the post-1949 writings of Fang and Wu Qiyuan were anonymous in their work for ECAFE and the UN.

The foregoing data make it clear that China sustained a severe loss of intellectual resources during this period. In the initial years, the new government tried hard to persuade Chinese scholars to return home and help build the new China. But those who answered this call often experienced persecution.[9] Things were not always easy for those who left (Egan 1987, p. 198). Quite a number ended up teaching in small and less well-known colleges: Moravian College, Park College, Northeast Missouri State Teachers College, Lebanon Valley College, Berea College, Bluefield College, and Aquinas College.

Universities

University Economics programs in China were not much affected for the first couple of years after 1949. A few Marxist professors were moved from obscure and remote positions into top-ranked universities.[10] One or two required courses in (Marxist) political economy were introduced. Participation in land reform interrupted classes in 1951. In 1952 more drastic measures occurred. Faculty were required to participate in extensive political study and "rectification". They were pressured to write "study conclusions" which were really confessions of their past misdeeds; many of which were published. "A professor of economics [Chang Chung-yi (Zhang Zhongyi)] confessed that he had for more than ten years taught the economics of the capitalists without understanding its reactionary character and eventual doom; he had thus served as 'the unpaid spokesman of the monopolistic capitalists'." (Chen 1960, pp. 69, 203)

The university system was reorganized: Christian colleges were forced to close, and their faculty and students were absorbed into national institutions.[11] Qinghua was transformed into a polytechnical institution without Economics. In social sciences, research was no longer stressed in the universities. Instead, an expanded role was given to separate research institutions, of which the most important was the Institute of Economics

(IOE, 1954) under the Chinese Academy of Sciences. The IOE absorbed most of the staff formerly under Academia Sinica.[12] As the scope of the government expanded, Marxist economists moved into staff and administrative positions.[13]

In October, 1950, the government opened a new flagship institution—China People's University ("Renda") in Beijing.[14] Its activities were concentrated on social and political topics.

> "A strictly 'party' institution . . . , the People's University drew both its faculty and students largely from middle ranking party functionaries who, through many years of faithful service, had proven their loyalty and devotion to what the party stood for. (Hu 1972, p. 65)

The Economics chair was Song Tao, a graduate of Northwest Associated Universities who had been teaching at Northwest University—both schools being before 1949 in Communist-dominated territory. However, the leading Renda Economics faculty were not political hacks. Zheng Linzhuang and Rao Yusu were transferred in from Yanjing. Dai Shiguang and Zhao Renjun moved from Qinghua, as did Wang Chuanlun.[15] Zhou Zuoren moved from Beida to Renda.

In 1953 there was a concerted effort to shift the Economics curriculum over to the Russian model for all universities. Russian professors came to teach, and Chinese professors such as Xu Yunan and Ma Yinchu made an effort to use Russian. Stalin's *Economic Problems of Socialism in the USSR* was translated and studied as a text. Feuchtwang and Hussain noted that "The essential feature of Stalin's text is that planning is not regarded as a problem, but rather as an activity that requires little more than common sense and elementary bookkeeping."[16] Chen Daisun reported using a Russian text by Rosenberg for history of economic thought.[17] There were two or three Russian Economics professors at Beida, the first named Karatief. They lectured in Russian and used interpreters. There were three or four Russian Economics professors at Renda, one named Bodlief.[18] In 1949–56 there was no significant translation of western economic material into Chinese.

Graduate study in Economics was largely concentrated at Renda. Study in the West by Chinese graduate students virtually ceased as China became relatively sealed off from the rest of the world. Table 15-4 summarizes these changes, using data on the graduate education of Chinese Economics professors from the 1990 Directory.

Table 15-4. Location of Graduate Study by Economics Professors Listed in 1990 Directory

Year*	West	Renda	Beida	Nankai	Fudan	Total**
1950	9	1	0	1	3	17
1951	5	2	0	0	1	15
1952	2	30	1	2	1	47
1953	0	27	0	0	1	33
1954	1	10	0	0	0	12
1955	0	21	1	0	0	25
1956	1	26	3	0	1	33
1957	0	4	1	0	2	9
1958	0	3	0	0	0	6

* Year graduate study completed.

** Includes categories not shown separately. Four went to the USSR and one to Japan.

Source: Compiled from Economics listings in *Biographical Dictionary of Professors in Chinese Universities and Colleges*, 1990.

Gao Hongye joined the Renda faculty in 1957, having completed a doctorate at Colorado with a dissertation on aggregate consumption functions. As he recalled, the faculty were young and did not have strong academic backgrounds. Many were revolutionary veterans. The Russians had just been there but most had left. Most textbooks were derived from the Russian materials; they were intended to be used all over the country. There were required courses in political economy, Marxian philosophy, and history of the Chinese and Soviet Communist parties. Gao did not teach immediately because of the disruptions of attending the anti-rightist campaign; there were meetings "all the time".

A short time after, Gao was asked to translate the first ten chapters of Paul Samuelson's introductory text (*Economics*, 5th edition). This was to be a required text throughout the country. It was completed in 1964. The book was not viewed as a tool for understanding economic reality, but as an artifact to help understand the West.[19]

The waning of Renda graduate enrollments in the late 1950s corresponded to an attack on its domination of higher education. It was criticized as a "huge beehive of doctrinairism" in 1957 (Hayhoe 1993, p. 491). Another factor was the de-emphasis on graduate study: an undergraduate degree plus political correctness was viewed as adequate preparation for teaching in a university.

The new Communist regime gave priority in its early years to enlarging education at all levels. However, emphasis in higher education was on science and technology with political and administrative subjects second. Economics and finance did not rank high, as can be seen from Table 15-5.

Table 15-5. Students in Economics and Finance Compared with all Students in Higher Education, 1949–1985

	Enrollment*		Graduates*	
Year	Economics & Finance	All	Economics & Finance	All
1949	n.d.	n.d.	3	18
1952	22	191	7	32
1953	14	212	11	48
1954	n.d.	n.d.	6	47
1957	12	441	4	56
1958	n.d.	n.d.	2	72
1962	12	830	3	177
1965	18	674	2	186
1970	**	48	0.6	103
1975	7	501	0.9	119
1977	8	625	5	194
1980	37	1144	1	147
1985	148	1703	24	316

* All the numbers refer to thousands, i.e. 22 = 22,000.

** Very small.

n.d. = No data.

Sources: *China Statistical Yearbook 1990*, p. 666; Taylor 1981, pp. 98, 123; Orleans 1971, pp. 372–373. Orleans 1971 estimated there were 49,000 graduates in finance and economics in 1949–58 (p. 379).

In 1952 Economics and finance still accounted for more than 10 percent of enrollments and 20 percent of graduates, but then declined. Not until the late 1970s did Economics return to a position of consequence.

The Soviet-Marxist emphasis did not obliterate western economics from the curriculum. Because of Marx's acknowledged debt to the classical economists, it was still appropriate to teach about Adam Smith and Ricardo.[20] Many senior economists turned to Chinese economic history, because Mao wanted to call attention to the (supposed) historical roots of socialism in China.

Many of the western-trained economists found the new regime's approach to statistics upsetting. Dai Shiguang was in conflict with the authorities who wanted statistics simply to serve political and administrative purposes. He preferred to stress social and economic phenomena. Ms. Cui Shuxiang taught statistics at the newly formed Central Institute of Finance and Banking in Beijing. She reported that all schools were required to use the Russian-based texts which used no mathematics beyond square roots. Within CAS, Wu Baosan experienced similar problems. His pioneering work in national-income measurement was cast aside, replaced by the crude measurement of gross material output by methods which were full of double counting.[21] However, such issues were swamped by the government's tendency to treat all kinds of economic data as "state secrets", putting them off limits to all but a few insiders.

The flavor of instruction in Economics was well conveyed by Chou Hsun (Zhou Xun):

> When I was at Peking University [1957–66], I spent a total of . . . three semesters . . . learning political economics. However, the emphasis . . . was not on the basic theory . . . but on the problems in implementing the current economic policies of the government such as 'the three banners' and 'walking on two legs.' In those three semesters Chinese economic policy changed repeatedly: at one time it was to promote 'mess halls in rural villages' which the commentaries being handed out on political economics referred to as the 'organizing element' in Mao Tse-tung's 'socialist political economics'; a half a year later the Party sent down orders eradicating the 'village mess halls' and wiping out all mention of them in the commentaries with a single stroke. (Chou 1979–80, p. 109)

Malthus and the Population Question

In September, 1949, Mao Zedong declared:

> It is a very good thing that China has a big population . . . The absurd argument of Western bourgeois economists like Malthus that increases in food cannot keep pace with increases in population . . . has been completely exploded by the realities in the Soviet Union and the Liberated Areas of China after their liberation." (Quoted Tien 1973, p. 178.)

The new government improved many aspects of public health and provided family allowances to government workers. They prohibited induced abortion, sterilization, and importation of contraceptives (Wang 1999, pp. 63, 88–89, 110–111). These measures accelerated population growth. In August, 1953, the State Council "quietly instructed the Ministry of

Health to help the masses to control reproduction . . ." (p. 175). A year later Shao Lizu urged birth control in addressing the State Council. Emphasis was on the microeconomic goals of reducing poverty in individual households and protecting the health of women and children by voluntary birth control. Shao took pains to cite Lenin denouncing neo-Malthusianism (Tien, p. 177; Wang 1999, pp. 89–91).

Another warning that the issue was ideologically charged came from Beida Professor Zhao Jing, who claimed in 1955 that "The reactionary population 'theories' of the Malthusian and Neo-Malthusian schools had long been, by means of voluminous booklets and journals and through extensive use of university lecture halls, diffused in Old China." (Quoted Tien, p. 182.) He vigorously attacked the alleged Malthusian views of Wu Jingchao, Chen Changheng, Chen Da, and Liang Shuming.[22]

However, by separating the micro and macro elements, the authorities (including Zhou Enlai and Mao himself) were able to endorse government encouragement of birth control in 1956–57. At an important conference in March 1957, even the macro arguments were deployed. And they took center stage in a long article by Wu Jingchao. Wu noted the heavy costs of child-raising; with fewer births those resources could be used for capital formation. He also noted the problem of finding jobs for the prospective entrants into the labor force.

In 1956–57, Wang Yanan published several items on the population issue, affirming the view that birth control was desirable but that Malthusianism was evil. He noted the importance of "the study of population theory at this time [because] the contemporary imperialist and colonialist scholars are attempting to pave the way ideologically for imperialists to enslave and massacre the peoples in the backward regions by duping them with so-called neo-Malthusianism . . ." (Wang 1969, p. 3)

In February, 1957, Mao Zedong himself suggested that "steps must be taken to keep our population for a long time at a stable level", citing problems of food adequacy and sufficient jobs (Tien, p. 188). In the Spring of 1957, restrictions on sterilization and abortion were removed. Publicity was also given to the provisions of the Marriage Law of 1950 specifying minimum ages for marriage of 18 for women and 20 for men. Within a few months, however, the population issue was caught up in the anti-rightist campaign.

The Anti-Rightist Campaign

Confident that his policies were successful and popular, Mao argued in

May, 1956, for free discussion: "let a hundred flowers bloom; let a hundred schools of thought contend". Intellectuals were encouraged to air their grievances against the Party—and these were numerous and vehement.

A characteristic criticism came from economist Wu Dakun, who had returned from Washington State in 1951 to teach at Renda. He pointed out that the authorities had come to judge professors by their "willingness to submit to discipline. 'Discipline' means that the professor lectures in class exactly according to the outline or lecture notes previously approved by the 'leadership'."[23]

Economist Ko Pei-chi (Ge Beiji) of Renda pointed out that "there is an acute shortage of pork, and the common people find the commodity unavailable. Some people attribute this to the elevation of living standards. Who are the people who enjoy a higher standard of living? They are the Party members, and cadres . . ." (Quoted MacFarquhar 1960, p. 87.)

A group of prominent western-trained economists submitted a memo of criticisms and suggestions.[24] They complained that "Our financial and economic policies and measures have either been borrowed blindly from Soviet Russia's precedents or have been sheer trial and error, subjectivism and recklessness personified, based on no objective economic laws whatsoever . . ." (MacFarquhar, p. 118) They went on to say that "economic practice is separated from economic science in our country [and] our economic policy has become the prisoner of 'routinism'".[25]

They recommended that the government strengthen the links between economic studies and government agencies,[26] let the economic scholars have more information about economic policies, aid economic scholars by providing them with necessary documents and research aids, promote interactions between economists who are Party members and those who are not, reduce dogmatism: try to extract useful insights from western ("bourgeois") economics; learn the essence of Marxism rather than word-by-word repetition.

Chen Zhenhan also made provocative statements at an open forum at Beida in 1956 sponsored by anthropologist Fei Xiaotong. Chen made clear his dissatisfaction that persons like himself, with backgrounds in western economics, were excluded from policy analysis: "walls exist" between Party-member and non-Party-member economists. Chen identified some operational problems of the current economic system, including monopoly and motivation: "profit is the motivation under capitalism, while there is no such motivation under socialism". Chen "criticized the excessive and ceaseless political work and movements which left academics and scientists 'too exhausted to pursue any useful research'", Chen "denigrated . . . so-called Marxist-Leninist social science research in the Soviet Union which, in his view, after 40 years still lagged far behind international (western) levels" (Lin 1981, p. 9).

These comments urged the regime to utilize the sensible optimizing elements of traditional western economics. Chen Zhenhan and Xu Yunan nominated three: Keynes's concept of the multiplier, the general concept of the margin, and statistical methods, particularly those based on probability analysis.

Permissiveness quickly gave way to repression.[27] "By the end of the year [1957], over 300,000 intellectuals had been branded 'rightists', a label that effectively ruined their careers in China. Many were sent to labor camps or to jail . . ." (Spence 1990, p. 572)

The manifesto of the economists drew an outraged response centered on Keynesian analysis.[28] Three of the six targeted economists were Harvard PhDs—Chen Zhenhan, Wu Baosan, and Luo Zhiru. Xu had studied with Keynes at Cambridge, and ironically, Xu's translation of Keynes's *General Theory* was published in 1957.[29] Noted Cambridge economist Joan Robinson visited China in 1953. She was probably referring to Hsu (Xu) when she wrote "H., whom you remember as a rather ivory-tower intellectual at Cambridge . . . is very happy and completely absorbed in the New China . . ." (1954, p. 334) Fan Hong, also a Cambridge student but also a long-time Marxist and now a leader of the Beida Economics department, led the attack on these points: "Keynesian economic theories defend capitalism . . . They are anti-science and anti-people. Chen Chen-han and his follower Xu Yunan advocate criticism of Marxism and acceptance of Keynesian theories of general employment. Their aim is to revive monopoly capitalism." Fan denounced as "erroneous" such elements of the *General Theory* as the concept of full employment, the marginal productivity theory of wages, the concept of marginal productivity of capital, and the liquidity preference theory of interest.[30] Wu Bannong of CAS responded to the specifics of Chen's defense of Keynesianism: "In Marxism, the necessary labor time and average profit rate are both concepts of 'average'. Therefore, accepting Keynesian concepts means denying Marxism. . . . Statistics has a class nature in itself. Only Marxist political economics can analyze social phenomena effectively. Besides, statistics itself cannot solve economic problems in the society."[31]

Xiang Chong (Zhong) also assailed Chen's defense of marginal analysis:

> Jevons, who originated the marginal school, lived during a time when capitalism turned downward. He tried to use 'scarcity' to hide the truth that capitalism exploits the people.

Wang Yanan was a long-time Marxist faculty member of Amoy (Xiamen) University, catapulted into the presidency of that institution after 1949. Wang announced confidently that "Marxism cannot become dogmatism, because Marxism is under the guidance of a materialist perspective on the world, and because Marxism represents the new-born working class, which undertook cruel battles with the capitalists."

Of the thirteen criticisms published by the government, the one by Sun Yefang came closest to having some objectivity. Sun pointed out that "all comprehensive statistical data published by the National Statistical Bureau Publishing House are allocated to China Science College and to 30 other universities where they are open to the Economics departments". Economists were invited to discussions in formulating the second 5-year plan. The success of "rightist" Wu Jingchao in researching investment and employment in the Northeast illustrated cooperation by government units.[32]

A separate attack was directed against Ma Yinchu, who had been installed as president of Peking University in 1951 (Hsia 1961). In 1956–57, Ma began campaigning for measures to reduce population growth, and also criticized the government's development strategy. According to Walker 1963, "Ma followed his lengthy surveys of the writings of Malthus and Keynes with equally long but unconvincing protestations that his views were 'fundamentally different'." (p. 118) Though his views were not clearly expressed, Ma was advocating greater attention to consumer demand and greater use of the market mechanism.

Between April 1958 and November 1959 Ma's ideas "were attacked by some two hundred critics from academic and literary circles".[33] Demographer Chen Da had a similar experience. He published several statements in 1957 urging birth control programs and criticizing the scientific accuracy of the recent census. He was appropriately denounced and dismissed from the Scientific Planning Commission. Although his "rightist" label was rescinded in 1961, his morale was damaged and he produced no more research (Boorman 1967, I, pp. 235–239).

Chen Zhenhan, Wu Baosan, and the other "rightists" noted here were removed from their teaching or research positions. Chen was excluded from teaching for 22 years, ultimately rehabilitated in 1979. Ma Yinchu was removed as president of Beida in 1960. They were not physically abused, but the "struggle sessions" were emotionally devastating (Arkush 1981, p. 262). They continued to draw their salaries, but were humiliated and cut off from scholarly interchanges.

Xiang Jingyun (PhD Wisconsin 1941), who held a high post in the National Resources Commission, was removed from office and sent into exile in Yunnan (Antoinette Stepanek 1992, pp. 219–222). Other economists persecuted as "rightists" included Yang Jingnian, Fu Zhufu, Li Huafang, Chang Chung-yi (Zhang Zhongyi), Li Pao-chen (Baozhen), Tao Ta-yung (Dayong), Tang Chung-tai (Chongtai), and Pu Shan.

The anti-rightist campaign significantly diminished the scope for rational scientific discourse concerning public policy.[34] China had already lost a major element of human capital in the diaspora of economists. Now the remaining western-trained economists were effectively ostracized.[35] Perhaps the greatest loss was their potential ability to receive new and improved economic ideas from the West. And there was no new generation of students bringing innovative ideas back to China.

The Great Leap

Mao quickly followed the anti-rightist movement with campaigns to mobilize mass projects for water control and irrigation. In mid-1958 the government moved to end private agricultural enterprise and organize all rural residents into giant communes. Flamboyant rhetoric celebrated the immense increases in production supposed to result.[36] Vast numbers of "backyard" steel furnaces were created, and families were pressured to donate their cooking pots and other household items to be melted as scrap. This was the "Great Leap Forward". It was a disaster of cosmic proportions:

> As China's investment in industry rose to an amazing 43.4 percent of national income in 1959, grain exports to the Soviet Union were also increased to pay for more heavy machinery. The average amount of grain available to each person in China's countryside, which had been 205 kilos in 1957 and 201 kilos in 1958, dropped to a disastrous 183 kilos in 1959, and a catastrophic 156 kilos in 1960 . . . The result was famine on a gigantic scale, a famine that claimed 20 million lives or more between 1959 and 1962. Many others died shortly thereafter from the effects of the Great Leap—especially children, weakened by years of progressive malnutrition.[37]

In July, 1960, the Soviet experts working in China were suddenly withdrawn. China became even more isolated from the rest of the world. Between 1957 and 1965, rural consumption per capita increased only 1.7

percent per year, and urban consumption levels remained almost unchanged. "Infant mortality in China in 1965 may still have been as high as 165 per 1000 . . . Life expectancy at birth in 1965 is estimated to have been 44 years." (Perkins 1988, pp. 638, 640)

Fortunately, the government dismantled its most destructive policies, particularly the rural communes. Farmers were again permitted to cultivate private plots, and private rural markets reopened. Government encouragement of birth control resumed by 1963 and set off a decline in birth rates from over 40 per thousand in 1963 to about 20 per thousand in 1980.[38]

For the next few years there was greater openness in the intellectual realm as well. In the period 1957–65, nearly 50 western economics books were translated into Chinese. These included Keynes's *General Theory*, Chamberlin and Robinson on imperfect/monopolistic competition, Hicks's *Value and Capital*, Klein's *Keynesian Revolution*, as well as a large number of older works of mainstream economics.[39] In 1961, the Shanghai Society of Economics convened forums on Adam Smith, Ricardo, Marshall, and Keynes (Goldman 1981, p. 23). Renda introduced (and sustained) a course in linear programming, producing a textbook in that area in 1962. Also at Renda, former Yanjing professor Zheng Linzhuang was asked in 1962 to teach a course on "foreign agricultural economics", after not being able to undertake research in this area since 1949 (Halpern 1985, p. 249).

Sun Yefang was an important contributor to the debate on socialist economic policy. Sun had studied in Moscow—he worked with Wassily Leontief—and was familiar with the efforts of Oskar Lange and Yevsei Liberman to use some of the tools of western microeconomics for socialist policy-making. In 1957 Sun became acting director of the Economic Research Institute. In the improved atmosphere following 1961, he pressed for giving individual enterprises more autonomy, relying on market signals, particularly profits.[40]

The Cultural Revolution

The reaction against the starvation attending the Great Leap brought a restoration of market institutions in some degree.[41] This return to "bourgeois" behavior outraged Mao and his allies. Campaigns against "reactionary" tendencies in drama and literature escalated in 1966 to a major attack on the persons in power throughout the society—many of whom had developed serious misgivings about Mao's policies. Upheavals were particularly vigorous in schools and universities.

According to Cyril Chihren Lin:

> At the very start of the Cultural Revolution economic reformers were identified and attacked . . . and in due course almost all economists . . . and indeed the whole discipline of economics were accused of 'economism.' At the early phase of the Cultural Revolution the attack on economists was spearheaded against the Chinese Academy of Sciences Economic (and Philosophy) Research Unit where Sun Yefang was acting director . . . Eventually the attack on theoretical and academic economists was widened to include the professional economists and planners in government economic departments at both central and local levels. The government planning and management machinery ceased to function when their personnel were dispersed to the countryside for reform-through-labor and 'criticism, struggle, transformation' exercises . . . Senior economists were more harshly treated: Wang Yanan died under persecution, Sun Yefang was imprisoned for seven years . . . Xu Dixin was placed under 'office arrest' for nearly six years during which he reread *Capital* scores of times.[42]

Once again persons with connections to the West were among the scapegoats. No significant translations of western economic works were published in 1968–76. The universities were closed, some for as long as ten years. Mao leveled attacks against intellectuals as such, and vast numbers of professors, students, and researchers were sent "to the countryside".[43] Chen Hansheng was placed under house arrest 1966–68, and his wife was tortured to death (Yu 1995–96, p. 276).

Civil war raged in some areas. By 1970 the peak of intensity had passed, and the authorities gradually moved to restore order. Fortunately the Cultural Revolution did not have a damaging effect on production comparable to the Great Leap. But it did great damage to China's educational system.

President Nixon's visit in 1972 heralded a relaxation of repressive tensions. Educational institutions resumed operation, but for a time gave great emphasis to recruiting students from among the "workers, peasants, and soldiers" and to promoting ideology.

Nobel-laureate-to-be James Tobin visited China in 1972. He reported that:

> Academic economics is not in good shape . . . The curriculum is largely ideological and certainly nonquantitative.[44] . . . A course in the history of bourgeois economic thought is offered, starting with Adam Smith and stopping with Keynes and Chamberlin . . . Developments in economics in the West in the last thirty years are simply unknown, and our Chinese friends were

> genuinely surprised by our insistence that many of these developments were relevant and useful to a socialist economy. Their general attitude was that bourgeois economics must be irrelevant since it is concerned with profit maximization, an objective repudiated by socialist economies. (Tobin 1975, p. 44)

Much of the economic literature of the Mao era is reviewed in Lin 1981. Of the 79 authors cited, only five were on our lists of western-educated economists, and they included the contributions of Ma Yinchu, Chen Zhenhan, and Wu Baosan to the hundred-flowers debacle.[45] Other sources which we scanned for western-trained economists include Nairuenn Chen, Cheng 1957, Li 1962, Perkins 1966, Skinner 1965, and Prybyla 1970.

After Mao Zedong died in 1976, the intensity of totalitarian repression was greatly reduced. Many of the persecuted intellectuals returned to more nearly normal lives. Chen Zhenhan and Wu Baosan were restored to their positions with Beida and CASS. Sun Yefang was freed in 1975 and again became an active participant in the discussions of economic policy.[46] Maddison 1998 noted that over the entire period 1952–78:

> there was a major acceleration in the pace of growth, with GDP rising threefold and per capita income by 80 per cent . . . The acceleration in performance was due to a massive increase of inputs of physical and human capital . . . Human capital was improved by significant advances in education and health. However, the productivity picture was dismal. In spite of its growth acceleration, China grew somewhat less than the world economy as a whole. (p. 16)

This achievements came at a terrible cost in terms of misery—the mass starvation of the Great Leap, the extensive murders and persecutions of land reform and the Cultural Revolution. Much of the capital so hastily accumulated was misdirected. The environment sustained serious damage from industrial pollution and from agricultural mismanagement.

Toward Market Economy

We can only briefly note the fascinating developments in China's economy since 1976. The initial major changes occurred in agriculture, where the "responsibility system" restored the autonomy of the family farm.[47] Opportunity was extended for such activities as transportation and marketing of farm products and rural construction. In urban areas, individuals regained the right to engage in business for themselves, with greater freedom to choose employment and place of residence. This brought an explosion of new enterprises in retailing and services, with attendant improvement in living conditions for most residents.

In 1978, a new constitution affirmed a commitment to family planning. And in 1979 the government formally adopted the policy of limiting each married couple to one child. Although very unpopular, the policy succeeded in bringing down population growth and enabling many families to avoid poverty. Noting the extreme swing from the anti-Malthusian diatribes of the 1950s, Lee and Feng (1999) argued that "Malthusian or neo-Malthusian theory continues to provide virtually the sole justification and motivation for China's unprecedented family planning program."[48]

Just as anti-Malthusian views faded away, so did anti-Keynesianism. Demand management became a central feature of government economic policy. China's mixed economy, with its many disequilibrium markets, came to resemble the sort of neo-Keynesian model advanced by Barro and Grossman (1976).[49]

The universities were rehabilitated and enlarged. The older western-trained economists were restored to positions of status and respect.[50] However, university faculty rosters contained many appointees from the years when faculty were selected for revolutionary service and ideological fervor. Around 1980, Chinese students once again began to appear in American universities. Western economists began coming to China.[51] The United States government Fulbright program brought economists beginning in 1983. In 1984 the Ford Foundation initiated its special training program in Economics, directed by Gregory Chow. This book is an outgrowth of the author's opportunity to participate in both of these programs. Chinese universities were particularly eager to create programs in economic management, and incorporated many economic tools and concepts into such programs.[52]

Economist Robert Dernberger visited China in 1980 and learned that "More than 100,000 economists are said to be working in China's research institutes, universities, and research units . . ." (Thurston and Parker 1980, p. 107) Most of these must have been at best recipients of undergraduate degrees, considering the meager enrollment in university economics programs.[53]

Robert Hsu (1991) offered this assessment:

> Soon after 1978 . . . a paradox became clear to me . . . I firmly believed that, in view of China's long history of intellectual accomplishments, Chinese

> economists would have much to contribute to world economics . . . On the other hand, it was obvious that many articles in Chinese economics journals in the late 1970s and early 1980s were superficial and dogmatic, unworthy of the term "economic analysis" . . . [T]he Marxist ideology became a severe constraint on the development of economics in China once it was adopted as the state ideology or dogma. (p. ix)

The Chinese economy experienced immense improvement after 1976. Chinese people enjoyed domestic stability, personal freedom, and law and order, to an extent unparalleled in modern Chinese history. However, the government remained under the domination of the Communist Party, and the government continued to exercise extensive interventions and participations in the economy.

Under Mao Zedong, information on such everyday matters as the names of university faculty or staff of research institutions were not published. However, after 1980 there was a great outpouring of biographical material on academic people. Three such publications have been used throughout this study.[54] Pooling their information gives us 871 names of economists who enjoyed some measure of esteem after 1949. Information about them is shown in Table 15-6.

Table 15-6. Birth Dates and Foreign Study of 871 Prominent Chinese Economists Post-1949

Birth date	All	Foreign Study				
		U.S.	Europe	Japan	USSR	Total
–1914	223	49	37	21	6	113
1915–19	131	36	7	5	0	48
1920–24	163	27	2	3	4	36
Subtotal	517	112	47	29	10	198
1925–43	352	0	0	0	14	14
Total	871*	112	47*	29	24	212

* Total includes two without dates, one of whom studied in France.
Sources: See note 54.

Despite the attrition from emigration, change of jobs, retirement, and death, one fifth of the prominent economists born in 1924 or before were U.S.-trained, and nearly 10 percent had studied in Britain or continental Europe. The proportions of the different foreign-study components match well the proportions in our total student populations reported in Chapters 4 to 6. Economists born in 1925 and after reported only negligible foreign study—the low proportion who studied in the Soviet Union is striking.

A different type of sample of Chinese economists can be derived from trip reports of western visitors. These include Reynolds (1981), Thurston-Parker (1980), Watson (1987), and especially Hu (1984). These identify 196 different economists and their work units. Of these, 30 are in our list as having studied in the United States, and another four studied in Britain. This result of 17.3 percent is close to the 18.3 percent yielded by Table 15-6.[55]

These data suggest that western-trained Chinese economists continued to be a significant element among senior university faculty and research staff during the first 30 years of Communist rule. Andrew Watson remarked in 1987:

> The senior scholars fall into two groups, those trained outside China before 1949 with a grounding in Western-style economics and those trained in the Soviet Union or in China during the 1950s. Both have experienced a renaissance of their work. The former have been re-appointed to prominent positions, have re-established contacts with their early roots and are playing an important role in the examination of foreign scholarship. The latter, many of whom were active in earlier periods of debate over economic reform, have been rehabilitated after the criticisms of the Cultural Revolution and provide the main force in the shaping of reformist economic scholarship. (p. 85)

Significance

In this book we have described in detail the large movement of Chinese to study Economics in western universities and return to positions in universities, business, and government. Our data demonstrated that returned students in Economics played a major role in Chinese universities, often constituting a third or more of the senior faculty. They also took on major positions in government (Sun Fo, Chen Gongbo, T. V. Soong, and He Lian). The upsurge in the number of returning economists was matched by an increase in university enrollments in Economics and by an explosion in the number of economic publications. However, the vast majority of the authors had not studied abroad. The same was true of the personnel of the rapidly expanding research organizations, the authors of translations of western economic works, and membership in the Chinese Economic Association. The return of western-educated Chinese economists helped bring about the emergence of a large, diverse, and vigorous economics profession consisting primarily of persons who did not study overseas—most of them, one presumes, graduates of the Chinese universities working as teachers, writers, business and government employees.

Wang Yi-chu (1966), who surveyed the entire spectrum of Chinese studying abroad in the twentieth century, disparaged the whole process. Study in the West, he believed, worsened the alienation of Chinese intellectuals from the mass of the people. And Yeh Wen-hsin (1990) implicitly condemned the "alienated" character of Chinese universities.

These criticisms were vastly overstated. The alienation of Chinese intellectuals was rooted in the traditional image of the scholar and in the class character of Chinese society.[56] The university experience is usually alienating even in the West, particularly for a young person who is the first in the family to attend university.[57] American land-grant universities were among the least alienating institutions in the world, structured as they were to provide practical instruction in agriculture and the mechanic arts, and drawing many students from rural backgrounds. Many Chinese economists were trained at Cornell, Michigan, Wisconsin, and Illinois. John Lossing Buck and his associates at Nanjing University did their best to recreate that land-grant college atmosphere in China. The same impulse was evident in the work of John Bernard Tayler at Yanjing and Fang Xianting at Nankai. Modernization was bound to be an alienating experience for a society where traditional ways were so pervasive and deep-rooted.

The most penetrating criticism is that returned students failed to deal with the problems of rural China. But they offered many sensible suggestions which the government failed to follow. Leftist critics seemed to feel there were simple remedies available, presumably involving the displacement of various putative "exploiters". The Communist experience has helped put these issues in better perspective. Rural poverty can only be alleviated by raising productivity and moving workers into non-agricultural activities—both measures which had been advocated by Buck and the Nanjing staff since the early 1920s.

To be sure, the predominant economic ideas of western-trained Chinese economists had many flaws (shared with western economists). They were unduly taken with the western fads for imperfect competition and Keynesian economics, both of which exaggerated market failure. They were too gullible regarding Sun Yat-sen's heavily collectivist proposals for economic development and his support for protectionist restrictions on imports. They retained populist prejudices toward landlords, moneylenders, and merchants. They vastly exaggerated the damage done by western imperialism. They unduly neglected the quantity theory of money and thus were "soft on inflation" in the 1940s. But by the 1940s China was producing world-class economists, many of whom defected to the West. The Communist regime chose to exile or immobilize its inherited economists, whose insights might have enabled the post-1949 regime to choose less disastrous economic policies.

It is useful to compare China's intellectual experience with Japan's. Japanese universities did not produce the kind of hands-on activist programs associated with the economists at Yanjing, Nanjing, and Nankai, but they produced more activists in the political arena. There were many Marxists among Japanese economists. Those Japanese economists who adopted mainstream western economics were able to progress further in the technical side involving mathematics and econometrics.

Indian economists followed British rather than American economics. This produced a prevalent outlook of "soft socialism" which was reflected in Indian economic policy after independence. The interventionist bias of the "license raj" was blamed for sluggish economic growth. Neither Japan nor India relied so much on overseas study in the development of their own professional economists, nor on westerners teaching Economics. India did produce a Nobel Prize winner (Amartya Sen, educated in England); China and Japan have not as of 2006.

Whatever were the shortcomings of western economics in 1949, they were at least being vigorously addressed in the West with emotional vigor and intellectual rigor in the atmosphere of free inquiry over the next quarter-century. The isolationism and intellectual nihilism of Mao's regime prevented China from either contributing to or drawing from this process.

The experience of China since 1949 helps put in perspective what happened in the previous half-century. The experiences with Marxian communism world-wide were disasters. In simplest terms, these regimes were based on force and fraud. While pretending to draw on concepts of human betterment and social justice, they manifested cruelty to an extreme degree. Much of this derived from Marx's emphasis on the evil of the bourgeoisie and on class struggle. Post-1949 Chinese experiences demonstrated just how difficult it was to improve significantly the real incomes and living conditions of China's rural residents.

Western economists from Adam Smith onward took for granted an institutional structure which would secure law and order, protect property rights and contractual obligations, restrain the predatory impulses of government officials, promote monetary stability, and provide basic infrastructure such as transportation. China lacked these, and for that reason much western economic analysis was of limited relevance. Similar considerations restricted the relevance of Japan's experience. Japan had relatively strong and responsible government. Despite abuses, Japanese occupation helped prepare Manchuria, Taiwan, and South Korea for subsequent superior economic performance.[58]

One can criticize western economics for failure to celebrate sufficiently the superior economic performance of free competitive markets.[59] Ralph Hawtrey noted in 1946 that "Economic faith [in free competitive markets] was better established at the beginning of the twentieth century than it had ever been. Yet somehow it has been weakened—almost extinguished." (p. 355) For much of the twentieth century western economists were quick to identify market failures and prescribe government interventions. Only with much more experience did the western world discover that such plausible measures as public housing, minimum-wage laws, transfer payments to low income families, and government ownership and operation of industries were often very disappointing.[60]

China needed to hear the lessons which Liang Qichao and Yan Fu were advocating around 1900—that private business enterprise was potentially a moral activity, one which would bring benefit to the general population. The Communist triumph was in some degree a triumph of pre-capitalist populism and primitivism, hostility toward merchants, landowners, and moneylenders—a situation where the general attitude of the public (especially outside the cities) had not caught up with Adam Smith. China's economic reform process after 1976 has revived the educational process begun by Liang and Yan.

Western microeconomic theory devoted much attention to welfare economics and the theory of optimal resource allocation. Before the 1980s, the Chinese Communist regime devoted no significant attention to the serious problems of optimization for government enterprises or government planning.[61] A poignant case involved Yu Guangyuan, who graduated from Qinghua in 1936 with a degree in physics. He went behind Communist lines and worked as an editor. After 1949 he became Associate Director of the Scientific Planning Committee. In 1963 he drafted a book in which he plainly undertook to reinvent the wheel—that is, to develop a concept of optimization within the acceptable Marxian frame of discourse, with no recourse to western economic analysis. Most of the manuscript was lost, but some fragments were ultimately published in Yu 1978 (*Biographies of Contemporary Chinese Economists*).

So on balance we can identify some real shortcomings of western economics in providing useful guidance for the Chinese. But we must also recognize that Chinese often did not exercise good judgment in deciding which elements of western economics to pursue or to ignore.

Notes

Chapter 1

1. Throughout this book, Chinese names are presented with family name first and personal name second. Initially each name is given in whatever westernized form the individual used. Thereafter most names are given in the current westernized form of pinyin. A glossary presents prominent names in traditional westernizations, pinyin, and hanzi (Chinese characters).
2. The reader is warned that our data sets are incomplete and imperfect. All generalizations are approximations.
3. Young Back Choi 1996 presents a similar but highly condensed analysis for Korea since 1945. Aiko Ikeo stresses the transfer of western economic ideas into Japan through books, journals, and visiting professors; but gives little attention to Japanese studying Economics in the West (1993, p. 195; 1996, p. 129).
4. We identified 79 Economics doctorates in Britain for Indian students through 1950, compared with 149 doctorates in the U.S. for Chinese. The total number of thesis degrees plus theses not completed were 176 for Indians in Britain and 447 for Chinese in the U.S. The Chinese total is about 2.5 times that for India. On India, see Ambirajam 1981, 1996. Thesis degrees in England are documented in Bilboul 1975. Sources for Chinese thesis degrees are detailed in Chapter 4.
5. Not all students returned to China. On the other hand, our tabulation omits students for whom we have no dates. These are roughly offsetting biases.
6. Hu Jichuang 1982 indicates there were 562 economic translations published in 1919–49. We generated a sample of 318 items covering 1900–49. Some are citations from Hu, some from the Nankai bibliographies (Chapter 14) and many were compiled for this study by Wang Jianye and Yan Zhijie from library shelf lists. Of our sample, 187 were western items, 65 Japanese and 18 Russian (remainder unknown). Many of the items translated were textbooks and I did not list them in Table 1-3. Translators were identified for only 230.
7. This information was kindly furnished by Sun Chung-hsing, translated by Lin Suren.
8. More precisely, Yan Fu's well-known translation appeared in 1902. However, in 1896, a Chinese translation of the Japanese translation of Smith was published by Nanyang College in Shanghai. Reynolds 1993, p. 111.

9. "China's leaders . . . launched the largest family planning program in the twentieth century on the basis of little more than nineteenth-century social theory. Government policy seems to have virtually embraced the original Malthusian paradigm without full consideration of its consequences." Lee and Feng 1999, p. 21.
10. Nobel-Prize-winner W. Arthur Lewis published his *Theory of Economic Growth* in 1955. He remarked that "the only twentieth century economist who came anywhere near to a general survey of economic growth was J. A. Schumpeter, in his *Capitalism, Socialism and Democracy* . . .", published in 1942 (1955, p. 21). Lewis was modest regarding the insights of economics in explaining successful growth and development (p. 418).
11. Maddison 1998, p. 13. He estimates that China's per capita gross domestic product decreased about ten percent between 1820 and 1952. p. 40. The fact of China's past glories left a powerful influence on Chinese intellectuals. In contrast to Maddison, Lee and Wang 1999 argue that "the Chinese standard of living at the time of Malthus was not only comparable to the West's; it even rose, if not monotonically or uniformly, in recent centuries, and not just in recent decades." (p. 11)
12. However, Englishman John A. Hobson recognized a different aspect of China's economic potential in his influential *Imperialism* (1902): "China might turn the tables upon the Western industrial nations, and, either by adopting their capital and organizers or . . . by substituting her own, might flood their markets with her cheaper manufactures, and refusing their imports in exchange might take her payment in liens upon their capital, reversing the earlier process of investment until she gradually obtained financial control over her [former] patrons and civilizers." (p. 309)
13. The western term "college" was often used in the early twentieth century to refer to Chinese secondary schools, many of which gradually extended their scope into university-level instruction. Kuno 1928 approaches this issue analytically.
14. Potential confusion of names arises from the fact that one of the missionary colleges initially called itself Peking University (later transformed into Yanjing University).
15. Moving the capital created a linguistic problem for westerners. "Peking" meant "northern capital", a name which was inappropriate after 1927. Chiang changed its name to "Peiping", meaning "northern peace".
16. The Chinese Social and Political Science Association was organized in 1915–16 and had a significant economic component. Their English-language quarterly journal, the *Chinese Social and Political Science Review* (*CSPSR*), first appeared in April 1916. Its first issue had three major economic articles. However, Sun 1987 described the organization as "more of a club for diplomats . . . than an academic association . . ." (p. 238)

17. Not only were many of the German "historicists" socialists (admittedly in a vague sense of the term), but so were quite a few of the leading economic theorists. Alfred Marshall considered himself a socialist, as did A. C. Pigou, Leon Walras, and Knut Wicksell. The leading American theorists were an exception.
18. See Chapter 11, also Trescott 2002.
19. A good survey of "academic Marxism" before 1949 appears in Sun 1987, ch. 7; also Douw 1991. On Shen, see Sun pp. 278–279; *Contemporary Social Scientists in China*, v. VI.
20. The clearest example of this possibility was the valiant protest of Ma Yinchu in the 1950s against Communist policies tending to encourage population growth. Although initially he was persecuted for his views, they ultimately prevailed. See Chapter 15.
21. "The late Maoist economy was characterized by enormous supply-side slack, and the balanced budgets of the period had done nothing to eliminate it. In other words, the situation inherited by the Dengist regime was akin to one of Keynesian unemployment, and therefore demand expansion offered an obvious means to unlock the economy's economic potential." Bramall 2000, p. 309.

Chapter 2

1. My inquiries in China, Europe, and America have failed to locate a copy of *Political Economy.* A copy of the *Treatise on Commerce* is held by the American Philosophical Society in Philadelphia. They are discussed in Tsien 1954.
2. The number of students enrolled in the Economics course was 9 in 1879, 8 in 1888, and 12 in 1893. Biggerstaff 1961, pp. 121n, 128–133.
3. Fryer's Chinese collaborator was Yin Zuxi. I have written about this book at much greater length: Trescott 1989.
4. Wang Kangzheng's letter to the author, Feb. 15, 1988.
5. Burton had written "certain propensities implanted in mankind, which, when viewed alone, have a selfish, narrow, and almost degrading aspect, are when contemplated in relation to each other, a wise provision for enabling man to advance his own welfare, happiness, and virtue." (1852, p. 51) The translation drastically changed this to say "God created man with the gift of a selfless nature so that people can get along well. But in the pursuit of wealth, one man often sacrifices another's interest. This is against the will of God. We must study and think out a method to get rich and increase wealth without going against God's will." All quotations from the translation are re-translations by Mr. Wang Kangzheng.

   Burton presented a lengthy example illustrating the spontaneous workings of supply and demand in provisioning London (pp. 52–53). The translation removed the supply and demand references. Where Burton stressed that British institutions were designed "to give them [supply and demand] free room to work" (p. 52), the translation merely identified their purpose as "let everybody obey the regulations".

6. So Kwan-wei 1950, pp. 49–52, 187–190.
7. Yih (Yi) Menghong 1985, p. 4. While Jevons is now best known for his pioneering work in introducing marginal-utility analysis around 1870, that topic does not appear in the very elementary *Primer*.
8. One of the earliest doctoral dissertations in Economics by a Chinese in the U.S. was "Economic Principles of Confucius and his School", by Chen Huan-chang (Huanzhang—Columbia, 1911).
9. *The Economist*, Jan. 21, 1995, p. 39. The diverse aspects of Confucianism are reviewed in Tai ed., 1989. Confucian values are credited for high rates of saving and devotion to education.
10. Portions of this section appeared in Trescott 1989.
11. An English translation is available: Thompson 1958. There are also extensive quotations and comments in Hsiao 1975, pp. 435–513.
12. Thompson 1958, pp. 211, 228. A Chinese translation of Bellamy's *Looking Backward* (1888) appeared in 1891. Bernal 1976, pp. 18–31.
13. Yan translated slightly more than half of the original, omitting Smith's digressions on variations in the value of silver (pp. 176–217) and on banks of deposit, particularly the Bank of Amsterdam (pp. 446–455). On the other hand, Yan did translate many of the comments of Thorold Rogers, editor of the edition of Smith which Yan used. And he added 310 notes of his own. Lai 2000, pp. 17–23.
14. Mao told Edgar Snow that at age 19 (in 1912) he began to study on his own in the Changsha public library. "I read Adam Smith's *Wealth of Nations*, and Darwin's *Origin of Species*, and a book on ethics by John Stuart Mill. I read the works of Rousseau, Spencer's *Logic*, and a book on law written by Montesquieu . . ." Snow 1938, pp. 142, 147–148.
15. See especially Lai 1997, 2000; also Zhu 1993.
16. Yan Fu entitled his translation Yuan Fu (= Origins of Wealth).
17. Marx's *Theories of Surplus Value* traces his central economic ideas, notably the labor theory of value, through Smith and Ricardo. This link to Marx enabled Chinese economists to teach Smith's ideas during Mao Zedong's ascendancy.
18. Much of the following appeared in Trescott and Wang 1994 and is reproduced with the kind permission of the publishers of the *Journal of the History of Economic Thought*.
19. Hsiao 1975. A corrosively negative view of Kang and Liang is given in Seagrave 1992, pp. 198–272.
20. Dr. Wang and I prepared a working paper containing his entire translation side-by-side with the parallel texts from Cossa and Ingram: Wang and Trescott 1986.

21. Wieger 1931 translated portions of this into French and summarized the rest—pp. 123–128. See also Levenson, pp. 130–131, 150–152, and Nathan 1985, pp. 53–54.
22. "On the Circumstances of the Struggles of Peoples", in Liang's *Ying-ping-shi Hou-chi Wen-chi* (1916), v. 4, pp. 10–35 at p. 11. This was translated for me by Wang Kangzheng.
23. Reynolds, pp. 114–126. A good illustration of the problem of terminology involved the currency reform proposals advanced in 1904 by the Jenks commission. The proposals were doomed by opposition from Chang Chih-tung arising from misunderstandings reflecting defective Chinese translations. Wei 1914, p. 101.

Chapter 3

1. Portions of this chapter appeared in Trescott 1994 and are reproduced with the kind permission of Blackwell Publishing.
2. A translation appears in Wei 1994, pp. 3–18.
3. He also recommended encouraging the production of opium in some backward areas. Wei 1994, p. 16.
4. Wang 1965, p. 172; Yu 1989, p. 87; Sharman 1965, p. 169; Bernal 1976, pp. 49–60.
5. Schiffrin 1957; Schiffrin and Sohn 1959; Lin 1972; Lindholm and Lin 1977; Wang 1966, pp. 347, 351–352.
6. George 1960, pp. 107, 109, 111–114, 121–122, 128, 308, 459, 470, 482–483, 494, 498, 503, 521, 527, 539.
7. Sun probably was not familiar with George's 1869 efforts to restrict Chinese immigration as harmful to the U.S. working class. Barker 1955, pp. 122–123.
8. The following section summarizes material developed in Lai and Trescott 2005.
9. Liang 1906a, pp. 16–17. Sun and his colleagues also drew on Ely. Ely was a devotee of the Christian Social Gospel who had studied in Germany and admired Bismarck's reforms. His writings were soon translated in China and were extensively used in Chinese universities. Ely defended state ownership of "natural monopolies" such as railroads, but was very skeptical about comprehensive socialist programs. Ely 1893, pp. 308–312.
10. Quoted Bernal 1976, p. 69; compare Sun 1943, p. 433. Henry George's tax proposal became known as the "single tax" because of his confidence that it would yield enough revenue to replace all other taxes. Sun expressed similar expectations in 1906: "After China's social revolution is accomplished, private individuals will never again have to pay taxes. The collection of land revenues alone will make China the richest nation on earth." Quoted Wei 1994, p. 48.
11. Wei 1994, pp. 66–67. However, rural land in China was bought and sold only infrequently.

12. Bernal 1976 has examined the early lengthy debates on land policy in great detail. While some of Sun's associates advanced specific land nationalization proposals, Sun did not endorse them and may not even have read them. Bernal, pp. 136–195, especially 193; see also Scalapino and Schiffrin 1957; Wilbur 1976, pp. 214–217.
13. Wilbur 1976, pp. 212–214. Henry George opposed what we would now term "land reform" and also rejected the idea of outright land nationalization. George 1960, pp. 324, 404.
14. Sun Yat-sen's widow Soong Qingling later told Edgar Snow, "He made it all up on the spur of the moment. It all depended on the political situation and the audience . . . But he was always a Socialist . . . He had very clear objectives in his mind—land to the tillers, social ownership of production, industrial modernization, equality of education and work opportunities for all and an end to foreign imperialism." Quoted Snow 1958, p. 92. See also Schiffrin 1980, p. 253.
15. *Encyclopedia* 1987, p. 381. The region in question remained in the 1990s relatively undeveloped. Dolon Nor in 1991 still had no rail service.
16. By the 1920s, Chinese students were learning about Malthus from courses in the history of economic thought. The case for voluntary birth restraint was developed in the successive editions of Chen Chang-heng's book *On the Population of China* which first appeared in 1918 and was in its 8th edition by 1928. Chen had been a graduate student at Harvard and held a series of high government positions. Tien 1973, pp. 168–170; *China Year Book* 1935; *Who's Who in Modern China*, p. 23. Wu Ching-chao (Jingchao) in 1944 commented on the influence of Sun on government policy, noting that "It is very difficult to advocate birth control just at the present." (Quoted MacNair 1944, p. xxxii.)
17. Hou 1974, p. 97. Sun's brief reference to a timetable for development shows this: "First, we must begin to build means of communication, railroads and waterways, on a large scale. Second, we must open up mines . . . Third, we must hasten to foster manufacturing." (1943, p. 438; also 1928, pp. 26, 138–140) Sun's rhetoric often sounds like a call to a "great leap". Sun 1921, p. 172; see also pp. 36, 114, 174, 194–196; Wei 1994, p. 221; Gasster 1968, pp. 79, 94–95; Schiffrin 1980, p. 116.
18. Sun 1943, p. 415; for similar references see pp. 367–369, 384, 389, 413, 436, 443. Myers 1989, p. 243.
19. The *China Year Book* of 1931 noted that "The first organization taken over by the Nanking [Construction] Commission was the Chihli River Commission of Tientsin . . . with the result that the only efficient conservancy service in the country . . . , has been completely destroyed." (pp. 76–77)
20. G. Chen 1934, pp. 352–353; "State Plans . . .", 1934, pp. 206–207; Chen Kung-po 1933. Wu Yuan-li 1946 gives a concise and focused review of policy proposals and actions; pp. 34–39.

21. Gregor and Chang 1983 argued that Taiwan's "entire [development] program was not only infused with the developmental spirit characteristic of his ideology, it embodied most of its critical programmatic components." (p. 32)
22. Contrary to Cheng 1989, which simply characterized Taiwan's land reform program as "the land redistribution program Sun advocated in 1924" (p. 250), Hou 1974 correctly remarked that "It will never be known . . . whether this kind of program ran across Sun's mind." (p. 111) See also Shen 1964, pp. 40–48; Thorbecke 1979; Li 1988, pp. 59–62.
23. Ho 1978, pp. 135–139. The campaign to limit population growth was greatly aided when Sun Fo was persuaded to support it. Li 1988, pp. 72–76.
24. Thus Li Kuo-ting, principal architect of Taiwan's economic policy, stated that in the 1950s, "we tried to develop all our industries to conform to Dr. Sun Yatsen's teaching . . ." (Li 1980, p. 11; see also p. 66.) And Henry Wan Jr. notes that "It would be wrong to regard the economic policies of Taiwan as far-sighted if not infallible. Many projects cherished by the government did not flourish." (Wan 1992, pp. 45–46, citing steel and shipbuilding among others.) In 1998, *The Economist* concluded "In a region where economic success is usually attributed to grand industrial policy and national champions, Taiwan has neither. When its government has tried to promote industries or create big conglomerates, it has usually failed . . . Taiwan, which . . . has not had much success with central planning, has created an environment where the entrepreneurial potential of its people can be fully realized." (Taiwan Survey, Nov. 7, 1998, p. 9)
25. Ian Little gives particular credit to K. Y. Yin and K. C. Yeh. Little wrote: "Tsiang told me that he believed the deal was clinched by his giving to Yin a copy of James Meade's *Planning and the Price Mechanism* . . ." (Little 1979, p. 475; my thanks to Arthur Waldron who provided the reference.) See also Tsiang 1980, 1989; Klein, Nerlove and Tsiang, 1980.

    According to Chin Chung, "it was the successful export drive of labor-intensive products . . . that explained, in good part, the miraculous growth of the Taiwan economy over the past 40 years." (1992, p. 7) Aside from brief references to agricultural exports, Sun did not discuss exports.

    The key roles of Jiang and Liu were celebrated in a conference at Cornell in 1996: Thorbecke and Wan 1996.
26. Alley 1954, p. 121. According to the *People's Daily*, the PRC has created a system which "has made Sun Yatsen's ideal a reality" (Oct. 15, 1991; compare Zhang 1991, p. 27). Mao Zedong's important manifesto, "On the People's Democratic Dictatorship", issued June 30, 1949, on the eve of the Communist take-over, has extensive references to Sun; Mao 1975, pp. 413–424. Chang and Gordon 1991 review Communist commentaries on Sun; pp. 140–144, 158–160.
27. On Mao's use of "the myth of Sun Yatsen", see Kindermann 1969.

Chapter 4

1. An earlier version of this appeared in Trescott 2000.
2. By 1955 approximately 2,000 Chinese students had been aided in their U.S. study by Boxer funds. Wilma Fairbank 1976, p. 114.
3. These data imply a very high proportion of Economics students continuing into graduate study, which is consistent with many other data. Our method of classifying students counts some whose ultimate specialty would not have been listed as Economics—Chen Da and Wu Jingchao for example.
4. In a series of studies analyzing the AEA lists of doctoral candidates, Lewis Froman (1930, 1942, 1952) tabulated the undergraduate institutions attended by each. For each of the three time periods (1904–28, 1929–40, and 1941–50) China ranked second to Canada. Of course many Chinese obtained undergraduate degrees in the U.S., but so did many Canadians.
5. Mason 1982. Dorfman 1959 devotes an entire chapter to Taussig and his Harvard colleagues, principally Carver and Charles Bullock—pp. 236–253.
6. Egan describes the case of Chang Wen-li (Zhang Wenli) who came with Yanjing Dean William Hung to study with Carver. "Carver told Hung that Chang was the brightest student he had ever had . . ." and arranged for him to work with the U.S. Department of Agriculture. Chang was recruited to the Soviet Union where he worked successfully to develop cotton culture. Egan 1987, pp. 108, 132–133, 188, 208.
7. A convenient collection of 2–3 page abstracts of Harvard dissertations was published annually by the university from 1926 through 1945.
8. Condliffe to E. W. Kemmerer, January 24, 1929, in Kemmerer Collection, Seely Mudd Manuscript Library, Princeton University. In the same letter, Condliffe noted that Hsiao was working in the Ministry of Finance helping prepare tariff schedules. "He struck me as being a very able statistician."
9. Qiu became for many years the distinguished librarian of the Harvard-Yenching Institute in Cambridge.
10. According to Don Moggridge, "it could be argued that Chicago, Harvard, and LSE [London School of Economics] . . . provided graduate students with the best analytical training in economics available in the late 1930s and 1940s. At Harvard there had been the changing of the guard that brought Schumpeter, Leontief, Haberler, and Hansen to the department, . . . By way of contrast. the theoretical training of economists at Columbia left much to be desired. C. P. Kindleberger, who was there as a student, reports that in the 1930s, 'economics education at Columbia was not exciting' and that 'there was no core of economic theory'." Moggridge 1995, pp. 227–228. See the enthusiastic reports on mid-1930s Harvard by Richard Musgrave and Wolfgang Stolper in Hageman 1999, pp. 65–68, 102–105.
11. Letter to the author, November 18, 2002. Pu's dissertation undertook to "analyze the effect of technological progress on the volume of employment"

in basically Keynesian models of industrialized societies. The dissertation included no references to China and very little relevance to China. The high quality of Pu's work is reflected in a note he published in *Econometrica* (Pu 1946) commenting on work by Lawrence Klein dealing with aggregating from the level of the individual firm up to the macro-economy. Klein cited Pu's assistance in his *Keynesian Revolution* (1947, p. ix).

12. Information from Tian Xiao-hua; Bartke 1987; Hoyt 1990.
13. On Yale see Kelley, 1974, pp. 182, 252, 281, 316; Barber 1988, pp. 156–163.
14. Slosson 1910, pp. 445–451. On Columbia's Economics program, see Rozwadowski 1988; Dorfman 1955.
15. Rutherford 2000, 2004. This theme is further developed in Chapter 8; see also Trescott 1992. The Institutionalist influence led to a downplaying of economic theory. Kenneth Arrow, a graduate student at Columbia in 1940–42, noted the absence of any required course in price theory (Dimand 1998, p. 462).
16. All nine of these were published in the series *Columbia Studies in History, Economics and Public Law*.
17. Ji's data on Chinese agricultural history were analyzed and extended in Perkins 1969, pp. 333–344. His dissertation on Chinese public works for water control received the Seligman Prize as the outstanding dissertation of 1936 and was translated into Japanese in 1939. *Who's Who in China* 1950, pp. 42–43.
18. Chao 1917, pp. 76–77; information in University of Illinois Archives.
19. *Who's Who in China* 1936, p. 135; Perleberg 1954, p. 120.
20. Of 72 Chinese students receiving graduate Economics degrees from Penn, 19 were from Jiaotong. University of Pennsylvania Archives.
21. *Who's Who in China* 1925, pp. 533–535; *China Year Book* 1935.
22. The University of Chicago may have been an exception. Emmett 1998 suggests Chicago's doctoral program was more rigorous and theory-centered and less given to advocacy-oriented policy studies (pp. 141–146). This may help explain why, of the 49 Chinese identified as graduate students at Chicago, only three completed doctorates. Even before Milton Friedman's arrival in 1948, Chicago was distinguished for its faculty commitment to free markets and skepticism about government economic activism. Reder 1982.
23. Author's interview with Chen Daisun, May 1992. Some of Dittmer's research appears in his 1918 article, which indicates he spent three years at Qinghua.
24. *China Handbook* 1937–45; "Survey of Recent Studies on Chinese Economy, 1927–1947".
25. Xiang was profiled at length by Roger Evans of the Rockefeller Foundation (diary, April 23, 1947). In 1947–49 he worked closely with Joseph and Antoinette Stepanek. They met him again in 1992, at which date he was still living in China, having been rehabilitated in 1979. Antoinette Stepanek 1992, pp. 219–222.
26. "Feng's aim was to 'humanize' agricultural science and get it outside the walls

of the college or laboratory. Research 'should be so conducted that its results can be put into practice by the average Chinese farmer and its progress be made to go hand in hand with his practice in farming'." Hayford 1990, pp. 71–72, 88–90. Feng 1931 is a good brief overview of Chinese farming.

27. Perleberg 1954, p. 222. His textbook (1934) was favorably reviewed by Lee Shison 1935. After his defection, Tung published a number of studies in Chinese highly critical of land reform on the mainland. These and other matters are reviewed in his English-language book *Communist China and the Chinese Problem* (Tung 1975) which is polemical but persuasive.
28. Klein, Nerlove, and Tsiang 1980; Thorbecke and Wan 1999. Liu and Jiang were the only Chinese economists whose international reputation led to their inclusion in the first edition of Mark Blaug's *Who's Who in Economics* (1983). The second edition (1986) added Alpha Chiang and Cheng Pao-lun, discussed below.
29. Perleberg 1954; "Research Notes", July, 1935, p. 393. George Wei observed that most American firms operating in the Shanghai area "dealt with the legal aspects of their businesses in China through this agency" (Wei 1997, p. 127).
30. Information from Princeton University Alumni Office.

Chapter 5

1. On LSE, see Dahrendorf 1995, Hayek 1946. Many of the students who received the BSc (Econ.) degree had specializations outside Economics proper, such as political science, sociology, or international relations.
2. Hicks was a student in the early PPE program and found it unimpressive. Hamouda 1993, p. 6. See also Flexner 1930, p. 289; Harrod 1951, pp. 121–122n. Michael Lindsay (1938), who brought Keynesian Economics to Yanjing, was much more impressed.
3. Flexner (1930) noted the essentially liberal-arts quality of British schools of commerce: "The Birmingham School undertakes little or nothing that could not . . . be done . . . by the faculty of arts . . . Some research in the economic history of the area is carried out; for the rest, the work falls into economics, economic history, transportation, and modern languages . . ." (p. 257)
4. These were Jen (Ren) Kainan (LSE 1914–19); Li Chien-nung (Jiannong—LSE 1913–16); and Yang Tuan-lu (Duanliu—LSE 1913–20). They were joined later by Liu Pinglin (Binglin—LSE 1920–23). LSE *Register* 1895–1932; Wuhan University faculty lists; *Biographies of Contemporary Chinese Social Scientists*; 1942 roster; *China Handbook* 1937–1945, p. 676.
5. Davin 1987, p. 55; also Yuan 1963, p. 108.
6. Tawney 1932. He spent much of 1931 in China and drew on the intellectual and social resources of Nankai, Nanjing, and Yanjing Universities. He was particularly impressed with the ideas of John Tayler, whom he had known at LSE. Terrill 1973 is the best review of his life and ideas. Tawney was also joint

author of an important study of Chinese education (Becker et al., 1932) and edited a volume of essays (mostly leftist) on Chinese agricultural problems (Institute of Pacific Relations 1938). Dahrendorf described him as a "romantic moralist", who perhaps felt that "modernity itself is the evil" (p. 126; see also pp. 232–241).

7. Several of Robbins's LSE course syllabi are reproduced in MacCormick 1992, pp. 31–34. The book provides many useful comments on the personnel and activities at LSE in the 1930s and 1940s.
8. Several of Hicks's LSE course syllabi are reproduced in MacCormick 1992, pp. 86–89.
9. Lewis moved to Manchester in 1948; his path-breaking study on "Economic Development with Unlimited Supplies of Labor" appeared in 1954.
10. Several of Hayek's syllabi for LSE courses are reproduced in MacCormick 1992, pp. 45–48, 102. Hayek's most esteemed essays on the informational and organizational deficiencies of collectivism are assembled in *Individualism and Economic Order* (Hayek, 1948).
11. Information from Lai Cheng-chung.
12. Hamouda 1993, p. 13; Dahrendorf 1995, pp. 187–203, 213, 221. Hicks 1983, p. 357; Robbins 1971, pp. 123–135.
13. We have not included Fei Hsiao-tung (Xiaotong—LSE PhD 1938) who became China's most distinguished anthropologist, and whose research dealt extensively with economic topics (Arkush 1981). The same treatment befalls L. K. Tao (Tao Menghe—BSc LSE 1913 in sociology), long-time Beida professor and director of the Institute of Social Research. *China Handbook* 1950.
14. His dissertation defense was conducted by Hayek and Hicks (who was then at Manchester) at the Liberal Club in London. Chen and Mo 1992, pp. 34–35.
15. Tsiang 1943. During the War, LSE operations were moved to Cambridge. In 1989, Tsiang reminisced: "It was certainly a very exciting time for us young students. We were free while in Cambridge to attend the lectures of teachers of both schools. To hear the traditional Marshallian theory and that of the Austrian school expounded by [D. H.] Robertson and Hayek and then to hear the same theories mercilessly attacked and ridiculed by Mrs. [Joan] Robinson and others was a very thrilling experience." Tsiang 1989, pp. 1–2. Compare Arndt 1997, p. 157; Dahrendorf 1995, pp. 184–189, 215–216, 345.
16. The CIER was established in 1981. When the author visited them in 1992, they had a staff of 114 people, of whom 71 were directly engaged in economic research. *Chung-Hua Institution for Economic Research 1991–1992*.
17. Hilda Tayler Brown to the author, January, 2005.
18. Mr. Anthony Twist kindly searched the Cambridge University records to retrieve Chinese names.
19. Tseng and Lo entered diplomatic service. *Who's Who in China* 1920, pp. 188–189; 1925, pp. 745–746; *China Year Book* 1931. Zhang Wei returned to teach

Economics at Beida and Qinghua; he also held government positions. *China Year Book* 1925–26.

20. The gist of his article was that "it's all in Marx". Fan-hung 1939; Howard and King, 1992, pp. 96–100. Yan taught at Beida after 1946. In 1957 he led the attacks against Chinese Keynesians during the anti-rightist campaign. *Biographies of Contemporary Chinese Economists*; letter, Yan Zhijie to author, October 18, 1993.
21. This does not include Otto van der Sprenkel, a graduate of LSE, who taught Economics at Nankai in 1948–49 and prepared an interesting book on the Communist take-over (van der Sprenkel 1951).
22. Carlson 1999 reviews the German influence on American economics.
23. Coats 1988, p. 347, quoting John Higham. Students aspiring to an academic career were expected to prepare a habilitation, more nearly comparable to an American doctoral dissertation. I do not think any Chinese did this.
24. Kreissler 1987, pp. 91–96. Economics was apparently taught at Tongji, as Shen Laiqiu taught there 1940–42.
25. Liaison between Chiang and Hitler was facilitated by Liang Ingwen, who received an Economics doctorate from the University of Greifswald in 1930. Liang had served as head of the Chinese Trade Bureau in Berlin, then became a secretary to Chiang. Kirby 1984, p. 155.
26. We compiled the list by scanning the annual volumes of *Jahresverzeichnis* . . . and from Yuan 1964. We examined as many of the dissertations as possible to decide whether they qualified as Economics or not. The search was conducted chiefly in the Library of Humboldt University (Berlin) and in the Bibliotheque Nationale in Paris. Of the 82 dissertations, 66 were examined. Of these, 55 identified the supervising professors and 50 contained biographical information about the student.
27. I included most of the Chinese contributors to Predohl 1937, since several of them are among our doctorates. The list also includes other Chinese who published economic materials in German language.
28. The Nazi preoccupation with "Aryan" race purity apparently did not lead to antipathy toward Chinese and other Orientals. Liang 1978 has many useful observations on this topic.
29. Stolper 1997, p. 95. Ignaz Jastrow was a prolific writer on law, history, and economics. He published books on Adam Smith, money and finance, commercial policy, unemployment insurance, and social policy. He directed one Chinese dissertation.
30. Schumpeter 1954, pp. 852, 1154. Grossekettler 1989 identifies a Freiburg "school" resembling the Chicago School, enlisting neo-liberal economists and jurists concerned with creating a free economy for Germany. Diehl's student was Tchang (Zhang) Pi-kai who wrote on the excessive subdivision of Chinese farm land. Zhang returned to teach at the Central Political Institute and

worked closely with Xiao Zheng. In 1949 he moved to Hong Kong and was a founder of New Asia College, later absorbed into the Chinese University. Information from an anonymous referee.

31. Sombart's *German Socialism* (1934) supported much of the Nazi program including its fanatical nationalism and anti-semitism. Seligman 1962, pp. 14–21; Harris 1941, which notes Sombart's denial of universal "laws" in economics, and his skepticism about the moral value of capitalism (pp. 832–835); also Schumpeter 1954, pp. 816–817n.
32. There is a recent biography of Jessen: Schluter-Ahrens 2002.
33. Wu's vita is in his dissertation, in Yale University Library.
34. The division of labor between the schools can be confirmed by comparing a 1935 BTH dissertation on profitability of ocean shipping (Lehmann 1935). The bibliography contains many of the same sources on statistical methods, but microeconomics is completely missing from the bibliography and the body of the work. Besides Wu Tao-kun, we listed four other dissertations in technische hochschulen.
35. Pribram was one of nine German economists identified by Schumpeter in 1933 as deserving assistance in fleeing Germany. Stolper 1994, p. 12. He also taught at Vienna; Leonard 2004, pp. 290, 298. He was on the staff of the Social Security Administration in 1942; see Pribram 1942.
36. Schumpeter 1954, pp. 854–855; Salomon 1945, pp. 603–604; Heimann 1944.
37. "Spann's lectures . . . were a war against individualism, atomism, psychologism, Marxism, and all the 'other dead sciences,' as he called them . . . Spann rejected individualist accounts, which he said were premised on a mistaken belief in individual freedom, a refusal to recognize the centrality of society . . . Spann championed 'Universalism,' an organic view with roots in German Romanticism" (Leonard 2004, p. 291). In China, Ma Yinchu was much impressed with Spann's ideas. Leonard also discusses at length Hans Mayer, whose teaching dealt much more directly with mainstream economic theory.
38. *China Handbook* 1937–45, p. 656; *Who's Who in China* 1950, 1954.
39. Besides his dissertation on China's iron and steel industry, Wang published a book in 1935 praising the Third Reich. Liang 1978, pp. 40, 78. Yang Shuren moved to Taiwan in 1949 for a long career in the business school of National Taiwan University.
40. Arndt 1937; Shen's biography to 1947 is in Archives of the United Board for Christian Higher Education in Asia, Box 165, Folder 3081, Yale Divinity School.
41. Hayhoe 1987, p. 111. We have identified one French-trained economist who taught at Franco-Chinese, namely Wang Sihua who joined in 1930. *Biographies of Contemporary Chinese Social Scientists*, IX.
42. Between 1926 and 1946, 473 Chinese went through the Lyons program. Of

these, 89 were in social sciences and law. Hayhoe, p. 112; Wang Yi-chu 1966, pp. 109–110.

43. Since most dissertations were not done in departments designated specifically as Economics, we examined as many as possible for significant economic content and to obtain the names of the advising professors. We examined 66 French dissertations, chiefly in the Bibliotheque Nationale and the University of Paris.
44. This was called "Mention Sciences Economiques". Lille had such a program also.
45. Comments on the academic specialties of French and German professors are based primarily on listings of their books in the *National Union Catalog*. Dockes et al. 2000 presents commentaries on Simiand, Nogaro, Aftalion, Gide, Rist, and Pirou.
46. Weisz 1983, p. 188. Hauser pioneered in economic history research based on statistical data. A representative dissertation under his direction was by Chao Zoo-biang (Zhao Zubang). His 176-page *Etude sur le Commerce Exterieur de la Chine de 1864 a 1932* (1932) provided very detailed descriptive statistics on trade and payments between China and other individual countries. But there is no significant analysis to explain the patterns.
47. Levi-Strauss 1945, pp. 514–515; Schumpeter 1954, pp. 820–821; Seligman 1962, pp. 40–41; Hicks 1932; Gillard and Rosier, eds., 1996.
48. Levi-Strauss 1945, p. 515; also Desrosieres 1991, pp. 224–227. Because of his courageous support for the French resistance, Halbwachs was deported to Buchenwald concentration camp, where he died in 1944. Clark, pp. 132, 145, 189, 209.
49. Granet's career is admirably summarized in Freedman 1973, which notes Granet's "unswerving adherence to democratic socialism" (p. 28).
50. Paris, 1937. Lu Yuwen went into government administration, becoming ultimately Commissioner of Reconstruction for Xinjiang Province in 1945. *China Handbook* 1937–45, p. 679.
51. Escarra's appointment as adviser to the Chinese government pre-dated 1923. Escarra, 1923. He helped translate into French some of Liang Qichao's writings on Chinese law. Escarra 1940, p. 256.
52. There are numerous citations to Liu's dissertation in Durand 1960, which concludes Liu's estimates of China's population were much too low (p. 246).
53. I excluded several Netherlands students who apparently came from Dutch East Indies (Indonesia).
54. Koung 1927 (Gong Xianming) listed several of his courses at Louvain. Political economy was taught by Defournay. The other three were law courses on such matters as labor legislation and social insurance, the topics Gong taught in the Labor University in 1930–31. Chan and Dirlik 1991, p. 136.

Chapter 6

1. The Christian college source materials often give the academic credentials of faculty members, and these have been one source of data for the student files. This might produce an upward bias in the proportion of Christian college graduates in our student files. However, there is no such bias in our PhD and ABD lists. Comparing those with the GS and MA files revealed the following:

	Christian college graduates	Chinese university graduates	CHR/CH
PhD	39	50	0.78
ABD	21	31	0.68
MA	141	188	0.75
GS	74	108	0.69

These data do not imply any upward bias in the Christian college share of GS and MA students.

2. The Japanese-educated component of CHINFAC is probably understated. We have made no systematic study of Japanese-educated economists; the numbers cited here are simply fall-out from listings compiled for other purposes.
3. Of the 82 people in the 1942 roster claiming foreign study, 46 were already identified in our files from other sources. Of the 26 claiming graduate study of Economics in the U.S., 22 were already in our files from other sources, and 4 were added, all in the GS category. Of 35 claiming European study (removing one duplication), 21 were in our files and 14 were added. The data in the directories of recent professors do not suggest we have underestimated those who studied in continental Europe—see Table 7-6.
4. Although the contours of Table 6-6 echo those of Table 6-2, the relative share of the four U.S. Economics categories does not. A main reason is that several people listed in the GS category, such as Wang Jizu and Gao Hongye, subsequently completed PhDs and returned to China.
5. *Biographies of Kuomintang Leaders*, 1948; copy in University of Washington Library. Listings are alphabetical but not paginated.
6. The presence of western-trained economists aided in the interface with visiting western economic experts such as those from the League of Nations and the Kemmerer Commission (which dealt extensively and productively with T. V. Soong). Arthur Young, who came to China with the Kemmerer group and remained until after the War, was very close to the process of attracting foreign investment and has written persuasively about it. Young 1971; 1997, pp. 90–107.
7. We did not tabulate the Chinese (such as He Lian) who began their collegiate studies in a Christian college and completed undergraduate study in the U.S. All three Pu brothers studied at missionary Shanghai University before completing undergraduate studies at Michigan and doctorates at Harvard.

8. According to Wang Yi-chu 1966, the Qinghua preparatory program sent 1,268 students to the U.S., of whom 10.38 percent (131 or 132) studied Economics, pp. 111–112. Our total is larger because it counts persons listed for either undergraduate or graduate study of Economics.
9. Completed thesis topics from Bilboul 1975; uncompleted thesis topics from lists in *Economica* 1926–33 and *Register of Research in the Social Sciences* 1943–50; four topics which looked like student research were taken from various biographical sources.

Chapter 7

1. The reader is reminded that the data are incomplete. Tables report faculty and students for whom we have found data.
2. Lutz, pp. 30–31, 65–66. Sheffield's text was still being used in 1915. North China Union College, "Course of Study and General Information", January, 1915 (Burke Library, Union Theological Seminary).
3. Canton Christian College catalogues 1901–02, 1903–04, in Archives of the United Board for Christian Higher Education in Asia, Record Group 11, Box 181, Folder 3246, Yale Divinity School Library (hereafter YDS). Wisner used as a text Jevons's *Primer*, presumably the Chinese translation by Joseph Edkins noted in Chapter 2.
4. One of the earliest and most durable was Louis Richard S. J., who had been a professor at the Naval Training School, island of Jersey, in 1894–1901 and taught the elementary course, history of political economy, and economic geography of China. Pierre Vigne, who was teaching finance in 1939, was a former sea captain. Louis des Courtils was an official in the municipal administration of the French Concession. 1939 English language catalogue, Shanghai Archive.
5. Aurora information from documents in Shanghai Archive, collection Q242. A list of doctoral theses through 1933 enumerates 25 items, only three of which are clearly Economics.
6. FCU, Lingnan catalogues; Lingnan "List of Faculty and Administrative Staff" (typed), RG 11, UBCHEA 42/1074, YDS.
7. "Christian Education in China", 1922, pp. 219–220. The report, probably influenced by J. B. Tayler, stated forthrightly that "the fundamental cause of poverty in China is over-population" (p. 235). It recommended research into (1) "the economic position of handicrafts of different kinds as affected by the introduction of machinery, factory organization, and other new elements; (2) changes in the character of land tenure in progress in China and the social consequences involved; (3) experiments in industrial cooperation and in factory organization; (4) redistribution of population in relation to industrial and agricultural development; (5) the causes of famine and the economics of famine relief." (p. 227)

8. Lunt 1925, p. 66; American Economic Association, 1938, p. 26; 1942, p. 32.
9. Lunt 1925, p. 220; American Economic Association, 1942, p. 93; Lamberton 1955, pp. 74, 119–120.
10. These data were compiled by the author from course descriptions in individual catalogues.
11. Joanne Sawyer, Hiram College Archivist, kindly supplied materials about Sarvis at Hiram. For economic writings by Sarvis, see his 1925a and b.
12. Sullivan was interned by the Japanese in 1942, but was able to teach Economics to some of his fellow prisoners. After returning to the U.S. on the famous repatriation vessel *Gripsholm*, he joined the State Department as an authority on labor conditions in Asia. He was killed in a plane crash in 1957. McDonald Sullivan kindly provided information concerning his father.
13. When Dickson Leavens interviewed Sullivan and Chao in April, 1934, he observed, "The university is shortstaffed, they are carrying heavy teaching loads, and have to spread over the whole field of economics and accounting." Typed memorandum in James Harvey Rogers papers, Yale University Archives, April 11, 1934.
14. "Ely was the giant of ethical economics, and his *Outlines* . . . remained the best-selling economics textbook in the country [U.S.] until the Second World War." Bateman, 1998, p. 37. This is an excellent review of the content and role of the Social Gospel movement. See also Rader 1966; Dorfman IV (1959), p. 211. Ely's *Outlines* had been translated into Chinese by 1910: Shao 1950, p. 44.
15. Carver contributed a section on human resources to *Foundations of National Prosperity*. In his introduction, Ely remarked of this: "he preaches a stern gospel, but we must admit that measures that give temporary relief and lead in the end to softness, flabbiness and degeneration deserve only condemnation" (Ely 1917, p. vi).
16. See Dorfman IV (1959), pp. 179–180. Clay's book was also published in an American edition.
17. Chinese Christian Educational Association, 1926, p. 120.
18. Chen Xiqing had graduated from FCU in 1927 and had just completed a PhD at Yale dealing with cooperatives.
19. *Fukien News*, Spring, 1937; in Box 122, Folder 2568, RG 11, UBCHEA, YDS.
20. The very low numbers for Lingnan were balanced by a high percentage of students majoring in business; averaging 20 percent for 1932, 1933, and 1936.
21. Biographical materials are in Box 160, Folder 3027, RG 11, UBCHEA, YDS.
22. Ibid.; Day 1955, p. 134. Lee also published (1927) a condensed English translation of Sun Yat-sen's *Three People's Principles*. Chang and Gordon 1991, p. 208, n. 45.

23. Answer to Questionnaire from United Service to China, Oct. 20, 1947, Box 109, Folder 2409, RG 11, UBCHEA, YDS.
24. Yin Hong kindly copied this in Shanghai; mimeographed.
25. "Yenching University: Announcement of Courses 1947–1948", Box 308, Folder 4747, RG 11, UBCHEA, YDS.
26. In Box 181, Folder 3250, RG 11, UBCHEA, YDS.
27. "Condensed schedules"—mimeo, in Box 197, Folder 3389A, RG 11, UBCHEA, YDS.
28. Four of the nine were members of Nanking's CAF, a measure of the high morale and cohesion of that organization. They were Chen Tsu-kwei (Zukgu), Pan Hongsheng, Swen Wenyu, and Tsui Ruh-tsuin (Cui Yujun). The other five were Edwin Chen (FCU), Wu Jixian (Lingnan), Lee Ba-en, and Hu Chow-yuan (Zhouyuan—Hangchow), and Zhao Shaoding (St. John's).
29. Carl Remer returned to teach one year at St. John's after receiving his doctorate from Harvard, but I did not include him among the PhDs.

Chapter 8

1. I have reviewed Tayler's career at greater length in Trescott 1992, 1993, and 1997. Materials have been reproduced with the kind permission of the *Journal of Economic Issues, Annals of Public and Cooperative Economy*, and University Press of America.
2. Biographical information was kindly furnished by Tayler's daughters, Hilda Tayler Brown and Gladys Tayler Yang. See also Trescott, 1992, 1993, 1997.
3. Peking University (Christian), *Bulletin* No. 3, "Announcement . . . 1920–21", Archives of the United Board for Christian Higher Education in Asia (UBCHEA), Record Group 11, Box 308, Folder 4744, YDS, pp. 6, 46.
4. Tayler 1923, p. 337. In 1928, Tayler wrote "The joint-family system has been the strength and weakness of China. Informed with the spirit of ancestor worship, it created at once the stability arising from filial piety and the stagnation resulting from excessive regard for the past; it has subordinated the young to the old, the living to the dead, and women to child-bearing, through early marriage and the reckless multiplication of the race." (p. 17) For an affirmative view of Chinese institutions as foundations for economic development, see Perkins 1975, pp. 3–18, especially p. 7.
5. Wagner 1938a, pp. 281, 284, 293. Maxwell Stewart, who subsequently became a prolific writer on economic topics, began his Yanjing experience (1926–30) as an English teacher, then transferred to sociology. In 1930 he helped the Economics Department develop a statistics laboratory. Dora Bent mimeographed circular, Jan. 21, 1930, in Box 314, Folder 4813, UBCHEA, YDS, p. 4; *Who's Who in America*, v. 25 (1948–49), p. 2375; Stewart 1928; Stewart and Fang 1930. Stewart served as editor of *The Nation* magazine

1934–47 and edited a series of Public Affairs Pamphlets until 1970. Field 1983, p. 167. Stewart wrote more than a dozen books on economic topics.

6. The only known copy is in the library of Peking University and was kindly located for me by Professor Yan Zhijie. Wagner also prepared a companion volume, *Yenching Readings in Economics*, printed without a date, probably 1936 or 1937. Of the approximately 425 pages, 90 were devoted to materials composed by Wagner. About 115 pages contained materials reproduced from elementary economics textbooks. The remainder were items relating to China, particularly by Shanghai University sociologist Herbert Lamson. Copy in Beida Library.
7. Chinese economic terminology was just becoming standardized; the Ministry of Education had published a standard lexicon of economic terms in 1936. Franklin Ho 1972, pp. 88–90.
8. Compare Slichter pp. 19–20 and 45–52 with Wagner chapters 1 and 2. Slichter (pp. 636–646) was probably her source for the view that union pressure or a minimum wage law could raise wages without substantial harm to employment. 1938b, pp. 222–224.
9. Chen 1934, p. 375. Note Chen's apparent lack of concern for the oppressive features of Stalin's and Mussolini's dictatorships.
10. "The Yenching School of Applied Economics" (pamphlet, Box 315, Folder 4825, UBCHEA, YDS); handwritten notations "1928" and "a proposal which did not materialize".
11. *The Leader*, Sept. 29, 1929; clipping in Box 314, Folder 4813 UBCHEA, YDS.
12. Tayler to General William Crozier, Dec. 5, 1932; Box 361, Folder 5564, UBCHEA, YDS. A more extended description is in "North China Industrial Service Union", a pamphlet of Feb., 1933, in the Burke Library, UTS.
13. Reynolds 1975, p. 459; Lu Guangmian, "The Marketing of Hisho Cotton" (typescript), Box 313, Folder 4797, UBCHEA, YDS.
14. A biography of Zheng is in *Contemporary Social Scientists in China*, v. 3, pp. 183–191.
15. This view was presented by Chen Xuqing—BA Illinois, Nankai faculty, and Wu Jingchao—PhD Chicago, Qinghua faculty. Alitto 1979, pp. 270–271; Douw 1991, pp. 122–126; Chiang 2001, pp. 69–71, 126–128. Yan Yangchu's biographer sarcastically expressed the issue thus: "Why was the village poor? The structural causes of rural misery were not the ignorance, disease and selfishness which Yen saw, but imperialism and feudalism . . . For the next fifty years this was to be the capsule dismissal of rural reconstruction, along with the observation that Oil King Rockefeller bankrolled the operation." Hayford 1990, p. 162.
16. Dora Bent mimeographed circular, Jan. 21, 1930; Box 314, Folder 4813, UBCHEA, YDS.

17. Yenching University *Bulletin*, "Announcement of Courses 1927–28"; Box 308, Folder 4745, UBCHEA, YDS, pp. 28–31.
18. "Alumni Bureau makes Survey of Graduates", typed, Feb. 23, 1937; Box 310, Folder 4773, UBCHEA, YDS; *News Bulletin*, April, 1939, p. 1.
19. Tayler to D. W. Edwards, Sept. 16, 1942; Box 42, Indusco Collection, Columbia University Archives.
20. Joseph Stepanek, an American engineer who came to China with UNRRA in 1947, reported enthusiastically about the cooperatives he encountered; Stepanek 1992, pp. 211–222.
21. Taylor, although primarily a historian, was initially attached to Economics. On his subsequent distinguished career, see Pye 2000.
22. Lindsay 1975, p. 46. The book, which consists chiefly of Lindsay's photographs of this and subsequent adventures, is not paginated. I numbered pages counting the title page as 1.
23. On Lindsay, who became Lord Lindsay of Birker on his father's death in 1946, see Burke's *Peerage* 1999, v. 2, p. 1719; Lindsay 1975, and Li Hsiao-li's untitled, undated autobiographical manuscript in the Hoover Institution Library at Stanford.
24. Chen "joined the staff of a certain Sino-Japanese research institute established by the Japanese organ, Hsing Ya Yuan. The function of the Institute, as far as we know, is to investigate into ways and means for the exploitation of the material resources of North China by the Japanese." "Annual Report of the College of Public Affairs . . . for the Academic Year 1942–1943 to the Rockefeller Foundation", RG 1, Series 601, Box 23, Folder 210, p. 2, Rockefeller Archive (hereafter RA). Chen was discredited by his apparent collaboration; rumor has it he moved to the Philippines when the Japanese war ended in 1945.
25. After a brief stint with the State Department, she held various positions at the Shipley School in Bryn Mawr, Pa. In 1963 she initiated a program using volunteers to tutor black children from Philadelphia, a program which by 1974 was serving 250 children. Biographical information from Wellesley Alumnae Office.
26. Band 1948; Lindsay 1975; Shewmaker 1971, pp. 131–135; Stein 1945, pp. 366–378.
27. Lindsay 1950, pp. 29–34; 1955, pp. 273–277; 1975. A recurrent theme was this: "the Communists have done a good job wherever their Marxist-Leninist theory is irrelevant . . . Where Marxist-Leninist doctrine applies, common sense vanishes." 1975, p. 102. In 1954 Lindsay returned to China as interpreter for a British Labour Party delegation which included Clement Atlee and Aneurin Bevan.
28. M. C. Balfour to Wu Wen-tsao, Nov. 19, 1943, in RG 1, Series 601, Box 22, Folder 204, RA.

29. Chao to M. C. Balfour, March 11, 1947; RG 1, Series 601, Box 22, Folder 207, RA.
30. Roger Evans, "Travel Diary, 1947", RG 1.1, Series 601, Box 51, Folder 430, pp. 66, 73, RA.
31. Interview with Hong Junyan, January, 1990. Professor Hong was a Yanjing student during the transition and then joined the Beida faculty. He was this author's supervisor and mentor in 1983–84, for which much gratitude is due. Hong described Shen as a "peddler" economist, an opportunist. He was denounced as a rightist in 1957 and was abused again during the Cultural Revolution, contributing to his death. A biography of Shen is in *Brief Biographies of Contemporary Chinese Social Scientists* 1982, v. 1, pp. 150–164.
32. Obituary from Yale University, September, 1996.
33. Clipping from Wellesley Alumnae newsletter, August, 1940, kindly supplied by Wellesley Alumnae Office. In the same note, she wrote, "I am working with others . . . at Yenching, trying to break down the age-old Chinese tradition that students and scholars demean themselves by working at anything but their books. We have established a Student Self-Help Committee which attempts to provide work for needy students."
34. Of the 339 on China topics, the largest numbers dealt with money, banking and prices (73), public finance (54), international trade and finance (40), and agriculture (33). Of those not specifically dealing with China, 22 were studies in business administration and 19 were on specific western economists or doctrines.

Chapter 9

1. Portions of this chapter appeared in Trescott 1997 and are reproduced with the kind permission of University Press of America.
2. For biographical information on John see Pugh 1973, Stross 1986; on Pearl, see Conn 1996, Thomson 1994.
3. Buck 1973, p. 11. Significantly, a survey of 181 CAF graduates in 1931 identified 67 in agricultural education and 28 agricultural officials, but no farmers, p. 12. Financial aspects of CAF development are reviewed in Trescott 1997.
4. These initial paragraphs are largely based on Taylor and Taylor, 1952, pp. 54–96.
5. In 1928, Paul Hsu played a major role in drafting the pioneering enabling legislation for rural cooperatives in Jiangsu Province. In 1930 he entered Cornell, receiving a master's degree in 1932 with a specialty in cooperatives. In 1935 he took a position with the Bank of Communications, working with loans to cooperatives, a position he still held in 1943. Buck 1973, p. 70; *China Handbook*, 1937–43, p. 753.
6. Terrill 1973, pp. 67–71; Buck 1973, pp. 34–35. There were 18 index citations

to Buck ("the most distinguished foreign authority on Chinese agriculture"—p. 73) and at least four other CAF staff were cited. Other leading "citees" were Nankai's Fang Xianting (15), J. B. Tayler (14), L. K. Tao (13), and D. K. Lieu (10).

7. "A Unique Opportunity" typescript, CAF Department of Agricultural Economics, June 1931. In Record Group 1, Series 601, Box 20, Folder 181, RA.
8. "List of Members of Faculty for the College of Agriculture and Forestry", 1934, Box 198, Folder 3398, UBCHEA Archives, Record Group 11, YDS.
9. However, by 1936, CAF surveys were being processed by punch cards on a "Hollerith machine". Department of Agricultural Economics, Annual Report to Rockefeller Foundation, October 1935–September 1936; RG 1, Series 601, Box 19, Folder 170, RA.
10. Pearl's autobiography (1954) deals only elliptically and scornfully with her husband—his name is never mentioned. Conn 1996 and Thomson 1994 give a fuller picture. Thomson reminds us that "it was by roughing it with Lossing through countless villages across the North China plain . . . that Pearl Buck discovered the Chinese peasant. Nothing else in her life . . . would ever be quite so important as that discovery." (p. 9) Hayford 1994 points out that *The Good Earth* "is curiously lacking in detailed description of just what it is that Wang Lung and his family do. We are not even sure of what crops they grow, much less of their agricultural techniques . . ." (p. 23)
11. Buck and Curtiss 1946. Wu Naichun helped me interpret this book, which I photocopied at the library of Nanjing Agricultural University.
12. The English language set of *Economic Facts* was reprinted in its entirety in 1981 by Garland Press.
13. Buck 1930, pp. 27–28. These issues did not disappear. Fleischer and Liu 1992 argued that if plot holdings in contemporary China were consolidated, productivity could be significantly increased.
14. Buck 1930a, p. 314. "The real problem . . . is not primarily how to reduce labor, but how to diversify it, and how to enlarge the farm business by more intensive farming so as to increase rather than to decrease the number of working days in the year." (Buck 1930b, p. 450)
15. The CAF curriculum demonstrated this awareness of social problems in the rural economy. In addition to numerous technical courses, the 1931 catalogue listed courses in "Agricultural Policy", "Rural Problems", and "History of Land Tenure in China". The latter dealt with "such topics as the history of land systems, taxation, equity in land ownership, tenant disputes, land adjustment, colonization, land surveying, etc." *University of Nanking Catalog*, December, 1931, pp. 58–59; UBCHEA Archives, Box 197, YDS.
16. Buck 1930, pp. 409–411. Buck found that 5.9 percent of the farm operators

were Christians, a proportion which seems too high to be credible for the entire country.

17. Buck had published his survey instrument of 1922, with about a thousand questions, recommending it for other researchers. However, efforts to use it in 1928 by the Institute of Social Sciences yielded unusable results. (Chiu 1933, pp. 162–165). Chiu criticized Buck's use of correlation coefficients in a 1926 survey: "the character of such rough data from careless sampling does not warrant the use of such refined technique . . ." (p. 176) By implication, CFE must have been better, although Chiu felt the samples were not representative (p. 186).
18. For example, the survey of farm size in CFE (p. 46) found a mean size of 7.01 acres (median 5.26), while LU found a mean size of only 4.18 acres (median 3.31) (p. 268). There was surprisingly little overlap in the localities surveyed. Of the 17 localities surveyed for crop yields in CFE, only five were among the 161 covered by LU. These show substantial discrepancies for some very basic data. We compared data on crop yields per unit of land for the five individually and also the attendant estimates for the entire country, taking the ratio of CFE/LU estimates. There are 22 individual data points, and only three of them show yield estimates that differ by less than 10 percent. For Su (Anhwei) the average of 7 ratios is 1.72 and for Kaifeng (Honan) an average for four items was 3.37. The best average was Wuchin (Wutsin—Kiangsu) with 0.95 for four items, but those individually ranged from 0.53 to 1.51. Ironically, for the entire country, ratios for ten items averaged out to 1.04, but the individual items ranged from 0.74 to 1.35. CFE, pp. 203–204; LU: Statistics, pp. 209–210.
19. Buck 1937, pp. 458–460. The "locality survey" was apparently completed by the investigator after gathering opinion from local authorities, but we are not told much about this (see pp. viii–ix). At any rate, 82 percent of localities reported improvement.
20. Buck recommended "A land program of keeping or restoring the land in the hands of those who work it . . ." (p. 21).
21. See Chiao 1933; Buck and Chiao 1928. These and other demographic materials are assessed in Hou 1968 and Aird 1968. Li Zhuomin characterized Chiao as "probably the most outstanding rural sociologist in China" (Li 1959, p. 199).
22. The article pays tribute to the quality of the data set and provides the most definitive review of Chinese rural demography for the pre-1949 period. Important results are that marital fertility was relatively low, despite the early and universal marriage by women (but not men), but that "the pattern of adjusted marital fertility rates appears to be similar to the pattern . . . that is characteristic of populations in which there is little or no control of births." (p. 613) Birth rates and death rates were high and close together, both about 41 per thousand. These are very consistent with a Malthusian view of China's

economy, an issue which has been challenged in recent literature. Lavely and Wong 1998; Lee and Wang 2000; Lee, Campbell and Wang 2002.

23. Committee for the Study of Silver Values and Commodity Prices 1935; Lewis was also the author of the chapter on prices in LU. Warren and Pearson had stressed the link between U.S. farm prices (many of which were determined in export markets) and the value of gold. Since China was on a silver standard, Lewis shifted the emphasis to silver.
24. His contract with the Treasury allowed him to devote half-time to other activities, but his compensation was entirely from the Treasury. The touchy relationship between this situation and his missionary status as of 1936 is explored in documents in the Presbyterian Historical Library, RG 82, Box 52, Folders 14 and 15. U.S. State Department cables contain summaries of some of Buck's reports. From these it appears his major task was simply to report gossip from China relating to silver and Chinese monetary conditions. See microfilm M973, roll 428, items #516, 553, 560, 572, 648, 696–697, 759, 804–805, 848, 854a, 931–933, 950, 962 (1935–36), National Archives.
25. A survey of 294 CAF graduates of 1924–46 revealed that 35 of them were working for the Farmers Bank. Buck 1973, pp. 50, 61.
26. Reynolds, pp. 417–424; interviews with Wang Yinyuan and Wang Xixian, June 24, 1992.
27. Buck's survey of graduates 1924–45 showed 37 had studied in the U.S., 1973, p. 61.
28. This includes Feng Rui and Tang Qiyu, both of whom graduated from CAF in 1920 before there was a real program in agricultural economics.
29. An extensive roster of faculty is given in Buck 1973, pp. 70–73; it lists their degrees and some information on what they did later. The CAF published extensive annual reports in English; many are in Yale Divinity School and Rockefeller Archive.
30. I did not include Wang Lien, whose name does not appear as teaching faculty. Wang completed a doctorate in Germany in 1936 and wrote 6 articles for *Economic Facts*, presumably as research staff.
31. College of Agriculture and Forestry, 1933. Wan Kwoh-ting (Guoding), who directed the compilation, was head of the Division of Agricultural History in the Department of Agricultural Economics.
32. Thus Stross's chief chapter on Buck's 1930s work is entitled "Myopia". He repeatedly makes sniping remarks about Buck's competence with the Chinese language. My interviews with Stanley Warren, A. B. Lewis, Wang Yinyuen, and Wang Xixian made it clear that Buck was sufficiently fluent in speaking and listening to talk shop with Chinese farmers. Pugh 1973 presents a much more positive view of Buck's work. The shortcomings of Buck's surveys were common to all the rural surveys of the period: compare Chiang 2001 on Chen Hansheng's work—pp. 164–221, 265–267.

33. Good examples are the 60 different items extracted in *Agrarian China* (Tawney 1939).
34. Interviews with Stanley Warren, August 1, 1990, Ardron Lewis, Feb. 29, 1991; Wang Yinyuan and Wang Xixian, June 24, 1992. Buck's work was highly praised by Glenn Hedlund, who became Chair of Agricultural Economics at Cornell following his sojourn at Nanjing. Hedlund 1962.
35. Information from interviews with the last two and from *Biographical Dictionary*, 1990.

Chapter 10

1. Li Dazhao studied political science and Economics at Nanyang before removing to study in Japan.
2. Yang Dali 1990. Chi Hua, who was ABD in Economics at Columbia from 1924, taught at Beiyang in 1929. *Who's Who in China* 1936, p. 42.
3. At Nanyang in 1902 "the students were forbidden to read Rousseau and Liang Qichao's *Renovation of the People*. In protest . . . over 100 students left the school, accompanied by Cai Yuanpei, who was teaching there at the time." Some of the dissidents were active in forming Aurora University in 1903. "The authorities responded by transforming Nanyang . . . into a Commercial College of the First Class . . ." in 1905. Hayhoe 1983, pp. 324–325
4. *Comprehensive Dissertation Index 1861–1972*, v. 27, p. 373.
5. Sites 1904, pp. i–11. Sites joined the faculty of Fukien Christian University when it opened in 1915 and taught there until 1927. Fukien Union College catalogues 1916–23, Archives of the United Board for Christian Higher Education in Asia, Record Group 11, Box 109, Folder 2397, YDS; "Personnel of Western Faculty", Box 109, Folder 2406.
6. Kuno 1928 reported "Students in both Nanyang and [Peking Jiaotong] are required to study English, French and Chinese; Political Science and Economics. In Economics alone, they have to take more than 100 units." (pp. 53–54) The Jiaotong institutions continue to operate and have a reputation for academic excellence.
7. In 1923 the students created the Nanyang University Economics Association. By 1925 it had over one hundred members, and produced in 1929 a two-volume "Collection on Economic Problems". Jiaotong University Documents, pp. 196–197; 1932 Catalogue, p. 49.
8. *Who's Who in China* 1936, p. 138 lists 16 books in Chinese and two in English.
9. According to Professor He Lian of Nankai, Li was "a popular teacher . . . He taught courses in economics, history of economic doctrines, public finance, and money and banking in four different universities . . . I met him in the summer of 1926 in Shanghai and asked him how he did it. He said that he went from one university to another on a rickshaw from morning until late afternoon.

The results were disastrous; like other teachers, he did not have time to prepare for the courses he taught. He repeated the same lectures from year to year. He had no time or funds for research, no time to update the material he used, and no time for his students." (Ho 1967, pp. 72–73, quoted Chiang 2001, pp. 16–17.)

10. Yuan 1934, p. 458. A similar view of Li was offered by Hu 1982 in reviewing his textbook writing.
11. Letter from Dean N. Nikiforoff, Nov. 24, 1932 to International Education Board, in Series 1, Box 27, Folder 385, RA. Harbin's most noted economics student was Evsey Domar, best known for his contribution to the Harrod-Domar model of economic growth. Blaug 1985, pp. 54–55.
12. National Sun Yatsen University 1936, pp. 2–5, 176. "In the entrance examinations . . . of 1924, applicants . . . were asked to assess the economic benefit of the Canton-Hankow rail line, to characterize the socioeconomic and geographic contours of the North China Plan, the Yangzi River Delta, and the Pearl River Delta, as well as to comment on how best to coordinate the economic developments in these three macro-regions—questions that had been dealt with at length" in Sun Yat-sen's writings. Yeh 1990, p. 31.
13. Gunn 1931, p. 51. On Gunn's return visit in December, 1932, the university president told him that the social science professors "are too theoretical. He is anxious for them to be more realistic and deal with Chinese problems." Dec. 13, 1932, RG 12.1, Box 23, RA. However, Chiu 1933 reported that faculty conducted agricultural surveys beginning in 1920 (p. 201).
14. National Sun Yatsen University 1936, pp. 46–47. The University was also in process of establishing a Research Institute of Chinese Economic History. In 1934 the university began to publish its own *Quarterly Journal of Social Sciences*.
15. League of Nations 1935, p. 21. Our faculty listings for Zhongshan are very incomplete. Of 45 identified, 25 had studied in the West. Six studied graduate level Economics in the U.S. and three others had some U.S. study. Eighteen had studied in western Europe, including twelve in Germany, and eight had studied in Japan. National Sun Yatsen University 1935 is our only direct name list; many others are from biographical references.
16. Another 10,000 were enrolled in "colleges" of law and political science, which were really secondary schools. They were operated for profit and their academic reputations were not good. Their required courses did not include Economics as such, but did include money and banking, accounting, and statistics. In 1909 there had been as many as 46, reporting an astonishing 111,000 students. By 1923 the government was driving them out of business. Cameron 1931, p. 86; Hayhoe 1993, p. 481. See Sun 1987 on the close link with similar institutions in Japan (pp. 67–69, 86–87).

17. These and subsequent 1931 enrollment figures are from "General Conditions . . ." 1931. This source omits many universities.

    In 1931 the League of Nations sent three western professors to National Central (in geology, English, and geography). Later a League staff member told Rockefeller Foundation representative Selskar Gunn "that the visiting professorships at the National Central University are a complete failure. The attitude of the students is intolerable. They insist upon setting the hours for lectures, etc., and then do not come. If they do come they do not understand English. Furthermore, they open all of the personal mail of the professors and are highly impudent. All of the three professors who are now teaching agree that their work has been useless." Selskar Gunn, "China Diary", April 13, 1933, quoting Rene Charron.
18. One of the more interesting was He Haoruo (PhD Wisconsin), discussed in Chapters 4 and 15. Selskar Gunn of the Rockefeller Foundation visited NCU in 1931 and concluded that "little or no research work is done in the Social Sciences". 1931, p. 59. However, in 1934 NCU initiated its own *Journal of Social Science*. Professor Zhu Xie published several important studies of public finance, including survey data documenting "the extra-legal supplementary taxes which . . . local governments imposed on the rural population". Fairbank and Liu 1961, pp. 337, 339. Zhu had received a doctorate from Berlin in 1931.
19. *China Year Book* 1934; *China Handbook* 1937–43, p. lxii; ibid., 1937–45, p. 694; *Who's Who in Modern China* 1954, p. 222.
20. *Who's Who in China* 1936, p. 276; Yuan, p. 459.
21. Chiu 1933 called it "the oldest and most important agricultural college in North China. It has good personnel especially in its department of agricultural economics, which was established in 1927; but because of limitation of funds it has not done as much as the ability of its personnel warrants" (p. 210). Dong, who had formerly worked with the China International Famine Relief Commission, organized a large-scale agricultural survey in 1932, collecting data from the members of cooperatives organized by CIFRC.
22. *Who's Who in China* 1940; *Who's Who in Modern China* 1954, p. 222; Lee 1934.
23. Our faculty listings are very incomplete. Of the 27 identified, 16 had studied in the West, including seven in Britain, eight in graduate-level Economics in the U.S.
24. "General Conditions of all the Universities of the Country" (1931), typescript, in United Board Archives, RG 51, Box 309, Folder 4762, YDS.
25. *Brief Biographies of Contemporary Chinese Social Scientists*, VIII, pp. 158–174; *Survey of Public Wuhan University*, 1933, 1936; both Chinese language.
26. *China Handbook* 1937–45, p. 676; Hu Jichuang, 1982.
27. Hu Jichuang (1982) ranked Pan's textbook *Economic Principles* the best of its kind.

28. The People's College was also referred to as Shanghai University, not to be confused with the missionary college of the same name. Chan and Dirlik 1991, p. 37; Chiang 2001, pp. 136–148. Yeh notes it also functioned as a trade school and offered courses in banking systems, monetary theories, social and economic policies (p. 145).
29. Chan and Dirlik, p. 98. In 1930 a faculty member articulated the goals of this research as follows:

    "[W]e should conduct an investigation of . . . number and size of the labor force, their living conditions, their wages and income, their skills and productivity, labor-capital relations, and industrial development . . . [W]e should study the data collected . . . to understand . . . their causes and consequences so that we could come up with proposals for improvement of the labor situation." (pp. 69–70)

    The topics paralleled very closely those stressed by He Lian and Fang Xianting in their Nankai studies.
30. Zhu Dongjiu held faculty positions at Fudan, China Academy, Jinan, and Great China, as well as Laoda. He was the author of two textbooks: *Methods of Economic Research* (1930) and *Wage Theory* (1929). Hu Jichuang 1982.
31. Hayhoe 1996, pp. 52–54. Yeh 1990 presents Ministry of Education enrollment estimates for 41 institutions in 1934, totalling approximately 28,000 (pp. 282–283).
32. Becker 1932, pp. 28, 143, 159–161, 165–167. Perhaps the most frequently quoted passage in the report was this: "A visitor who examines the plan of work in History, Political Science, or Economics, in some universities of China may be pardoned if he feels uncertain whether it is designed for Western students who are studying China, or for Chinese students who are studying the West." (p. 165) The statement totally contradicts the point the authors were presumably trying to make.
33. Gunn diaries, Dec. 2, 1932; RG 12.1, RA.
34. Tawney himself made several of these points in *Land and Labour*—1932, pp. 178–179.
35. P. 91. A Dutch professor characterized National Central 1942 as "the second best University in China, the best being the Associated Universities in Kunming." Payne 1945, p. 93.
36. *China Annual* 1944, pp. 512–513. This was a publication of the puppet regime and did not include names of authors or editors.
37. Ou 1977, p. 105. C. C. Cheng provided useful information on this university, which he attended. It closed in 1949 but was later reincarnated in Taiwan.
38. The drastic decline in publications dealing with China's economy is documented in Chapter 14.

39. Ou 1977, p. 102. "Higher education" here is broader than the university sample we have reported for earlier dates.
40. Sun 1987 lists the required and (numerous) elective courses for 1939 and also 1912, 1913, 1944, and 1948; pp. 319–320.
41. Chen Daisun and Fang Xianting are discussed in detail in the chapters on Qinghua and Nankai respectively. Zhao Lanping was discussed above, as was Yang, who drafted the initial course list. Chen Changheng's principal employment was with the national government, where he was chair of the Financial Affairs Committee of the Legislative Yuan 1928–48. He also held faculty positions in Peking and Nanjing but no specifics are given (*China Year Book* 1935; *China Handbook* 1937–45, p. 638; *Who's Who in Modern China* 1954, p. 23) Biographical information on Zhu is in his dissertation (Chu 1933) and *China Handbook* 1937–45, p. 647.
42. Of the 101 respondents, 93 reported a current academic position, 32 listed one previous post, and 31 listed two. Combined, these represented employment at 55 different schools.
43. As in Table 6-1, these cover the entire period through 1949 and make no allowance for date or length of service.
44. Fairbank 1976, pp. 47, 50. She wrote "it was characteristic of the times that economics was the overwhelming first choice of students, preparing themselves, they hoped, for employment in Government or banking where there was a possibility of riding the inflationary tide instead of drowning in it." She quoted a departmental administrator who wrote "The [U.S.] *Quarterly Journal of Economics* is desired by almost every Chinese economist who had discussed the matter with the Committee, and in view of the large number of economists who will make use of the material the Committee had made a special request therefore." (p. 47) A copy of the special Chinese-printed edition of Fairchild is in the Beida library.
45. Hu Jichuang 1982. We added Nankai textbooks which Hu unaccountably omitted.
46. Fairbank 1976 refers briefly to the post-war "reestablishment of the mission-founded Chinese language school, the College of Chinese studies" (p. 179).
47. AEA *Directory*, 1938. Coons gave a series of lectures to the College of Chinese Studies published under the title "Economic Reconstruction in China"—Coons 1934.
48. Details are in Chapter 14; principal sources were the Skinner bibliographies and the quarterly Nankai listings.

Chapter 11

1. The next few paragraphs draw heavily on Chiang 1986, pp. 133–150, 156–174. Much of this material was included in Trescott 1995, 1997, 2002. Portions

are reproduced with the kind permission of Harvard University Press, *History of Political Economy*, and University Press of America.

2. He subsequently translated into Chinese Fisher's book on *The Making of Index Numbers* as well as a number of Fisher's short economic essays for the general public. Allen 1993, pp. 190–192.
3. He discovered that the actual collection of price data was very difficult. Many trades had specialized vocabularies; in addition, weights and measures were frustratingly non-standardized. He needed to employ retired tradespeople to assist in data collection. Ho 1967, pp. 97–98.
4. Ho 1967, p. 72. Our course surveys indicate there were such courses.
5. There are brief biographies of both He and Fang in Wang 1994.
6. Fong 1930. Fong also had an experience very rare for Chinese studying in the U.S.—he worked for the Ford Motor Co. for three months in the summer of 1925. He described the experience as including "working on the assembly line, shoveling coal into the furnace, mediation in family disputes, visiting the municipal morgue for identification or examination of employees killed in accident, etc." Fong 1975, p. 28.
7. Zhang was sometimes properly skeptical about what they were doing. Chiang reports this dialogue with Franklin Ho concerning his index-number work: "What do you need all these figures for? What are you trying to find out?" "Well, my statistical studies can prepare us for the scientific reconstruction of China." "Well, your procedure often reminds me of a man who tries to locate an elephant with a microscope." (Chiang, p. 84)
8. Franklin Ho candidly admitted that the textbooks "under present circumstances in China, will have to be largely translations or adaptations from the best products of western experiences" but assured that they would be "made fit for Chinese consumption". Yen, Zhang, and Ho to E. E. Day, July 30, 1931, in Folder 432, Box 51, Series 601, RG 1.1, p. 4, RA.
9. "A Prospectus of Nankai Institute of Economics", 1931, in Folder 439, Box 52, Series 601, RG 1.1, RA, p. 2.
10. Chiang 1986, pp. 195–202. Seven major articles were published from this project, of which six concerned taxation and county finance.
11. As projected in 1933, the survey would have been comparable in scope to those of John Lossing Buck at Nanjing University. "Report on the work of the Institute for 1932–1933", May 22, 1933, Memorandum A, p. 2; Folder 432, Box 51, Series 601, RG 1.1, RA. This over-ambitious project was not carried out.
12. "Report on the work of the Institute for 1932–1933", May 22, 1933, Folder 432, Box 51, Series 601, RG 1.1, RA, p. 5.
13. "Personnel of the Teaching and Research Staff, Nankai Institute of Economics, 1932–1933" (mimeo); attached to letter from He to Edwin Day, Folder 432, Box 51, Series 601, RG 1.1, RA; Chiang, p. 193.
14. Wu went to Harvard and Li to LSE.

15. Interview with Wu Baosan April 27, 1992. Wu spent most of his career with the Institute of Social Science, later the Chinese Academy of Social Science (CASS). While at Nankai, Wu was the major author of a 1937 textbook in elementary economics, adapted from the popular American textbook by Yale professors Fairchild, Furniss, and Buck (*Elementary Economics*, 2nd ed., 1930, 2 vols.). He 1967, p. 82.
16. "Report of the Nankai Institute of Economics . . . 1933–1934", Folder 433, Box 52, Series 601, RG 1.1, RA, p. 5. The initial conception of the graduate program was to be "somewhat similar to that of the Institute of Economics of the Brookings Institution in Washington, D.C". "Report on the work of the Institute for 1932–1933", May 22, 1933, Folder 432, Box 51, Series 601, RG 1.1, RA, p. 8.
17. He developed his text as he taught the course, beginning with American works by Harley Lutz (*Public Finance*) and Edwin R. A. Seligman (*Essays in Taxation*), and incorporating material about China as he could locate it. Ho 1967, pp. 80–81. The textbook was adopted by "more than a dozen leading universities". "Report of the Nankai Institute . . . July 1, 1935 to June 30, 1936", Folder 439, Box 52, Series 601, RG 1.1, RA, p. 15. The Institute's initial plans for textbook production were another example of "boundless ambition". A report of December, 1933, projected no fewer than 20 textbooks or similar teaching materials. "Work of the Institute, July, 1932–December, 1933", attached to letter, He and Zhang to Gunn, December 21, 1933, Folder 433, Box 51, Series 601, RG 1.1, RA, p. 3.
18. "Report of the Nankai Institute of Economics, July 1, 1935 to June 30, 1936", Folder 439, Box 52, Series 601, RG 1.1, RA.
19. "Nankai Institute of Economics: Its History and Work 1927–1936" 1937, pp. 19–21.
20. See especially Fong 1933, pp. 350–351; 1934a, pp. 453–455; 1935b; 1937. China is, according to Fang, "a free market in the true sense of the word . . ." (1937, p. 267), but one searches in vain for any affirmation of the virtues of free markets.
21. Cipolla 1976, pp. 139–145, who noted that "the people of the town intuitively developed feelings for union and cooperation." (p. 144) Fernand Braudel wrote that "the social structures in both India and China automatically rejected the town and offered, as it were, refractory, sub-standard material to it" (1973, p. 410). Fang touched on this: 1937b, p. 922. See also Cipolla 1976, pp. 117–122, 139–145; Arkush 1981, p. 302 n. 7.
22. There was probably a reason for this change of outlook in 1936. In that year the government appeared to be making a decisive move toward state-owned industrial development with substantial aid from Germany, following a treaty for barter exchanges in 1934. See Kirby 1983.
23. When he composed his memoirs in the 1960s, He commented (in reference to

the 1930s) "Although formulators of policy claimed [Sun Yat-sen's] *San Min Chu I* as the basis of their action, there is no basic principle of development outlined there." (Ho 1967, p. 148) During his government service, He worked unsuccessfully to try to obtain agreement on a substantive interpretation of Sun's views. Ho 1967, pp. 294–300.

24. Fong 1936a, b. In all fairness, Fang's extremely valuable survey of specific industrial developments in China contains several references warranting skepticism about government. For instance, regarding electric power, "too often . . . nationalization has so far consisted simply of expropriation with subsequent deterioration of services", Fong 1936c, p. 64; see also pp. 71–74.
25. Protectionism was never a big element in the He-Fang policy outlook. But they constantly alluded to the damage being done by competition from foreign imports. By the mid-1930s China had high tariff rates, but troubled relations with Japan prevented rigorous enforcement, especially in Northeast China.
26. His experiences are recounted in detail in Ho 1967.
27. *Nankai University Doctoral Programs and Advisors*, 1990, pp. 341–343; Wang 1994; interview with Bao Juemin, June 14, 1992.
28. Li's doctoral research focused on international aspects of China's silver-based monetary system. It yielded two articles in the (U.S.) *Quarterly Journal of Economics* (Li 1935, 1939).
29. "Nankai Institute of Economics: Its Work in War-time, 1937–1940", Folder 439, Box 52, Series 601, RG 1.1 RA, p. 16; author's interviews with Chen Zhenhan and Cui Shuxiang, May 1992, April 1999; Li 1981, pp. 8–9.
30. "Work of the Institute, July, 1932–December, 1933", op. cit., pp. 6–7.
31. These comments can be well illustrated by the textbook which underlay the Nankai principles book—Fairchild, Furniss, and Buck's *Elementary Economics* (1930, 1931). (See note 15 above.) The 1,200 pages presented a staggering amount of factual material in a very verbose style. The micro theory of firms and factors was developed at length, but in a strictly partial equilibrium manner with little in the way of evaluations. Opportunities to moralize about market economy were missed at such key points as discussion of property rights (I, 18–21) and the functions of money (I, 392). Economic development was treated only through discussion of "historical stages" in which the increases in output and productivity received only minuscule attention (I, pp. 68–69).
32. "Work of the Institute, July, 1932–December, 1933", mimeo, attached to letter from He and Zhang to Selskar Gunn, December 21, 1933, RA Project 1.1, Series 601: China, Box 52, Folder 433.
33. From the various Nankai reports to the Rockefeller Foundation in the Rockefeller Archive.
34. "Nankai Institute of Economics . . . Eighth Annual Report to the Rockefeller

Foundation July 1, 1939 to June 30, 1940", Folder 439, Box 52, Series 601, RG 1.1, RA.

35. The graduate class numbered nine students. Their first year program included seminars in economic theory offered by Li Zhuomin and Fung Chuan-tchs (Chuanshi, newly hired with doctorate from Vienna), history of economic thought by Fang, and economic history by recent Yale PhD Rockwood Chin. German language was required; this exposed the graduate students to distinguished economist Tuan Maolan. Tuan had received a PhD from Columbia in 1928 and was serving as senior secretary in the Ministry of Foreign Affairs. "Nankai Institute of Economics . . . Eighth Annual Report . . ." "Chinese Who's Who", in *China Handbook* 1937–1943, p. lxii.
36. This operation was closed down in April, 1939. "Nankai Institute of Economics: Its Work in War-time, 1937–1940", Folder 439, Box 52, Series 601, RG 1.1, RA. This was not the only product of the Rockefeller rural-reconstruction program. In 1938 He Lian became head of the Agricultural Credit Administration and established a program to improve the organization of rural credit cooperatives. A number of Nankai people were involved. Ho 1967, pp. 221–225.
37. There was much criticism of the Chinese government's economic program during the war. Critics argued it was designed to enrich insiders by giving the government monopoly control over important industries. Reynolds, 1975, pp. 144, 170–173. He's memoirs and much other evidence suggest he was a reluctant participant and that the impulses toward government monopoly were coming from other sources. Ho 1967, especially pp. 382–400.
38. Fong 1975, p. 45; 1942a, p. 67.
39. Sang Hengkang published "An Explanation of Full Employment" (June 1942) and "From Marx's Theory of Crisis and Keynes' Theory of Employment to China's Economic Policy" (January, 1943). Yang Shujin produced "Theory of Full Employment and China's Wartime Economic Policy" (October, 1942) and "On the Price Theory of J. M. Keynes" (November, 1943). Qian Rongkun wrote "Keynes' Theory of Interest" (March, 1944). Professor Chen Zhenhan published "The Monetary Theory of J. M. Keynes" (August, 1943). See citations in "Annual Report of the Nankai Institute of Economics . . . July 1942–June 1943", Appendix V (Folder 440); "Nankai Institute . . . Twelfth Annual Report to the Rockefeller Foundation July 1, 1943 to June 30", 1944, pp. 15, 17 (Folder 440); Franklin Ho to Marshall Balfour, March 13, 1945 (Folder 437, all in Box 52, Series 601, RG 1, RA).
40. He to Marshall Balfour, March 13, 1945, Folder 437, Box 52, Series 601, RG 1, RA; Fong 1975, p. 70.
41. Roger Evans, "Travel Diary, 1947", Folder 430, Box 51, Series 601, RG 1.1, RA, pp. 66, 73.
42. Chin had been born in the U.S. to Chinese parents and thus could claim U.S.

citizenship. American Economic Association 1964, p. 52. Later he held faculty positions at Berea, Wheaton, and University of Connecticut.

43. He to Balfour, May 11, 1944; Folder 437, Box 52, Series 601, RG 1, RA; "Fourteenth Annual Report of the Nankai Institute of Economics, 1945–46", Folder 438, idem.
44. "Application from the China Institute of Economics to the Rockefeller Foundation . . .", He to Joseph Willits, June 14, 1947, Folder 601S, Box 51, Series 601, RG 1.1, RA.
45. Report of interview with Roger Evans, June 1, 1949, Folder 438, Box 52, Series 601, RG 1, RA. Courses dealing with socialism were relatively common in Chinese universities prior to 1949. Zhou Enlai was a loyal alumnus of the Nankai secondary school and helped shield the university from the worst of political abuse. Van der Sprenkel, Guillain and Lindsay 1951 describes the Communist take-over at Nankai.
46. Interviews with Chen and Yang, June 17, 1992; *Nankai University Doctoral Programs and Advisors*, pp. 79–80, 90–92; *Biographical Dictionary of Professors in Chinese Universities and Colleges*, p. 1027.
47. One notable exception was the addition of Wang Chi-tsu (Jizu), who had completed a PhD at Illinois in 1954. Wang worked in the Ministry of Foreign Affairs until joining Nankai in 1962. *Nankai University Doctoral Programs and Advisors*, 1990, pp. 94–97. Professor Wang graciously arranged extensive interviews with Nankai senior faculty in 1992.
48. A comparative assessment of Chinese university Economics programs is given in Hu 1984. The present author visited Nankai in 1983, 1984, 1992, and 1999.
49. Besides public finance and principles, textbooks actually published covered commercial law, municipal administration in the U.S. (!) and personnel administration. Fang produced *Studies in Chinese National Economy* (1938) in two volumes. Thus they did not exactly bestride the mainstream of economics. However, drafts covering economic history and economic geography were duplicated for classroom use. "Report on the Work of the Institute for 1932–1933", Folder 432, Box 51, Series 601, RG 1.1, RA, p. 3.
50. Evans "Travel Diary, 1947", p. 44 (May 1, 1947), quoting Father E. S. deBreuvery of Aurora University, Shanghai. Folder 430, Box 51, Series 601, RG 1.1, RA. For examples of theoretical sophistication in Nankai writings, Li Zhuomin's 1939 and 1941 items serve well. My own favorite is a brief article on inflation by Cui Shuxiang (Mrs. Chen Zhenhan). With concise logic it destroyed the numerous false theories of inflation and established the central role of currency-financed government deficits (Tsui 1941).
51. In 1937 Fang had written, "Other factors . . . play an important part in forcing the process of industrialization on a fundamentally agricultural society, but that the state is primarily responsible for nurturing it to its growth and maturity cannot be disputed." (Fong 1937, p. 259) And see Fong 1942a, pp. 78–81.

52. He to Gunn, March 3, 1941, Folder 434, Box 52, Series 601, RG 1, RA. This was indeed a bad year for He. In August his son was killed in an air raid. He himself was in Hong Kong when the Japanese took it in December, but managed to escape two months later. Ho 1967, pp. 320 ff. He's disillusion with the unlimited-government interpretation of Sun Yat-sen's ideas apparently began in 1938, when He was appointed director of the Economic Department of the newly-formed San Min Zhuyi Youth Corps. Ho 1967, pp. 299–300.
53. Roger Evans travel diary, entry April 22, 1947; Folder 430, Box 51, Series 601, RG 1.1, RA.

Chapter 12

1. Lund, 1956. By then the name "Peking University" had already been taken by a Methodist missionary college which was the principal predecessor of Yanjing. Names were further confused when Peiping University (separate from Beida) was created in 1927.
2. Cai also favored the German style in Economics, reflected in his appointments. In 1933 he wrote a preface for *Historical School Economics*, by Chu Chien-tsi (Zhu Jianzi), indicating that historical economics was superior to either classical or Marxian Economics.
3. Dewey was in China from May 1919 to July 1921, and Russell from October 1920 to July 1921. Sun 1986, p. 384.
4. Li studied political science and economics at Beiyang College of Law and Political Science, then attended Waseda University in Japan 1914–16. In 1920 he was appointed professor of history, political science, economics, and law. "He taught courses on modern political science, historiography, historical materialism, socialism and social movements, social legislation." (Chow, p. 54)
5. Alitto characterized Tao, as of 1918, as "China's best-known sociologist" (1979, p. 67).
6. Liang had never been abroad and did not have a university degree. He had achieved prominence as a student of Buddhism through self-study. Alitto 1979, pp. 48, 56–60. By the time of his Beida appointment (1917) he already displayed strong commitment to non-violence, as well as "faith in both the innate goodness of the masses and the ability of an elite—formed along moral . . . rather than political lines—to elicit the latent power of the people" (p. 61). Liang's ideas are presented in this book, mainly devoted to the influx of western economic ideas, because he offered an original indigenous Chinese approach to economic development.
7. Chen's autobiography describes his long career as an intelligence agent for Moscow; summary in Yu 1995–96; Chiang 2001, pp. 159–221.
8. Boorman 1967–71, II, pp. 252–255. Ku served briefly as Minister of Railways

in 1932 and was president of National Central University 1941–43.

9. *Who's Who in Modern China* 1954, p. 130.
10. Otte reported he had "received his first training in commercial statistics in the Maritime Customs Service in China . . . 1901 to 1917. He taught statistics at the Customs College at Peking from 1913 to 1915 and in 1925 for one term at the National University." (Otte 1933, p. 242) He published extensively on China's economy.
11. "He established close ties with Shanghai businessmen and industrialists so that he could improve his understanding of conditions and practices in this economic center of China . . . an essential precondition to the application of Western economic principles and methods to the development of the Chinese economy." (Boorman 1967–71, II, p. 476)
12. As late as 1947, Ma wrote "The various difficulties and dangers confronting our economy have not been due to too rapid a development of capitalism. Rather, they are attributable to the tardiness and slowness in the development of capitalism." Quoted Hsia 1961, p. 58.
13. *Biographies of Contemporary Chinese Economists*; Chow Tse-tung 1960, p. 244; Roy 1971, p. 125.
14. *Who's Who in China* 1925, pp. 781–782.
15. Yu worked for the Ministry of Education and became in 1930 director of the Customs College in Peking. *China Year Book* 1931, p. 649.
16. Chen did receive financial support for a translation of Marx's *Capital* from the China Foundation for the Promotion of Education and Culture in 1933–34. The annual reports of the Foundation are in the Beida Library.
17. "On June 3 1921, after Peking's teachers in eight institutions of higher education had gone unpaid for several months, a demonstration by students and teachers marching to petition at the presidential palace was dispersed by gunfire with many casualties." Sun 1986, p. 385 n. 60.
18. Chen 1993 describes the disruptions of 1927–30: pp. 170–178.
19. Selskar Gunn Travel Diary, 1931, Folder 129, Box 12, Series 601, RG 1, RA, p. 60.
20. Zhao wrote "while I was working as a compiler in the National Bureau of Historical Research in Peking from 1920 to 1922 I was greatly impressed by the abundance of historical documents on Chinese economic history, but at the same time I was disappointed to find that the English Classical economics had nothing in common with Chinese economic conditions . . . [A]fter receiving instruction . . . from [Columbia] Professors Seligman, Seager, Mitchell and Simkhovitch . . . I realized that the modern tendency of economic theory is to put great emphasis upon comparative study, historical treatment and the institutional approach." (Chao 1930, p. 7)
21. A biographical sketch of Zhao with bibliography appears in *Contemporary Social Scientists in China*, v. 2, pp. 259–271.

22. He worked for the Institute of Social Research in 1929 and was co-author of monographs on cotton marketing in Hebei Province and a survey of village families in the vicinity of Peking.
23. "[A] large part of its research has thus far been confined to the compilation of treatises on economic conditions and principles not related to China." "Research Notes", *Nankai Political and Social Science Quarterly* 8:2 (July 1935, p. 391).
24. The following section is based on Peking University 1933, translated by Xiao Zhijie and Liu Yixin.
25. In the following sections, all the books have been checked against standard bibliographic sources to give authors' full names and most probable dates of publication. A few titles have been corrected.
26. Peking University 1935; translated for me by Liu Yixin.
27. To be sure, China's economy, agricultural and commercial as it was, did not conform to the Keynesian model. But China's depression was essentially imported, and understanding it required an understanding of what was going on in the western countries.
28. There is a copy in the Beida Library.
29. These are listed in "A Classified Catalogue of the Western Books of the Former National Tsinghua University Kept by the National Peking University Library", May, 1942, pp. 3–82, 3–83, 3–93. (Copy in Beida Library)
30. "One professor in the economics department, in teaching 'The History of Economic Thought' for second-year students, read verbatim from an old English-language book. The students dubbed that class 'third-year English.'" Israel ed. 1982–83, p. 141. The only professor identified with this course was Zhao Naituan.
31. Roger Evans Travel Diary, Record Group 1.1 Projects, 601 China, Box 51, Folder 601S, RA, May 9, 1947.
32. He credited Marx with anticipating Keynes in showing that a) people's failure to spend all their income is a crucial source of shortfall in aggregate demand, and b) that the rate of interest depends on money supply and money demand. Both propositions can easily be found in earlier writers.
33. Fan 1947. Wu Naichun interpreted Fan's book for me.
34. *Contemporary Social Scientists*, pp. 268–271. In addition, this lists nine substantial undated journal articles, probably from the period 1946–49.
35. Interviews with Lai Rungyuan (1999) and Du Du (1992).
36. These data on faculty and students do not cover SWAU personnel not explicitly allocated to Beida. The totals do not precisely match those in Table 10-6, which include foreign teachers and prorated SWAU students.
37. Klein and Clark 1971; Israel and Klein 1976, pp. 77–78; Bartke 1987, pp. 56–57.

Chapter 13

1. *The Tsinghuapper* (yearbook), v. 2, 1917, pp. 16, 18 (Library of University of California, Berkeley); *Who's Who in China* 1936, p. 170.
2. The actual surveys were carried out in 1922 by university students, including four from Qinghua, identified only as "Mr. Yang, Mr. Hsiung, Mr. Chang and Mr. Wang". Malone and Tayler 1923–24, I, pp. 100–101.
3. Qinghua transcript of Ku Te-ming dated June 1922, kindly supplied by Shirley Horowitz of Johns Hopkins University, where Ku completed a BA in 1924.
4. Chen remained with Qinghua until 1951. He published a textbook on population problems in 1934 and a monograph on overseas Chinese in 1938. Moving with Qinghua to Kunming during the War, he also headed the government's Institute of Census Research. This work led to his book *Population in Modern China* (1946). Boorman 1967–71, I, pp. 235–238.
5. Chu published numerous articles on such topics as China's silver currency and its depreciation, Chinese government finance, and statistical practices and services of other countries. *Who's Who in China* 1925, pp. 215–216; 1931, p. 111.
6. Information on Li and other Qinghua faculty are based primarily on Chinese-language faculty lists in Qinghua University 1994.
7. The archival materials identify employment in the mid-1930s for most students. This is supplemented by our data file on Chinese economists, drawn from numerous biographical sources and university records. Since this file stresses faculty, this category is over-represented in Table 13-1.
8. Wang Yi-chu (1966, pp. 374, 420) spoke disparagingly of the returned students in general, but his criticisms seem more relevant to the generation of students whose undergraduate study was done in the U.S.
9. *Who's Who in China* 1950, p. 74; *China Handbook* 1937–45, pp. 654–655.
10. *Draft History of Qinghua University*, pp. 222–225.
11. Liu had also studied at Penn and Northwestern and taught mainly business subjects at Qinghua. Bilboul 1975; Yuan 1963.
12. Israel 1982–83, pp. vi–vii. By 1932 Qinghua had the largest university library in China. In 1937, 69 of the 94 full professors had studied in the U.S. Israel and Klein 1976, pp. 51, 53.
13. Chen spent a year in Europe and attended Charles Rist's lectures at the Sorbonne in Paris. Interview with Chen Daisun, May, 1992.
14. Volume I of his collected writings (Chen 1989) contains 38 items published in 1934–41. They average 7 pages in length; many appeared in newspapers. However, when in 1935 Qinghua initiated a periodical entitled *Social Science*, Chen contributed a number of substantial essays. These included a study of the concept of equilibrium in economic analysis and its relationship to the dynamics of the real world, and another on the accounting problems caused by inflation. In several of his articles, Chen indicated his support for government economic planning and control, particularly after the War began.

15. Xiao remained with Qinghua intermittently until 1941, moving to Kunming. In 1937–38 he headed the College of Law and Literature at National Yunnan University. From 1944 to 1949 he was chancellor of the National Chung-cheng University in Kiangsi Province. *Who's Who in China* 1950, p. 83.
16. J. B. Condliffe to Edwin Kemmerer, January 24, 1929, in Kemmerer papers, Seelye Mudd Library, Princeton University. Condliffe characterized Zhao as "a very able statistician".
17. *China Yearbook* 1925–26. Zhang, who left Qinghua in 1937, held several government positions.
18. Selskar Gunn China Diary 1931 (typescript), RG 1, Series 601, Box 12, Folder 129, RA, p. 65.
19. Interviews with Harry Price and Chen Daisun; Fairbank 1982, pp. 103–198. Fairbank met Chen several times after Qinghua moved to Kunming and reported on the evident hardship and dedication he observed—pp. 192, 231.
20. Another was possibly Liang Fang-chung, who claimed a Qinghua MA (1933) in a recent biographical directory. He worked as a researcher with the Institute of Social Science 1934–43, studied (no degrees) at Harvard and London School of Economics during the War, and became a professor at Zhongshan University (Guangzhou) after 1949. *Biographies of Contemporary Chinese Economists*, 1987, pp. 483–486.
21. Wu's dissertation was published: Wu, 1939. In reviewing the book, Li Zhuomin wrote that the study "was in fact planned when the author was studying in the graduate school at the National Tsing Hua University". Li 1941. Tsui 1941 cites five of Wu's articles in *New Economist* and *Today's Critic* dealing with price controls.
22. Lee published several articles in American journals and also translated into Chinese the book *Land Economics* by Richard T. Ely and George Wehrwein. See Lee 1947a, 1947b, 1948.
23. Dai had been in the Economics graduate program at Qinghua. Israel and Klein 1976, p. 56.
24. Roger Evans Travel Diary (typescript), 1947, p. 69; RG 1.1, Series 601, Box 51, Folder 601S, RA.
25. Chen's thoughtful essay "Economic Freedom and Political Freedom" expressed concern about the problems of inequality and instability arising from market economy. (Chen 1989, pp. 455–460.) But it is not a research article. And it is the only item dated subsequent to 1941 in the collected works. Chen 1998 v. 1 is a smaller selection from among basically the same items.
26. Tsui 1941 cites three of Wu's articles in *New Economist*. In 1945 he published a pamphlet on "Industrial Planning in China" (Wu 1945).
27. Chen 1998, v. 2 contains many reflections about Chen's career from colleagues and students.
28. Interview with Wu Baosan, April 27, 1992.

29. Aside from Chen Daisun, there are very few former Qinghua professors in the various biographical publications which were so numerous in the 1980s. However, the directories concentrated on survivors, and many of the Qinghua veterans had passed away. Qinghua provided its share of the victims for the anti-rightist campaign—Chen Da, Xu Yunan, Wu Jingchao.

Chapter 14

1. Kuno 1928 noted that "it has long been the practice of leading American universities to allow Oriental students to write Masters' or Doctors' theses on purely Oriental subjects . . . In fact, the Masters' and Doctors' degrees have been conferred because the students have supplied valuable information imported from their native lands, and not because of meritorious work or any ability demonstrated by the individual student through research work done in American universities." (p. ix)
2. The development of certification around 1940 brought about formal recognition of research and publication as part of the criteria for tenure and promotion. Ou 1977, pp. 109–110.
3. Liu spent most of his career outside the academic realm, but did serve during the War as Dean, College of Commerce, National University of Chongqing. He was Chinese representative to the Statistical Commission of the UN 1946–49 and commercial counsellor to the Chinese Embassy 1946–52, remaining in the U.S. until his death in 1962. *New York Times*, May 8, 1962, p. 39; *Who's Who in China* 1936, p. 170.
4. C. S. Chen 1931; *Who's Who in China* 1936, pp. 26–27. Chen also taught at National Central and Central Political Institute.
5. Liu had taught at several Chinese universities and was connected with National Central in 1933. See Chinese-language faculty roster for Nanjing University, 1933–34 (YDS); Qinghua University archival source discussed in Chapter 6.
6. Bateman 2001. Bulmer 1991 and Converse 1987 provide background on the development of social surveys in the U.S.
7. By this time Gamble could cite results from four other investigators. Gamble 1933, p. 322. The studies show no concern for assessing variance around the mean to evaluate sampling errors.
8. Chiu, p. 218. D. K. Lieu said Chen's surveys "are all of the best grade of statistical work done in this country . . ." Lieu 1931, p. 112*.
9. Malone and Tayler 1923–24. Chiu 1933 discussed this project at length: pp. 239–243. He criticized the lack of attention to sampling procedures, and indicated much of the field data were never processed and reported—a situation which seems to have been fairly common in the early studies.
10. The Nanjing studies are summarized in Chiu, pp. 161–199. Buck's enthusiasm for survey research outran prudence and patience. He produced a lengthy manual and model questionnaire for agricultural field research which covered

46 pages and which suffered from complexity, vagueness, and excessive generality. It proved wasteful of time and money when people tried to apply it. Chiu, pp. 164–165.

11. Dealey 1925; Chan and Dirlik 1991, p. 218; Shao 1950, pp. 56–66.
12. See the insightful comments on this problem by anthropologist Fei Xiaotong 1940, pp. 179–180. Shortcomings of Fei's own surveys are enumerated in Arkush 1981, pp. 298–299. Converse notes that sampling theory was introduced by Arthur Bowley in 1912–13, but "Bowley's application of sampling theory to the survey does not seem to have had much impact on actual practice in the United States until the 1930s". Converse 1987, p. 35; see also Hennock 1991, pp. 205–213.
13. Sheng 1925, p. 1. Yang studied in Japan 1906–11 and at the London School of Economics 1913–20. On returning to China, he worked for the Commercial Press in Shanghai until 1928 when he headed the newly established Institute of Social Sciences under Academia Sinica. In 1930 he became Professor of Economics at National Wuhan University, serving at times as Dean of the Law School, Chair of the Economics Department, and Dean of Students. *Biographies of Contemporary Chinese Social Scientists*, VIII.
14. He translated Fisher's *Making of Index Numbers* into Chinese. Allen 1993, pp. 190–192.
15. Lin 1928, p. v. Lin was a Nankai graduate with no overseas experience.
16. Yang 1928. Yang was a graduate of Beida. After several years as a researcher, he completed a master's degree at Michigan and joined the Beida faculty. Although his 1928 study did not calculate sampling error, he did compare his consumption data with those of two other surveys, pp. 14–16.
17. Gunn China diary, p. 83.
18. Nankai 8:1 1935, p. 167. Myers 1970 surveys and criticizes Chen's studies, pp. 15–16. The AS annual report for 1929 boasted that Chen and his assistant, Wong Ying-seng, "have established a new classification of the land cultivators and the land owners, completely refuting" those used by the government and by John Buck. "Academia Sinica with its Research Institutes" 1929, p. 51.
19. Chiang 2001, p. 170. Chen's problems in dealing with "the universal pattern of development" are detailed at pp. 174–179, 192–195, 204–207. Recall Liang Shuming's scornful dismissal of efforts to fit China into any western-style stage theory (see above, p. 224). Chen's survey project in Wuxi discovered there were fourteen different types of farm households. There was no standard measure of land area: 173 different sizes of the common unit were encountered. Chiang, p. 172.
20. "Academia Sinica with its Research Institutes" 1929, pp. 49–50.
21. Fong 1935a, pp. 167–170. The Institute's journal dealing with Chinese economic history is described in detail in Fairbank and Liu pp. 234–235. Editors included Tang Xianglong, Zhang Yinlin, Liang Fangzhong, and Wu Han.

22. This includes five identified in "Academia Sinica with its Research Institutes" 1929.
23. *Social Sciences in Nanjing*. No dates are given in the source.
24. *AEA Directory* 1969. Liang worked for the Asian department of the International Monetary Fund 1946–69.
25. Chiu Chin-chang studied in Japan and later joined the faculty of West China Union University. Very possibly other fellows also studied in Japan; we have no systematic file on Japan.
26. These included Wang Ching-yu (Jingyu) and Chang (Zhang) Youyi, both of whom became distinguished Chinese economic historians. Author's interview with Wu Baosan April 27, 1992. Both are listed in the Nanjing sample analyzed above.
27. Liu's national-income estimates were subsumed into a much more comprehensive work—Liu and Yeh 1965. His career and publications are reviewed in Klein et al., 1980.
28. Her prior studies are identified (using the name Djang Siao-mei), along with her thesis topic, in "List of Theses . . ." 1929, p. 237. See also Fairbank and Liu, pp. 248, 264, 292, 364. Her predecessor as head of the research department was Tang Yu-jen (Youren), who had studied in Japan. *China Year Book* 1935, p. 405. During the war Ms. Chang also directed the Chinese Economics Research Institute in Chongqing (Fong 1941, p. 177).
29. Publications of the two banks are described (and praised) in Fairbank and Liu 1961, pp. 261–265. Ji attended the Bretton Woods Conference in 1944 as H. H. Kung's secretary. Klehr and Radosch, p. 21.
30. Evans also described in detail the economic history research by Wang Leiming of the Bank research staff. Evans 1947, pp. 89–90. Three other U.S. PhDs were with the Central Bank in 1947: Chou Shun-hsin (Shunxin), Fong Shou-kwei (Shangui), and Wu Yuanli. "China Institute of Economics", 1947.
31. I have excluded a few items: translations of works by western authors, collections of statutes, regulations published by government agencies, tariff rates, railway freight rates, business manuals, doctoral dissertations. Since it is not easy to identify all publications of government agencies, the figures in Table 14-2 should be viewed as approximations.
32. [Nankai] *Monthly Bulletin on Economic China*, 7:9, Sep. 1934, p. 393.
33. Zhang then proceeded to the U.S. and completed a master's degree at Illinois in 1939, returning to faculty positions in China. *Biographical Dictionary of Professors*; *Social Science Biographical Directory*.
34. This organization was led by Xiao Zheng and connected with the Central Political Institute. Xiao had studied in Germany in 1929–32 and was an enthusiastic advocate of Sun Yat-sen's land proposals. Douw 1991, pp. 167, 219–242. According to Douw, of the 23 directors of the Association, two had studied in the U.S., five in Japan, four in Germany, and one in France. "It is

generally agreed that students . . . educated in Japan and Western Europe were more 'political' than those from the USA." (p. 228)

35. According to Douw, this organization consisted chiefly of staff members of government agencies, notably ministries of railways and of industry. None of the six leaders mentioned by Douw had studied Economics in the West. pp. 165–166, 176–177.
36. We added the articles listed in Tsui 1941 and Ou 1942.
37. One issue was missing; v. 5, number 3.
38. These were also supplied by Professor Sun Chung-hsing and translated by Liu Yixin and her mother, Professor Lin Suren. We have all of volume 1, numbers 1 and 4 of volume 2, and number 2 of volume 3.
39. The editors identify the positions held by many of the authors: 31 held government positions, 16 were connected with universities, and 26 worked for research organizations, chiefly Academia Sinica.
40. Here as in the preceding tabulations, we recorded only the author's name and the year of publication.
41. These are Brandt 1989; Faure 1989; Hou 1965; Myers 1970; Liu and Yeh 1965; Rawski 1989; Eastman 1974 (Chapter 5); and Perkins 1969. Because of the qualitative element, I thought it appropriate to include doctoral dissertations which are not included in the other parts of Table 14-5.
42. These proportions are mirrored in the participants in the annual meetings of the Chinese Economic Association 1926–37. As noted in Chapter 1, of 514 names, 55 studied graduate-level Economics in the U.S. and nine in Europe.
43. This is a reminder that our tabulation does not exclude Chinese whose western study came after their publications.
44. There may also be sampling bias. Our data on non-doctoral students in the continental countries come from "Who's Who" types of publications which may contain a higher proportion of published authors.
45. My tabulations for the Nankai and Skinner lists are initially in name-years. I selected the eleven top scorers in the Nankai lists (8 or more) and from the Skinner Chinese list (6 or more). I took the top three in the *QJE*—recall these are not necessarily articles about China's economy. Finally, I included the seven top scorers from western citations shown in Table 14-6 (5 or more). These yielded 23 separate names. Summing the separate numbers of publications would be inappropriate since the same items are listed in more than one source. The Nankai listings cover the years 1912–42 for books and 1934–42 for periodicals. The *QJE* was published in the years 1930–37.
46. The bibliography of Beida's Zhao Naituan lists 61 newspaper items, of which 13 were in *Ta Kung Pao*. *Contemporary Social Scientists in China*, v. 2. Nankai faculty published extensively in this newspaper. Fang Xianting edited several volumes reprinting such articles. Fong 1938 contained 94 items by over 30 authors, mostly Nankai people (Wu Ching-chao 1940). Similar

collections appeared in 1940, 1943, and 1945. Skinner and Hsieh 1973 gives details.

47. His entry in *Who's Who* 1950 (p. 14) lists five books and five translations. He was a researcher for the Sun Yat-sen Institute and the National Land administration. Feng Hefa was a graduate of the Labor University who subsequently studied in Japan and became a member of the Fudan faculty. Chan and Dirlik 1991, pp. 142, 156–157.
48. Wu Jingchao was identified as "Counselor, Ministry of Economic Affairs, now in the United States". Liang was Director of Research, Farmers Bank of China. Holland, 1944, pp. 217–218.
49. "China Institute of Economics", RA 1947–49.
50. The research director was Liu Sien-wei (Xian), who had completed a doctorate at Paris in 1940 and was living and working in France. Of the 22 Chinese officers and members of the Research Council, 11 had done Economics graduate study in the West and eight held Economics positions with Chinese universities. Lieu 1948, p. vi. Their first pamphlets were by geologist Chang Chi-yun (Zhang Jiyun), Kao Ping-shu (Gao Pingshu, Ministry of Economic Affairs), and Peng Shin-wei (Xinwei), professor of money and banking at Fudan. The Institute also sponsored publication of Wu 1946 and Lieu 1948.
51. From 1926 until 1939, *Ta Kung Pao* ("The Impartial") was headed by Wu Ting-chang (Dingzhang). Wu was a Japanese-educated banker who held a number of official positions after 1935. *China Handbook* 1937–45; *Who's Who* 1953; He Lian memoirs p. 139. Items appearing in its supplement, the *Nankai Economic Weekly*, were sometimes quite sophisticated. Nankai's Yuan Wen-pu published articles on Alfred Marshall, the law of diminishing returns, and Austrian monetary theories.
52. A 1929 survey of 4,722 national government civil employees found their educational background to be as follows:

Returned students:	Number	Percent (%)
Europe	185	3.9
U.S.	277	5.9
Japan	329	7.0
Other higher ed.	1,570	33.3

Both the number of government employees and the proportion with higher education undoubtedly increased after 1929. Lin 1931, p. 165*.

53. This is a brief summary of my extended study of Fang's work: Trescott 2002.
54. Fong, Lin, and Koh 1942, summarizing the "Draft Outline of the Principles for China's Post-war Economic Reconstruction" prepared by the Chinese Economic Reconstruction Society.
55. Douw, pp 122–125; Arkush 1981, pp. 115, 200, 305–306. Ironically, Wu seems to have shared Liang Shuming's conviction that only exposure to the

West dislodged China from a relatively static agricultural society. Wu 1946, p. 462.

56. Quoted MacNair 1944, p. xxxii. Wu blamed the attitude of officials on the influence of Sun Yat-sen. Wu played a major role in the Malthusian controversy which broke out in 1957; discussed in the following chapter.
57. Wu 1944, p. 80. Coming at the time of the Bretton Woods discussions, these considerations were very much on the agenda.
58. Li 1946, p. 492. The unwary reader must be alert to the likelihood that anti-Japanese feeling was often the basis for ritual complaints about imports, foreign investment, and the Treaty Ports.
59. The customary dig at merchants was qualified: "In spite of exploitation on the part of middlemen—a class newly emerged and having special significance for commercial development—the income and hence the standard of living of peasants producing such products was raised." (p. 502)
60. Sun Fo, 1942. For other illustrations of the illusion of benevolent and competent dictatorship, see Grieder 1981, pp. 345–347.
61. Graham Peck, who lived in China as a journalist in the 1940s, stressed the degree to which government monopolies alienated business people from the KMT. 1950, pp. 552–554.
62. The English-language versions were published by Philip Jaffe, publisher of *Amerasia* magazine and a prominent American leftist and critic of Chiang Kai-shek (Klehr and Radosch 1996). Jaffe assured his readers that "Communism is not the issue in China and . . . no human power can convert today's backward Chinese economy into the basis for a Communist state" p. 329. On Tao, see Fairbank 1976, pp. 134–135; Peck, pp. 541, 580.
63. A representative sample of traditional wisdom is that government should "transport goods from any locality where prices had dropped because of a surplus, to places where prices had risen because of shortages" (p. 272). It would be churlish to suggest that market forces tend to do this.
64. Wu 1946, p. 6. This is the most impressive of the Sino-International economic pamphlets.
65. Pp. 48–49. Wu's rather general criticisms can be matched with specific details in the publications cited by Hsu 1942.
66. For examples, see Gideon Chen 1934 and He Lian 1936. It is instructive that anti-Communist Shansi warlord Yen Xishan attempted to develop an industrialization program explicitly imitating the Soviet model. Gillin 1965.
67. Chou 1963 illustrates the ambivalent treatment of China's inflation. Although he asserted the primary role of money (pp. 14, 173), the book devoted very little space to money. Chou was a Yanjing graduate who completed a PhD at Columbia in 1945. He worked in the Central Bank, left China in 1949 and ultimately served a long career at the University of Pittsburgh.
68. Using logarithmic first differences for data in Chang 1958, pp. 371–373.

69. P. 45. Eastman 1984 devoted an entire chapter to the destructive effects of the gold-yuan "reform" of 1948: pp. 172–202, 264–273.
70. Chang's data indicate that prices increased 135 percent per year, 1937–48, while money (currency plus deposits) rose 107 percent (Chang, pp. 371–375).
71. Tsui 1941, p. 185. Chu Tsu-hui 1941, published soon after, illustrates this point of view. After identifying "inflation of the Chinese currency" as one of five possible causes of rising prices, Chu stated that "without the manipulation of greedy speculators, Chinese price movement would not show such unreasonable changes" (p. 296). Thus he felt government price control was appropriate. Chu was a member of the research staff of the Central Bank, formerly professor of statistics at Wuhan University. Ironically, his 1926 MA thesis at Wisconsin had been on "The Influence of Credit on the Level of Prices". He was ABD at Harvard.
72. Monetary expansion was not cited by any of the authors who had not studied in the West. D. K. Lieu, whose overseas study was at the undergraduate level, explicitly denied that money was an important factor. As late as 1948 he still granted it only a minor role: Lieu 1948, pp. 88–89.
73. Huang had completed an MA in Economics at Yale and was working for the World Bank. Both Wu 1956 and Chang 1958 stressed the monetary cause.
74. Sun 1987 concluded that "no Chinese social scientists were known to have formulated any internationally recognized theories out of their studies of Chinese society," p. 164.

Chapter 15

1. Among agencies which evacuated to Taiwan was the Joint Commission on Rural Reconstruction, taking about half its staff. Interview with James Chang (former member of JCRR staff), June 23, 1990. Its last days on the mainland are graphically chronicled in Stepanek 1992, pp. 46–53. JCRR contributed much to Taiwan's economic development.
2. A valuable perspective on the land "reform" was provided by Dong Shijin (PhD Cornell, 1924), who fled to Taiwan after teaching agricultural economics in several mainland universities: "It is not a reform in any sense, and its objectives are beyond the realm of the land question. It is a fierce, ruthless warfare against the landowners and 'rich farmers'." Tung 1975, pp. 34–35; see also Domes 1980, pp. 4–9; Lindsay 1960. The American Federation of Labor estimated that five million Chinese were killed. Tung, p. 47. According to Perkins 1969, about 43 percent of cultivated land was redistributed, pp. 87–89.
3. One of the Chinese negotiators in the peace talks was Pu Shan, known as Pu Shou-shan when he received his Harvard PhD in Economics in 1949. His two brothers, also Harvard Economics doctorates, also returned to work for the Communist government. Information from Tian Xiaohua, Anthony Koo, and Hoyt 1990.

4. Prices rose by roughly 25 percent in 1952–55, then were effectively stabilized. Cassou 1976, p. 85. American sinologist Knight Biggerstaff, who was in China in 1949, reported, "Some time in June [1949] a savings system was set up by the [newly created] People's Bank of China under which money could be deposited in the form of savings units based on the current prices of rice, cloth, coal and cooking oil . . . When the deposit units plus interest were withdrawn, the depositor was paid the number of People's yuan required to buy an equivalent amount of those commodities . . ." (Biggerstaff 1979, p. 10) Such a system had earlier been proposed by Jiang Shuojie. See also Bodde 1950, p. 138; Campbell and Tullock 1954. A currency reform in March, 1955, issued new renminbi in a ratio of 10,000 old to one new. Prybyla 1970, p. 200.
5. Persons remaining in China were identified chiefly from interviews, bibliographies and from biographical materials published in the 1980s. These are limited to prominent economists and of course omit most deceased persons. Persons leaving China were identified mainly from AEA directories and publications. Both listings are very incomplete. Students on whom we do not have post-1949 information are much more likely to have remained in China. However, we compiled a separate list of 42 persons who were employed in the U.S. during the 1940s and could easily have remained.
6. Four other early NTU faculty were on our list of (former) mainland Economics faculty, including Japan-trained Zhao Lanping. Lee Wen-fu kindly obtained the NTU faculty lists for me.
7. Aside from Chang and D. K. Lieu, the list is confined to persons who are in our student files. Many additional distinguished Chinese economists, such as Gregory Chow, could be added whose graduate study came later.
8. The collection appears in the *Tsing Hua Journal of Chinese Studies*, III:2 and IV:1, June, 1963. There were also articles by Rockwood Chin (Berea), Chou Shun-hsin (University of Pittsburgh), Kuo Tse-chiu (?), Wang Nien-tzu (UN), Wu Ta-yeh (ECAFE), and Chen Cheng-sieu (?).
9. However, several of the late returnees were apparently well protected: Wang Jizu, Gao Hongye, and Wu Dakun, for example. Information from interviews with Wang and Gao, 1992; for Wu, see Halpern, 1985, p. 305.
10. An example was Ji Taoda, who became chair of the Nankai department in 1949. He had studied in Moscow in 1927–30 and taught thereafter at Shanxi University. Shen Zhiyuan was moved into Yanjing under similar circumstances. He had studied in Moscow and taught at Jinan, Beiping, and Northwest Universities. *Contemporary Social Scientists in China*, 1989, v. III, VI. Beida was a notable exception, where Ma Yinchu became president in 1951 and Chen Daisun moved into the economics chair. Yong Wenyuan became Dean and Secretary-General of the newly formed Shanghai College of Finance and Economics. He had been an underground Communist agent at Wisconsin,

where his 1948 master's thesis was on Marx's theory of unemployment (Loh 1962, p. 35).

11. Hayhoe 1993. In 1953 there were created a series of universities of finance and economics. The Shanghai institution received numerous faculty transferred from local missionary colleges, notably St. John's and Aurora.
12. IOE was formally under the Chinese Institute of Science until 1977. The staff went to the National Revolution School in 1950, studying Marxism with Chinese instructors. They participated in land reform alongside university faculty and students. Wu Baosan served as deputy director until 1957 when he was removed in the anti-rightist campaign. Interview with Wu Baosan April 27, 1992. The first head of IOE was Di Zhaobai, "a basically self-educated Marxist economist . . ." In 1957 he was replaced by Sun Yefang (Halpern 1985, pp. 72, 152).
13. "The political economists, a group of Party functionaries who were generally autodidacts (or Party-didacts) in the field of economic theory, established their leadership over general economic work . . . [in 1953–57] pushing aside the small number of western-educated economic specialists or relegating them to secondary positions." Clausen 1983, p. 68. Prominent among the new economists were former members of Chen Hansheng's circle, notably Xue Muqiao and Sun Yefang.
14. Officially Renda evolved out of two institutions earlier established in the Communist-dominated northeast: North China United University (established 1939) and Northern University (established 1946). See People's University 1990 (?), p. 12. These may be the same schools mentioned in reference to Song Tao below.
15. Wang was a graduate of Southwest Associated Universities who did graduate work at Qinghua with Xu Yunan, assisting in his translation of Keynes. Wang studied at Glasgow and Cambridge 1948–51, then returned for a brief stint at Qinghua. Author's interviews, April, 1992.
16. 1983, p. 10; Clausen 1983, p. 57. This is a measure of how little attention Marxism gave to optimization, and how little attention pre-1949 Chinese economists had given to optimal decision-making in a collectivist system.
17. This was *History of Economic Theory* by D. I. Rosenberg. Two Russian books bearing Stalin's name were widely used in China: *Soviet Socialist Economic Problems*, and *Textbook of Political Economy*.
18. Interview with Chen Daisun and Wang Chuanlun, April 9, 1992.
19. Interview with Gao Hongye, April 21, 1992.
20. Most of Marx's *Theories of Surplus Value* is a commentary on Smith and Ricardo. According to Wang Chuanlun, Xu Yunan was transferred to Beida in 1952. He became fluent in Russian and worked with Russian professors there. His teaching focused on Marx and the theory of surplus value. Interviews, April, 1992.

21. Interviews with Cui and Wu, Spring, 1992.
22. Chen Zhangheng had done graduate study at Harvard and in 1918 published a book on Chinese population which went through numerous editions over the following decade. He held a number of high positions in the KMT government. In 1957 he was a staff member of the Shanghai Museum of Literature and History (Tien 1973, p. 213). On Wu Jingchao, see above pp. 256, 280–282.
23. Chen 1960, p. 97. This practice was still widespread in 1983.
24. Much of the "Manifesto of the Economists" (October, 1957) is reproduced in MacFarquhar, pp. 117–120. The authors were Chen Zhenhan, Xu Yunan, Luo Zhiru, Gu Chunfan, Wu Baosan, and Ning Jiafeng. Much of what follows is based on the Chinese-language document, "Opposing Bourgeoisie's Revival in Social Science", published by the government in January, 1958. Liu Yixin prepared the translation for the author. See also Walker 1963, pp. 116–117; Halpern, 1985, p. 81.
25. Wu Baosan offered his own restatement of the exclusion. "Now there are only two roads for the old economists to take. One is to study economic history and the other to study international economy." Quoted MacFarquhar, p. 82.
26. The principal western-trained economist to hold a high position in economic administration was Ji Chaoding (PhD Columbia). He served on numerous bodies dealing with international economic and trade problems. Boorman 1967–71, I, pp. 293–297.
27. According to a Beida student, Party crackdown against dissidents came within days of the principal "bloomings", generating a campus atmosphere of fear and tension. Liu Shui Sheng 1959.
28. During the brief thaw in 1956, Beida offered a course in Keynesian economics. Chen 1960, p. 126. On June 12, 1956, a forum in Beijing debated "whether there were any useful elements in Keynes's theories", MacFarquhar, p. 117.
29. Ning Jiafeng had a graduate degree from LSE. Gu Chunfan was described as a self-taught but erudite economist who had been vice minister of posts and telegraph under the KMT and remained in government after 1949. *Who's Who in Modern China* 1954, p. 108
30. According to Halpern, Fan "in 1950 had been the first professor at Beijing University to enter the [Communist] Party . . ." 1985, p. 192. Fan's Marxist anti-Keynesianism was already manifest in his 1939 article in *Review of Economic Studies* (Fan-hung 1939).
31. Wu Bannong earlier used the name Leonard Wu. He received an MA from Columbia and worked for the Institute of Social Research and the Institute of Pacific Relations. In 1949 he chaired the Restitution Committee of the Chinese Delegation to Japan. He remained in China working for the Chinese Academy of Social Sciences. Interview with Wang Jizu, June 11, 1992; Cheng 1956, p. 184.
32. Evidence that western-trained economists were not altogether excluded is

provided by Li Zhuomin's 1959 study of China's industrialization in 1952–57. Li cited 135 Chinese authors of post-1949 items on China's economy. Of these, eleven were in our student lists, included such notables as Zhang Peigang and Chen Da.

33. Hsia, p. 62. Ironically, Ma published strongly anti-Keynesian ideas in 1958, joining the chorus of attacks on Chen and other Keynesians. Boorman 1967–71, II, p. 477. Walker 1963 notes that one critic denounced Ma for bourgeois ideas associated with Cournot and Marshall (p. 122).
34. The lengthy quotations of the population debate reproduced by Tien 1973 (Chapter 5) mostly maintained an objective and scholarly tone prior to the anti-rightist furor.
35. With the exception of long-time Marxists Fan Hong, Wang Yanan, and Ji Chaoding. On Fan and Wang, see Halpern, pp. 149–50, 192–193. Chu Hsueh-fan (Xuefan) and Chien Chang-chao (Qian Changzhao) were western-trained economists who continued in high office under the new regime. Chien had studied at LSE and Oxford in 1919–23. He held high posts in the KMT government until successfully shifting allegiance in 1949. His chief position subsequently was in the "KMT Revolutionary Committee" within the Communist apparatus. Bartke 1987, pp. 289–290; *Who's Who in China* 1950. Chu studied Economics in the Harvard graduate program in 1941. He worked in the KMT postal administration and was active in the Shanghai labor movement. In 1951 he became Minister of Posts and Telecommunications. Perleberg 1955, p. 55.
36. Much of the spirit is captured in the title of a 1959 article: "Let the Sulfuric Acid Basic Construction Projects Enter Production Ahead of Schedule Opposing Rightism, Arousing Diligence, and Attaining a More Rapid Leap Forward". Cited Nairuenn Chen 1963, p. 157.
37. Spence 1990, p. 583; see also Tung 1975; Becker 1996. In many areas officials refused to release grain from storage to relieve the suffering. Part of that problem was the prevalence of fictitious statistical data, a worsening problem. According to Prybyla, "The statistical blackout which descended on the country after 1959 has no precedent in the history of any modern nation." 1970, p. 6.
38. "[U]rban fertility began a rapid decline in 1963 in response to a government campaign to limit births. Rural fertility [began] a sustained decline in 1971 in response to the "wanxishao" (later, longer, fewer) campaign." Lavely, Lee, and Wong 1990, p. 814; also Robinson 1975, p. 28.
39. Information on translations was gathered by Yan Zhijie and Wang Jianye.
40. Naughton 1986, p. 139; Lin 1981, pp. 13–15; Halpern 1985, pp. 269–296.
41. The turn-around in rural marketing did not come until late 1961, and had to overcome "the traditional Chinese disparagement of tradesmen and commercial enterprise . . . A campaign to combat the lingering stigma attached to trade was launched in the fall in 1964 . . ." Skinner 1965, pp. 376–377.

42. Lin 1981, p. 38. Two English-language samples of verbal attacks on Sun were published in *Chinese Economic Studies* in 1971 (Revolutionary-Mass-Criticism Group . . . 1970; Writing Group . . . 1970). The second contains a remarkable reference comparing Sun to nineteenth century French economist Leon Baptiste Say, "master of philistine bourgeois economics" (pp. 286–287).
43. Intellectuals as a group "were classified as the 'stinking ninth category' of class enemies, coming after the eight other categories: landlords, rich peasants, counterrevolutionaries, bad elements, anti-CCP rightists, renegades, enemy agents, and capitalist roaders, all of whom were seen as detrimental to the CCP interest and subjected to the proletarian dictatorship." Du 1992, p. 62.
44. Tobin and Lloyd Reynolds were both struck by the paucity of statistical data on China's economy, a reflection of the disorder arising from the Cultural Revolution. Tobin 1975, p. 26; Reynolds 1975, pp. 22–23.
45. In 1966 the quarterly *Chinese Economic Studies* was introduced, publishing translations of (mostly) Chinese-language writings on China's economy. We tabulated 85 names of Chinese authors down through volume 12:2 (Winter 1978–79). Of these, only two had studied in the West—Wang Yanan and Wu Jingchao. The studies published over this period are good evidence of the abysmal quality of Chinese economic discourse of the period.
46. A significant indicator of intellectual liberation was the 1978 revival of *Jingji Yanjiu* (Economic Research), a leading economic periodical which had been shut down in 1966. Wang 1979, p. 3.
47. Although farm families were given control of land use—including the right to rent it out— they did not and do not (2007) own the land. Because they cannot pledge land as collateral for loans, no effective mortgage market has developed.
48. P. 21. Much of their book is devoted to refuting "the Malthusian mythology of Chinese population". They cite the long-time practice of infanticide as somehow contradicting Malthusian analysis. To Adam Smith and Malthus, of course, the practice was symptomatic of the chronic shortage of food and land.
49. An application of the Barro-Grossman model to China is presented in Wang Zhaoping's dissertation—1992.
50. Chen Daisun, Gao Hongye, Wang Chuanlun, and Lu Guangmian all became members of the National People's Consultative Committee.
51. See Herschede 1985; Hu Teh-wei 1984.
52. However, in 1983–84 Beida was still teaching a course on the U.S. economy which concentrated on the collusive monopolistic "interest-groups" which supposedly controlled the economy. Beida students were still required to study Marxist "political economy", but I never found any who could discuss Marxist economics coherently.
53. According to Du Ruiqing 1992, "the enrollment of students of finance and economics, which was 18,120 in 1965 . . . was down to 6570 in 1976 . . ." As

late as 1987, "among all the full-time university faculty in China, only 12.6 percent had graduate training" (pp. 15, 69).

54. The English-language professors' directory lists about 17,000 full professors as of October, 1987. We tabulated 647 economists. About half were born in 1924 or earlier. For comparison, there were in 1989 about 19,000 full-time teachers of economics in institutions of higher learning, but only 3400 held professorial rank (*China Statistical Yearbook* 1990, p. 667). *Biographies of Contemporary Chinese Economists* (Chinese language) gave us 104 names, 22 of them deceased. The *Social Science Biographical Directory* (Chinese language) provided 297 names of economists, including 43 deceased. Wu Naichun and Ma Lingjie translated these references for me.
55. In contrast, Robert Hsu's 1991 survey of Chinese economic theories 1979–1988 cites 193 Chinese economists, none of whom appear in our student lists. I believe his sources are overwhelmingly people in government (including the think-tanks) rather than in universities.
56. Yung-chen Chiang 2001 notes "the elite and outsider roles of social scientists and social researchers in China during the Republican period". Referring mainly to the rural surveys, he states "Whether they were the . . . social engineers of the Anglo-American type, or rural reform advocates of the low-brow intellectual brand, or Chen [Hansheng] and his fellow advocates of revolution, they were all outsiders and elite as far as their subjects were concerned, alien in their world view, vocabulary, mannerism, clothing and even language." (p. 267)
57. "[Go] to London, Paris, Berlin, or Rome. Smell the alienation that hovers over thousands of young people as they wander among those forbidding buildings collectively known as Humboldt University or Sorbonne. Plumb their frustrations as they sit in vast lecture halls, listening to professors reading from ancient, yellowed notes . . . Think about college years as perennial reenactment of the emigrant experience. It is leaving home, going to a faraway place; it is the grueling encounter with strange new worlds of ideas and cultural techniques, both alluring and intimidating." (Joffe 2000)
58. "Taiwan was an area where government-by-law, literacy and education, and the economic and social development, after half-a-century of Japanese rule, had all reached such high levels that no province in China, except for the small enclaves around the treaty ports and perhaps Manchuria, could match it on any realistic terms." (Hsieh 1972, p. 629)
59. Nobel-Prize winner James Buchanan (1990) recalled his initial graduate studies in 1940 as follows: "I surveyed the workings and structures of the institutions of Roosevelt's New Deal; I came to understand central banking theory and policy; I learned something about taxation and budgetary processes; I learned a bit of elementary statistics . . . But neither in these courses nor in my prior undergraduate experience did I have proper exposure to the central principle

of market organization. I remained blissfully ignorant of the coordinating properties of a decentralized market process, an ignorance that made me vulnerable to quasi-Marxist arguments and explanations about economic history and economic reality . . ." (p. 165)

60. George Stigler, referring to the period before the 1960s, noted that "even when economists took an active and direct interest in a policy issue, they did not make systematic empirical studies to establish the extent and nature of a problem or the probable efficiency of alternative methods of solving the problem" (1975, p. 49).

61. James Tobin observed from his 1972 visit that the Chinese economists "regarded it as entirely natural that people should grow up to work in the locales where they were born, even if their marginal products—my word, of course, not theirs— might be higher somewhere else . . . Our suggestion that it might be desirable to shift people from poorer land to better land was stoutly resisted. If for historical reasons people happen to live on unpromising terrain, they and their children must simply put more Maoist energy and ingenuity into improving the situation . . ." (Tobin 1975, p. 39; Galbraith 1973, p. 83)

References

"A Survey of Recent Studies on Chinese Economy, 1927–1947", [prob. H. D. Fong], undated typescript. Rockefeller Archive, Record Group 1.1 Projects; Series 601 China, Box 51, Folder 601S.

"Academia Sinica with its Research Institutes" (pamphlet). Shanghai: Science Press, 1929.

Aird, John S. "Population Growth", in Eckstein, ed., 1968, pp. 193–327.

Alitto, Guy S. *The Last Confucian: Liang Shu-ming and the Chinese Dilemma of Modernity*. Berkeley: University of California, 1979.

Allen, Robert Loring. *Irving Fisher: A Biography*. Cambridge, MA: Blackwell, 1993.

Alley, Rewi. *The People Have Strength*. Beijing: the author, 1954.

Ambirajan, S. "The Aftermath of Empire", in Coats, ed., 1981, pp. 98–132.

———. "The Professionalization of Economics in India", in Coats, ed., 1997, pp. 80–96.

American Economic Association. Directory of Members, various titles, various dates.

American University Men in China. Shanghai: Comacrib Press, 1936.

Arkush, R. David. *Fei Xiaotong and Sociology in Revolutionary China*. Cambridge, MA: Harvard University Press, 1981.

Arndt, Paul. *Der Arbeitslohn in China* [Wages in China]. Leipzig: Buske, 1937.

Arndt, Heinz W. "Economist Down Under", in Hagemann, ed., 1997, pp. 151–176.

Arrigo, Linda Gail. "Landowner Concentration in China: The Buck Survey Revisited", *Modern China*, 12:3 (July, 1986), pp. 259–360.

Backhouse, Roger E. "The Changing Character of British Economics", in Coats, ed., 1997, pp. 33–60.

Band, Claire and William. *Two Years with the Chinese Communists*. New Haven: Yale University Press, 1948.

Barber, William J., ed. *Breaking the Academic Mould: Economists and American Higher Learning in the Nineteenth Century*. Middletown, CN: Wesleyan University Press, 1988.

Barclay, George, Ansley J. Coale, Michael A. Stoto, and T. James Trussell. "A

Reassessment of the Demography of Traditional Rural China", *Population Index*, 42:4 (October, 1976), pp. 606–635.

Barker, Charles Albro. *Henry George*. New York: Oxford University Press, 1955.

Barker, Randolph, Radha Sinha, and Beth Rose, eds. *The Chinese Agricultural Economy*. Boulder CO: Westview Press, 1982.

Barnett, Suzanne Wilson and John K. Fairbank, eds. *Christianity in China: Early Missionary Writings*. Cambridge, MA: Harvard University Press, 1985.

Barr, Pat. *To China with Love: The Life and Times of Protestant Missionaries in China 1860–1900*. London: Secker and Warburg, 1972.

Barro, Robert J. and Herschel I. Grossman. *Money, Employment and Inflation*. New York: Cambridge University Press, 1976.

Bartke, Wolfgang. *Who's Who in the People's Republic of China*. Armonk, NY: M. E. Sharpe, 1981, 1987.

Bateman, Bradley W. "Clearing the Ground: The Demise of the Social Gospel Movement and the Rise of Neoclassicism in American Economics", in Morgan and Rutherford, eds., 1998, pp. 29–52.

———. "Make a Righteous Number: Social Surveys, the Men and Religion Forward Movement, and Quantification in American Economics", in Klein and Morgan, eds., 2001, pp. 57–85.

Bauer, Wolfgang and Shen-chang Hwang. *German Impact on Modern Chinese Intellectual History: A Bibliography of Chinese Publications*. Wiesbaden: Franz Steiner, 1982.

Becker, C. H., M. Falski, P. Langevin, and R. H. Tawney. *The Reorganisation of Education in China*. Paris: League of Nations, 1932.

Becker, Jasper. *Hungry Ghosts: Mao's Secret Famine*. New York: Free Press, 1996.

Bedeski, Robert E. "The Concept of the State: Sun Yat-sen and Mao Tse-tung", *China Quarterly*, 70 (June, 1977), pp. 338–354.

Bennett, Adrian Arthur. *John Fryer: The Introduction of Western Science and Technology into Nineteenth Century China*. Cambridge, MA: Harvard University Press, 1967.

Bernal, Martin. *Chinese Socialism to 1907*. Ithaca: Cornell University Press, 1976.

Biddle, Jeff. "Institutional Economics: A Case of Reproductive Failure?", in Morgan and Rutherford, eds., 1998, pp. 108–133.

———. "Statistical Economics, 1900–1950", *History of Political Economy*, 31:4 (Winter, 1999), pp. 607–651.

Biggerstaff, Dwight. *The Earliest Modern Government Schools in China*. Ithaca: Cornell University Press, 1961.

———. "Nanking Letters 1949" (mimeo). Ithaca: Cornell University, 1979.

Bilboul, Roger R., ed. *Retrospective Index to Theses of Great Britain and Ireland 1716–1950*, v. 1: Social Sciences and Humanities. Oxford: European Bibliographical Center-Clio Press Inc., 1975.

Biographical Dictionary of Professors in Chinese Universities and Colleges. Beijing: Higher Education Press, 1990.

Biographies of Contemporary Chinese Economists 當代中國經濟學家錄, Liu Zhinan and Zhong Jianmin, eds. Guangdong People's Press, 1987 (Chinese language).

Biographies of Contemporary Chinese Social Scientists 中國現代社會科學家傳略, Gao Zhengde, ed. Shanxi People's Press, 1982 (Chinese language), 2 titles.

"Biographies of Kuomintang Leaders" (mimeo), prepared by Chinese Communist Party 1945; translated 1948 by Committee on International and Regional Studies, Harvard University.

Blaug, Mark. *Great Economists Since Keynes*. 2nd ed. Northampton, MA: Edward Elgar, 1985.

——— and Paul Sturges, eds. *Who's Who in Economics*. Cambridge, MA: MIT Press, 1983; 2nd ed. Brighton, UK: Wheatsheaf Press, 1986.

Bodde, Dirk. *Peking Diary: A Year of Revolution*. New York: Henry Schurman, 1950.

Bonnichon, Andre. "La Faculte de Droit de l'Universite l'Aurore", *Bulletin de l'Universite l'Aurore*, III:1:3 (1940), pp. 298–307.

Boorman, Howard L. *Biographical Dictionary of Republican China*. New York: Columbia University Press, 1967–71.

Bowen, Howard R. *Graduate Education in Economics*. American Economic Review Supplement, September 1953.

Bramall, Chris. *Sources of Chinese Economic Growth, 1978–1996*. Oxford: Oxford University Press, 2000.

Brandt, Loren. *Commercialization and Agricultural Development: Central and Eastern China 1870–1937*. New York: Cambridge University Press, 1989.

Brandt, Vincent. "Landlord-Tenant Relations in Republican China", *Papers on China*, 17 (1963) pp. 192–234.

Braudel, Fernand. *Capitalism and Material Life 1400–1800*. New York: Harper and Row, 1973.

Bray, Francesca. *Agriculture*, v. 6 Part II of *Science and Civilization in China* (Joseph Needham, ed.). New York: Cambridge University Press, 1984.

Breit, William and Roger Spencer, eds. *Lives of the Laureates: Ten Nobel Economists*. Cambridge, MA: MIT Press, 1990.

Brief Biographies of Contemporary Chinese Social Scientists (Gao Zheng-de, ed.). Shanxi People's Press, 1982.

Buchanan, James. "Born-Again Economist", in Breit and Spencer, eds., 1990, pp. 163–180.

Buchanan, Keith. *The Transformation of the Chinese Earth*. New York: Praeger, 1970.

Buck, Paul, ed. *Social Sciences at Harvard 1860–1920*. Cambridge, MA: Harvard University Press, 1965.

Buck, John Lossing. "The Chinese Church and Country Life", *Chinese Recorder*, 54:6 (June, 1923), pp. 319–326.

———. "The Building of a Rural Church: Organization and Program in China", *Chinese Recorder*, July, 1927a.

———. "Farm Ownership and Tenancy in China" (pamphlet). Shanghai: Committee on Christianizing the Economic Order, 1927b.

———. *Chinese Farm Economy*. Chicago: University of Chicago Press, 1930a.

———. "Chinese Rural Economy", *Journal of Farm Economics*, 7:3 (July, 1930b), pp. 440–456.

———. *Land Utilization in China*. Nanking: University of Nanking, 1937.

———. Oral history interview with Gould Colman, 1962, Cornell University Archives.

———. "Food Grain Production in Mainland China Before and During the Communist Regime", in *Food and Agriculture in Communist China*, Buck, Owen L. Dawson, and Yuan-li Wu, eds. Stanford: Hoover Institution, 1966, pp. 3–72.

———. "The Agricultural Economy of China, 1927–1937, as Exemplified by the Work at the University of Nanking", in Sih, ed., 1970, pp. 171–193.

———. "Development of Agricultural Economics at the University of Nanking, Nanking, China, 1926–1946", Cornell International Agricultural Development Bulletin 25, 1973.

———. "Land and Agricultural Resources", in Yuan-li Wu, ed., 1973, pp. 45–69.

———. "An Agricultural Survey of Szechwan Province, China". Chungking: Farmer's Bank of China, 1943. Reprinted in *Three Essays on Chinese Farm Economy*. New York: Garland Press, 1980.

——— and Chiao Chi-ming. "The Composition and Growth of Rural Population Groups in China", *Chinese Economic Journal*, March, 1928, pp. 219–236.

Buck, Pearl S. *My Separate Worlds*. New York: John Day, 1954.

Bulmer, Martin, Kevin Bales, and Kathryn Kish Sklar, eds. *The Social Survey in Historical Perspective*. New York: Cambridge University Press, 1991.

Burke's Peerage and Baronetage, 106th ed. Chicago: Fitzroy Dearborn, 1997.

[Burton, John Hill]. *Political Economy for Use in Schools and for Private Instruction* [佐治芻言]. Edinburgh: Chambers Brothers, 1852, 1873.

Butterfield, Kenyon. *The Rural Mission of the Church in Eastern Asia*. New York: International Missionary Council, 1931.

Bye, Raymond. *Principles of Economics*, 3rd ed. New York: F. S. Crofts, 1936.

Cameron, Meribeth. *The Reform Movement in China, 1898–1912*. Stanford, CA: Stanford University Press, 1931.

Campbell, Colin D. and Gordon C. Tullock. "Hyperinflation in China, 1937–49", *Journal of Political Economy*, 62:3 (June, 1954), pp. 236–245.

Carlson, Benny. "Wagner's Legacy in America: Re-opening Farnam's Inquiry",

Journal of the History of Economic Thought, 21:3 (September, 1999), pp. 289–310.

Carver, Thomas Nixon. *Principles of Rural Economics*. Boston: Ginn and Co., 1911.

———. *Principles of Political Economy*. Boston: Ginn and Co., 1919.

———. *Reflections of an Unplanned Life*. Los Angeles: Ward Ritchie, 1949.

Cassou, Pierre-Henri. "The Chinese Monetary System", *Chinese Economic Studies*, 9:4 (Summer, 1976), pp. 82–97 (orig. 1973).

Chan, Ming K. and Arif Dirlik. *Schools into Fields and Factories: Anarchists, the Guomindang and the National Labor University in Shanghai 1927–1932*. Durham: Duke University Press, 1991.

Chang, Hao. *Liang Ch'i-ch'ao and Intellectual Transition in China, 1890–1907*. Cambridge, MA: Harvard University Press, 1971.

Chang, John K. *Industrial Development in Pre-Communist China*. Chicago: Aldine, 1969.

Chang Kia-ngau. *The Inflationary Spiral: The Experience in China, 1939–1950*. New York: John Wiley, 1958.

Chang, Maria Hsia. "Sun Yat-sen's Program for the Economic Modernization of China", in Gregor and Chang, eds., 1983, pp. 4–25.

Chang Pei-kang. *Agriculture and Industrialization*. Cambridge, MA: Harvard University Press, 1949.

Chang, Sidney H. and Leonard H. D. Gordon. *All Under Heaven . . . Sun Yat-sen and his Revolutionary Thought*. Stanford, CA: Hoover Institution, 1991.

[Chang] Tschang Yen-yu. *Soziale Frage und standische Sozialpolitik in Wesen und in China* (The Social Question and Social Policy in Theory and in China). Vienna: Oskar Andreas, 1935.

Chao, G. T., ed. *Who's Who of American Returned Students*. Peking: Tsinghua College, 1917.

Chao Nai-tuan. *Richard Jones: An Early English Institutionalist*. New York: Columbia University Press, 1930.

Chen Chang-sheng. "Some Phases of China's Population Problem", *Bulletin de l'Institut International de Statistique*, 25:2 (1931), pp. 18*–54*.

———. "The Chinese Census of Population since 1712", *Bulletin de l'Institut International de Statistique*, 25:2 (1931), pp. 122*–134*.

Chen Daisun. *The Works of Chen Daisun* 陳岱孫文集 (2 vols.). Beijing: Peking University Press, 1989 (Chinese language).

———. *Chen Daisun xueshu jingyao yu jiedu* 陳岱孫學術精要與解讀. Fukien: Fukien Renmin Chubanshe, 1998.

Chen, Gideon (Chen Chi-tien). "International Relations", in *Report of the Conference on Christianizing Economic Relations*, Shanghai, 1927, pp. 63–65.

———. "Recent Social and Moral Problems and Attitudes", *Chinese Christian Year Book* (1929), pp. 95–106.

———. "Chinese Government Economic Planning and Reconstruction", in Lasker and Holland, eds., 1934, pp. 352–382.

Chen Huan-chang. *The Economic Principles of Confucius and his School*. New York: Columbia University Press, 1911 (2 vols.).

Chen Kung-Po. "China's Four-Year Industrial Plan", *Chinese Economic Journal*, 13:3 (September, 1933), pp. 203–220.

Chen Li-fu. "The Function of the Commission on Land Research and Planning" (pamphlet). Nanking: International Relations Committee, n.d. (1934?).

Chen, Nairuenn. *The Economy of Mainland China, 1949–1963: A Bibliography of Materials in English*. Berkeley, CA: Social Science Research Council, 1963.

Chen Ta. *Population in Modern China*. Chicago: University of Chicago Press, 1946.

———. "Les Problemes Demographiques en Chine" (pamphlet). New York: UNESCO, 1950.

Chen, Theodore H. E. *Thought Reform of the Chinese Intellectuals*. Hong Kong: Hong Kong University Press, 1960.

Chen Tsu-yu and Mo Chi-peng, eds. *The Reminiscences of Dr. S. C. Tsiang*. Taipei: Institute of Modern History, Academia Sinica, 1992 (Chinese language).

Chen, Warren. "An Estimate of the Population of China in 1929", *Bulletin de l'Institut International de Statistique*, 25:2 (1931), pp. 55*–87*.

Chen, Xiaoching Diana. "Curricula and Academic Professionalization at Peking University 1898–1937". PhD dissertation, University of Chicago, 1993.

Chen Zen, Sophie H., ed. *Symposium on Chinese Culture*. Shanghai: China Institute of Pacific Relations, 1940.

Cheng, Chu-yuan. *Income and Standard of Living in Mainland China*. Hong Kong: Urban Research Institute, 1957.

———. "The Doctrine of People's Welfare: The Taiwan Experiment and its Implications for the Third World", in Cheng, ed., *Sun Yat-Sen's Doctrine in the Modern World*. Boulder: Westview, 1989, pp. 244–275.

Cheng Yu-kwei. *Foreign Trade and Industrial Development of China*. Washington: University of Washington Press, 1956.

Cheung, Steven N. S. "Will China Go 'Capitalist'?" (pamphlet). London: Institute of Economic Affairs, 1982.

Chiang Kai-shek. *China's Destiny* and *Chinese Economic Theory*. New York: Roy Publisher, 1947.

Chiang Yung-chien. "Social Engineering and the Social Sciences in China, 1898–1949". Unpublished PhD dissertation, Harvard, 1986.

———. *Social Engineering and the Social Sciences in China, 1919–1949*. New York: Cambridge University Press, 2001.

Chiao Chi-ming. "A Study of the Chinese Population", *Milbank Memorial Fund Quarterly Bulletin*, 11:4 (October, 1933), reprinted in Myers ed., 1980.

Chiaotong University. *General Catalogue*, 1931–32, 1935–36 (English language); 1932 (Chinese language).

———. *Selected Editorial Materials of History of Jiaotong University* 交通大學校史資料選編, 1986 (Chinese language).

China Academy. *Graduation Commemoration Book* 中國公學畢業紀念刊, 1941.

The China Annual, 1944. Shanghai: Asia Statistics Co. (published by puppet regime).

"China Institute of Economics", typescript materials, Rockefeller Archive: Record Group 1.1 Projects; 601 China, Box 51, Folder 601s, 1947–49.

China International Famine Relief Commission. *Herr Raiffeisen among Chinese Farmers*. Peiping, CIFRC, 1930.

China Year Book. Tientsin and Shanghai, various issues.

Chinese Christian Educational Association. "The Christian College in the New China". Shanghai, 1926; Box 448, Folder 6008, RG 51, YDS.

[Chinese Government Information Office]. *China Handbook*, 1937–43, 1937–45. New York: Macmillan.

Chiu, Alfred Kaiming. "Recent Statistical Studies of Chinese Rural Economy, 1912–1932". Unpublished PhD dissertation, Harvard University, 1933.

———. "Agriculture", in MacNair, ed., 1946, pp. 467–491.

Choi, Young Back. "The Americanization of Economics in Korea", in Coats, ed., 1997, pp. 97–122.

Chou Hsun. "The Present State and Future Outlook for Social Science Research in Communist China", *Chinese Law and Government* 12:4 (Winter, 1979–80), pp. 85–119.

Chou Shun-hsin. *The Chinese Inflation 1937–1949*. New York: Columbia University Press, 1963.

Chow Tse-tung. *The May Fourth Movement*. Cambridge, MA: Harvard University Press, 1960.

Christian Education in China: The Report of the China Educational Commission of 1921–1922. Shanghai: Commercial Press, 1922.

Chu Tsu-hui (C. H.). "The Price-fixing Policy of War-time China", *China Quarterly* (Shanghai) 6:2 (Summer, 1941), pp. 296–306.

Chung, Chin. "Impacts on Domestic and Host Economies of Taiwan's DFI toward Mainland China". Taipei: Chung-Hua Institution for Economic Research, unpublished MS, 1992.

Chung-Hua Institution for Economic Research, 1991–1992 (pamphlet). Taipei, 1992.

Chungshan University. "Condition of Chungshan University" 國立中山大學現狀(民國廿四年), 1935 (Chinese language).

———. *History of Chungshan University 1924–1949* 中山大學校史. Shanghai: Shanghai Education Press (Chinese language).

Church, Robert L. "The Economists Study Society: Sociology at Harvard, 1891–1902", in Paul Buck, ed., 1965, pp. 18–90.

———. "Economists as Experts: The Rise of an Academic Profession in the United States, 1870–1920", in Stone, ed., 1974, v. II, pp. 571–609.

Cipolla, Carlo M. *Before the Industrial Revolution: European Society and Economy, 1000–1700*. New York: Norton, 1976.

Clark, Terry Nichols. *Prophets and Patrons: The French University and the Emergence of the Social Sciences*. Cambridge, MA: Harvard University Press, 1973.

Clausen, Soren. "Chinese Economic Debates after Mao", in Feuchtwang and Hussain, eds., 1983, pp. 53–73.

Coats, A. W., ed. *Economists in Government*. Durham, NC: Duke University Press, 1981.

———. "The Educational Revolution and the Professionalization of American Economics", in Barber, ed., 1988, pp. 340–375.

———, ed. *The Post-1945 Internationalization of Economics*. Durham, NC: Duke University Press, 1997.

Coe, John L. *Huachung University*. New York: United Board, 1962.

Cohen, Paul A. *Between Tradition and Modernity: Wang T'ao and Reform in Late Ch'ing China*. Cambridge, MA: Harvard University Press, 1974.

College of Agriculture and Forestry, University of Nanking. *Agricultural Index to Periodicals and Bulletins in Chinese and in English Principally Published in China, 1858–1931*. University of Nanking, 1933 (University of Illinois Library).

Committee for the Study of Silver Values and Commodity Prices, Ministry of Industry. *Silver and Prices in China*. Shanghai: Commercial Press, 1935.

Committee on Relation of the Church to China's Industrial and Economic Problems. "The Church and the Economic and Industrial Problems of China". Peking, 1923 (Peking University Library).

Comprehensive Dissertation Index. Ann Arbor, MI: University Microfilms, 1973.

Condliffe, J. B., ed. *Problems of the Pacific*. Chicago: University of Chicago Press, 1930.

Conn, Peter. *Pearl S. Buck: A Cultural Biography*. New York: Cambridge University Press, 1996.

Contemporary Social Scientists in China 中國當代社會科學家. Beijing Library Editorial Department and Editorial Department of Jilin Library Association, eds. 1982–85 (Chinese language).

Converse, Jean. *Survey Research in the United States: Roots and Emergence*. Berkeley: University of California, 1987.

Coons, Arthur. "Economic Reconstruction in China" (pamphlet). Peiping: College of Chinese Studies, 1934 (University of Illinois Library).

Corbett, Charles Hodge. *Shantung Christian University (Cheeloo)*. New York: United Board, 1959.

Cossa, Luigi. *Guide to the Study of Political Economy*. London: Macmillan, 1880.

———. *An Introduction to the Study of Political Economy*, translated by Louis Dyer. London: Macmillan, 1893.

Cottrell, Allin F., ed. *New Perspectives on Keynes*. Durham, NC: Duke University Press, 1995.

Cressey, George B. "Christian Higher Education in China; A Study for the Year 1925–1926" (pamphlet). Shanghai: China Christian Educational Association, 1928.

———. "The Source of China's 'Vegetable Civilization'", *New York Times Book Review*, May 1, 1938.

Dahrendorf, Ralf. *LSE: A History of the London School of Economics and Political Science 1895–1995*. Oxford: Oxford University Press, 1995.

Davin, Delia. "Imperialism and the Diffusion of Liberal Thought: British Influences on Chinese Education", in Hayhoe and Bastid, eds., 1987, pp. 33–56.

Day, Clarence Burton. *Hangchow University*. New York: United Board, 1955.

Dealey, James Q. "A Chinese Village Survey", *Journal of Applied Sociology*, 9:3 (January, 1925), pp. 174–178.

Deng Maomao. *Deng Xiaoping, My Father*. New York: Basic Books, 1995.

Desrosieres, Alain. "The Part in Relation to the Whole: How to Generalise? The Prehistory of Representative Sampling", in Bulmer, Bales, and Sklar, eds., 1991, pp. 217–244.

Dimand, Robert W. "Fisher and Veblen: Two Paths for American Economics", *Journal of the History of Economic Thought*, 20:4 (December, 1998), pp. 449–465.

Dittmer, Clarence G. "An Estimate of the Standard of Living in China", *Quarterly Journal of Economics* 33:1 (November, 1918), pp. 107–128.

Dockes, Pierre et al., eds. *Les Traditions Economiques Francaises 1848–1939*. Paris: CNRS Editions, 2000.

Domes, Jurgen. *Socialism in the Chinese Countryside*. London: C. Hurst, 1980.

Donnithorne, Audrey. *China's Economic System*. New York: Praeger, 1967.

Dorfman, Joseph. "The Department of Economics", in Hoxie, ed., 1955, pp. 161–206.

———. *The Economic Mind in American Civilization*, v. 3 & 4. New York: Viking Press, 1949, 1959.

Douw, Leo. "The Representation of China's Rural Backwardness 1932–1937". PhD dissertation, Leiden University, 1991; kindly supplied by Linda Arrigo.

Drake, Fred W. "Protestant Geography in China: E. C. Bridgman's Portrayal of the West", in Barnett and Fairbank, eds., 1985, pp. 89–106.

Du Ruiqing. *Chinese Higher Education*. New York: St. Martin's Press, 1992.

Duncan, Kenneth. *Essentials of Economics*. Shanghai: Commercial Press, 1930 (orig. 1914).

Durand, John D. "The Population Statistics of China, A.D. 2–1953", *Population Studies*, 13:3 (March, 1960), pp. 209–256.

Duus, Peter. "Science and Salvation in China: The Life and Work of W. A. P. Martin", *Papers on China*, 10, 1956.

Eastman, Lloyd E. *The Abortive Revolution: China under Nationalist Rule, 1927–1937*. Cambridge, MA: Harvard University Press, 1974.

———. *Seeds of Destruction: Nationalist China in War and Revolution 1937–1949*. Stanford: Stanford University Press, 1984.

———. "Nationalist China during the Nanking Decade 1927–1937", in Fairbank and Feuerwerker, eds., 1986a, pp. 116–167.

———. "Nationalist China during the Sino-Japanese War 1937–1945", in Fairbank and Feuerwerker, eds., 1986b, pp. 547–608.

Echinard, Yann and Anne LeRoy. "Lucien Brocard: Un Economiste Francais Novateur, Original et . . . Meconnu", in Dockes, et al., op. cit. 2000, pp. 169–182.

Eckstein, Alexander. *China's Economic Development*. Ann Arbor, MI: University of Michigan Press, 1975.

———, Walter Galenson, and Ta-chung Liu, eds. *Economic Trends in Communist China*. Chicago: Aldine, 1968.

Edkins, Joseph. *Chinese Currency*. Shanghai: Presbyterian Mission Press, 1901.

———. *The Revenue and Taxation of the Chinese Empire*. Shanghai: Presbyterian Mission Press, 1903; reprinted 1981 by Garland Press.

———. *Banking and Prices in China*. Shanghai: Presbyterian Mission Press, 1905 (Beijing National Library).

Edmonds, Richard Louis. "The Legacy of Sun Yat-Sen's Railway Plans", *China Quarterly*, No. 111 (September, 1987), pp. 421–443.

Edwards, Dwight W. *Yenching University*. New York: United Board, 1959.

Egan, Susan Chan. *A Latterday Confucian: Reminiscences of William Hung (1893–1980)*. Cambridge, MA: Harvard University Press, 1987.

Ely, Richard T. *Outlines of Economics*. New York: Chautauqua-Century Press, 1893.

——— and George Ray Wicker. *Elementary Principles of Economics*. New York: Macmillan, 1904.

———, Ralph H. Hess, Charles K. Leith, and Thomas Nixon Carver. *The Foundations of National Prosperity*. New York: Macmillan, 1917.

Emmett, Ross B. "Entrenching Disciplinary Competence: The Role of General Education and Graduate Study in Chicago Economics", in Morgan and Rutherford, eds., 1998, pp. 134–150.

Encyclopedia of New China. Beijing: Foreign Language Press, 1987.

Escarra, Jean. "Le Probleme de l'Exterritorialite en Chine" (pamphlet). Paris: Librairie de la Societe du Recueil Sirey, 1923.

———. *China Then and Now*. Peking: Henri Vetch, 1940.

Evans, Roger F. "China Diary" (typescript). Rockefeller Archive, Record Group 1.1 Projects, Series 601 China, Box 51, Folder 601S, 1947.

Fairbank, John K. *Chinabound: A Fifty-Year Memoir*. New York: Harper and Row, 1982.

——— and Kwang-ching Liu. *Modern China: A Bibliographic Guide to Chinese Works, 1898–1937*. Cambridge, MA: Harvard University Press, 1961.

——— and Albert Feuerwerker, eds. *The Cambridge History of China*, v. 13: *Republican China*. New York: Cambridge University Press, 1986.

Fairbank, Wilma A. *America's Cultural Experiment in China 1942–1949*. Washington: Government Printing Office, 1976.

Fairchild, Fred R., Edgar S. Furniss, and Norman S. Buck. *Elementary Economics*. New York: Macmillan, rev. ed., 1930, 1931 (2 vols.).

Fan Hong. *Modern Monetary Theory* 現代貨幣學. 1947 (Chinese language).

——— [Fan-hung]. "Keynes and Marx on the Theory of Capital Accumulation, Money and Interest", *Review of Economic Studies* 7:1 (1939), pp. 28–41.

Faure, David. *The Rural Economy of Pre-Liberation China*. Hong Kong: Oxford University Press, 1989.

Fei Hsiao-tung. Review of "A Study of the Rural Economy of Wuhing, Chekiang", *Nankai Social and Economic Quarterly* 11:1 (January, 1940), pp. 178–180.

Fei, John C. H. "A Bird's Eye View of Policy Evolution", in K. T. Li, 1988, pp. 26–46.

Feng Rui. "Agriculture", in Chen Zen, ed., 1931, pp. 224–236.

Fenn, William P. *The Effect of the Japanese Invasion on Higher Education in China*. Shanghai: China Institute of Pacific Relations, 1940.

———. *Christian Higher Education in Changing China, 1880–1950*. Grand Rapids: Eerdmans, 1976.

Feuchtwang, Stephan and Athar Hussain. "Introduction", in *Chinese Economic Reforms*. New York: St. Martins, 1983, pp. 1–50.

Feuerwerker, Albert. *China's Early Industrialization*. Cambridge, MA: Harvard University Press, 1958.

———. "The Chinese Economy 1912–1949", *Michigan Papers in Chinese Studies* #1, Ann Arbor, 1968.

———. *Economic Trends in the Republic of China, 1912–1949*. Michigan Papers in Chinese Studies #31, Ann Arbor, 1977.

Field, Frederick Vanderbilt. *From Right to Left: An Autobiography*. Westport, CN: Lawrence Hall, 1983.

Fish, John Charles Lounsbury. *Engineering Economics: First Principles*, 2nd ed. New York: McGraw-Hill, 1923.

Fleischer, Belton and Yunhua Liu. "Economies of Scale, Plot Size, Human Capital, and Productivity in Chinese Agriculture", *Quarterly Review of Economics and Finance*, 32:3 (Fall, 1992), pp. 112–123.

Flexner, Abraham. *Universities: American, English, German*. New York: Oxford University Press, 1930.

Fong, H. D. (Fang Hsien-ting). *Triumph of Factory System in England*. Tientsin: Chihli Press, 1930.

———. "Rural Industries in China", in Lasker and Holland, eds., 1933, pp. 299–351.

———. "Bibliography on Silver and China", [Nankai] *Monthly Bulletin on Economic China*, 7:12 (December, 1934), pp. 513–524.

———. "Rural Industries in China's Reconstruction", *Monthly Bulletin on Economic China*, 7:11 (November, 1934a), pp. 449–455.

———. "Economic Statistics in China", *Monthly Bulletin on Economic China*, 7:1 (January, 1934b), pp. 15–27.

———. "Research Notes", *Nankai Social and Economic Quarterly*, 8:1 (April, 1935), pp. 163–177.

———. "Bibliography on the Land Problems of China", *Nankai Social and Economic Quarterly*, 8:2 (July, 1935), pp. 325–384.

———. "Rural Weaving and the Merchant Employers in a North China District: II", *Nankai Social and Economic Quarterly*, 8:2 (July, 1935), pp. 274–308.

———. "Economic Ills and their Control in China" 中國經濟之癥結與統制, *Quarterly Journal of Economics and Political Science*, 4:3 (April, 1936a), pp. 521–561 (Chinese language).

———. *Toward Economic Control in China*, Shanghai: China Institute of Pacific Relations, 1936b.

———. "Industrial Capital in China", *Nankai Social and Economic Quarterly*, 9:1 (April, 1936c), pp. 27–94.

———. "Industrial Organization in China", *Nankai Social and Economic Quarterly*, 9:4 (January, 1937a), pp. 919–1006.

———. "Industrialization and the Rural Industries in China", *China Quarterly* (Shanghai), 2:2 (Spring, 1937b), pp. 259–279.

———. (ed.) *Studies in Chinese Economy*. Changsha: Commercial Press, 1938 (2 vols.)

———. "Industrialization for China's Southwest", *China Quarterly*, 4:2 (Spring, 1939), pp. 299–306.

———. "A Brief Survey of Economic Literature on China during the War", *Nankai Social and Economic Quarterly*, 12:1 (January, 1941), pp. 169–182.

———. "The Prospect for China's Industrialization", *Pacific Affairs*, 15:1 (March, 1942a), pp. 44–60.

———. "The Postwar Industrialization of China", National Planning Association Pamphlets 12 & 13, 1942b.

———. "Recollections of Early Research on Chinese Economy", *Tsing Hua Journal of Chinese Studies*, 3:2 and 4:1 (June, 1963), pp. 69–84.

———. *Reminiscences of a Chinese Economist at 70*. Singapore: South Seas Society, 1975.

——— and Franklin Ho. "A Survey of Recent Studies on Chinese Economy, 1927–

1947" (typescript). Rockefeller Archive, Record Group 1.1 Projects; Series 601 China, Box 51, Folder 601S.

———, K.Y. Lin, and Tso-fan Koh. "Problems of Economic Reconstruction in China". Shanghai: China Institute of Pacific Relations, 1942 (reprinted Garland Press, 1981).

Fraser, Stewart, ed. *Education and Communism in China*. London: Pall Mall Press, 1971.

Freedman, Maurice. "Marcel Granet, 1884–1940, Sociologist", in introduction to Freedman's translation of Granet, *The Religion of the Chinese People*. Oxford: Blackwell, 1975 (orig. 1922).

[French Ministry of Education]. *Catalogue des Theses et Ecrits Academiques* (annual, 1912–1950).

Friedman, Donald J. *The Road from Isolation: The Campaign of the American Committee for Non-Participation in Japanese Aggression*. Cambridge, MA: Harvard University Press, 1968.

Froman, Lewis A. "Graduate Students in Economics 1904 to 1928", *American Economic Review*, 20:2 (June, 1930), pp. 235–247.

———. "Graduate Students in Economics, 1904–1940", *American Economic Review*, 32:4 (December, 1942), pp. 817–826.

———. "Graduate Students in Economics", *American Economic Review*, September 1952, pp. 602–608.

Fu, Poshek. *Passivity, Resistance and Collaboration: Intellectual Choices in Occupied Shanghai 1937–1945*. Stanford, CA: Stanford University Press, 1993.

Fudan University Catalogue 私立復旦大學一覽, 1937 (Chinese language).

Galbraith, John Kenneth. *A China Passage*. Boston: Houghton Mifflin, 1973.

Galenson, Walter, ed. *Economic Growth and Structural Change in Taiwan*. Ithaca: Cornell University Press, 1979.

Gamble, Sidney. *How Chinese Families Live in Peiping*. New York: Funk and Wagnalls, 1933.

———. *Ting Hsien: A North China Rural Community*. New York: Institute of Pacific Relations, 1954.

——— and John S. Burgess. *Peking: A Social Survey*. New York: George H. Doran, 1921.

Gasster, Michael. "Reform and Revolution in China's Political Modernization", in Wright, ed., 1968, pp. 67–96.

"General Condition of All the Universities of the Country" (mimeo, 1931). Yale Divinity School, RG 51, Box 309, Folder 4762.

George, Henry. *Progress and Poverty*. New York: Schalkenbach Foundation, 1960 (orig. 1879).

[German Ministry of Education]. *Jahresverzeichnis der Deutschen Hochschulschriften* [Annual Directory of Dissertations in German Higher Education], 1912–1950.

Gillard, L. and Michel M. Rosier. *Francois Simiand (1873–1935): Sociologie, Histoire, Economie*. Paris: Editions des Archives Contemporaine, 1996.

Gillin, Donald G. "China's First Five-year Plan: Industrialization under the Warlords as Reflected in the Policies of Yen Hsi-Shan in Shansi Province, 1930–1937", *Journal of Asian Studies*, 24:2 (February, 1965), pp. 245–259.

Goldman, Merle. *China's Intellectuals: Advise and Dissent*. Cambridge, MA: Harvard University Press, 1981.

Granet, Marcel. *Chinese Civilization*. Kathleen Innes and Mabel Brailsford, trans. London: Routledge and Kegan Paul, 1930.

Gray, Jack. *Rebellions and Revolutions: China from the 1800s to the 1980s*. New York: Oxford University Press, 1980.

Gregor, A. James and Maria Hsia Chang. "The Thought of Sun Yat-Sen in Comparative Perspective", in Cheng, ed., 1988, pp. 103–137.

Gregor, A. James, Maria Hsia Chang, and Andrew B. Zimmerman. *Ideology and Development: Sun Yat-Sen and the Economic History of Taiwan*. Berkeley: University of California, 1981.

———. *Essays on Sun Yat-Sen and the Economic Development of Taiwan*. Baltimore: Maryland International Law Society, 1983.

Grieder, Jerome B. *Intellectuals and the State in Modern China*. New York: Free Press, 1981.

Grossekettler, Heinz G. "On Designing an Economic Order. The Contributions of the Freiburg School", in Walker, ed., 1989, pp. 38–84.

Gunn, Selskar. "China Diary" 1931; typescript. RA; RG 1, Series 601, Box 12, Folder 129.

Gurvitch, George and Wilbert Moore, eds. *Twentieth Century Sociology*. Freeport, NY: Books for Libraries Press, 1971 (orig. 1945).

Hageman, Harald, ed. *Zur Deutschsprachenigen Wirtschaftswissenschaftlichen Emigration nach 1933* (The Emigration of German-Speaking Economists after 1933). Marburg: Metropolis-Verlag, 1997.

Halpern, Nina P. "Economic Specialists and the Making of Chinese Economic Policy, 1955–1983". PhD dissertation, University of Michigan, 1985.

Hamouda, O. F. *John R. Hicks: The Economists' Economist*. Cambridge: Blackwell, 1993.

Hamrin, Carol Lee and Timothy Cheek, eds. *China's Establishment Intellectuals*. White Plains, NY: M. E. Sharpe, 1986.

The Handbook of the Chinese Students in U.S.A. New York: Chinese Students Handbook Co., various years 1924–35.

Handy, Robert. *The Social Gospel in America 1870–1920*. New York: Oxford University Press, 1966.

Harris, Abram L. "Sombart and German (National) Socialism", *Journal of Political Economy*, 50:6 (December, 1941), pp. 805–835.

Harrod, Roy. *The Life of John Maynard Keynes*. New York: Harcourt Brace, 1951.

Hawtrey, Ralph G. "The Need for Faith", *The Economic Journal*, 56:223 (September, 1946), pp. 351–365.
Hayek, Friedrich A. "The London School of Economics 1895–1945", *Economica*, No. 49 (February, 1946), pp. 1–31.
———. *Individualism and Economic Order*. Chicago: University of Chicago Press, 1948.
Hayford, Charles W. *To the People: James Yen and Village China*. New York: Columbia University Press, 1990.
———. "The Good Earth, Revolution, and the American Raj in China", in Lipscomb, Webb, and Conn , eds., 1994, pp. 19–27.
Hayhoe, Ruth. "Towards the Forging of a Chinese University Ethos: Zhendan and Fudan, 1903–1919", *China Quarterly* 94 (June, 1983), pp. 323–341.
———. "Catholics and Socialists: The Paradox of French Educational Interaction with China", in Hayhoe and Bastid, eds., 1987, pp. 97–119, 302–308.
———. "Chinese Universities and the Social Sciences", *Minerva*, 31:4 (1993), pp. 478–503.
———. *China's Universities, 1895–1995: A Century of Cultural Conflict*. New York: Garland Press, 1996.
——— and Marianne Bastid, eds. *China's Education and the Industrialized World*. Armonk, NY: M. E. Sharpe, 1987.
Hebert, Robert F., ed. *Perspectives on the History of Economic Thought*. Brookfield, VT: Edward Elgar, 1993.
Hedlund, Glenn. Oral history interview with Gould Colman, 1962, Cornell University Archives.
Heimann, Eduard. "Franz Oppenheimer's Economic Ideas", *Social Research*, 11:1 (February, 1944), pp. 27–39.
Hennock, E. P. "Concepts of Poverty in the British Social Surveys from Charles Booth to Arthur Bowley", in Bulmer et al., eds., 1991, pp. 189–216.
Herschede, Fred. "Economics as an Academic Discipline at Nanjing University", *China Quarterly* No.102 (June, 1985), pp. 304–316.
Hewa, Soma, and Philo Hove, eds. *Philanthropy and Cultural Context*. Lanham, MD: University Press of America, 1997.
Hicks, John R. Review of Simiand, *Le Salaire*, *Economic Journal*, September, 1932, pp. 451–474.
Hipps, John B. *History of the University of Shanghai*. Board of Founders, 1964.
History of Fudan University 復旦大學志. Shanghai: Fudan Daixue Chubanshe, 1985 (Chinese language; Beijing National Library).
History of Social Sciences in Nanjing 南京社會科學志 (Chinese language).
Ho, Franklin. "An Index of the Physical Volume of Foreign Trade in China, 1868–1927", in *Problems of the Pacific*, J. B. Condliffe, ed., 1930, pp. 300–312.
——— and H. D. Fong. "Industrialization in China: A Study of Conditions in Tientsin" (pamphlet). Tientsin: Nankai, 1929a.

———. "Extent and Effects of Industrialization in China" (pamphlet). Tientsin: Nankai, 1929b.

———. "Industries", in Chen Zen, ed., 1931, pp. 237–280.

———. "Analysis of Chinese Economy and its Way Out" 中國經濟病症之解剖與診斷, *Quarterly Journal of Economics and Political Science*, 4:2 (January, 1936a), pp. 227–259 (Chinese language).

———. "Rural Economic Reconstruction in China" (pamphlet). Shanghai: China Institute of Pacific Relations, 1936b.

———. "Reminiscences of Ho Lien [Franklin L. Ho]" (typescript). Special Collections, Columbia University Libraries, 1967.

Ho, Samuel P. S. *Economic Development of Taiwan, 1860–1970*. New Haven: Yale University Press, 1978.

Hofheinz, Roy Jr. and Kent E. Calder. *The Eastasia Edge*. New York: Basic Books, 1982.

Holcombe, Arthur N. *The Chinese Revolution*. Cambridge, MA: Harvard University Press, 1930.

Holden, Reuben. *Yale in China*. New Haven: Yale in China Association, 1964.

Holland, W. L. "Supplementary Note on I. P. R. Research in China", *Pacific Affairs*, 17:2 (June, 1944), pp. 217–218.

Hou Chia-chu. "The Structure and Determinants of Tenure System in Modern China: 1900–1940", in Hou and Yu, eds., 1979, pp. 163–182.

——— and Tzong-shian Yu, eds. *Modern Chinese Economic History*. Taipei: Academia Sinica, 1979.

Hou Chi-ming. "Some Reflections on the Economic History of Modern China (1840–1949)", *Journal of Economic History* 23:4 (December, 1963), pp. 595–605.

———. *Foreign Investment and Economic Development in China 1840–1937*. Cambridge, MA: Harvard University Press, 1965.

———. "Manpower, Employment and Unemployment", in Eckstein, Galenson, and Liu, eds., 1968, pp. 329–396.

———. "Sun Yat-sen's Economic Philosophy and Policy", in Sih, ed., 1974, pp. 91–117.

Hou Ho-ji and Wu Chi-jin. 1984. *Modern Chinese Economic Thought* 中國近代經濟思想史稿, vol. 3, Heilongjiang (Chinese language).

Howard, M. C. and King, J. E. *A History of Marxian Economics*, vol. II, 1929–1990. Princeton: Princeton University Press, 1992.

Hoxie, R. Gordon, ed. *A History of the Faculty of Political Science, Columbia University*. New York: Columbia University Press. 1955.

Hoyt, Edwin P. *Korea 1950: The Day the Chinese Attacked*. Minnesota: Paragon House, 1990.

Hsia, Ronald Hsiu-yung. "The Intellectual and Public Life of Ma Yin-chu", *China Quarterly*, No. 6 (April–June, 1961), pp. 53–63.

Hsiao Kung-chuan. *A Modern China and a New World: Kang Yu-wei, Reformer and Utopian, 1858–1927*. Seattle: University of Washington Press, 1975.

Hsiao, Theodore E. *The History of Modern Education in China*. Shanghai: Commercial Press, 1935.

Hsieh, Winston. "An Unfinished Pyramid in the Field of Twentieth Century Chinese Studies", *Journal of Asian Studies* 31:3 (March, 1972), pp. 615–631.

Hsin Ying. "The Theory of Industrial Development in Economically Undeveloped Areas". PhD dissertation, University of Michigan, 1947.

Hsu, Robert C. *Chinese Economic Theories, 1979–1988*. New York: Cambridge University Press, 1991.

Hsu Yung-ying. "Critics of Economic Control in China", *Pacific Affairs*, 15:2 (June, 1942), pp. 222–229.

Hu, C. T. "The Chinese People's University: Bastion of Marxism-Leninism", in Niblett and Butts, eds., 1972, pp. 63–74.

Hu Jichuang. "Basic Economic Theories of China from the 1920s to the 1940s" 二十–四十年代中國的經濟基本理論, *Learned Journal of Beijing Institute of Trade and Finance*, September 1982, pp. 52–69 (Chinese language).

———. *Outline of Modern History of Chinese Economic Thought* 中國近代經濟思想史大綱, v. 3. Beijing: China Social Science Press, 1984 (Chinese language).

———. *A Concise History of Chinese Economic Thought*. Beijing: Foreign Languages Press, 1988.

Hu Sien-tsin. "Inflation and Inflation Control in China, 1937–1947". PhD dissertation, University of Illinois, 1948.

Hu, Teh-wei. *The State of American Economic Studies in the People's Republic of China* (mimeo). Washington: U.S. Information Agency, 1984.

Huang, Andrew Chung. "The Inflation in China", *Quarterly Journal of Economics*, 62:3 (August, 1948), pp. 562–575.

Huang Fu-ching. *Chinese Students in Japan in the Late Ch'ing Period*. Tokyo: Centre for East Asian Cultural Studies, 1982.

Huang Hua. "A True Account of John Stuart's Departure from China", *Beijing Review*, 33:43 (October 22–28, 1990), pp. 32–35.

Huang, Philip C. C. *The Peasant Family and Rural Development in the Yangtze Delta, 1350–1988*. Stanford, CA: Stanford University Press, 1990.

———. "A Reply to Ramon Myers", *Journal of Asian Studies*, 50:3 (August, 1991), pp. 629–633.

Huang Sung Kang. *Li Ta-chao and the Impact of Marxism on Modern Chinese Thinking*. Paris: Mouton, 1965.

Huenemann, Ralph William. *The Dragon and the Iron Horse: The Economics of Railroads in China, 1876–1937*. Cambridge, MA: Harvard University Press, 1984.

Hughes, T. J. and D. E. T. Luard. *The Economic Development of Communist China, 1949–1958*. London: Oxford University Press, 1959.

Hunt, Michael H. "Pearl Buck—Popular Expert on China, 1931–1949", *Modern China*, 3:1 (January, 1977), pp. 33–64.

Ikeo, Aiko. "Japanese Modern Economics, 1930–1945", in Hebert, ed., 1993, pp. 192–202.

———. "The Internationalization of Economics in Japan", in Coats, ed., 1997, pp. 123–141.

Ingram, John Kells. *A History of Political Economy*. New York: Macmillan, 1888, 1915.

Israel, John, ed. "Draft History of Qinghua University", *Chinese Education*, 15:3–4 (Fall–Winter, 1982–83).

Israel, John. "The Idea of Liberal Education in China", in Morse, ed., 1983, pp. 89–117.

——— and Donald W. Klein. *Rebels and Bureaucrats: China's December 9ers*. Berkeley: University of California Press, 1976.

Joffe, Josef. "Swarthmore and Liberal Arts", in "Voices from Swarthmore" (pamphlet), Swarthmore College, 2000.

Johnson, Harry G. *The Shadow of Keynes: Understanding Keynes, Cambridge and Keynesian Economics*. Oxford: Blackwell, 1978.

Jones, Byrd L. "A Quest for National Leadership: Institutionalization of Economics at Harvard", in Barber 1988, pp. 95–131.

Kelley, Brooks Mather. *Yale: A History*. New Haven: Yale University Press, 1974.

Kindermann, Gottfried-Karl. "Sun Yat-senism as a Model for Syncretistic Ideologies of Developing Countries", in Lowenthal, ed., 1969, pp. 149–176.

King, Wei-shin. "Republic of China's System of Land Taxation", in Lindholm and Lin, 1977, pp. 56–66.

Kirby, William C. "Kuomintang China's 'Great Leap Outward': The 1936 Three Year Plan for Industrial Development", *Illinois Papers in Asian Studies* II, 1983, pp. 43–66.

———. *Germany and Republican China*. Stanford: Stanford University Press, 1984.

Klehr, Harvey and Ronald Radosch. *The Amerasia Spy Case*. Chapel Hill: University of North Carolina, 1996.

Klein, Donald W. and Anne B. Clark. *Biographic Dictionary of Chinese Communism, 1921–1965*. Cambridge, MA: Harvard University Press, 1971.

Klein, Judy L. and Mary S. Morgan, eds. *The Age of Economic Measurement*. Durham, NC: Duke University Press, 2001.

Klein, Lawrence. *The Keynesian Revolution*. New York: Macmillan, 1947.

Klein, Lawrence R., Marc Nerlove, and S. C. Tsiang. "Ta-Chung Liu, 1914–1975", in *Quantitative Economics and Development: Essays in Memory of Ta-Chung Liu*, Klein, Nerlove, and Tsiang, eds. New York: Academic Press, 1980, pp. xiii–xix.

Koung Shien-ming. *Comment Remedier a la Situation Tragique des Travailleurs*

Chinois (How to Remedy the Tragic Condition of Chinese Workers). Louvain: Desbarax, 1927.

Kreissler, Francoise. "Technical Education as Keys to Cultural Cooperation: The Sino-German Experience", in Hayhoe and Bastid, eds., op. cit., 1987, pp. 81–96.

Kuhn, Philip A. "The Development of Local Government", in Fairbank and Feuerwerker, eds., 1986, pp. 329–360.

Kuno, Yoshi S. "Educational Institutions in the Orient with Special Reference to Colleges and Universities in the United States; Part II: Chinese Educational Institutions". Berkeley: University of California, mimeo, 1928.

Lai Cheng-chung. "European Cooperativism in Chinese Perspective", *Annals of Public and Co-operative Economy*, 59:3 (July–September, 1988), pp. 369–377.

———. *Adam Smith and Yen Fu: Western Economics in Chinese Perspective*. Sinchu (Taiwan): National Tsing Hua University, 1997.

———, ed. *Adam Smith Across Nations*. Oxford: Oxford University Press, 2000.

——— and Paul B. Trescott. "Liang Qichao, Sun Yatsen, and the 1905–7 Debate on Socialism", *International Journal of Social Economics*, 32:12 (December, 2005), pp. 1051–1062.

Lamberton, Mary. *St. John's University, Shanghai, 1879–1951*. New York: United Board, 1955.

Lampman, Robert J., ed. *Economists at Wisconsin: 1892–1992*. Madison: University of Wisconsin Press, 1993.

Lardy, Nicholas R. "Food Consumption in the People's Republic of China", in Barker, Sinha, and Rose, eds., 1982, pp. 147–162.

Lasker, Bruno and W. H. Holland, eds. *Problems of the Pacific, 1933*. Chicago: University of Chicago Press, 1934.

Lavely, William, James Lee, and Wang Feng. "Chinese Demography: The State of the Field", *Journal of Asian Studies* 49:4 (November, 1990), pp. 807–834.

Lavely, William and R. Bin Wong. "Revising the Malthusian Narrative: The Comparative Study of Population Dynamics in Late Imperial China", *Journal of Asian Studies*, 57:3 (August, 1998), pp. 714–748.

League of Nations. "Report . . . by the Director of the Section for Communications and Transit . . . on his Mission to China", Geneva, 1935.

Leavens, Dickson. *Silver Money*. Bloomington, IN: Pantagraph Press, 1939.

Lee, James Z. and Wang Feng. *One Quarter of Humanity: Malthusian Mythology and Chinese Realities, 1700–2000*. Cambridge, MA: Harvard University Press, 1999.

———, Cameron Campbell, and Wang Feng. "Positive Checks or Chinese Checks?", *Journal of Asian Studies*, 61:2 (May, 2002), pp. 591–607.

Lee, Shison. Review of Tung, *Agricultural Economics, Nankai Social and Economics Quarterly*, v. 8 (1935), pp. 409–411.

Lee Shu-ching. "The Theory of the Agricultural Ladder", *Agricultural History*, 21: 1 (January, 1947a), pp. 53–61.

———. "Pattern of Land Utilization and Possible Expansion of Cultivated Area in China", *Journal of Land and Public Utility Economics*, 23:2 (May, 1947b), pp. 142–152.

———. "The Heart of China's Problem, The Land Tenure System", *Journal of Farm Economics*, 30:2 (May, 1948), pp. 259–270.

Lehmann, Gunther. *Mathematisch-graphische Untersuchung uber die Rentabilitatsverhaltnisse von Frachtschiffen* (Mathematical-graphical Investigation of the Rate of Return from Freight Shipments). Berlin: Triltsch and Huthbert, 1935.

Leng, Shao Chuan and Norman D. Palmer. *Sun Yat-sen and Communism*. New York: Praeger, 1960.

Leonard, Robert. "'Between Worlds', or an Imagined Reminiscence by Oskar Morgenstern on Equilibrium and Mathematics in the 1920s", *Journal of the History of Economic Thought*, 26:3 (September, 2004), pp. 285–310.

Levenson, Joseph R. *Liang Ch'i-ch'ao and the Mind of Modern China*. Cambridge, MA: Harvard University Press, 1959.

Levi-Strauss, Claude. "French Sociology", in Gurvitch and Moore, eds., 1971, pp. 503–537.

Lewis, W. Arthur. *The Theory of Economic Growth*. London: George Allen and Unwin, 1955.

Li, Anthony C. *The History of Privately Controlled Higher Education in the Republic of China*. Washington: Catholic University, 1954.

Li, Choh-ming. "The Effect of Depreciated Exchange upon Merchandise Movements", *Quarterly Journal of Economics*, 49:3 (May, 1935), pp. 495–502.

———. "The Theory of International Trade under Silver Exchange", *Quarterly Journal of Economics*, 51:4 (August, 1939), pp. 491–521.

———. Review of *An Outline of International Price Theories* by Chi-yuen Wu, *Nankai Social and Economic Quarterly* 12:1 (January, 1941), pp. 200–203.

———. "Economic and Social Research in Wartime China", *Pacific Affairs*, 17:2 (June, 1944), pp. 209–216.

———. "Inflation in Wartime China", *Review of Economics and Statistics*, 27:1 (February, 1945), pp. 23–33.

———. "International Trade", in MacNair, ed., 1946, pp. 492–506.

———. *Economic Development of Communist China*. Berkeley: University of California Press, 1959.

———. *Statistical System of Communist China*. Berkeley: University of California Press, 1962.

Li Chuan-shih. *Principles of Business Economics*. Shanghai: Commercial Press, 1924.

———. *Business Statistics*. Shanghai: Commercial Press, 1927.

Li, K. T. *My Views on Taiwan's Economic Development*. Taipei, 1980.

———. *The Evolution of Policy behind Taiwan's Development Success*. New Haven: Yale, 1988.

Liang, Ernest P. *China: Railways and Agricultural Development, 1875–1935*. Department of Geography, University of Chicago Research Paper No. 203, 1982.

Liang, Hsi-huey. *The Sino-German Connection*. Amsterdam: van Gorcum, 1978.

Liang Qichao. "Concise History of Economic Thought" (orig. 1903), *Yin-ping-shih Wen-chi* 飲冰室文集, 12, 1–61 (Chinese language).

———. "Is Social Revolution Necessary to Today's China?"「社會革命果為今日中國所必要」, *Xinmin Congbao* 新民叢報 86: 5–52, 1906a (Chinese language).

———. "More Refutations of Minbao's Views on Land Nationalization"「再駁某報之土地國有論」, *Xinmin Congbao*, nos. 90–92 (1906b), Chinese language. Most reprinted in the *Collected Writings of Liang Qichao* 19:1–54.

———. "On the Circumstances of the Struggle of Peoples" (orig. 1902–03), *Yin-ping-shih Ho-chi Wen-chi* 飲冰室合集文集, 4, 10–35 (Chinese language), 1916. Note: the foregoing are various editions of Liang's collected works, all whimsically identified as "Yin-ping-shih": "From the Ice-Drinker's Studio". Date, publisher, place are not always shown.

Lieberthal, Kenneth. *Revolution and Tradition in Tientsin 1949–1952*. Stanford: Stanford University Press, 1980.

Lieu, D. K. "A Brief Account of Statistical Work in China", *Bulletin de l'Institut International de Statistique*, 25:2 (1931), pp. 88*–121*.

———. *The Growth and Industrialization of Shanghai*. Shanghai: China Institute of Economic and Statistical Research, 1936.

———. *China's Economic Stabilization and Reconstruction*. New Brunswick: Rutgers University Press, 1948.

Lin, Cyril Chihren. "The Reinstatement of Economics in China Today", *China Quarterly*, no. 85 (March, 1981), pp. 1–48.

Lin, Peter Wei. "A Statistical Study of the Personnel of the Chinese National Government", *Bulletin de l'Institut International de Statistique*, 25:2 (1931), pp. 135*–208*.

Lin, Sein. "Sun Yat-sen and Henry George: The Essential Role of Land Policy in their Doctrines", *American Journal of Economics and Sociology*, 33:2 (April, 1972), pp. 201–220.

Lin Sung-ho. *Factory Workers in Tangku*. Peiping: China Foundation, 1928.

Lin Wei-ying. *China under Depreciated Silver 1926–1935*. Shanghai: Commercial Press, 1935.

———. "Behavior of Prices in China since the War", *China Quarterly*, 4:2 (Spring, 1939), pp. 265–276.

Lindholm, Richard W. and Sein Lin. *Henry George and Sun Yat-sen: Application and Evolution of their Land Use Doctrine*. Cambridge, MA: Lincoln Institute, 1977.

Lindsay, Michael. "The Oxford Modern Greats Course and its Application to Yenching", *Chinese Social and Political Science Review*, 12:1 (April–June, 1938), pp. 59–71.

———. *Notes on Educational Problems in Communist China, 1941–47*. Westport, CN: Greenwood Press, 1977 (orig. 1950).

———. *China and the Cold War*. Melbourne: Melbourne University Press, 1955.

———. "Agrarian Policy and Communist Motivation", *China Quarterly*, no. 1 (January–March, 1960), pp. 15–17.

———. *The Unknown War: North China, 1937–1945*. London: Bergstrom and Boyle, 1975.

Lipscomb, Elizabeth J., Frances E. Webb, and Peter Conn, eds. *The Several Worlds of Pearl Buck*. Westport, CN: Greenwood Press, 1994.

Little, Ian D. "An Economic Renaissance", in Galenson, ed., 1979, pp. 448–507.

Liu Shui Sheng (pseud.). "Life in a Chinese University", *Atlantic Monthly*, 204:6 (June, 1959), pp. 89–92.

Liu Ta-chung. *China's National Income 1931–36*. Washington: Brookings, 1946.

———, C. Twanmo, and K. C. Yeh. *Production of Food Crops on the Chinese Mainland: Prewar and Postwar*. Santa Monica: Rand Corporation, 1964.

——— and Kung-chia Yeh. *The Economy of the Chinese Mainland: National Income and Economic Development, 1933–1959*. Princeton: Princeton University Press 1965.

Liu Zhinan and Zhang Jianmin, eds. *Biographies of Contemporary Chinese Economists* 當代中國經濟學家錄. Guangzhou: Guangdong People's Publishing House, 1987 (Chinese Language).

Lo, Jung-pang, ed. *K'ang Yu-wei: a Biography and a Symposium*. Tucson: University of Arizona Press, 1967.

Loh, Robert. *Escape from Red China*. New York: Coward-McCann, 1962.

Lowenthal, Richard, ed. *Issues in the Future of Asia*. New York: Praeger, 1969.

Lund, Renville C. "The Imperial University of Peking". PhD dissertation, University of Washington, 1956.

Lunt, Carroll, ed. *The China Who's Who (Foreign)*. Shanghai: Kelly and Walsh, 1925.

Lutz, Jessie Gregory. *China and the Christian Colleges 1850–1950*. Ithaca: Cornell University Press, 1971.

———. "Karl F. A. Gutzlaff: Missionary Entrepreneur", in Barnett and Fairbank, eds., 1985, pp. 61–87.

MacCormick, Brian J. *Hayek and the Keynesian Avalanche*. New York: St. Martin's, 1992.

MacFarquhar, Roderick, ed. *The Hundred Flowers*. London: Atlantic Books, 1960.

MacNair, Harley F., ed. *Voices from Unoccupied China*. Chicago: University of Chicago Press, 1944.

———, ed. *China*. Berkeley: University of California Press, 1946.

Maddison, Angus. *Chinese Economic Performance in the Long Run*. Paris: OECD, 1998.

Mallory, Walter H. "Rural Cooperative Credit in China", *Quarterly Journal of Economics*, 45:3 (May, 1931), pp. 484–498.

Malone, Carroll B. and John B. Tayler. "The Study of Chinese Rural Economy", *Chinese Social and Political Science Review*, 7:4 (October, 1923), pp. 88–101; 8:1 (January, 1924), pp. 196–212; 8:2 (April, 1924), pp. 230–259.

Mao Tse-tung. "On the People's Democratic Dictatorship" (orig. 1949), in *Selected Works of Mao Tse-tung*. Peking: Foreign Language Press, 1975, IV, pp. 411–424.

Mao, Y. K. "Discussion of 'Henry George, His Enduring Contribution to Progress'", in Lindholm and Lin, 1977, pp. 52–53.

Martin, Michael F. "Rural Living Conditions in Pre-Liberation China: A Survey of Three Recent Studies", *Journal of Peasant Studies*, 19:1 (October, 1991), pp. 122–137.

Mason, Edward S. "The Harvard Department of Economics from the Beginning to World War II", *Quarterly Journal of Economics*, 97:3 (August, 1982), pp. 383–433.

Meier, Gerald M., ed. *From Classical Economics to Development Economics*. New York: St. Martin's Press, 1994.

Meisner, Maurice. *Li Ta-chao and the Origins of Chinese Marxism*. Cambridge, MA: Harvard University Press, 1967.

[Ministry of Education, China]. "Required Courses for Colleges" 教育部〈大學科目表〉, 1940 (Chinese language).

———. "Name List of Teachers in 3-year Colleges and Above"「專科以上學校教員名冊第一冊」(Chinese language), 1942.

Minyi 民意 (Hu Hanmin 胡漢民 and Wang Jingwei 汪精衛). "Reply to the Criticism of Socialism in Xinmin Congbao no. 86"「告非難民生主義者」(駁〈新民業刊〉第四年14號社會主義論), *Minbao* 民報 12: 45–155, 1907 (Chinese language).

Moggridge, Donald E. "The Diffusion of the Keynesian Revolution: The Young and the Graduate Schools", in Cottrell, ed., 1995, pp. 223–241.

Morgan, Mary S. and Malcolm Rutherford, eds. *From Interwar Pluralism to Postwar Neoclassicism*. Durham, NC: Duke University Press, 1998.

Morse, Ronald A., ed. *The Limits of Reform in China*. Boulder, CO: Westview Press, 1983.

Musgrave, Richard A. "Crossing Traditions", in Hagemann, ed., 1997, pp. 63–80.

Myers, Ramon. *The Chinese Peasant Economy*. Cambridge, MA: Harvard University Press, 1970.

———. *Selected Essays in Chinese Economic Development*. New York: Garland Press, 1980.

———, ed. *Bulletins of the Social Research Department 1928–1933*. New York: Garland Publishing Co., 1982, pp. 3–16.

———. "The Principle of People's Welfare: A Multidimensional Concept", in Cheng, ed., 1989.

———. "How Did the Modern Chinese Economy Develop? A Review Article", *Journal of Asian Studies*, 50:3 (August, 1991), pp. 604–628.

Nance, W. B. *Soochow University*. New York: United Board, 1956.

"Nankai Institute of Economics: Its History and Work 1927–1936". Tientsin: The Institute, June, 1937 (pamphlet).

Nankai University Doctoral Programs and Advisors. Tianjin, Nankai University, 1990.

Nathan, Andrew J. *A History of the China International Famine Relief Commission*. Cambridge, MA: Harvard University Press, 1965.

———. 1985. *Chinese Democracy*. New York: Knopf.

National Sun Yat-sen University. *The National Sun Yat-sen University: A Short History*. Canton: the University, 1936 (Beida Library).

National Union Catalog: Pre-1956 Imprints. London: Mansell, 1973.

Naughton, Barry J. "Sun Yefang: Toward a Reconstruction of Socialist Economics", in Hamrin and Cheek, eds., 1986, pp. 124–148.

Niblett, W. Roy and R. Freeman Butts, eds. *Universities Facing the Future*. San Francisco: Jossey-Bass, 1972.

Orleans, Leo. "Education and Scientific Manpower", in Fraser, ed., 1971, pp. 363–388.

———. "Soviet Influence on China's Higher Education", in Hayhoe and Bastid, eds., 1987, pp. 184–198.

Ou Pao-san. "Recent Discussion on China's Food Problem", *Pacific Affairs*, 15:3 (September, 1942), pp. 345–359.

———. "International Payments in National Income", *Quarterly Journal of Economics*, 40:2 (February, 1946a), pp. 289–298.

———. "A New Estimate of China's National Income", *Journal of Political Economy*, 54:6 (December, 1946b), pp. 547–554.

——— and Wang Foh-shen. "Industrial Production and Employment in Pre-war China", *Economic Journal* 56, 223 (September, 1946), pp. 426–434.

Ou Tsuin-chen. "Education in Wartime China", in Sih, ed., 1977, pp. 89–123.

Pang Bin-chin. *Der Aussenhandel zwischen Deutschland und China und die deutsch-chinesische Aussenhandelspolitik* (Trade between Germany and China and Sino-German Trade Policy). Erlangen: Richard Weissman, 1937.

Payne, Robert. *Forever China*. New York: Dodd, Mead, 1945.

Peake, Cyrus. *Nationalism and Education in Modern China*. New York: Howard Fertig, 1970 (orig. 1932).

Pearson, Heath. "Was There Really a German Historical School of Economics?", *History of Political Economy* 31:3 (Fall, 1999), pp. 547–567.

Peck, Graham. *Two Kinds of Time*. Boston: Houghton Mifflin, 1950.

Peiping University. *Name List of Faculty and Staff* 國立北平大學教職員錄, 1933.

Peking Government University. *Preparatory College Bulletin*, June, 1915 (Union Theological Seminary).

Peking University. *Graduation Commemoration Book* 畢業同學紀念冊, 1925 (Chinese language).

———. *A Survey of National Peking University* 國立北京大學一覽, 1933 (Chinese language).

———. *Peking University Graduates, 1911–1948*, 1948 (Chinese language).

———. *History of Peking University 1898–1949* 北京大學校史（1898–1949）. Beijing: Peking University Press (Chinese language), 1984.

———. College of Law, Department of Economics, Catalogue of Courses 法律學院經濟學系課程一覽, 1935 (Chinese language).

Pelzer, Karl J. *An Economic Survey of the Pacific Area; Part I. Population and Land Utilization*. Shanghai: China Institute of Pacific Relations, 1941.

"People's University of China" (brochure, the university), Beijing, 1990.

Perkins, Dwight H. *Market Control and Planning in Communist China*. Cambridge, MA: Harvard University Press, 1966.

———. "Government as an Obstacle to Industrialization: The Case of Nineteenth-Century China", *Journal of Economic History* 27:4 (December, 1967), pp. 478–492.

———. *Agricultural Development in China*. Chicago: Aldine Publishing Co., 1969.

———, ed. *China's Modern Economy in Historical Perspective*. Stanford: Stanford University Press, 1975.

———. "Reforming China's Economic System", *Journal of Economic Literature*, 26:2 (June, 1988), pp. 601–645.

Perleberg, Max, ed. *Who's Who in Modern China*. Hong Kong: Ye Olde Printerie Press Ltd., 1954.

Persky, Joseph. "The Neo-Classical Advent: American Economics at the Dawn of the 20th Century", *Journal of Economic Perspectives*, 14:1 (Winter, 2000), pp. 95–108.

Pomeranz, Kenneth. *The Great Divergence: China, Europe, and the Making of the Modern World Economy*. Princeton: Princeton University Press, 2000.

Porter, Robin Scarland. "The Christian Conscience and Industrial Welfare in China". Unpublished PhD dissertation, University of London, 1977.

———. *Industrial Reformers in Republican China*. Armonk, NY: M. E. Sharpe, 1994.

Predohl, Andreas, ed. Symposium on China's Industrialization, *Weltwirtschaftliches Archiv*, 45:2 (March, 1937).

Pribram, Karl. "Employment Stabilization through Pay Roll Taxation", *Quarterly Journal of Economics*, 57:1 (November, 1942), pp. 142–152.

Price, Harry B. "Population Pressure in China", *Democracy*, 1:2 (May 15, 1937).

Prybyla, Jan S. *The Political Economy of Communist China*. Scranton: International Textbook Co., 1970.

Pu, Shou-shan. "A Note on Macroeconomics", *Econometrica*, 14:1 (January, 1946), pp. 299–302.

———. "Technological Progress and Employment". PhD dissertation, Harvard, 1949.

Pugh, Jim. "J. Lossing Buck, American Missionary: The Application of Scientific Agriculture in China, 1915–1944". Unpublished thesis, Swarthmore College, 1973 (copy in Presbyterian Historical Library, Philadelphia).

Putman, John J. "Special Economic Zones: China's Opening Door", *National Geographic*, 164:1 (July 1983), pp. 64–83.

Pye, Lucian W. "George E. Taylor (1905–2000)", *China Quarterly*, no. 163 (September, 2000), pp. 843–844.

Qinghua University. *Survey of Public Qinghua University: Course Catalogue*, 1935 (Chinese language).

———. *Draft History of Qinghua University*. Beijing: Zhonghua Publishing House (Chinese language).

———. *Selected Documents of History of Tsinghua University* 清華大學史料選編 (3 vols.). Beijing: Qinghua University, 1994 (Chinese language).

Rader, Benjamin G. *The Academic Mind and Reform: The Influence of Richard T. Ely in American Life*. Lexington: University Press of Kentucky, 1966.

Rawski, Thomas G. *Economic Growth in Prewar China*. Berkeley: University of California 1989.

Reder, Melvin W. "Chicago Economics: Permanence and Change", *Journal of Economic Literature*, 20:1 (March, 1982), pp. 1–38.

Register of Research in the Social Sciences (annual), 1943–50.

Remer, Charles F., ed. *Readings in Economics for China*, 2nd ed. Shanghai: Commercial Press, 1924 (orig. 1922).

"Research Notes", *Nankai Social and Economic Quarterly*, various issues.

Revolutionary-Mass-Criticism Group of Workers . . . "Criticism against Sun Yeh-fang and Struggle-Criticism-Transformation on the Economic Front", *Chinese Economic Studies*, 4:4 (Summer, 1971), pp. 255–267.

Reynolds, Bruce. "Observations on Six Months in the PRC", *China Exchange News*, 9:4 (December, 1981), pp. 5–8.

Reynolds, Douglas R. "The Chinese Industrial Cooperative Movement and the Political Polarization of Wartime China, 1938–1945". Unpublished PhD dissertation, Columbia University, 1975.

———. *China 1898–1912: The Xinzheng Revolution and Japan*. Cambridge, MA: Harvard University Press, 1993.

Reynolds, Lloyd G. "China's Economy: A View from the Grass Roots", *Chinese Economic Studies*, 8:3 (Spring, 1975), pp. 8–24.

Robbins, Lord [Lionel]. *Autobiography of an Economist*. London: Macmillan, 1971.

Robinson, Joan. *Letters from a Visitor to China*. Cambridge: Students' Bookshops, 1954.

———. *Economic Management in China*. London: Anglo-Chinese Educational Institute, 1975.

Rostow, Walt W. "Development as a Societal Problem in a Colonial Setting", in Meier, ed., 1994, pp. 144–172.

Roy, David Tod. *Kuo Mo-jo: The Early Years*. Cambridge, MA: Harvard University Press, 1971.

Rozwadowski, Franek. "From Recitation Room to Research Seminar: Political Economy at Columbia University", in Barber, 1988, pp. 169–202.

Rutherford, Malcolm. "Understanding Institutional Economics 1918–1929", *Journal of the History of Economic Thought*, 22:3 (September, 2000), pp. 277–308.

———. "Institutional Economics at Columbia University", *History of Political Economy*, 36:1 (Spring, 2004), pp. 31–78.

Salomon, Albert. "German Sociology", in Gurvitch and Moore, eds., 1971, pp. 586–614.

Sarvis, Guy W. "The Standard of Living in China and its Meaning", *Journal of Applied Sociology*, 9:3 (January–February, 1925a), pp. 187–195.

———. "The Social Situation in China", *Journal of Applied Sociology*, 9:4 (March–April, 1925b), pp. 277–282.

Scalapino, Robert and Harold Schiffrin. "Early Socialist Currents in the Chinese Revolutionary Movement", *Journal of Asian Studies*, 18:3 (May, 1959), pp. 321–342.

Schiffrin, Harold, "Sun Yat-Sen's Early Land Policy: The Origin and Meaning of Equalization of Land Rights", *Journal of Asian Studies*, 16:4 (August, 1957), pp. 549–564.

———. *Sun Yat-sen, Reluctant Revolutionary*. Boston: Little Brown, 1980.

——— and Pow-Key Sohn. "Henry George on Two Continents: A Comparative Study in the Diffusion of Ideas", *Comparative Studies in Society and History*, 2:1 (October, 1959), pp 85–109.

Schluter-Ahrens, Regina. *Der Volkswirt Jens Jessen* (The Political Economist Jens Jessen). Marburg: Metropolis-Verlag, 2002.

Schrader, David E. *The Corporation as Anomaly*. New York: Cambridge University Press, 1993.

Schran, Peter. *The Development of Chinese Agriculture, 1950–1959*. Urbana: University of Illinois, 1969.

Schumpeter, Joseph. *Capitalism, Socialism and Democracy*. New York: HarperPerennial, 1952.
———. *History of Economic Analysis*. New York: Oxford University Press, 1954.
Schwarcz, Vera. *The Chinese Enlightenment: Intellectuals and the Legacy of the May Fourth Movement of 1919*. Berkeley: University of California, 1986.
Schwartz, Benjamin. *In Search of Wealth and Power: Yen Fu and the West.* Belknap Press of Harvard University, 1964.
Scott, Roderick. *Fukien Christian University*. New York: United Board, 1954.
Seagrave, Sterling. *The Soong Dynasty*. New York: Harper and Row, 1985.
———. *Dragon Lady: The Life and Legend of the Last Empress of China*. New York: Knopf, 1992.
Seligman, Ben B. *Main Currents in Modern Economics*. Glencoe: Free Press, 1962.
Shao Bing-kun. "Methodology in the Development of Agricultural Economics in China". PhD dissertation, University of Wisconsin, 1950.
Sharman, Lyon. *Sun Yat-sen: His Life and its Meaning*. Hamden, CN: Archon Books, 1965.
Sheean, Vincent. *Personal History*. Boston: Houghton Mifflin, 1969 (orig. 1934).
Shen, T. H. *Agricultural Resources of China*. Ithaca: Cornell University Press, 1951.
———. *Agricultural Development on Taiwan since World War II*. Ithaca: Cornell University Press, 1964.
———. "Comment", in Hou and Yu, 1979, pp. 157–162.
Sheng T. [Chung]. "The Shanghai Wholesale Price Index Number" (pamphlet). Shanghai: Ministry of Finance, 1925.
Shewmaker, Kenneth E. *Americans and Chinese Communists: A Persuading Encounter*. Ithaca: Cornell University Press, 1971.
Sichuan University Catalogue 國立四川大學一覽, 1936.
Sih, Paul K.T., ed. *From Confucius to Christ*. St. John's University Press, 1952.
———, ed. *The Strenuous Decade: China's Nation-Building Efforts, 1927–1937*. New York: St. John's University Press, 1970.
———, ed. *Sun Yat-sen and China*. Jamaica, NY: St. John's Press, 1974.
———, ed. *Nationalist China during the Sino-Japanese War*. Hicksville, NY: Exposition Press, 1977.
Singer, Hans. "The Influence of Schumpeter and Keynes on the Development of a Development Economist", in Hagemann, 1997, pp. 127–150.
Sites, Clement Moore Lacey. "Syllabus of Introductory Economics: Comprising Production, Value and Distribution". Shanghai: Nanyang College, 1904 (Beida Library).
Skinner, G. William. "Marketing and Social Structure in Rural China, Part III", *Journal of Asian Studies*, 24:3 (May, 1965), pp. 363–399.
———. *Modern Chinese Society: an Analytical Bibliography*. Vol. 1: Publications

in western Languages, 1644–1972. Vol. 2 (with Winston Hsieh): Publications in Chinese, 1644–1969. Stanford, CA: Stanford University Press, 1973.

Slichter, Sumner. *Modern Economic Society*. New York: Henry Holt, 1931.

Slosson, Edwin E. *Great American Universities*. New York: Macmillan, 1910.

Smith, Adam. *The Wealth of Nations* [1776]. Oxford: Oxford University Press, 1976.

Snow, Edgar. *Red Star Over China*. New York: Random House, 1938.

———. *Journey to the Beginning*. New York: Random House, 1958.

Snow, Helen Foster. "Notes on the Chinese Student Movement" (typescript). Madison, CN: the author, 1961.

So Kwan-wei. "Western Influence and the Chinese Reform Movement of 1898". PhD dissertation, University of Wisconsin, 1950.

Social Science Biographical Directory 當代中國社會科學手冊. Ru Xi and Yi Kexin, eds. Beijing: Beijing Social Science Publishing House, 1989 (Chinese language).

Soothill, W. E. *China and the West*. London: Oxford University Press, 1925.

Southwest Associated Universities. *Documents* 國立西南聯合大學史料. Beijing, Peking University Library, 1998.

Spence, Jonathan. *To Change China: Western Advisers in China 1620–1960*. Boston: Little Brown, 1969.

———. *The Search for Modern China*. New York: W. W. Norton, 1990.

"State Plans for Industrial Development", *Chinese Economic Journal*, 15:2 (August, 1934).

Stein, Gunther. *The Challenge of Red China*. New York: McGraw-Hill, 1945.

Stepanek, Antoinette. *A Town Called Shaoyang: Witnessing Dynamic Changes in China*. Boulder, CO: Gold Hill Publications, 1992.

Stepanek, Joseph E. *A Town Called Shaoyang: Introducing Industry Appropriate to China*. Boulder, CO: Gold Hill Publications, 1992.

Stewart, Maxwell S. "China's Economic Challenge to the Missionary", *Chinese Recorder*, August, 1928, pp. 482–486

——— and Fang Fu-an. "A Statistical Study of Labor and Industry in China", *Chinese Economic Journal*, October 1930.

Stigler, George. *The Citizen and the State*. Chicago: University of Chicago, 1975.

Stolper, Wolfgang. "Facts without Planning", in Hagemann ed., 1997, pp. 95–126.

———. *Joseph Alois Schumpeter*. Princeton: Princeton University Press, 1994.

Stone, Lawrence, ed. *The University in Society*. Princeton: Princeton University Press, 1974.

Streeten, Paul. "An Autobiographical Sketch", in Hagemann, ed., 1997, pp. 177–206.

Stross, Randall. *The Stubborn Earth: American Agriculturalists on Chinese Soil, 1898–1937*. Berkeley: University of California, 1986.

Sun Ching-hsing. "The Development of the Social Sciences in China before 1949". PhD dissertation, Columbia University, 1987.

Sun, E-tu Zen. "The Growth of the Academic Community 1912–1949", in Fairbank and Feuerwerker, eds., 1986, pp. 361–420.

Sun Fo. *China Looks Forward*. New York: John Day, 1944.

———. "National Scheme of Railway Construction", *China Year Book, 1929–1930*, pp. 357–379.

Sun Yat-sen. *Memoirs of a Chinese Revolutionary: A Programme for National Reconstruction for China*. Phila: McKay, n.d. (prob. 1921).

———. "Socialism" [1914], in Remer, ed., 1924, pp. 659–661.

———. *The International Development of China*. London: Hutchinson, 1928 (orig. Eng. ed. 1922).

———. *San Min Chu I, The Three Principles of the People*. Translated by Frank Price. Chungking: Ministry of Information, 1943 (orig. 1927).

Ta-hsia (Great China) University Catalogue 大夏大學一覽, 1935 (Chinese language).

Tai Hung-chao, ed. *Confucianism and Economic Development: An Oriental Alternative?* Washington, DC: Washington Institute, 1989.

Tang, Anthony M. "Policy and Performance in Agriculture", in Eckstein, Galenson, and Liu, eds., 1968, pp. 459–507.

Tawney, Richard H. *Land and Labour in China*. London: George Allen and Unwin, 1932.

———, ed. *Agrarian China*. London: George Allen and Unwin, 1939.

Tayler, John B. "China's Industrial Future: Can She Develop a Distinctive Order?", *The World Tomorrow*, 6:11 (November, 1923), pp. 337–339.

———. "A Program for the Chinese Economic Society", *Chinese Social and Political Science Review* 10:4 (1926), pp. 845–859.

———. *Farm and Factory in China*. London: Student Christian Movement, 1928.

———. "A Policy for Small Scale Industry in China", in *The People's Livelihood*. National Christian Council: Shanghai, 1931, pp. 52–58.

———. "The Possibilities of Rural Industry in China", *Monthly Bulletin on Economic China*, 7:1 (January, 1934), pp. 47–59.

——— and W. T. Zung. "Labour and Industry in China", *International Labour Review*, 8:1 (July, 1923), pp. 1–20.

Tayler, Robert. *China's Intellectual Dilemma: Politics and University Enrolment*. Vancouver: University of British Columbia, 1981.

Taylor, Henry C. *An Introduction to the Study of Agricultural Economics*. New York: Macmillan, 1912 (orig. 1905).

——— and Anne Dewees Taylor. *The Study of Agricultural Economics in the United States, 1840–1932*. Ames: Iowa State University Press, 1952.

Teng Ssu-yu and John K. Fairbank, eds. *China's Response to the West*. New York: Atheneum, 1963.

Terrill, Ross. *R. H. Tawney and his Times*. Cambridge, MA: Harvard University Press, 1973.

Thompson, Laurence G. *Ta T'ung Shu: The One-World Philosophy of K'ang Yu-wei*. London: Allen and Unwin, 1958.

Thomson, James C. Jr. *While China Faced West: American Reformers in Nationalist China, 1928–1937*. Cambridge, MA: Harvard University Press, 1969.

———. "Pearl Buck and the American Quest for China", in Lipscomb, Webb, and Conn, 1994, pp. 7–15.

Thorbecke, Erik. "Agricultural Development", in Galenson, ed., 1979, pp. 132–205.

——— and Henry Wan, eds. *Taiwan's Development Experience: Lessons on Roles of Government and Markets*. Norwell, MA: Kluwer Academic Publishers, 1999.

Thurston, Anne F. and Jason H. Parker, eds. *Humanistic and Social Science Research in China: Recent History and Future Prospects*. New York: Social Science Research Council, 1980.

Thurston, Matilda and Ruth Chester. *Ginling College*. New York: United Board, 1955.

Tien, H. Yuan. *China's Population Struggle*. Columbus: Ohio State University Press, 1973.

Ting, Leonard G. Review of King, *Essays on China's Railway Problems*, *Nankai Social and Economic Quarterly*, 8:2 (July, 1935).

———. Review of Lieu 1936, *Nankai Social and Economic Quarterly*, 9:4 (January, 1937), pp. 1102–1105.

Tobin, James. "The Economy of China: A Tourist's View", *Chinese Economic Studies*, 8:3 (Spring, 1975), pp. 25–46.

Trescott, Paul B. "Scottish Political Economy Comes to the Far East: The Burton-Chambers Political Economy and the Introduction of Western Economic Ideas into Japan and China", *History of Political Economy*, 21:3 (Fall, 1989), pp. 481–502.

———. "Institutional Economics in China: Yenching University, 1917–1949", *Journal of Economic Issues* 26:4 (December, 1992), pp. 1221–1255.

———. "John Bernard Tayler and the Development of Cooperatives in China, 1917–1945", *Annals of Cooperative and Public Economics*, 64:2 (Spring, 1993), pp. 209–226.

———. "Henry George, Sun Yat-sen and China", *American Journal of Economics and Sociology*, 53:3 (July, 1994), pp. 363–374.

———. "Economics at China's Nankai University, 1926–1949", paper presented to History of Economics Society, South Bend, Indiana, June 1995.

———. "How Keynesian Economics Came to China", paper presented to Annual European Conference on the History of Economic Thought, Lisbon, February 10, 1996.

———. "American Philanthropy and the Development of Academic Economics in China before 1949", in Hewa and Hove, eds., 1997, pp. 157–181.

———. "Graduate Study in Economics by Chinese in the U.S., 1900–1950", *Taiwan Journal of Political Economy*, 3:1 (Fall, 2000), pp. 1–15.

———. "H. D. Fong and the Study of Chinese Economic Development", *History of Political Economy*, 34:4 (Winter, 2002), pp. 789–809.

———, Wang Jianye, and Yan Zhijie. "The Introduction of Western Economic Ideas into China", paper presented to History of Economics Society, Fairfax, VA, May, 1985.

——— and Zhaoping Wang. "Liang Chi-chao and the Introduction of Western Economic Ideas into China", *Journal of the History of Economic Thought*, 16 (Spring, 1994), pp. 126–145.

Tribe, Keith, ed. *Economic Careers: Economics and Economists in Britain 1930–1970*. London: Routledge, 1997.

Triviere, Leon. "Birth Control in China", *Contemporary China*, II (1956–57), pp. 94–99.

Tsiang Sho-chieh. "A Note on Speculation and Income Stability", *Economica*, N. S. November, 1943, pp. 286–296.

———. *The Variations of Real Wages and Profit Margins in Relation to the Trade Cycle*. London: Pitman, 1947.

———. "Exchange Rate, Interest Rate, and Economic Development: The Experience of Taiwan", in Klein, Nerlove, and Tsiang, eds., 1980, pp. 309–346.

———. "Fashions and Misconceptions in Monetary Theory and Their Influences on Financial and Banking Policies", in Tsiang, *Finance Constraints and the Theory of Money*. New York: Academic Press, 1989, pp. 107–130.

———. *The Reminiscences of Dr. S. C. Tsiang* 蔣碩傑先生訪問紀錄. Taipei: Academia Sinica, 1992 (Chinese language).

Tsien, Tsuen-hsuin. "Western Impact on China through Translation", *Far Eastern Quarterly*, 13:3 (May, 1954), pp. 305–327.

Tsui Shu-hsiang. "Chinese Economic Problems under Recent Discussion: I. Prices", *Nankai Social and Economic Quarterly*, 12:1 (January, 1941), pp. 183–195.

Tung Shih-tsin. *Communist China and the Chinese Problem*. Taipei: China Publishing Co., 1975.

van der Sprenkel, Otto B., Robert Guillain, and Michael Lindsay. *New China: Three Views*. New York: John Day, 1951.

van Slyke, Lyman. "Liang Sou-ming and the Rural Reconstruction Movement", *Journal of Asian Studies*, 18:5 (1959), pp. 457–474.

Wagner, Augusta, ed. *Yenching Readings in Economics*, n.d. (probably 1936 or 1937, Peking University Library).

———. *An Introduction to Economics for Chinese Students*. Peiping: Yenching University, 1938 (Peking University Library).

———. *Labor Legislation in China*. New York: Garland Press, 1981 (orig. 1938).

Walker, Donald A., ed. *Perspectives on the History of Economic Thought*. Brookfield, VT: Edward Elgar, 1989.

Walker, Kenneth. "Ideology and Economic Discussion in China: Ma Yin-chu on Development Strategy and his Critics", *Economic Development and Cultural Change*, 11:2 Part 1, (January, 1963), pp. 113–133.

Wan, Henry Jr. "The Market Transition in Taiwan: Any Relevance for PRC?". Unpublished MS, Cornell University, 1992.

Wang Foh-shen. "China's Industrial Production 1931–1946". Nanking: Institute of Social Sciences, Academia Sinica, 1948, reprinted in Myers, ed., 1980.

Wang, Gabe T. *China's Population: Problems, Thoughts and Policies*. Brookfield, VT: Ashgate Publishing Co., 1999.

Wang, George C. Editor's Introduction, *Chinese Economic Studies*, 12:3 (Spring, 1979), pp. 3–5.

Wang Wenjun, ed. *Historic Figures in Nankai* 南開人物志. Tianjin: Nankai University, 1994 (Chinese language).

Wang Yanan. "The Marxist Population Theory and China's Population Problem", *Chinese Economic Studies*, II:3, 4 (Spring/Summer, 1969).

Wang, Y. C. [Yi-chu]. "The Influence of Yen Fu and Liang Ch'i-ch'ao on the *San Min Chu I*", *Pacific Historical Review*, 34:2 (May, 1965), pp. 163–184.

———. *Chinese Intellectuals and the West*. Chapel Hill: University of North Carolina, 1966.

Wang, Zhaoping. "Shortages, Work Effort, and Price Adjustments—A Look at China's Economic Reforms since the late 1970s". PhD dissertation, Southern Illinois University, 1992.

——— and Paul B. Trescott. "Liang Chi-chao and the Introduction of Western Economic Ideas into China". Working Paper, Southern Illinois University, 1986.

Warren, George. *Farm Management*. New York: Macmillan, 1913.

Watson, Andrew. "Social Science Research and Economic Policy Formulation: The Academic Side of Economic Reform", in Yahuda, ed., 1987, pp. 67–88.

Wei, C. X. George. *Sino-American Economic Relations, 1944–1949*. Westport, CN: Greenwood Press, 1997.

Wei, Julie Lee, Ramon H. Myers, and Donald G. Gillin, eds. *Prescriptions for Saving China: Selected Writings of Sun Yat-sen*. Stanford, CA: Hoover Institution, 1994.

Wei Wen Pin. *The Currency Problem in China*. New York: Columbia University Press, 1914.

Weisz, George. *The Emergence of Modern Universities in France, 1863–1914*. Princeton: Princeton University Press, 1983.

West, Philip. *Yenching University and Sino-Western Relations, 1916–1952*. Cambridge, MA: Harvard University Press, 1976.

Who's Who in China. Shanghai: Weekly Review, 1920, 1925, 1931, 1936, 1940, 1950. Entire set reprinted 1973.

Who's Who of the Chinese Students in America. Berkeley, CA: Lederer, Street and Zeus, 1921.

Wieger, Leon. *Chine Moderne, II Le Flot Montant*. Hien-Hien, 1921.

———. *Chine Moderne, III Remous et Ecume*. Hien-Hien, 1922.

———. *Chine Moderne, Tome 1: Prodromes*. Hien-hien, 1931.

Wiens, Thomas B. "The Microeconomics of Peasant Economy: China, 1920–1940". New York: Garland Press, 1982 (orig. Harvard PhD dissertation, 1973).

Wilbur, C. Martin. *Sun Yat-sen, Frustrated Patriot*. New York: Columbia University Press, 1976.

Wong, J. Y. *The Origins of an Heroic Image: Sun Yat-sen in London, 1896–1897*. New York: Oxford University Press, 1986.

Woodbridge, George, ed. *UNRRA*. New York: Columbia University Press, 1950 (3 vols.).

Woodhead, H. G. W., ed. *China Year Book*. 1925: Tientsin Press, 1926; 1931: Shanghai: North China Daily News and Herald.

World Bank. *China, The Transport Sector*. Washington, 1985.

Wright, Mary Clabaugh, ed. *China in Revolution: The First Phase 1900–1913*. New Haven, CN: Yale University Press, 1968.

Writing Group of the Kirin Provincial Revolutionary Committee. "Class Struggle in the Field of Socialist Construction and Economics", *Chinese Economic Studies*, 4:4 (Summer, 1971), pp. 268–289.

Wu Chi-yuen. *The Theory of International Price Relationships: An Historical Study*. London: G. Routledge, 1939.

———. "The Chinese Dollar: July 1937 to July 1940", *Nankai Social and Economic Quarterly*, 12:1 (January, 1941), pp. 53–113.

Wu Ching-chao. Review of Fong 1938, *Nankai Social and Economic Quarterly*, 11:1 (January, 1940), pp. 191–192.

———. "Economic Reconstruction and Planning: Wartime and Post-war", in MacNair, ed., 1944, pp. 65–80.

———. "Industrial Planning in China" (pamphlet). Shanghai: China Institute of Pacific Relations, 1945 (LSE Library).

———. "Economic Development", in MacNair, ed., 1946, pp. 455–465.

Wu Tao-kun. *Mathematisch-statistische Untersuchung zur chinesischen Industrie* (Mathematical-statistical Investigation into Chinese Industry). Jena: Neuenhahn, 1937.

Wu Yuan-li. "Capital Formation and the Economic Order: An Analytical Study (with Special Reference to the Case of a Poor Country)". PhD dissertation, LSE 1946a.

———. "China's Economic Policy—Planning or Free Enterprise?" (pamphlet). New York: Sino-International Economic Research Center, 1946b.

———. *An Economic Survey of Communist China*. New York: Bookman Associates, 1956.

———, ed. *China: A Handbook*. New York: Praeger, 1973.
Wuhan University catalogues 國立武漢大學一覽, 1933 and 1936 (Chinese language).
Yahuda, Michael B. *New Directions in the Social Sciences and Humanities in China*. New York: St. Martin's Press, 1987.
Yang Dali. "Beiyang University, 1885–1912: Charles D. Tenney and the Politics of Educational Entrepreneurship", paper presented at Workshop on History of Christian Higher Education in China, Yale University, 1990.
Yang, Simon (Yang Hsi-meng). "An Index of the Cost of Living in Peiping" (1928), reprinted in Myers 1982.
Yeh Wen-hsin. *The Alienated Academy: Culture and Politics in Republican China, 1919–1937*. Cambridge, MA: Harvard University Press, 1990.
Yen Fu. *Yuan Fu* 元富 (Chinese-language translation of Smith's *The Wealth of Nations*) [1902]. Taipei: Commercial Press; excerpts translated by Lai Cheng-chung.
Yih Meng-hong. "Some Notes on the Influx of Western Economics into China by the end of 19th Century and at the Beginning of 20th Century", manuscript, 1985.
Yonay, Yuval P. *The Struggle over the Soul of Economics: Institutionalist and Neoclassical Economists in America between the Wars*. Princeton: Princeton University Press, 1998.
Young, Arthur. *China's Nation-Building Effort, 1927–1937*. Stanford, CA: Hoover Institution Press, 1971.
———. *Cycle of Cathay*. Vista, CA: Ibis Publishing, 1997.
Young, Warren and Frederic S. Lee. *Oxford Economics and Oxford Economists*. London: Macmillan, 1993.
Yu Guangyuan. "The Concept of Economic Effects in the Production of Material Values under the condition of Socialism", *Chinese Economic Studies*, 12:4 (Summer, 1979), pp. 6–55.
Yu, Maochen. "Chen Hansheng's Memoirs and Chinese Communist Espionage", *Bulletin of the Cold War International History Project*, 1995/96, pp. 274–276.
Yuan Tung-li. *A Guide to Doctoral Dissertations by Chinese Students in America 1905–1960*. Washington: Sino-American Cultural Society, 1961.
———. *A Guide to Doctoral Dissertations by Chinese Students in Great Britain and Northern Ireland, 1916–1961*. Reprinted from *Chinese Culture Quarterly*, Taipei, 1963.
———. *A Guide to Doctoral Dissertations by Chinese Students in Continental Europe, 1907–1962*. Reprinted from *Chinese Culture Quarterly*, Taipei, 1964.
Yuen Wen-pu. Review of Li Chuan-shih, "Contemporary Chinese Economic Thought", [Nankai] *Monthly Bulletin on Economic China*, 7:11 (November, 1934), pp. 458–459.

Zhang Haipeng. "The Revolution of 1911 and Sun Yat-sen", *Beijing Review*, October 14–20, 1991, pp. 24–27.

Zhu Shaowen. "Adam Smith in China", in Mizuta and Sugiyama, eds., 1993, pp. 279–291.

Zong Shenyuan and Tao Zunqian, eds. *Biographical Dictionary of Professors in Chinese Universities and Colleges*. Beijing: Higher Education Press, 1990.

「反對資產階級社會科學復辟」第二輯（中國科學院召開的社會科學界反右派鬥爭座談會發言集）。北京：〈科學〉出版社. "Opposing Bourgeoisie's Reviving in Social Science", second volume (The Collection of the Speeches at the Anti-Rightists' Meeting in Social Science Circle, Summoned by Academy of Science). Beijing: Publisher of *Science*, January, 1958. Translated by Liu Yi-xin.

Glossary

The Wade-Giles romanization has been converted to pinyin according to *The Chicago Manual of Style*, 15th Edition, p. 426. Chicago: The University of Chicago Press, 2003. However, some names are spelled in their common printed forms as appeared in written works. Hanzi have been provided where they are known.

Wade-Giles	*Pinyin*	*Hanzi*
Chang Chi-wen	Zhang Qiyun	張其昀
Chang Chi-yun	Zhang Qiyun	–
Chang Chia-hsiang	Zhang Jiaxiang	張家驤
Chang Chun-ming	Zhang Chunming	張純明
Chang Chung-yi	Zhang Zhongyi	張重一
Chang Hsi-chang	Zhang Xichang	張錫昌
Chang Hsiao-mei, Djang Siao-mei	Zhang Xiaomei	張肖梅
Chang Hsin-yi, C. C.	Zhang Xinyi	張心一
Chang Jen-chieh	Zhang Renjia	張人價
Chang Kia-ngau	Zhang Jiaao	張嘉璈
Chang Ko-wei	Zhang Guowei	張果為
Chang Lu-luan	Zhang Luluan	張履鸞
Chang Pei-kang	Zhang Peigang	張培剛
Chang Teh-chang	Zhang Dechang	張德昌
Chang Teh-tsui	Zhang Decui	張德粹
Chang Tien-tse	Zhang Jianze	張天澤
Chang Wei	Zhang Wei	張瑋
Chang Wen-li	Zhang Wenli	張文理
Chang (Tschang) Yen-yu	Zhang Yenyu	張彥如
Chang Yin-lin	Zhang Yinlin	張蔭麟
Chang Yuan-ju	Zhang Yuanruo	–
Chang Yun-fu	Zhang Yunfu	張雲伏

Wade-Giles	*Pinyin*	*Hanzi*
Chao Cheng-hsin	Zhao Chengxin	趙承信
Chao Ching	Zhao Jing	趙靖
Chao Jen-tsun	Zhao Renjun	趙人雋
Chao Lan-ping	Zhao Lanping	趙蘭坪
Chao Nai-tuan	Zhao Naituan	趙迺摶
Chao Shao-ting	Zhao Shaoding	趙紹鼎
Chao Zoo-biang	Zhao Zubang	趙祖邦
Chen Chang-heng	Chen Changheng	陳長蘅
Chen Chen-han	Chen Zhenhan	陳振漢
Chen Cheng-mo	Chen Zhengmo	陳正謨
Chen Chi-hsiu	Chen Qixiu	陳啟修
Chen Chi-tien, Gideon	Chen Qitian	陳其田
Chen Chin-tao	Chen Jintao	陳錦濤
Chen Chiu	Chen Qiu	陳虬
Chen Chung-shen	Chen Zhongshen	陳鐘聲
Chen Dai-sun	Chen Daisun	陳岱孫
Chen Dao	Chen Dao	陳道
Chen Han-sheng	Chen Hansheng	陳翰笙
Chen Hsi-ching, Francis	Chen Xicheng	陳希誠
Chen Huan-chang	Chen Huanzhang	陳煥章
Chen Hui-shen	Chen Huishen	陳慧生
Chen Kung-po	Chen Gongbo	陳公博
Chen Lu-chen	Chen Luzhen	陳鷺振
Chen Pao-ying	Zhen Baoying	–
Chen Shao-kwan	Chen Zhaokun	陳兆鯤
Chen Shao-te	Cheng Shaode	程紹德
Chen Shao-wu	Chen Shaowu	陳紹武
Chen Ta	Chen Da	陳達
Chen Tao	Chen Dao	–
Chen Tsu-kwei	Chen Zukgui	陳祖檠
Chen Tu-hsiu	Chen Duxiu	陳獨秀
Chen Yin-fang	Chen Yinfang	陳蔭枋
Cheng Lin-chuang	Zheng Linzhuang	鄭林庄
Cheng Pao-lun	Zheng Baolun	鄭寶崙
Cheng Yu-kuei	Zheng Youkui	鄭友揆

Wade-Giles	*Pinyin*	*Hanzi*
Chi Chao-ting	Ji Chaoding	冀朝鼎
Chi Hua	Ji Hua	紀華
Chi Shien-yien (Luther Jee)	Ji Shenen	朱神恩
Chi Tao-da	Ji Taoda	季陶達
Chia Shi-yi	Jia Shiyi	賈士毅
Chiang Chung-I, Alpha	Jiang Zhongyi	蔣中一
Chiang Shu-huan	Jiang Shuhuan	–
Chiao Chi-ming	Qiao Qiming	喬啟明
Chien Chang-chao	Qian Changzhao	錢昌照
Chien Chia-chu	Qian Jiaju	千家駒
Chien Rong-kun	Qian Rongkun	錢榮堃
Chin Kuo-chen	Jin Guozhen	金國珍
Chin Kuo-pao	Jin Guobao	金國寶
Chin Quock-ping, Rockwood	Chen Guoping	陳國平
Chin Tsan	Qin Zan	秦瓚
Chiu Kai-ming, Alfred	Qiu Kaiming	裘開明
Chou Hsien-sung	Zhou Xiansong	周賢頌
Chou Hua-chang	Zhou Huazhang	周華章
Chou Kuei	Zhou Gui	–
Chou Ping-lin	Zhou Binglin	周炳琳
Chou Shun-hsin	Zhou Shunxin	周舜莘
Chou Teh-wei	Zhou Dewei	周德偉
Chou Tso-jen	Zhou Zuoren	周作人
Chow Ling, Frank Chou	Zhou Lin	周林
Chu Bin-yuan	Zhu Binyuan	朱彬元
Chu Bing-nan	Zhu Binglin	朱炳林
Chu Chi (Chu Hsieh)	Zhu Xie	朱偰
Chu Chi-sheng	Zhu Jisheng	朱繼聖
Chu Chien-tsi	Zhu Jianzi	–
Chu Chun-yi, Jennings P.	Zhu Junyi	朱君毅
Chu Chung-tao, Tahmy	Zhu Zhongdao	朱中道
Chu Pao-ying	Zhu Baiying	祝百英
Chu Tien-yu	Zhu Dianyu	朱甸余
Chu Tsu-hui	Zhu Zuhui	朱祖晦
Chu Tung-chiu	Zhu Tongjiu	朱通九

Wade-Giles	*Pinyin*	*Hanzi*
Chuan Han-sheng	Quan Hansheng	全漢昇
Chuan Kuo-bao	Quan Guobao	全國寶
Chun Pao-hsun	Zhu Baoxun	朱保訓
Chun Tsi-yi	Zhun Ziyi	–
Di Chao-bai	Di Chaobai	狄超白
Ding, Edwin (Chen Hsing-yueh)	Chen Xingle	陳興樂
Fan Hong	Fan Hong	樊弘
Fei Ching-han, John	Fei Jinghan	費景漢
Fei Hsiao-tung	Fei Xiaotong	費孝通
Feng He-fa	Feng Hefa	馮和法
Feng Hua-teh	Feng Huade	馮華德
Feng Kuei-fen	Feng Guifen	馮桂芬
Feng Rui	Feng Rui	馮銳
Fong Hsien-ding, H. D. Fong	Fang Xianting	方顯庭
Fong Shou-kwei	Fang Shangui	方善桂
Fu Chu-fu	Fu Zhufu	傅筑夫
Fung Chuan-tchs, Fun Tschavsch	Fung (Deng) Chuanshi	(馮)鄧傳詩
Gao Hong-ye	Gao Hongye	高鴻業
Han Fei-zu	Han Fei	韓非
Ho Feng-shan	He Fengshan	何鳳山
Ho Hao-jo	He Haoruo	何浩若
Ho Kuo-liang, Alfred K.	He Guoliang	何國梁
Ho Lien, Franklin	He Lian	何廉
Ho Ping-yin	He Bingxian	何炳賢
Ho Ssu-yuen	He Siyuan	何思源
Hong Jun-yan	Hong Junyan	–
Hou Chi-ming	Hou Jiming	侯繼明
Hou Shu-tung	Hou Shutong	侯樹彤
Hou Wen-ping	Hou Wenbing	胡文炳
Hsia Hsiu-yung, Ronald	Xia Xiuyong	夏修永
Hsiang Ching-yuen	Xiang Jingyun	向景雲
Hsiao Cheng	Xiao Zheng	蕭錚
Hsiao Chu	Xiao Chu	蕭處
Hsu Chen, Paul	Xu Cheng	徐澄
Hsu Chi-ching	Xu Zhijing	徐致靖

Wade-Giles	*Pinyin*	*Hanzi*
Hsu Chih, Mongton	Xu Chi	徐遲
Hsu Shi-lian, Leonard	Xu Shilian	許士廉
Hsu Ti-hsin	Xu Dixin	許滌新
Hsu Yu-nan	Xu Yunan	徐蔚南
Hsueh Hsien-chou	Xue Xianzhou	薛仙舟
Hsueh Mu-chiao	Xue Muqiao	薛暮橋
Hu Chi-chuang	Hu Jichuang	胡寄窗
Hu Kyi-yuan	Hu Jiyuan	胡繼瑗
Huan Kuan	Huan Kuan	桓寬
Huang Cho	Huang Zhuo	黃卓
Huang Chung, Andrew	Huang Zhong	黃中
Huang Feng-hua	Huang Fenghua	黃鳳華
Huang Han-liang	Huang Hanliang	黃漢梁
Huang Hsien-ju	Huang Xianru	黃憲儒
Huang Hua	Huang Hua	黃華
Huang Khai-loo	Huang Kailu	黃開祿
Huang Yi-sun	Huang Yisun	黃貽孫
Jao Yu-su (Mrs. Liu)	Rao Yusu	饒毓蘇
Jen Kai-nan	Ren Kainan	任凱南
Jen Tsung-chi	Ren Zongji	任宗濟
Kan Nai-kuang	Gan Naiguang	甘乃光
Kang Yu-wei	Kang Youwei	康有為
Kao Ping-shu	Gao Pingshu	高平叔
King Shih-hsuan	Jin Shixuan	金世煊
Ko Fuh-ting	Ge Fuding	戈福鼎
Ko Pei-chi	Ge Beiji	–
Koo, Anthony Ying-chang	Gu Yingchang	顧應昌
Koung Shien-ming	Gong Xianming	龔賢明
Ku Chun-fan	Gu Chunfan	谷春帆
Ku Meng-yu	Gu Mengyu	顧孟余
Ku Ping-yuan	Gu Bingyuan	–
Ku Te-ming	Gu Deming	顧德銘
Kuan Shu-chuang (Mrs. Ting)	Dingguan Shuzhuang	丁關淑莊
Kuo Jui-chang	Guo Ruizhang	郭瑞璋
Kuo Shien-yen	Guo Xianyan	郭先彥

Wade-Giles	*Pinyin*	*Hanzi*
Kuo Ta-li	Guo Dali	郭大力
Kuo Tse-chiu	Guo Zeqiu	郭則虬
Kwok Yam-tong	Guo Yintang	郭蔭棠
Lau Tong-sun	Lou Tongsun	樓桐孫
Lee Ba-en, Elmer Lee	Li Peien	李培恩
Lee Ching-han, Franklin C. H.	Li Jinghan	李景漢
Lee Kan	Li Gan	李幹
Lee Shi-son, Ching-lin	Li Shison / Li Qinglin	–
Li Bing-hua	Li Binghua	李秉華
Li Chien-nung	Li Jiannong	李劍農
Li Choh-ming	Li Zhuomin	李卓敏
Li Chuan-shih	Li Quanshi	李權時
Li Hsi-sheng	Li Xisheng	李希聖
Li Hsiao-li	Li Xiaoli	李效黎
Li Hua-fang	Li Huafang	李化方
Li Hui-chien	Li Huiqian	李撝謙
Li Jui	Li Rui	李銳
Li Kuang-chung	Li Guangzhong	李光忠
Li Nai-lu	Li Nailu	李迺祿
Li Pao-chen	Li Baozhen	–
Li Pao-liu	Li Baoliu	李寶鎏
Li Shi-heng	Li Shiheng	黎世衡
Li (Lee) Shu-ching	Li Shuqing	李樹青
Li Ta	Li Da	李達
Li Ta-chao	Li Dazhao	李大釗
Li Tang	Li Dang	李儻
Li Teh-ying	Li Deyin	厲德寅
Li Ti-tsun	Li Dijun	李迪俊
Li Tzu-hsiang	Li Zixiang	李紫翔
Liang Chi-chao	Liang Qichao	梁啟超
Liang Ching-chun	Liang Qingchun	梁慶椿
Liang Fang-chung	Liang Fangzhong	梁方仲
Liang Ing-wen	Liang Yingwen	梁穎文
Liang Shu-ming	Liang Shuming	梁漱溟
Lieu Da-kuin (D. K.)	Liu Dajun	劉大鈞

Wade-Giles	*Pinyin*	*Hanzi*
Lin Lin	Lin Lin	林霖
Lin Tung-hai, Jefferson Lamb	Lin Donghai	林東海
Lin Wei, Peter	Lin Wei	林暐
Lin Wei-ying	Lin Weiying	林維英
Liu Ching-shan	Liu Jingshan	劉景山
Liu Nan-ming	Liu Nanming	劉南溟
Liu Ping-lin	Liu Binglin	劉秉麟
Liu Sien-wei	Liu Xianwei	劉先緯
Liu Ssu-yeh	Liu Siye	劉駟業
Liu Ta-chung, T. C. Liu	Liu Dazhong	劉大中
Liu Tien-chen, William	Liu Dianchen	劉甸忱
Liu Ting-mien	Liu Tingmian	劉廷冕
Lo Chieh-fu	Luo Jiefu	羅介夫
Lo Chih-ju	Luo Zhiru	羅志儒
Lo Mei-huan	Luo Meihuan	駱美奐
Lo Ting	Luo Ding	羅鼎
Lo Tsung-yi	Luo Zhongyi	羅忠詒
Lu Chung-tai	Lu Changdai	魯崇岱
Lu Kuang-mian	Lu Guangmian	盧廣綿
Lu Ping	Lu Ping	魯平
Lu Yu-wen, Lou Yee-wen	Lu Yuwen	盧郁文
Ly Juwan Usang, Li Chao-huan	Li Zhaohuan	黎照寰
Ma Chien-chung	Ma Jianzhong	馬建中
Ma Hsiang-po	Ma Liang	馬相伯 (馬良)
Ma Yin-chu	Ma Yinchu	馬寅初
Mai Chien-tseng	Mai Jianzeng	麥健曾
Meng Tien-pei	Meng Dianbei	–
Meng Yung-chien	Meng Yongjian	–
Ning Chia-feng	Ning Jiafeng	甯嘉風
Ou Pao-san	Wu Baosan	巫寶三
Ouyang Ping, Eo-yang Ping	Ouyang Ping	歐陽蘋
Pan Hong-sheng	Pan Hongsheng	潘鴻聲
Pan Kuang-chiung, Francis	Pan Guanghui	潘光迥
Pan Shu-lun	Pan Xulun	潘序倫

Wade-Giles	*Pinyin*	*Hanzi*
Pan Yuan-lai	Pan Yuanlai	潘源來
Pao Chueh-min	Bao Juemin	鮑覺民
Pei Peng-fei	Bai Pengfei	白鵬飛
Peng Hsueh-pai	Peng Xuepei	彭學沛
Peng Shin-wei	Peng Xinwei	彭信威
Pi Tsong-shi	Pi Zongshi	皮宗石
Poe Hsueh-feng, Dison	(Pu) Boe Xuefeng	浦薛鳳
Pu (Shou-)shan	Pu Shoushan	浦壽山
Pu Shou-chang	Pu Shouchang	浦壽昌
Pu Shou-hai	Pu Shouhai	浦壽海
Sang Heng-kang	Sang Hengkang	桑恒康
Shao Bing-kun	Shao Bingkun	邵丙昆
Shen Chi-yuan	Shen Zhiyuan	沈志遠
Shen Hsien-yao	Shen Xianyao	–
Shen Lai-chiu, Djini, Lionel	Shen Laiqiu	沈來秋
Shen Tsu-ting	Shen Zuding	–
Sheng Chun, T. Sheng	Sheng Jun	盛俊
Shih Chien-sheng	Shi Jiansheng	施建生
Sih, Paul (Hsueh Kuan-tsien)	Xue Guangqian	薛光前
Song Tao	Song Tao	宋濤
Soong Tze-ven (T. V.)	Song Ziwen	宋子文
SSu-ma Chien	Sima Qian	司馬遷
Sun Fo, Sun Ke	Sun Ke	孫科
Sun Han-ping	Sun Hanbing	孫寒冰
Sun Pi-chi, Patrick	Sun Biqi	孫碧奇
Sun Tsu-yin	Sun Zuyin	孫祖蔭
Sun Ye-fang	Sun Yefang	孫冶方
Sun Yi-chang	Sun Yirang	孫詒讓
Swen Wen-yuh	Sun Wenyu	孫文郁
Tai Shih-kuang	Dai Shiguang	戴世光
Tan Ssu-tung	Tan Sitong	譚嗣同
Tang, Anthony Chung-ming	Tang Zongming	唐宗明
Tang Chi-yu	Tang Qiyu	唐啟宇
Tang Ching-tseng	Tang Qingzeng	唐慶增
Tang Chung-tai	Tan Chongtai	譚崇台

Wade-Giles	*Pinyin*	*Hanzi*
Tang Chung-tzu	Tang Chongci	唐崇慈
Tang Hsiang-lung	Tang Xianglong	湯象龍
Tang Wen-kai	Tang Wenkai	唐文愷
Tang Yu-jen	Tang Youren	唐有壬
Tao Hsi-shen	Tao Xisheng	陶希聖
Tao Meng-ho, L. K. Tao	Tao Lugong / Menghe	陶孟和
Tao Ta-yung	Tao Dayong	陶大鏞
Tchang Pi-kai	Zhang Pijie	張丕介
Teng Han-chung	Deng Hanzhong	鄧漢鐘
Teng Wei-tsao	Teng Weizao	滕維藻
Tiao Pei-chan	Diao Peiran	刁培然
Ting Chen	Ding Chen	丁忱
Ting Ge, Leonard	Ding Ji	丁佶
Ting Wen-tsu	Ding Wenzhi	丁文治
Tsai Cheng-huan	Cai Zhenghuan	–
Tsai Chin-pin Tsen	Cai Jinping	蔡競平
Tsai Ko-hsuan	Cai Kexuan	蔡可選
Tsai Yuan-pei	Cai Yuanpei	蔡元培
Tseng Chao-cheng	Zeng Zhaocheng	曾昭承
Tseng Tsung-chien	Zeng Zongjian	曾宗鑒
Tsiang Sho-chieh, S. C. Tsiang	Jiang Shuojie	蔣碩傑
Tso Shi-kang, Sheldon	Zhu Shikang	祝世康
Tsui Ruh-tsuin	Cui Yujun	崔毓俊
Tsui Shu-hsiang	Cui Shuxiang	崔書香
Tu Tu	Du Du	杜度
Tuan Mao-lan	Duan Maolan	段茂瀾
Tung Hsiu-chia	Dong Xiujia	董修甲
Tung Kuan-hsien	Dong Guanxian	董冠賢
Tung Shih-tsin	Dong Shijin	董時進
Wan Chung-hsin	Wan Zhongxin	–
Wan Feng-chao	Wan Fengzhao	–
Wan Kwoh-ting	Wan Guoding	萬國鼎
Wang Bing-hou	Wang Binghou	王秉厚
Wang Chi-chang, C. Z. Waung	Wang Qichang	王啟常
Wang Chi-tsu	Wang Jizu	王繼祖

Wade-Giles	*Pinyin*	*Hanzi*
Wang Chia-hong	Wang Jiahong	王家鴻
Wang Chien-tsu	Wang Jianzu	王建祖
Wang Ching-chun	Wang Jingchun	王景春
Wang Ching-yu	Wang Jingyu	汪敬虞 (馥蓀)
Wang Chuan-lun	Wang Chuanlun	王傳綸
Wang Hsi-hsien	Wang Xixian	王希賢
Wang Hsien-chiang	Wang Xianqiang	王先強
Wang Ju-mei, Huang Hua	Wang Rumei	–
Wang Kang-shen	Wang Kangshen	王康生
Wang Nien-tzu, Samuel	Wang Nianzu	王念祖
Wang Si-hua	Wang Sihua	王思華
Wang Tao	Wang Tao	王韜
Wang Tsai-shan	Wang Caishan	–
Wang Ya-nan	Wang Yanan	王亞南
Wang Yin-sheng	Wang Yinsheng	王寅生
Wang Yin-yuan	Wang Yinyuan	汪蔭元
Wang You-chu	Wang Youzhu	–
Wei Wen-pin	Wei Wenbin	魏文彬
Wei Yuan	Wei Yuan	魏源
Wong Kuo-cheng, K. C.	Wong Guozhong	王國忠
Wong Wen-hao	Wong Wenhao	翁文灝
Wu Chi-tao	Wu Jidao	–
Wu Chi-yuen	Wu Qiyuan	伍啟元
Wu Ching-chao	Wu Jingchao	吳景超
Wu Han	Wu Han	吳晗
Wu Hsiang-chi	Wu Xiangzhi	吳向之
Wu Kai-in	Wu Jixian	胡繼賢
Wu Pun-nung, Leonard T. K.	Wu Bannong	吳半農
Wu Ta-chun	Wu Dajun	吳大鈞
Wu Ta-kun	Wu Dakun	吳大琨
Wu Ta-yeh	Wu Daye	吳大業
Wu Tao-kun	Wu Daokun	吳道昆
Wu Ting-chang	Wu Dingzhang	–
Wu Yuan-li	Wu Yuanli	吳元黎

Wade-Giles	*Pinyin*	*Hanzi*
Yan Zhi-jie	Yan Zhijie	晏智杰
Yang Chien	Yang Quan	楊銓
Yang Ching-nien	Yang Jingnian	楊敬年
Yang Hsi-meng, Simon	Yang Ximeng	楊西孟
Yang Ju-mei	Yang Rumei	楊汝梅
Yang Shu-chin	Yang Shujin	楊叔進
Yang Shu-jen	Yang Shuren	–
Yang Sueh-chang	Yang Xuezhang	楊雪章
Yang Tuan-lu	Yang Duanliu	楊端六
Yang, William Yu (Yang Wei)	Yang Wei	楊蔚
Yang Yin-pu	Yang Yinpu	楊蔭溥
Yao Tseng-yin	Yao Zengyin	姚曾陰
Yeh Yuan-long	Ye Yuanlong	葉元龍
Yen Chung-ping	Yan Zhongping	嚴中平
Yen Fu	Yan Fu	嚴復
Yen Jen-keng	Yan Rengeng	嚴仁賡
Yen Yang-chu, James	Yan Yangchu	晏陽初
Yin Liang-en	Yin Liangen	–
Yin Tsu-hsi	Yin Zuxi	–
Yu Chin-tang	Yu Jingtang	余井塘
Yu Hsiang-ling	Yu Xiangling	余相林
Yu Kuang-yuan	Yu Guangyuan	于光遠
Yu Tsune-chi, James	Yu Junji	于俊吉
Yu Tsuo-yi	Yu Zuoyi	–
Yu Wen-tsan	Yu Wencan	余文燦
Yu Yung-tzu	Yu Yongzi	于永滋
Yuen Wen-pu, Yuan Hsian-nen	Yuan Wenbo	袁文伯
Yung Wen-yuan	Yong Wenyuan	雍文遠

Index